DATE			

Britain and the
Sino-Japanese War, 1937-1939

Britain and the Sino-Japanese War, 1937-1939

A Study in the Dilemmas of British Decline

BRADFORD A. LEE

Stanford University Press, Stanford, California   1973
London: Oxford University Press

Stanford University Press
Stanford, California
London: Oxford University Press
© 1973 by the Board of Trustees of the
Leland Stanford Junior University
Printed in the United States of America
Stanford ISBN 0-8047-0799-5
Oxford ISBN 0-19-690405-6
LC 77-190526

To C.J.

Preface

THE PRINCIPAL aim of this book is to examine Britain's response to the undeclared Sino-Japanese war from its outbreak in July 1937 to the beginning of the European war in September 1939. In pursuing this goal, I have given considerable attention to British evaluations of Japanese expansionism, Chinese nationalism, and communism in East Asia. Another aim is to set Britain's reaction to the East Asian crisis within the larger framework of her overall foreign policy. This involves both comparing her Far Eastern and European policies, and elucidating the connection between them. In particular, I have explored appeasement in an East Asian context, and from the perspective thus provided have reappraised it in its European setting.

Anyone who deals with appeasement needs to begin with a definition. British statesmen in the 1930's used the word to describe any attempt to reduce international tensions. Historians have used it to describe everything from surrendering in the face of aggression to negotiating from overwhelming strength. To achieve some measure of precision, I shall define appeasement as the granting of concessions to a power in the hope of satisfying its desire for expansion or of weaning it from the use of force. The concessions may be economic, but usually take the form of tacit or explicit sanction for proposed or accomplished changes in the territorial or military status quo. Merely failing to resist conquest—as distinct from sanctioning it—is not appeasement.

The historical significance of appeasement is as vexed a question as its precise definition. Many historians have discussed appeasement in terms of Britain's moral sensibilities or weakness of will. These approaches, in my opinion, obscure the main point. Appeasement as practiced by British statesmen was above all a diplomatic strategy designed to maintain Britain's leading position in an unstable world. It was not the only strategy used or considered; indeed whether to appease or not was one of the dilemmas of British decline to which my subtitle refers. In Europe, of course, Britain adhered on the whole to a policy of appeasement during the late 1930's, but in East Asia she chose a firmer course. One of my primary concerns is to account for this contrast.

On this issue and others, I have relied heavily on the newly opened British Foreign Office and Cabinet papers for the 1930's at the Public Record Office in London. Voluminous and illuminating as these records are, they sometimes raise as many questions as they answer about the mainsprings of British policy. Reasons and rationalizations for certain of Whitehall's decisions seem hopelessly jumbled, and it is difficult to judge how deeply one should probe. My research has led me to concentrate on British assessments of Japanese and German aims and thinking. But I should note at the outset that these assessments may well have been influenced by other, more elusive, factors. There are indications, for example, that Neville Chamberlain's inclination to regard Germany's aims as limited stemmed in part from his distaste for all-out British rearmament and its presumed financial and political risks. And there are hints of unsounded psychological and cultural depths in British attitudes toward Japan. To do more than merely touch on either of these matters, however, would be to venture beyond the scope of this study.

Though I alone am responsible for the interpretations in this book, I am grateful to a number of scholars and institutions for their assistance. W. Roger Louis introduced me to the complexities of British foreign policy and also stressed the importance of clear and precise prose. Ian H. Nish guided me through the initial phase of my work and discussed with me certain problems of later phases. During the long stages of writing and revision I benefited from the encouragement and perceptive criticism of F. H. Hinsley. Along the way, I also received help in one form or another from E. H. Carr, the late Mary C. Wright, James B. Crowley, Martin Griffin, Chitoshi Yanaga, and the members of the International History Seminar at Cambridge University. For the financial assistance that supported my research, I must thank the Old Dominion Foundation (for a Mellon Fellowship); the Colony Trust (Berzelius Society); the National Science Foundation and the Yale University Political Science Department; Dean John Wilkinson of Yale; and Clare College and the Political Science Fund Committee at Cambridge University.

I am also grateful to the Controller of Her Majesty's Stationery Office for permission to quote from the British records; to the Harvard College Library for permission to include excerpts from the Joseph Grew Diary and the Jay Pierrepont Moffat Diplomatic Journals; and to Lady Vansittart for allowing me to use the Vansittart Papers at Churchill College, Cambridge University.

Finally, I should like to thank my parents and parents-in-law for help of various kinds and, above all, my wife, Connie, for humoring me in times of distress and interrupting her own studies to do some typing and proofreading.

B.A.L.

May 1972

Contents

Britain and the
Sino-Japanese War, 1937-1939

Chapter one

Britain Between East and West

BRITISH STATESMEN from Lansdowne to Churchill grappled with one overriding problem: how to maintain Britain's leading position in the world as her relative power declined. Rarely was this task more difficult than in the late 1930's. Neville Chamberlain and his colleagues faced a hostile and bewildering international environment born of economic depression, ideological conflict, and rapid shifts in the balance of world forces. The most alarming aspect of the situation was German and Italian pressure on the status quo in Europe and the Mediterranean. But Britain was also deeply concerned about East Asia. Japan seemed bent on dominating that region, and as she advanced deep into the Asian mainland after the Sino-Japanese conflict broke out in July 1937, vast British interests in China came under heavy pressure. Britain did not possess the strength to respond forcefully to these simultaneous challenges in the West and in the East, and her efforts to deal with the situation in one area were hampered by her difficulties in the other.

Clearly, the emergence of Japan as an antagonist did much to make the world situation in the late 1930's so treacherous for the Chamberlain government. To historians this development represents an important step toward the end of Western predominance in Asia. To the British at the time it seemed a bitter irony. In the critical periods before and during the First World War, Japan had been an ally. The alliance, concluded in 1902 and renewed in 1905 and 1911, enabled the British to leave the defense of their "informal empire" in China to Japan and concentrate on the troubled state of affairs in Europe. It benefited the Japanese as well, virtually ensuring that neither Germany nor France would help Russia in the Russo-Japanese War of 1904-5, and affirming Japan's status as a first-class power.

Noticeable strains nevertheless developed between the two island empires as early as the Chinese Revolution of 1911. Friction increased during the First World War when the Japanese took advantage of the European powers' preoccupation to expand their position in China. By the end of the war, Britain was very apprehensive about Japan's ambitions. Even so, she would have continued the alliance (at least in a modified form) had it not been for Canadian and, above all, American opposition. Britain still felt that close ties with the Japanese were necessary to the maintenance of her world position. She also hoped that the alliance might help her to restrain Tokyo in the future. But the United States, suspicious both of Japan and of the "old diplomacy," believed that the alliance in effect gave the Japanese a free hand to expand. London wanted to avoid a breach with the Americans, not least because it would exacerbate an already intense naval rivalry at a time when the British government wished to reduce defense spending.[1]

The related issues of naval armaments and the Anglo-Japanese alliance were resolved at the Washington Conference of 1921-22. A Five-Power Treaty fixed Japan's battleship strength at 60 percent of the tonnage of the United States and Britain and called for the signatories to refrain from building fortifications in a large area of the Pacific, including Hong Kong and the Philippines. This agreement ensured Japan's naval hegemony in the western Pacific. The Anglo-Japanese alliance was replaced by a Four-Power Treaty, which merely pledged the signatories—Britain, France, Japan, and the United States—to consult each other over conflicts of interest and instances of aggression in the Pacific. These two treaties had profound consequences for Britain's position in East Asia. Having severed her formal bond with the Japanese and having achieved her goal of naval limitation, she found herself without the means to protect her interests in that region. She had decided in 1921 to build a major naval base at Singapore, but construction proceeded intermittently. Even when the base finally opened in 1938, it was not ready to operate on a full wartime footing. In any case, there was no British fleet that could be stationed in the East, and Singapore was too far away to be of use in defending British interests in China. Under these circumstances, Britain had to depend on the frail reeds of American support and Japanese restraint.

The third agreement reached at the Washington Conference was the Nine-Power Treaty, which affirmed the independence and the administrative and territorial integrity of China, as well as the open-door principle. The signatories resolved to give China full opportunity to establish a stable and effective government, and promised to consider revising the "unequal treaties" that had been imposed on the Chinese in the previous eighty years. The language was noble but ambiguous. It contained no real break with the assumption that China should remain under foreign tutelage, and granted her only minor concessions, leaving her major desires such as tariff autonomy and the abolition of extraterritoriality unmet.

Within ten years, the Washington treaty order had collapsed in all but name. The conference had not created a community of interests among the participating powers, as was shown by the failure of the Peking Tariff Conference of 1925-26. Nor had the gathering at Washington taken into account the strength of Chinese nationalism and the growing influence of the Soviet Union in East Asia. Chiang Kai-shek and the Nationalists, with substantial Soviet assistance, sought in the mid-1920's to unify China. This ambitious undertaking was accompanied by an intense anti-imperialism, directed primarily at Britain. The May Thirtieth Incident of 1925 in Shanghai was followed by an effective anti-British boycott and by the overrunning of the concession at Hankow in early 1927.

As the Foreign Office noted later, its response to this Nationalist surge was "an enforced retreat, necessitating endless rearguard
actions, and in which our main effort [was] directed towards
preventing it from being turned into a rout."[2] The famous British
memorandum of December 1926—in which it was proposed that
the signatories of the Nine-Power Treaty should go as far as possible toward meeting China's "legitimate aspirations"—has usually been viewed as heralding a new policy of far-reaching concessions to Chinese nationalism, but the changed stance actually consisted of relinquishing non-essential rights in order to safeguard
essential ones. Britain's determination to protect her position in
China was demonstrated in January 1927, when she unilaterally
reinforced Shanghai with 12,000 troops. Yet relations between
Britain and the Nationalists did grow closer during 1927. Certainly, London's willingness to be conciliatory on some issues was
a factor in this development, but perhaps a more important
(though not unrelated) factor was Chiang's break with the Communists. From 1928 to 1931, British prestige with the Kuomintang
increased as London not only gave up its concessions in Hankow,
Amoy, Kiukiang, and Chinkiang and terminated its lease at Wei-
haiwei, but also recognized China's right to tariff autonomy.
However, on extraterritoriality, the future of Shanghai, and shipping rights, Britain took a rather firm stand. In fact, a Foreign
Office memorandum of 1930 asserted that whenever danger
threatened Shanghai, "British interests, both economic and political, are so great that British troops must be sent to protect the
settlement, just as though it were a British possession."[3]

Relations between London and Tokyo were relatively cordial
throughout the 1920's. No doubt Japan regarded the abrogation
of the Anglo-Japanese alliance as (in Churchill's words) "the
spurning of an Asiatic Power by the Western World"; but at this
stage there was little evidence to support the view, later expressed
by Sir Robert Craigie, that ending the alliance removed "one of
the main buttresses against the pursuit by Japan of a policy of
adventure and aggression."[4] Though British strategists saw Japan
as Britain's most likely enemy, they did not think a Japanese at-

tack very probable.[5] It was clear to the Foreign Office by 1930, however, that the "outward show of harmony" between London and Tokyo masked "an underlying divergence of interests," and that Japan's policy in China was "bound to take a somewhat different turn from our own."[6]

The divergence between Japanese and Western interests in East Asia became even more marked at the London Naval Conference of 1930. Hoping to retain naval hegemony in the western Pacific, Japan pressed for a 70-percent ratio in heavy cruisers. The United States wished to extend the 60-percent ratio for capital ships to all categories of vessels, and won Britain's support on this point. Japan feared that the lower ratio would enable the British and American fleets to undertake offensive operations in her home waters. Faced with a united Anglo-American front, however, she agreed to a compromise that allowed her a *de facto* 70-percent ratio until 1936 but undermined the principle of her naval domination in the western Pacific. The conference precipitated a severe domestic reaction in Japan and weakened civilian rule there. Moreover, it dealt a severe blow to the principle of Anglo-American-Japanese cooperation that had been the basis of Japan's foreign policy since 1922.[7]

Whatever remained of this principle was destroyed by the Manchurian crisis of 1931-33. Manchuria had long been of paramount strategic and economic importance to Japan. When the Kuomintang tried to assert its power there from 1928 to 1931, the Japanese military became quite concerned. The Kwantung Army engineered an incident at Mukden in September 1931 and proceeded to seize South Manchuria. After a change of cabinet in Tokyo later that year, Japan advanced into North Manchuria, establishing the client state of Manchukuo in March 1932. Shortly before this puppet government was formed, fighting between the Chinese and the Japanese had also broken out far to the south at Shanghai.

Preoccupied with a financial emergency at home and acutely aware of her vulnerability in East Asia, Britain desperately wanted to avoid a confrontation with Japan. There was widespread feeling among Conservatives and in the Foreign Office that, in view of Chinese incompetence and arrogance, Japan's grievances (though not her methods of seeking redress) were legitimate, and in any case Britain hoped to keep on good terms with the Japanese. At the same time, however, she hoped to work with the United States, to uphold the League of Nations, and to maintain her prestige with the Chinese.[8] The difficulty of reconciling these objectives was demonstrated in January 1932 when Henry Stimson, the American Secretary of State, announced that the United States would not recognize changes in Manchuria brought about by force. Stimson wanted the British to support this declaration, but they feared that it would offend Japan, and were also averse to acting in advance of the League. Their somewhat clumsy rejection of the initiative annoyed Washington. Returning to the charge in February, Stimson tried to convince Foreign Secretary Sir John Simon that London and Washington should "invoke" the Nine-Power Treaty. The British sidestepped this cryptic proposal,[9] though they did guide through the League a declaration embodying Stimson's earlier call for non-recognition. This failure of cooperation between Stimson and Simon led to mutual recriminations that did much to embitter Anglo-American relations in the ensuing years.

Rather than make gestures that might provoke Japan, Britain wanted to limit the consequences of Sino-Japanese hostilities by reconciling the two sides. Largely through her initiative, a truce was arranged in May 1932 at Shanghai—where the outbreak of fighting in late January had threatened her vast interests. Britain generally followed a conciliatory line at the League of Nations as well, but a confrontation nevertheless developed between Japan and the League. In October 1932 the Lytton Commission, appointed by the League Council to study the Manchurian question, acknowledged its complexity but recommended that Manchukuo should not be recognized. When in February 1933 the Assembly adopted a report based on the commission's work, Japan left the League in protest. Occupying Jehol in March, she pushed south of the Great Wall. In late May the Kwantung Army and local Chinese officials concluded the Tangku Truce, which in effect gave the Japanese a hold on most of Hopei north of Peking.

Perhaps the main consequence of the Manchurian crisis was that it sent Japan on a fateful quest for an autonomous national defense. By late 1933 Tokyo had decided to seek predominance in China and the military capability to meet any threat posed by the Soviet Union, the United States, and Britain. Publicly, this new policy was reflected in Japan's talk of an Asian Monroe Doctrine.[10] A precise indication of what she meant was given in April 1934, when a Japanese Foreign Ministry spokesman declared that Japan had a special responsibility for maintaining peace in East Asia and that she would oppose any foreign military and economic aid to the Chinese.

Tokyo's growing pretensions in China during 1933-34 strained Anglo-Japanese relations. Another important source of friction was trade rivalry. The president of the Board of Trade, Sir Walter Runciman, told the Cabinet in March 1933: "The very low wages paid in Japan, coupled with the low value of the yen, made it impossible for this country to compete. The position had passed beyond that of a sporadic attack by business men on the trade of another country and was approaching a national movement by Japan to capture the markets of Asia and beyond that continent."[11] The government, under heavy pressure from the Lancashire textile industry, proceeded to impose quotas on Japanese imports into British colonies. This aroused considerable resentment in Tokyo.[12]

Difficulties in East Asia were only part of London's worries. Only nine months after coming to power in January of 1933, Hitler had taken Germany out of the Disarmament Conference and the League of Nations. The withdrawal from the League, coming as it did in the same year as Japan's, aroused alarm in Britain, not least because it seemed to foreshadow a rapprochement between the two dissatisfied powers. In the winter of 1933-34, the Defence Requirements Committee examined British military deficiencies in light of the deteriorating world situation, and concluded that though Japan was the greatest immediate problem,

Germany was the ultimate, more fundamental menace. Believing that Britain lacked the resources to meet both the German and the Japanese threats, the committee recommended early in 1934 that London try to get on better terms with Tokyo.*

This recommendation, which prompted a sustained, high-level reappraisal of British policy in East Asia, received the measured support of Foreign Secretary Simon and the enthusiastic endorsement of Neville Chamberlain, then Chancellor of the Exchequer. The two ministers, worried by clandestine German rearmament under Hitler, shared the committee's view that Britain could not afford to have a hostile Japan at her back in the event of a European war.[13] Though strategic considerations were the principal justification for trying to improve relations with Tokyo, the Federation of British Industries, which sent a mission to East Asia in late 1934, felt that a rapprochement would yield commercial benefits as well.[14]

As Simon frequently pointed out, however, there were formidable obstacles in the way of an Anglo-Japanese understanding, and in the winter of 1934-35 these difficulties checked the drive for a rapprochement. A desire not to alienate the United States was a major obstacle. Chamberlain, who believed that London could not rely on Washington's help in East Asia, was more or less indifferent to the prospect of American resentment, but Simon and Prime Minister Ramsay MacDonald were unwilling to move closer to Tokyo at the expense of good relations with America. A closely related difficulty was the question of naval limitation.

---

* The records of the Defence Requirements Committee are in CAB 16/109. The committee's conclusions reflected the influence of Sir Warren Fisher, head of the civil service and permanent under-secretary of the Treasury, and of Sir Robert Vansittart, permanent under-secretary of the Foreign Office. Vansittart's distrust of Germany, which has received much scholarly attention, was shared by Fisher, who also disliked the United States. In one note to his colleagues on the committee, Sir Warren wrote that "it is essential in my view to get clear of our 'entangling' agreement with the U.S.A. who should be left to circle the globe with ships if they want, to gratify their vanity by singing 'Rule Columbia, Columbia rules the waves,' and to wait and see for how many years the politically all-powerful Middle West will continue to acquiesce in paying a fantastic bill related to no real requirement but primarily to indulge the braggadocio of Yahoodom." Note by Fisher, Jan. 29, 1934, CAB 16/109.

During the fall of 1934, Japan insisted on parity with the British and American fleets. When she failed to get her way, she denounced the Five-Power Treaty of 1922, pushing London closer to Washington.[15] Japan's hard-line China policy also helped to undermine the possibility of Anglo-Japanese cooperation. In return for economic concessions, London might conceivably have been willing to give Japan some political support in China. But in an important memorandum circulated to the Cabinet in January 1935, Sir George Sansom warned against such a bargain. Sansom, a noted historian of Japan and the commercial counsellor to the British embassy in Tokyo, predicted that time would reveal structural weaknesses in the Japanese economy. Arguing that Japan would therefore be more amenable later on, he recommended not hurrying to come to terms. Simon, referring to Sir George as "the greatest living authority" on Japan, told the Cabinet that "his opinion must be the authoritative one in this matter."[16]

As Britain's hopes for an understanding with the Japanese faded, she began trying to negotiate a comprehensive European settlement with Hitler. The Foreign Office's plan, accepted by the Cabinet at the turn of 1934-35, was to seek concessions from Germany—her return to the League of Nations and her adherence to air, Danubian, and Eastern pacts—in exchange for the legalization of her rearmament. There was little in this scheme to attract Hitler, especially after he announced in March 1935 that he was reintroducing conscription and establishing an army of thirty-six divisions. This move undermined Britain's bargaining position, but she continued to negotiate. Though a controversial Anglo-German naval agreement was signed in June, the main negotiations for a European settlement came to a standstill later in the summer of 1935.[17]

The collapse of this first sustained attempt to reach agreement with Hitler coincided with a sharpening of the Italo-Abyssinian crisis. When Italy invaded Abyssinia in October 1935, the British faced a dilemma. They wanted to avoid war with Italy, not least because it might cripple their fleet. They also feared that

Anglo-Italian friction might push Rome into the arms of Berlin and encourage aggressive moves by Germany and Japan. But if they responded too timidly, the authority of the League would be undermined and the British public would be angry. These conflicting considerations led Britain to follow a "double policy" of conciliating Mussolini and at the same time pressing the League to adopt economic sanctions against him.[18] This contradictory course failed. The infamous Hoare-Laval plan to end the war caused such an uproar in Britain that the government disavowed it.* The sanctions antagonized Italy without stopping her, and they were lifted shortly after Abyssinia was defeated in May 1936.

One major result of the Abyssinian affair was that the Italians loomed as Britain's third potential enemy. A second result was that Hitler felt emboldened to reoccupy the demilitarized Rhineland in March 1936. Rather than challenge this German move, London made another effort to reach agreement with Berlin. Proposals offered by Hitler himself—an air pact, Germany's return to the League of Nations, and a security pact between Germany and her western neighbors—formed the basis of this second set of negotiations. The British were nonetheless unable to pin the Führer down, and by late 1936 the Foreign Office had lost hope of a genuine European settlement. Foreign Secretary Anthony Eden and his advisers were not averse to further negotiations, but their goal by this juncture was to play for time until Britain could build up her military strength.[19]

Though Germany and Italy dominated much of London's attention in 1935-36, the British by no means neglected East Asia. In June 1935 they announced that Sir Frederick Leith-Ross, the government's chief economic adviser, was going to China to investigate the economic situation there. The idea of this mission emerged from the deliberations of a Cabinet committee early in 1935, when the Chinese economy seemed about to collapse. The mission was meant not only to help the Nationalist government but also to make it clear to both Japan and China that Britain had,

---

* This Anglo-French plan would have ceded part of Abyssinia to Italy outright and given her economic control of another part.

in the words of the committee, "no intention of allowing ourselves to be ousted from our position in China and our fair share of the Chinese market."[20] Another, more ambitious, goal of the mission, according to Sir John Pratt of the Foreign Office, was "no less than a complete restitution of the whole complex of political relationships established by the Washington Conference and the Nine-Power Treaty as it had existed prior to Japan's seizure of Manchuria."[21] In short, the British hoped to persuade Japan to return to a policy of cooperation with the West. This naïve hope proved illusory: the Japanese merely intensified their efforts to dominate China. Their field armies were able to exclude the Kuomintang from Hopei and Chahar by the terms of the Ho-Umezu and Ch'in-Doihara agreements of June 1935. They then promoted a movement for autonomy in North China while their Foreign Ministry sought, albeit unsuccessfully, a comprehensive "friendship" treaty with the Chinese that would have made Nanking subservient to Tokyo.

The failure of the mission's political goals pushed its economic goals to the forefront. In November 1935, shortly after Leith-Ross's arrival in China, the Nanking government nationalized all silver stocks in the country and abandoned the silver standard in favor of a managed paper currency. Britain helped this reform to succeed by ordering her banks in China to hand over their silver holdings to the government. By the summer of 1936, Leith-Ross could report that the economic situation was promising, and that there was great potential in China for new British investment and increased trade.[22] His optimism stimulated activity. In the following autumn, for example, the Export Credit Guarantees Department appointed a special representative to China. This move was designed to ensure that the Chinese would purchase capital goods from British firms. China, for her part, negotiated for both a railway loan and a general loan.[23] As Britain's involvement in China's economic development increased, political relations grew closer, and her inclination to conciliate Japan diminished.

Upset but not deterred by this shift in Britain's stance, Japan sought in 1936 to consolidate her position in North China. In

November of that year, moreover, she tried to neutralize the Soviet Union's influence and power in East Asia by concluding the Anti-Comintern Pact with Germany. Sir Robert Vansittart of the Foreign Office voiced the apprehensions aroused in many British observers by this agreement:

At present the *appearance* is that of co-operation against communism; but the appearance convinces no one.... What the agreement clearly does do, however . . . is to introduce Japan into the orbit of European affairs at a particularly delicate and dangerous phase, and to increase the probability that, in given circumstances, Germany and Japan would now act together.[24]

Anticipating that Britain would be alarmed by the prospect of an increasingly dangerous interaction between her European and East Asian problems, Japan apparently hoped to exploit the Anti-Comintern Pact diplomatically to negotiate a *modus vivendi* with her.[25] Shortly before the agreement with Germany was signed, Japanese Ambassador Yoshida Shigeru told the British that his government wanted to reach an understanding with them. Yoshida, a staunch if ineffectual advocate of close relations between Britain and Japan, personally advanced some vague proposals about cooperation for the "protection" and reconstruction of China. The Foreign Office's reaction was cautious.[26] Convinced that there were elements of weakness in Japan's position—"the overshadowing presence of Russia, lack of financial strength and the enormous latent and elastic power of resistance which China possesses"—and determined to alienate neither Washington nor Nanking, Foreign Secretary Eden and his advisers wanted Britain to move slowly until the Japanese definitely moderated their policy and reached a détente with China.[27] London's response in early 1937 to Yoshida's approach therefore consisted largely of pointing out the difficulties in the way of a settlement. The Ambassador then asked Tokyo for concrete proposals, but apparently did not receive any before the outbreak of Sino-Japanese fighting in July 1937.[28]

While Britain was reacting cautiously to Japanese overtures in late 1936 and early 1937, she was actively seeking an improvement in her relations with Italy. From her standpoint, Mussolini's behavior in the second half of 1936 seemed exceedingly erratic. Soon after the Spanish Civil War began in July 1936, Italy and Germany intervened on the side of General Franco's insurgents, prompting the Soviets to support the government forces and arousing concern in London that the conflict might expand into a general European war. In November Mussolini proclaimed the Rome-Berlin Axis. During the same month, however, he indicated a desire for an understanding with London. Fearing the damage that a hostile Italy could do to Britain's lines of communication to the East, the Chiefs of Staff and a majority of the Cabinet wanted to seize this opening. Eden preferred a more circumspect attitude similar to that adopted toward Japan's approaches, but acceded to the wishes of his colleagues.[29] In January 1937 London and Rome concluded a "gentleman's agreement" in which they assured each other of their intention to respect the status quo in the Mediterranean. Anglo-Italian relations soon deteriorated again, however, as Mussolini sent more troops to Spain and issued anti-British propaganda. By the spring of 1937 Eden and some of his advisers believed that there was a greater immediate danger to peace from an incident created by Rome than from a move made by Berlin.[30]

At this juncture, Neville Chamberlain became Prime Minister. Eden remained as Foreign Secretary, a position that he had held since late 1935. The new Cabinet included two of his predecessors at the Foreign Office, Home Secretary Sir Samuel Hoare and Chancellor of the Exchequer Sir John Simon, as well as his successor in February 1938, Lord Halifax. As their critics have long insisted, these men had considerable shortcomings. Chamberlain not only was vain and obstinate, but also clung to a belief in negotiation and reason in an age when such values were scorned by his antagonists. Hoare (in A. J. P. Taylor's phrase) "suffered from excessive cleverness,"[31] Simon was doomed to vacillation by his own analytical mind, and Halifax languidly accommodated himself to unpleasant circumstances. Even Eden, whose reputation emerged unsullied from the 1930's, was rarely as resolute in his deeds as in his public pronouncements.

The Chamberlain Cabinet's unhappy record, however, was due

less to personal weaknesses than to the magnitude and intractability of the difficulties with which it had to deal. The fundamental problem was how to stave off war and maintain a leading position in the world at a time when Britain lacked the military and economic strength to cow Germany, Italy, and Japan. Chamberlain wanted to deal realistically yet decisively with this conundrum. He believed that policy should be in line with power. He also thought that conciliatory British initiatives would lead to a settlement in Europe, or at least to a reduction in tension there. Feeling that Germany was the principal disruptive force, and that the best way of countering Mussolini's disquieting attitude was to get on better terms with Hitler, Chamberlain made his initial approach to Berlin. Germany's Foreign Minister, Baron von Neurath, was invited to London. Von Neurath at first accepted this invitation, but then withdrew his acceptance in late June. The failure of this initiative did not discourage the Prime Minister from further efforts to reach agreement with Germany, though he thenceforth directed his attention toward Italy as well.

Chamberlain, having changed his stance since 1934, gave considerably less thought to conciliation in East Asia than in Europe. He did not inject vigor into the somewhat laggard discussions between the Foreign Office and Yoshida, nor did he even revive the moribund Cabinet Committee on Political and Economic Relations with Japan. In March 1937, however, while still Chancellor of the Exchequer, he had sent a memorandum to the United States suggesting an exchange of views on the possibility of improving Anglo-American-Japanese relations. Washington's cool response killed this idea.[32] At an Imperial Conference in May Australia proposed a Pacific non-aggression pact. Though the gathering endorsed this suggestion, the British thought it premature, and nothing came of it.[33]

No doubt one reason why Chamberlain concentrated on Europe was that the situation in East Asia seemed to be brightening. By early 1937 the Japanese General Staff had become more concerned than ever over the possibility of war with the Soviets, who had steadily increased their military forces in East Asia since the

Manchurian crisis. Fearing that its preparations against Moscow would be hampered by the outbreak of an incident in North China, the staff wanted to modify Japan's aggressive policy there. The civilian leaders were equally anxious to avoid hostilities with Nanking. Though the Japanese still wished to exclude the Kuomintang from the northern provinces, their attitude toward the Chinese grew noticeably milder.[34] From his vantage point in London, Eden stated in May that "there appeared to be signs of the dawn of a new era in the relations between China and Japan since Japan was apparently modifying her views with regard to the right way of dealing with China."[35]

The potency of two sources of friction, however, clouded the prospects for peace in East Asia. Relations between Japan and the Soviet Union grew increasingly strained, as was reflected in fighting between the two powers along the Amur River in June and early July of 1937. More important, Nanking was becoming militant. After the Manchurian crisis, Generalissimo Chiang Kai-shek had conciliated Tokyo so that he could gain time to build up his military strength and to suppress the Chinese Communists. But by 1936 widespread sentiment had developed in China for an end to the civil war and for a stronger stand against Japan. After the mysterious Sian Incident late in that year, the stubborn and taciturn Generalissimo finally moved toward an anti-Japanese united front with Mao Tse-tung.[36] Continued pressure by the Communist Party, the advice of German military advisers, and the growing Soviet and British interest in China apparently convinced Chiang in the spring and summer of 1937 to try to restore his authority in the northern provinces, or at least to resist any new Japanese encroachment there.[37]

Fighting between China and Japan broke out at Lukouchiao (Marco Polo Bridge) on July 7, 1937. This incident, unlike that at Mukden in 1931, was not engineered by the Japanese military. Neither side wanted war, but neither adopted a conciliatory stance. With one eye on nationalistic opinion in China, Chiang insisted on playing a part in any settlement, but Premier Konoe Fumimaro, who had recently come to power, refused to allow him

to interfere. A major war soon developed. Konoe, the widely respected scion of the Fujiwara clan, and Foreign Minister Hirota
Koki, instrumental in Japan's drive for predominance in China
since 1933, exhorted their countrymen to "chastise" and "rejuve-
nate" China.

Japan not only proceeded to push the Chinese into the interior,
but also threatened British interests in the occupied areas. Despite the growing German and Italian menaces nearer home,
everyone in London regarded Britain's position in China as too
important to be abandoned. Most British officials saw this position in economic terms. In the first six months of 1937, Britain
sent exports worth more than £4 million (over 1 percent of her
total) to China and imported Chinese goods worth approximately
£2.1 million.[38] Though in retrospect these amounts seem relatively small, many British leaders in the 1930's thought them significant. In May 1935, for example, Chamberlain and Sir Walter
Runciman asserted that "in the present state of world trade and
the consequent depression in our textile and heavy industries, it
is clearly out of the question for us to contemplate being pushed
out of our existing market in China or being deprived of our
share in the potential market which exists there, especially for
capital goods."[39] As for Britain's investments in China, one cautious estimate in 1937 put their value at £250 million, about 6
percent of British overseas holdings and 35 percent of all foreign
investments in China.[40] According to Sir Robert Craigie, who became ambassador to Japan in 1937, these holdings assumed "an
ever increasing importance" because of the "steady shrinkage of
our foreign investments throughout the world" since 1933.[41] Britain also had extensive shipping interests in China; indeed, British
ships carried 41.9 percent of the total tonnage of foreign, coastal,
and inland shipping in 1936.[42]

Important as these existing interests seemed, it was China's potential as a market and a field for investment that most impressed
the British. Convinced that the Nationalist economy had received
a tremendous boost from the Leith-Ross mission of 1935, they
viewed China as one of the few expanding markets in the world.

In May 1937 the Department of Overseas Trade published a report that gave a favorable picture of China's development, called attention to the apparent expansion of her markets since 1935, and pointed out her need for capital.[43] Such optimism, however, was not entirely justified. Even after the currency reforms of 1935, the Chinese economy was probably close to stagnation.[44] Even if the projected China market became a reality, moreover, the United States, Japan, and Germany—which had long been increasing their shares of China's trade at the expense of Britain's share—were the more likely beneficiaries. Nor was London's hope that China would be an increasingly attractive field for British investment wholly warranted. The Nationalist government was fostering monopolies in many economic sectors and imposing heavy taxes on enterprises in which there was foreign investment.[45]

A significant part of Britain's economic interests in China had grown out of her political position there, which was based on unequal treaties dating back to the 1840's. The British had concessions in Tientsin and Canton; administrative privileges at Hankow, Kulangsu, and Peking; and a predominant influence in the important International Settlement at Shanghai. In all these places, British nationals enjoyed extraterritorial "rights." It was these privileges that the Nationalists had attacked in the 1920's and early 1930's. Sino-Japanese friction after September 1931 had diverted Chiang Kai-shek's attention from these infringements of China's sovereignty. The British remained prepared to discuss these matters with him, but were definitely in no hurry to abandon their privileges.[46]

The Japanese advance on the Asian mainland not only endangered Britain's economic and political position in China, but also posed a strategic threat to her vast possessions and interests in South Asia and the western Pacific. She had formal control over Hong Kong, India, Burma, Malaya, Singapore, North Borneo, Brunei, and Sarawak; had large investments in Thailand and the Netherlands East Indies; and was largely responsible for the defense of Australia and New Zealand. If the British became involved in a war, it would be essential for them to maintain their trade with these areas, which supplied rubber, tin, oil, food, and other materials that were important in wartime.[47] So long as Japan was bogged down in China, Britain's interests to the south and the west seemed secure. But London feared that if the Japanese defeated Chiang Kai-shek, they would be emboldened to attack the British Empire in Asia and the Pacific. Britain therefore generally tended to view China as the Empire's first line of defense.

The Chamberlain government's task in East Asia after July 1937 was to find a way to protect its interests by either halting or diverting the Japanese advance. Four basic alternatives were open: a firm line, including economic sanctions against Japan and substantial financial, political, and perhaps even military assistance to China; a policy of benevolent neutrality that would favor China by giving her moral support and limited material aid, but at the same time avoid a confrontation with Japan; a genuinely impartial stance insofar as possible; or appeasement of the Japanese. This last alternative would have involved stopping all support for Chiang Kai-shek and recognizing Japan's predominant position in the northern provinces, if not in other parts of China as well. It might also have meant removing barriers against the flow of Japanese goods into the British Empire and lending Tokyo money for the development of occupied areas on the Asian mainland. In return, Britain would no doubt have pressed for guarantees that her interests in China would be respected, for an end to the war, and perhaps for a non-aggression pact.

In evaluating these possible courses, British leaders took into account many factors, least important of which were public opinion in Britain, the advice of commercial and financial interests, and the views of the Dominions. Public sentiment was distinctly anti-Japanese. Events in East Asia, however, were not a major issue in British politics in 1937-39. There was only sporadic pressure on the Cabinet for strong action against Japan, and Chamberlain and his colleagues were never pushed into taking steps they opposed on other grounds. The most that can be said of public opinion is that it reinforced the government's aversion to conciliating Japan. The influence exerted on policy by the City and by British commercial groups in China is more difficult to gauge, but seems slighter than in 1934-35. The traders and financiers were in close contact with the Foreign Office and other departments, and their objective—to protect Britain's economic position in China—was fully shared by the government. Even so, their advice was hardly decisive in the formulation of policy, partly because the Foreign Office believed that it was the best judge of how to deal with Japan and partly because different commercial and financial groups held widely varying views.* The Dominions, for their part, also disagreed over what course Britain should take. New Zealand favored a strong line, whereas Canada, South Africa, and Australia were opposed to any action that might provoke Japan. The views of the latter three were frequently cited by those officials in London who did not want to impose sanctions on Japan. On other issues, however, the Dominions had surprisingly little influence.

Three factors that did fundamentally shape Britain's Far Eastern policy were the European situation, the American attitude, and Britain's own military weakness. A rapid succession of crises in Europe after 1937 not only dominated most of London's attention, forcing East Asian problems into the background for much of the period, but also made clear the need for caution in China. The British feared that any precipitate move on their part in the East would have destabilizing repercussions in Europe. Also, they could not count on United States support. In a memorandum sent to London more than a month before the Lukouchiao Incident, the State Department indicated that it favored "parallel" rather than joint action with the British,[48] and the Roosevelt administration adhered to this posture fairly consistently in the ensuing years.

Had Britain been stronger militarily, she would have been less inhibited by European instability and American reticence. From

---

* Commercial groups generally favored a firm stand against Japan; but many financiers, especially in the early stages of the war, favored conciliating her.

1919 to 1932, however, British defense spending had been based on the assumption that there would be no major war for ten years. Even when Sino-Japanese fighting at Shanghai in 1932 led to the abandonment of this "ten-year rule," and the Defence Requirements Committee's recommendations were in, the Cabinet moved cautiously, fearing that large defense expenditures would be politically unpopular and economically harmful. Serious rearmament did not begin until 1936, when the Cabinet accepted a fairly comprehensive scheme to renovate and augment British forces; and even then the newly created post of Minister for Co-ordination of Defence was given to the rather phlegmatic Sir Thomas Inskip. Under his indecisive supervision, rearmament proceeded slowly.[49]

The Royal Navy, which would play the primary role in a war with Japan, started programs in 1936 that provided mostly for modernizing old ships and replacing obsolete ones. These measures were in line with the principle that Britain should be able to send to the Far East a fleet large enough to furnish "cover" against the Japanese fleet and still have a sufficient force to protect her home waters against the strongest European naval power. The Defence Requirements Committee had recommended in late 1935, however, that Britain should aim at a higher standard of naval strength, one that would enable her to place a fleet in the Far East "fully adequate to act on the defensive and to serve as a strong deterrent against any threat to our interests in that part of the globe" and, at the same time, to maintain in home waters "a force able to meet the requirements of a war with Germany."[50] After naval strategists worked out plans to put the new standard into effect, Sir Samuel Hoare (then First Lord of the Admiralty) brought the question before the Defence Plans (Policy) Committee in the spring of 1937. He warned his colleagues that the fleet, on its existing standard, could not safeguard the Empire in the East against Japan if Britain became involved in a European war.[51] The economy-minded Cabinet nonetheless postponed a decision on the higher standard in 1937-38.

Predictably, the Chiefs of Staff were quite concerned over the sluggish pace of British rearmament. In February 1937, for example, they warned that until Britain was rearmed, she would "be seriously handicapped if forced into war, either in the west or the east."[52] In June 1937 the Chiefs of Staff prepared a full appreciation of the problems that would be raised by the outbreak of Anglo-Japanese hostilities. The basis of Britain's strategy would be to send her fleet to Singapore as soon as possible after the war started; otherwise, India, Australia, and New Zealand would be open to attack. Yet, as they pointed out, the base at Singapore would not be ready to meet full wartime requirements until late 1940. The strategists warned, moreover, that it might take seventy days for the fleet to reach Singapore, during which time Britain's interests in the East would be at the mercy of the Japanese.[53]

Clearly, the British would be confronted with grave difficulties in the event of a war with Japan. But the principal cause for worry was the growing likelihood that a conflict on one side of the world would spread to the other side, and that Britain would find herself simultaneously at war with Germany, Italy, and Japan. As the Chiefs of Staff were to declare repeatedly in 1937-39, Britain's defense forces would not be strong enough for this in the foreseeable future. The menace of German air attacks aside, such a war would "introduce the problem of our security in the Mediterranean and Red Sea in its acutest form." The Chiefs of Staff declared, however, that anxieties about the situation in the Mediterranean should not keep a fleet from being sent to Singapore. If the Soviets somehow became involved in the war against Germany, Italy, and Japan, some of Britain's military problems might be alleviated, but the strategists feared that a Soviet victory over Japan could "result in the spread of some form of communism through China and the establishment of Soviet influence up to the borders of India and Burma."[54]

In summary, then, military weakness, together with the European crisis and American reluctance to cooperate, virtually precluded a hard-line policy toward Japan. But these constraints were less important in Britain's weighing of her remaining policy

options—benevolent neutrality, impartiality, and appeasement—
than were her evaluations of the rapidly changing situation in
East Asia. Was Japanese imperialism stronger than Chinese nationalism? Was there a limit to Japan's ambitions? Were there
moderate elements in the Japanese government with whom Britain could cooperate? Could communism succeed in China? To
what extent were the interests of London and of Chiang Kai-shek
"identical" or, at any rate, complementary? Britain pondered
these questions at length—and well she might, for the answers
to them held the key to her future in East Asia.

Chapter two

The Outbreak of Fighting in China

ON JULY 7, 1937, a company of Japanese soldiers on maneuvers and troops of the Chinese 29th Army exchanged fire in the vicinity of Lukouchiao, which was a railway junction not far from Peking. Late that night, a Japanese officer requested entrance to Wanping, a town near Lukouchiao, to search for a soldier who was allegedly missing. The Chinese refused, and a second skirmish soon broke out. Negotiations ensued and, though a third flurry of fighting took place on July 9, a local agreement between the two field armies was reached two days later. This understanding called for the Chinese to withdraw their troops from the area, enforce anticommunist measures, apologize for the incident, and punish those who were responsible.[1] The settlement did not mark the end of trouble, however, because by this time the central governments of Japan and China were deeply involved in the North China situation. Soon after receiving reports of the skirmishes, Tokyo had decided to try to "localize" the incident, but on July 10 Nanking announced that it reserved the right to reject any local agreement. Nanking also dispatched four army divisions to southern Hopei; these troop movements were particularly significant because Tokyo would regard them as a violation of the Ho-Umezu Agreement of 1935. Japan responded on July 11 both by warning Chiang Kai-shek not to interfere with a local settlement and by sending reinforcements to North China from Manchukuo and Korea. Thus, within four days of the initial fighting, the conflicting policies of the Chinese and Japanese governments were setting in motion a series of events that would result in large-scale hostilities.[2]

The first dispatch about the Lukouchiao Incident reached London on July 9, but the Foreign Office did not realize how grave the developments in East Asia were until further information arrived on July 12 and 13. Though preliminary reports indicated that apparently neither side had deliberately provoked the incident, the British feared that Japan might exploit it to strengthen her position in North China, and Foreign Secretary Eden therefore decided to press her to exercise restraint. On July 12 he warned Japanese Ambassador Yoshida that if the tension in the Peking area persisted or grew worse, conversations leading toward better relations between Britain and Japan "would hardly be possible."[3] Eden then instructed James Dodds, chargé d'affaires in Tokyo, to repeat this warning directly to Foreign Minister Hirota Koki as soon as possible. Dodds believed that the proper moment for this threat had not yet arrived, and thus when he saw Hirota on July 14 he moderated the language of Eden's warning.[4]

Meanwhile, on July 13, the Foreign Office had asked the Americans to join Britain in urging restraint on Tokyo. The State Department explained to Sir Ronald Lindsay, the British ambassador, that joint representations would only antagonize Japan, and that the United States accordingly preferred cooperation on "parallel but independent lines."[5] This rebuff disappointed Britain, but did not keep the Foreign Office from instructing Dodds again to counsel moderation to the Japanese. London also told Sir Hughe Knatchbull-Hugessen, the ambassador to China, to ask the Chinese to exercise restraint and not do anything that would make the situation worse.[6]

By mid-July, Britain's representatives in East Asia began to make judgments about the Sino-Japanese crisis. Dodds believed that "Japan did not want the incident, does not want to have to push it through, and is not being provocative."[7] He viewed British attempts to restrain Tokyo as pointless, if not counterproductive,* and he told London that a peaceful solution of the trouble "depends on the ability of [the] Chinese government to restrain its nationals."[8] Knatchbull-Hugessen was inclined to agree with Dodds that Japan had not engineered the incident and did not want it to spread. But, as Sir Hughe realized, China did not share this estimate of Japan's intentions and was preparing to resist what she regarded as a new act of Japanese aggression. In fact, Knatchbull-Hugessen had suspected for some time that Nanking was increasingly thinking in terms of extending its authority to the northern provinces and even to Manchuria. He had noted in March that the Chinese "are firmly resolved to bring to an end, sooner rather than later, the 'special position' which Japan is trying to build up [for] herself in the North."[9] In late April he had reported that China was making large-scale military preparations, and that, according to Foreign Minister Wang Ch'ung-hui, Nanking "intended sooner or later to recover Manchoukuo and would employ force if necessary."[10] Nevertheless, in the days following the Lukouchiao Incident, the Chinese assured Knatchbull-Hugessen that they had no aggressive intentions and wanted peace, though they did make it clear that they would not tolerate any step by Japan to consolidate her control of North China. Then on July 15 Sir Hughe was given a statement prepared by Chiang Kai-shek revealing that Nanking was ready for war and was moving troops north to resist the Japanese. To the Ambassador's alarm, this message seemed to indicate that the Chinese had finally decided to act decisively to assert their influence in the northern provinces. He immediately admonished Wang Ch'ung-hui that "it was impossible for me to make use of this statement in its existing form, that if it became known it would have the

---

* Dodds's assessment, particularly his belief that Japan should not be pressed, may have been influenced by the more experienced American ambassador, Joseph Grew. Grew's diary for July 15, 1937, comments: "He [Dodds] tells me everything that he is doing, shows me his telegrams and asks my advice." On July 23 Grew added that "we agree all along the line on estimates and policies. Our cooperation is so complete that it's almost as if he [Dodds] were a member of my own staff." See Grew Papers.

effect of another Ems telegram." Wang replied that he "fully realized" the implications of the statement, and that "it showed
Chiang Kai-shek's state of mind."[11]

In short, the reports of Knatchbull-Hugessen and Dodds indicated that, whereas Japan had not provoked the incident and
wanted to localize the trouble, China was very likely to resist any
such local settlement. This picture, which showed the Chinese as
the more belligerent of the principals, was accepted tentatively
and with reservations by the top figures in the Foreign Office.
Eden told the Cabinet that "so far as could be judged from the
information received by the Foreign Office, the present situation
in the neighbourhood of Peking had not been brought about by
deliberate Japanese initiative." But he was apprehensive that
Japan might take some action that would precipitate widespread
fighting.[12] Sir Alexander Cadogan, the deputy under-secretary, was
more skeptical: "In spite of reassuring messages from Tokyo, I
can't say I like the look of things. The Japanese assurances [that
they want a local settlement] remind me forcibly of six years ago,
and I couldn't like to put too much faith in them *yet*."[13]

All British officials agreed on the seriousness of the situation.
Knatchbull-Hugessen warned that trouble could not be avoided if
by localizing the dispute the Japanese meant carrying their control
of North China one step further and then returning to normal
conditions. The Chinese, he emphasized, would not accept such a
dénouement.[14] Sir Hughe seems to have put his finger on the
truth of the matter. Since the signing of the local agreement on
July 11 Japan had been trying to persuade the chairman of the
Hopei-Chahar Political Council, General Sung Che-yuan, to accept it. For the previous two years, General Sung had, in the words
of one observer, "out Chinesed the Chinese in devising obstructive
methods of irritating resistance to Japanese penetration."[15] But
on July 18-19, evidently convinced that Japan was not trying to
cause trouble this time, he consented to an understanding based
on the agreement. The Chinese troops who had been involved in
the fighting at Lukouchiao and Wanping began to withdraw.[16]

Thus the Japanese field army had once again "solved" the

North China problem in accordance with Tokyo's policy of excluding the Kuomintang from the region. Nanking, however, remained determined not to tolerate any such local settlement. In an *aide-mémoire* delivered on July 17, Tokyo had in effect demanded that the Chinese government refrain from interfering in the North China situation. Nanking responded the next day by reiterating its right to veto any settlement reached by local authorities.[17] This reply was followed by Chiang Kai-shek's famous speech at Kuling, in which he declared that China, though desiring peace, was nearing the limit of her patience and would not allow "one inch more" of her territory to be lost. Chiang also outlined four points that constituted the minimum basis for Sino-Japanese negotiations: Chinese sovereignty must be upheld; the status of the Hopei-Chahar Political Council was not to be altered; no official appointed by Nanking could be removed; and the disposition of General Sung's 29th Army must not be restricted.[18] It was now more apparent than ever that Japanese and Chinese policies toward North China were fundamentally at odds. In a word, Chiang sought a resolution of the crisis that would at the least restore the status quo ante and preserve what remained of his authority in the north, whereas Tokyo hoped to minimize his influence there.[19] Unless one or the other took a more moderate stand, a conflagration seemed likely.

Faced with this ominous spiral of events, London considered what steps, if any, should be taken to prevent the outbreak of war. Not surprisingly, the feasibility of mediation was carefully explored. As early as July 12 Quo Tai-chi, the experienced Chinese ambassador to London, had pressed Britain to mediate. The British had been reluctant to proffer good offices at that stage, because they felt that Japan would reject the offer.[20] Nevertheless on July 15 Dodds did hint in Tokyo that London would be willing to act in a mediatory capacity; this cautious approach elicited no response from the Japanese.[21] On the following day, the Chinese asked Britain to inform Japan that they were willing to agree to a mutual cessation of troop movements on July 17, after which arrangements could be made for the restoration of the status quo ante.[22] Without awaiting instructions from London, Dodds informed Tokyo of this standstill proposal,* but the Japanese indicated on July 18 that it was unacceptable.[23]

Even after Japan had rejected the proposal, Eden wanted London to keep on trying to avert war. If the British were silent, Tokyo might be encouraged to take some aggressive step, and he thus announced publicly on July 21 that conversations to improve Anglo-Japanese relations would not be held "so long as the present situation in North China persists."[24] Meanwhile, London was also trying once again to secure Washington's cooperation. At the suggestion of Prime Minister Chamberlain, Eden asked the United States on July 20 whether she would join the British in pressing the Chinese and Japanese to suspend troop movements and in putting forward proposals that might lead to a settlement.[25] On the following day, before the State Department had responded to this approach, the American ambassador in London, Robert Bingham, suggested on his own authority that Britain propose to Washington a joint trade embargo on Japan. Bingham, a staunch advocate of Anglo-American solidarity, explained his startling suggestion by arguing that "if some attempt were not made to call a halt to Japanese aggression there would soon be an end not only to the trade of both our countries with China, but also a total loss of the large investments both our countries possessed in the Far East." The Ambassador begged Eden to tell no one, least of all the State Department, that he had made the proposal.[26] When the Foreign Secretary informed Chamberlain of Bingham's suggestion, the Prime Minister said he hoped the idea would go no further because it might so seriously damage Anglo-Japanese relations

---

* In writing about the proposal some years later, Joseph Grew, then American ambassador in Tokyo, saw Japan's rejection as indicating she was not interested in avoiding hostilities with China. But Grew's assertion misses the point: Tokyo's response to Nanking's initiative was less a reflection of its attitude toward peace than of its overriding concern to exclude the Kuomintang from the local negotiations in North China. See Joseph C. Grew, *Turbulent Era: A Diplomatic Record of Forty Years, 1904-1945* (Boston: Houghton Mifflin, 1952), 2: 1050; and Grew, *Ten Years in Japan* (New York: Simon and Schuster, 1944), p. 230. The entry for July 20, 1937, in Grew's diary contains a more balanced statement on the Japanese position. See Grew Papers.

that Britain would be forced to spend "millions in defensive measures in the Far East."[27] Eden himself seemed unenthusiastic about an embargo, but he did hope that Bingham's proposal reflected a desire in Washington to support his approach of July 20. Hence, when the American reply of July 21 rejected the British plan and reiterated the State Department's preference for parallel action, he was deeply disappointed.[28] It was becoming increasingly clear that the United States intended insofar as possible to avoid involvement in the Sino-Japanese dispute. This intention was underscored when, on July 23, Lindsay advised Eden that Bingham was talking "nonsense" and was "miles . . . out of touch with the State Department."[29]

Surprisingly, the tension in East Asia appeared to ease somewhat at this time. The British consul-general at Peking told London that the War Office in Tokyo had ordered Japanese military authorities in North China to avoid further fighting.[30] Moreover, Chiang had apparently decided after all not to contest the local settlement that had been reached,[31] and some Japanese emissaries were making peace overtures to the Chinese. Optimism prevailed in Tokyo, where it was felt that Nanking intended nothing "beyond a war of words."[32] Notwithstanding these hopeful signs, tension began to build between the two field armies in North China, and on July 25 and 26 skirmishes occurred at Langfang and Peking. Acting with the approval of central headquarters in Tokyo, the commanding officer of the Japanese army in North China presented Sung Che-yuan with an ultimatum demanding the complete withdrawal of Chinese troops from the Wanping area within one day. On July 27, before the deadline, the Chinese troops at Wanping attacked the Japanese, and a fierce battle soon raged.[33] But rather than risk a crushing defeat, Sung withdrew his army, and the Japanese soon gained control of the whole area around Peking and Tientsin. That accomplished, the Japanese General Staff called a halt to further operations by the field army in hopes that a comprehensive political settlement of the North China problem could now be reached. By August 7 the Konoe Cabinet had formulated conditions for a settlement, and three

days later the Japanese ambassador in China transmitted an out-
line of Japan's terms to the Chinese Foreign Ministry.[34]

The reaction of British officials to all this warrants detailed
attention. From Tokyo, Dodds reiterated his belief that Japan did
not seek large-scale fighting with China, though he did concede
that the Japanese military was prone to aggravate the situation.
According to Dodds, the greatest threat to peace was Chiang Kai-
shek's deliberate exaggeration of the Japanese menace.[35]

Knatchbull-Hugessen disagreed. Whereas in his earlier cables he
had emphasized China's willingness to fight, he now stressed the
aggressive behavior of the Japanese army. Though Japan had not
provoked the incident, the Japanese military had reacted "extrav-
agantly" to it and

deliberately exploited it for the purpose of obtaining a settlement of the
North China situation once and for all. There was absolutely nothing
in the incident to justify the despatch of reinforcements from Manchuria
or Japan, and it is obvious that the Army misled the Japanese Government as to the seriousness of the situation and deliberately worked up
feeling.[36]

Sir Hughe was convinced that in light of this behavior and of
Japan's China policy since 1931, Chiang was not exaggerating the
Japanese threat. Chiang was willing to negotiate with Japan but
could not allow himself to be "jockeyed [into] blind acceptance
of some local settlement which will destroy [China's] position in
the north once and for all," because Chinese nationalistic opinion
would then oust him from power.[37] Hence Britain must not advise
him to accept Japan's proposals, nor even ask him to suspend
troop movements; so far as both Chiang's position and Britain's
interests in China were concerned, the "risks resulting from military defeat are definitely smaller than those from immediate acquiescence in Japanese demands."[38]

Thus by early August the Foreign Office was receiving markedly
divergent analyses of the situation from its representatives in East
Asia. In particular, there was much uncertainty about Japanese intentions. The Foreign Office had received widely varying versions
of the terms of the local settlement reached on July 19 and conflicting estimates of what further demands, if any, the Japanese

intended to press upon the Chinese. To make matters worse, the Chinese central government maintained that it knew nothing about the July 19 agreement and nevertheless insisted that Japan's demands were constantly increasing.[39]

Observers in the Foreign Office were understandably perplexed. Nigel B. Ronald of the Far Eastern Department adopted a philosophical approach to the conflict:

"China" is not a unit susceptible of clear definition: it is rather a vague concept sanctified by long usage. In a sense therefore it is itself a sham, as possessing so little definable reality. Perhaps it is this quality of unreality, quite as much as the Chinese predilection for all sorts of make-believe and self-deception, which so infuriates the Japanese with their passion for the orderly treatment of a recognisable and tangible objective reality.[40]

Throughout July, Ronald had hoped that China would conciliate the Japanese, but in August he decided that "the risks to British interests are probably quite as great whether the Chinese resist or acquiesce."[41] He agreed with Knatchbull-Hugessen's analysis of Japanese intentions, but his view of politics in China was not sanguine. "The Chinese," he wrote, "have gone on long enough playing at being soldiers, playing at being the constructors of a super-modern state. [Until they] are brought to face the fact that their whole political system is riddled with shams by seeing it reduced to ruins, they are likely to go on in the bad old way."[42]

Charles W. Orde, head of the Far Eastern Department, shared many of Ronald's opinions. He believed that the Chinese were "inveterate wrigglers and self-deceivers," and that they were "infuriating to live with even when one's desires are legitimate." But Orde pointed out that "this does not excuse the Japanese, whose desires are exorbitant."[43] Sir John Pratt, who had spent many years in the consular service in China, summed up his colleagues' attitude when he wrote that the Japanese had "behaved in a provocative manner," but that the Chinese had "as usual acted in a thoroughly irresponsible and idiotic manner. We may consider that Japan has used excessive force to deal with this menace, but we cannot prove it."[44]

The top officials in the Foreign Office saw the situation in less complex terms. Cadogan, a former ambassador to China, bluntly declared that "the Japanese have not got a leg to stand upon," inasmuch as the conflict resulted from their attempts to "further their policy of blatant aggression."[45] He insisted that the Japanese were far less concerned than the Chinese to keep the peace, and that in any future assessment of blame, Britain would have to side with the Chinese.[46] Eden, too, was apparently certain that Japan had aggressive intentions.[47]

Eden and Cadogan felt far more strongly than the lower-level officials that Britain should move to restrain Japan at once, but it was difficult to formulate a plan of action that would be both feasible and effective. As Pratt pointed out, "nothing but force will restrain Japan and neither we nor America are prepared to use force."[48] Certain less drastic steps were likewise impossible. On July 24 Britain probed the Germans to see whether they might cooperate in trying to restore peace in East Asia, but they showed no interest in the idea.[49] Four days later, and again on August 4, the Chinese ambassador in London asked whether the British would sell aircraft and other war matériel to China, but Eden refused, explaining that Britain's own rearmament and her prior commitments to other countries were absorbing all her supplies and production.[50] Meanwhile, the Soviet Union was hinting that she would be willing to join the British in collective action of some sort against Japan, but Nigel Ronald reflected the feeling in the Foreign Office when he asserted that Britain should associate herself with the Soviet Union only "as a very last resort," and that collaboration with Stalin would "constitute an evil day."[51] In fact, the British strongly opposed any Russian intervention in East Asia. And their concern was heightened by reports that Chiang Kai-shek was seeking assistance from Moscow. Britain's fear of Soviet intervention had little to do with the Chinese Communist Party; the Foreign Office held a very low opinion of the CCP's importance and capabilities.[52] Rather, the British feared that increased Soviet influence would be detrimental to Britain's position in China, as it had been in the 1920's, and would provoke the active intervention of Germany and Italy on Japan's behalf in the Sino-Japanese dispute. Hence the Foreign Office was relieved by later reports that the Soviets sought no great involvement.[53]

At this juncture, Eden felt there was nothing to do but approach the United States again. He did not want Britain to act alone, and he thought it vital to establish the basis of Anglo-American cooperation if the British were to weather future storms in both Europe and East Asia. Thus on July 28 Eden repeated to Ambassador Bingham his proposal of July 20. The American reply of July 30 asked Britain to specify the *modus vivendi* she envisaged in her proposal and suggested that perhaps she could call for an evacuation of "*all* foreign personnel" and all Chinese military forces from the Peking area.[54] The Foreign Office did not like the American suggestion, for it would be useless to ask the Japanese to withdraw their troops, and proposed instead that the United States and Britain assist the Japanese and Chinese in opening negotiations and smooth over any difficulties that might arise during these talks.[55] The Americans were not enthusiastic about the British plan, and in fact tended to think that London's policy since July 7 had been somewhat imprudent. Joseph Grew was particularly critical of Britain, describing the Foreign Office's diplomacy as naïve. It seemed to him that the British, with the exception of Dodds, failed to realize that representations would only antagonize Japan. Grew believed that the Foreign Office's attempt to use the Anglo-Japanese negotiations at London to restrain Japan was inept; such clumsy threats, he maintained, would poison Anglo-Japanese relations for some time to come. Even an offer of good offices was, in his opinion, likely to do as much harm as good.[56] Nevertheless, the State Department consented to separate and informal approaches to Tokyo by Grew and Dodds along the lines of the Foreign Office proposal. These feelers, made on August 10 and 11, were politely rebuffed by Foreign Minister Hirota, who informed the two representatives that Japan was already negotiating with China.[57]

Thus by the second week in August the situation in China was bleak. According to Knatchbull-Hugessen, the Chinese were ready "to fight to a finish."[58] Though the Japanese seemed anxious to

avoid large-scale fighting and were offering what they considered
to be generous terms, there was little chance that the negotiations
would result in a lasting settlement, because Japan wanted a "fundamental readjustment of Sino-Japanese relations" and China had
"already reached the very limit of concession."[59] Further fighting
was imminent, and Britain could do little to prevent it. The only
consolation for the British was that hostilities would apparently
be confined to North China. Britain's relatively minor interests
there would suffer gravely, but the major British interests in
Shanghai and South China would presumably be fairly safe.

Ominous tensions, however, were developing in the Shanghai
area. A fragile peace had existed there since the truce agreement
of 1932, which had created a demilitarized zone around the city to
be policed by so-called Chinese Peace Preservation Corps and
established a joint commission of Chinese, Japanese, and Western
nationals to supervise the agreement. In June 1937 the Japanese
called a meeting of the joint commission and charged that the
Chinese were violating the truce by expanding the Peace Preservation Corps, moving artillery and tanks into the demilitarized zone,
and building fortifications there. No action was taken because the
commission could not decide whether the 1932 agreement was
still valid. When war broke out in North China, Sino-Japanese
tension in Shanghai increased. By early August the area seemed
on the brink of war, and many panic-stricken Chinese nationals
fled into the International Settlement. According to the acting British consul-general in Shanghai, the Peace Preservation Corps,
which "were in fact regular soldiers," were "no longer under civilian control" and were adopting a more openly anti-Japanese attitude.[60] Meanwhile, Knatchbull-Hugessen was becoming alarmed
that the Chinese might shift the field of battle from North China
to Shanghai; as he later commented, "the Chinese authorities
seemed to have Shanghai so much in their minds."[61] On August
8 the Chinese Foreign Minister told Sir Hughe that if the Japanese
sent any reinforcements to Shanghai, China would attack.[62] On
the following day, a British War Office report argued that General
Alexander von Falkenhausen, the German military adviser to

Nanking, would try to convince Chiang Kai-shek to strike for a quick and decisive victory somewhere in China.* The report went on to predict that the Chinese might provoke an incident in Shanghai, "where they may be able to exploit the resulting Japanese reaction in their own favour" by winning Western support.[63]

For their part, the Japanese authorities in Nanking and Shanghai were showing caution.[64] The Japanese chargé d'affaires in Nanking told Knatchbull-Hugessen on August 9 that Japan wanted to avoid involving Shanghai in hostilities.[65] On the same day, a Japanese naval lieutenant and a seaman, apparently trying to launch a two-man attack on an airport, were shot by Chinese soldiers on the outskirts of Shanghai. Rather than use this peculiar incident as an excuse to take action against the Chinese, Japanese officials tried to ease the resulting tension.[66] However, Tokyo had already decided to reinforce the naval landing party that Japan, as one of the treaty powers, maintained at Shanghai. Presumably, the Japanese government's decision was prompted by its fear that the Peace Preservation Corps and other Chinese were threatening the lives and property of Japanese citizens in Shanghai.[67] The reinforcements, numbering a thousand men, arrived on August 11, and on the following day Nanking moved almost thirty thousand of its best troops into a nearby area. On August 12 the Japanese embassy in London assured the Foreign Office that Tokyo was "anxious to avoid trouble at Shanghai."[68] Nevertheless, a major conflict seemed inevitable.

These developments were of very great concern to Britain, especially since her vast investments in Shanghai were threatened. On August 2 the commander-in-chief of the British naval forces on the China Station told the Foreign Office that the time had already

* General von Falkenhausen told a member of the British embassy in China that the Chinese army, "if it followed the advice of [the] German advisers, was capable of driving [the] Japanese over the Great Wall," adding that "war on a national scale was a necessary experience for China and would unify her." Robert Howe later told the Foreign Office that these views were also expressed to the Chinese and were "to a great extent responsible for the strong stand by Chiang Kai-shek in the beginning." Howe to FO, Nov. 17, 1937, FO F9796/9/10. General von Falkenhausen also told Berlin in late July that China's military prospects in a war against Japan would be favorable. See DGFP, 1.465.

arrived for the government to try to prevent hostilities at Shanghai.[69] For the next two weeks the British searched for ways to keep the situation under control. From August 8 to August 13 the German, Italian, French, American, and British ambassadors to China acted together in seeking assurances from the Chinese and the local Japanese authorities that hostilities would not break out at Shanghai. Both sides gave such assurances, though each accused the other of trying to provoke a conflict. On August 12 the Japanese convened a meeting of the joint commission and charged that Chinese troop movements violated the 1932 truce agreement. They demanded the withdrawal of the Peace Preservation Corps, but the Chinese mayor of Shanghai said that he had no control over the corps, and that the request must be referred to Nanking.[70] On the following day, Dodds learned in Tokyo that Japan was willing to withdraw to her original positions and to reduce the number of her troops in Shanghai, if the Chinese would withdraw their forces and destroy their defenses near the International Settlement.[71] But this proposal was too late: fighting had already broken out and was spreading rapidly.

The battle for Shanghai was a horror from the start. On August 14, which came to be called Bloody Saturday, inexperienced Chinese pilots dropped bombs into the crowded streets of the International Settlement and the French Concession, killing almost two thousand civilians and wounding many more. That night Nanking declared that China was "in duty bound to defend her territory and her national existence" and was fighting "for the maintenance of international justice."[72] Tokyo responded on August 15 by announcing that "drastic measures" were necessary "to chastise the lawless Chinese troops" and by dispatching army units to Shanghai to bolster the badly outnumbered naval landing party.[73] The Sino-Japanese War, albeit undeclared, had begun.

The British reacted with repeated representations to both sides and various plans to put an end to the warfare. Their tone with China, including that of a protest against the erratic bombings of August 14, was generally mild; with Japan it was noticeably harsher. A British message to the Japanese Foreign Ministry on

August 16 insinuated that Japan was to blame for the hostilities and urged her to withdraw her landing party.[74] A further note, delivered on August 20, said that "world and British opinion hold Japanese actions responsible for the course of events at Shanghai" and stressed that "the magnitude of Japanese operations has been out of all proportion to the comparatively trivial incident . . . which gave rise to them."[75] A third communication, referring to Japanese action in Shanghai as "preposterous" and "glaring," was so severe that Dodds on his own responsibility toned it down before presenting it to Japan.[76] As Grew predicted, Britain's blunt representations only irritated the Japanese.[77]

British efforts to end the hostilities were no more successful than their representations. The first plan—devised by the consuls of the five Western powers in Shanghai, under the leadership of the British and American consuls—proposed a return to the status quo ante except that the Chinese would also withdraw the Peace Preservation Corps two miles away from the International Settlement. The plan collapsed when Chiang Kai-shek insisted that the powers guarantee Japan's execution of the agreement and when the Japanese objected that their troops were needed in Shanghai to protect their twenty thousand nationals.[78] A second scheme was worked out on August 16 by the Western ambassadors at Nanking. The five ambassadors, and particularly Knatchbull-Hugessen, believed that any solution based on a return to original positions was unworkable, and that the main obstacle to peace was the presence of Japanese military forces. Consequently, they proposed that the Japanese and Chinese troops should withdraw simultaneously, and that Japan, with Western assistance, should evacuate her nationals from Shanghai. The Japanese citizens would return after the Chinese troops had been completely withdrawn.[79] This proposal fell through when the consuls at Shanghai said that it would not work. The British nevertheless used it as the basis for another scheme, which they presented to China and Japan on August 18. This plan called for the withdrawal of Chinese and Japanese forces, but envisaged that British forces and the soldiers of other willing powers would protect Japan's nationals for the duration of the crisis. The Japanese replied on August 19, stating they "could not *at present* accept [the] proposal," because there were too few foreign troops in Shanghai to protect twenty thousand people and because it was the duty of the Japanese government to protect its citizens.[80] On the same day the United States informed Britain that she did not want to participate in the plan, since there was no evidence that Japan was interested in it.[81] The British immediately urged both the Japanese and the Americans to reconsider, whereupon Secretary of State Hull told Ambassador Lindsay that the "State Department is somewhat embarrassed at being pressed more than once to cooperate in this scheme." Hull went on to warn that "should messages come from London to the effect that [the] scheme has failed because [the] United States Government refused to participate," this might "cause recriminations to arise and would give a check to Anglo-American cooperation." As Orde pointed out, this message was "somewhat querulous" and confirmed that Washington was not eager to involve itself in East Asian difficulties by collaborating with London.[82] A second Japanese rejection of the scheme followed, and the British found themselves helpless spectators of the course of events in Shanghai.

Nor was the failure of these energetic efforts toward peace Britain's only cause for dismay at this point. There were also indications that Chiang Kai-shek was contemplating a shift away from the Western powers and toward the Russians in his search for reliable and substantial support. Sino-Soviet negotiations on a non-aggression pact and a mutual-assistance agreement had started in the spring of 1937, but the talks did not make much progress until August. A non-aggression pact was finally signed on August 21, at which time Moscow promised to grant a credit to Nanking. Though no formal agreement about the size and nature of the credit was reached until March 1938, the Russians began sending ammunition, equipment, military advisers, planes, and even pilots to China in the fall of 1937.[83] London's reaction to the non-aggression pact was reflected in Nigel Ronald's comment that "the Chinese mind certainly seems to work in a most inexplicable way"; the British believed that Nanking's action would only cause Japan to intensify her war effort.[84] In retrospect, the reasons for Chiang's move seem clear. By becoming involved in hostilities at Shanghai, he hoped to be able to use British and American desires to safeguard their interests there as a lever to force the Japanese to negotiate an agreement favorable to him. But when he realized that Western diplomacy was having little effect on Japan, he felt compelled to turn toward the Soviet Union.[85] An agreement with the Russians would divert some of Japan's attention away from Shanghai and North China and back to Manchukuo. The Soviet Union's thinking can also be reconstructed. The Japanese seizure of Manchuria in 1931-32, Hitler's rise to power in 1933, and the Tokyo-Berlin Anti-Comintern Pact of 1936 had brought the Russians face to face with the ominous possibility of war on two fronts. Relations between Japan and the Soviet Union were further strained by the outbreak of fighting between them along the Amur River in June and early July 1937. Tokyo's sudden involvement in a war with China at this juncture was undoubtedly a relief to the Russians, for much of Japan's resources and attention would obviously have to be diverted to the south, and lest the Japanese win a quick victory, Moscow decided to strengthen Chiang Kai-shek both materially and morally.

On August 23, two days after the signing of the Sino-Soviet understanding, Japan for the first time took the offensive against Chiang's forces in Shanghai, and thereafter she steadily pushed them away from the city. During September the Japanese were able to gain control of an area extending twenty miles beyond Shanghai, and by late October they had driven the Chinese out of Chapei. Even the thought of this Japanese success galled the British. Admiral Charles Little, commander-in-chief of Britain's China squadron, grumbled: "It is humiliating for the white man not to have the power to prevent them from damaging and making use of the fine city which he, and most especially the British, have laboriously built up and which is such an asset to the Far East."[86] Sir John Pratt predicted that a Japanese victory in Shanghai "would mean the final extinction of British interests in this re-

gion," and the ever-pessimistic Charles Orde observed all too accurately that "there is nothing we can do to influence the outcome
of the present struggle [at Shanghai], and we can but look forward
with gloom to the future."[87]

Clearly, during the Shanghai crisis the Foreign Office's attitude
toward Japan hardened further and Anglo-Japanese relations deteriorated perceptibly. Even so, the Far Eastern Department conceded that Tokyo had not wanted to become involved in fighting
at Shanghai. Pointing out that Nanking did not send its best troops
to North China in July, Ronald maintained that "the Chinese
staged the attack at Shanghai as promising an advantageous diver-
sion." China, he believed, calculated that fighting in the city would
damage British and American interests and hence bring the two
Western powers in on her side against the Japanese.[88] Though
neither Pratt nor Orde agreed completely with Ronald's argument, they both noted that Nanking had begun to make threatening military preparations in Shanghai quite some time before hostilities had broken out in the north. However, Orde felt that these
Chinese moves were excusable in view of Japan's past behavior,
and concluded that "it is impossible to put the responsibility entirely on either side if one confines oneself to Shanghai; taking a
wider view Japan must of course be held responsible." In Pratt's
view, otherwise similar to Orde's, Tokyo's aggressiveness since
the early 1930's not only justified Nanking's preparatory moves
but, in the final analysis, warranted placing the blame for hostilities at Shanghai squarely on Japan.[89] The implication of these
comments is clear: the question of immediate responsibility for
various incidents and even the outbreak of war was more or less
academic, because Japan's policy of aggression over the past four
to six years was the ultimate "cause" of all the trouble.

The first major Anglo-Japanese incident of the war occurred on
August 26, when Ambassador Knatchbull-Hugessen was seriously
wounded by bullets fired from two Japanese planes as he traveled
by car from Nanking to Shanghai.[90] Japan informally expressed
her "very deep regret" on the following day, but Eden pressed for
a formal apology, as well as for punishment of those responsible

and a guarantee that such incidents would not recur.[91] The British protest, delivered on August 29, was worded in such strong terms that Sir Robert Craigie, then just arriving as ambassador to Tokyo, later remarked that the note "cut the Japanese nation to the quick and turned them overnight from a friendly to a hostile race."[92] Craigie may have exaggerated slightly, but it is clear that London's verbal lashing made Japan very reluctant to satisfy the British requests. The Japanese told James Dodds not only that Chiang Kai-shek had been expected on the road where the incident occurred and that Knatchbull-Hugessen should have notified their military authorities before setting out on his journey, but also that they were not even convinced that their planes were responsible for the shooting.[93] On September 6 Japan gave the British an "interim reply" in which she expressed "profound regret," but stated that her investigations "have so far failed to produce any evidence to establish that the shooting was done by a Japanese aeroplane."[94] At a Cabinet meeting on September 8 both Chamberlain and Eden called this reply unsatisfactory. Eden wanted to withdraw Craigie, but Chamberlain suggested instead that a stinging note be sent to Tokyo to the effect that "apparently in matters of this kind Japan was unable to attain to the normal standards observed among civilised peoples." Eden feared that such a rebuke might cause the Japanese to sever relations with Britain. The meeting ended without a decision.[95] Meanwhile, Craigie, still pressing the British demands, was able after almost two more weeks of cajoling to get Tokyo to issue a vague admission of responsibility and another expression of "deep regret." Though Eden thought that this was still unsatisfactory, Chamberlain persuaded him to accept it, and London announced on September 21 that the incident had been resolved.[96]

At the same time, another issue was straining Anglo-Japanese relations. On August 16 Tokyo indicated that "circumstances may require [the] establishment of a system of searching merchant vessels for armaments" in the waters off Shanghai and Canton.[97] Nine days later the Japanese announced that they had closed to Chinese ships a large section of the coast south of Shanghai, and on

September 5 this "pacific blockade" was extended to cover almost all of the coast of China. Though only Chinese vessels were subject to the blockade, Japan reserved the right to hail all ships to ascertain their identity. She also insinuated that if vessels of third powers carried arms and ammunition to Chiang Kai-shek, she might in the future feel compelled to apply the blockade to them as well.[98]

The Japanese moves were scrutinized in London, where it was doubted that verifying the identity of all vessels was legal in the absence of a declaration of war. But Britain hesitated to raise this point, because she feared that Tokyo would respond either by carrying out its threat to prevent British ships from transporting munitions to China or by declaring war on China and instituting a full blockade. Either of these possible Japanese reactions would lead to serious disputes between Britain and Japan in the western Pacific and would also damage British trade with China.[99] To forestall such undesirable developments, the Chamberlain Cabinet decided on September 8 to tell Tokyo that Britain would agree to a carefully circumscribed verification procedure if Japan would refrain from more serious interference with British shipping.[100]

In taking this step, London was acting alone. As early as August 31, the Foreign Office had asked the United States whether she would cooperate to keep Japan from interfering with Anglo-American shipping, but Washington was no more inclined than before toward joint action.[101] In fact, the Americans were particularly anxious to avoid a dispute with Tokyo over shipping. On September 14 the Roosevelt administration announced that no government-owned ships would be permitted to carry munitions to either China or Japan, and that other American vessels would engage in such trade at their own peril.[102] This action was ill received in London. Nigel Ronald charged that the announcement showed "excessive timidity" and was "a wholly uncalled for blow for the unfortunate Chinese aggressee," and Sir Alexander Cadogan added that "it is due to their blind fright of becoming involved in any incident. . . . It is a poor performance, and a warning to us—if such were needed—of what to expect from them."[103]

The British, for their part, had set up a special Cabinet committee to consider what retaliatory moves could be made in case Japan ignored their proposal of September 8 and took drastic action against their shipping. The committee, at Chamberlain's suggestion, debated whether to reinforce Britain's naval strength in East Asia.[104] In view of the troubled European situation, such a step could not be undertaken lightly; hence it was fortunate that the drastic Japanese moves for which the committee was preparing did not take place. Presumably, Japan failed to exercise full belligerent rights because she wanted to avoid serious friction with "neutral" powers.

Not surprisingly, after the Knatchbull-Hugessen incident and the thinly veiled threat to interfere with British shipping, Anglo-Japanese relations were far from cordial. London was highly suspicious of Tokyo's intentions. The Foreign Office agreed wholeheartedly with an observation made by Dodds: "The Japanese . . . hope by force and diplomacy to extirpate occidental influence in Eastern Asia."[105] Most British officials would have liked to take effective action to restrain Japan. But they realized that any measures strong enough to halt the Japanese were likely to involve war, which could not be risked at this stage.

There were good reasons why the risk was too great. Germany and Italy posed such formidable threats to European stability and British security that Britain could not afford to become entangled in East Asia. The Germans were growing steadily stronger and, moreover, had not been very responsive to Chamberlain's initial approach to them as Prime Minister. In late June and July the Foreign Office received reports that a German move in Central Europe was imminent. The British calculated that Hitler was not yet ready for a new foreign adventure, but were nevertheless uneasy, particularly since the reports reminded them that Germany's aspirations were still largely unfulfilled.[106]

Italy's intentions and behavior in the summer of 1937 seemed even more sinister. Not only did she continue to support General Franco's insurgents in Spain, but she also strengthened her air bases in the Mediterranean, reinforced her garrison in Libya with two mechanized divisions, and fomented anti-British unrest in the troubled Arab world. These moves threatened Britain's dominant position in the Mediterranean and the Middle East, thus jeopardizing communications with India, East Asia, and Australasia.[107] Eden, who apparently feared a sudden attack by Mussolini, circulated a memorandum on June 15 calling for a new assumption to guide the Chamberlain government's defense preparations: "Italy cannot be considered as a reliable friend and must for an indefinite period be regarded as a possible enemy, especially if she can count on the goodwill and potential support of Germany, or if the United Kingdom were involved in difficulties elsewhere."[108] During the discussions of July 1 and 5 in the Committee of Imperial Defence, Chamberlain argued that it was absurd to contemplate fighting Italy in addition to Germany and Japan. The committee decided that the Italians need not be regarded as potential enemies, and the Cabinet approved this line on July 14.[109]

Chamberlain, fully supported by the Chiefs of Staff, was very anxious to reduce tension between London and Rome. In his opinion, Italy's disquieting behavior was due to her fear that the British were "harbouring a vendetta against her."[110] After a conciliatory speech by Eden on July 19, Mussolini and Chamberlain exchanged letters in which they assured each other of their desire for better relations and agreed that Anglo-Italian conversations should be held soon.[111] Though Eden remained suspicious of Rome's intentions, Chamberlain was confident that an understanding could be reached. He told Lord Halifax on August 7 that dictators were "men of moods. Catch them in the right mood and they will give you anything you ask for."[112]

The cordial atmosphere of late July did not last long. In August and early September British merchant shipping was sunk off the Spanish coast, presumably by Italian planes and submarines. A Foreign Office memorandum of September 2 warned that "the immediate future has never been more fluid and incalculable."[113] At the Nyon Conference in mid-September, Britain and France arranged a naval patrol of the Mediterranean that ended the sinkings. Chamberlain was not altogether pleased. He felt that this success came "at the expense of Anglo-Italian relations. . . . With intense chagrin they [the Italians] see collaboration between the British and French fleets. . . . It would be amusing, if it were not also so dangerous."[114] The Prime Minister, though somewhat exasperated by Italy, still hoped to begin talks with her. As he had earlier told the Cabinet: "A return to normal friendly relations between ourselves and Italy would undoubtedly weaken the Rome-Berlin axis and it might be anticipated that in the event of a dispute between ourselves and Germany the attitude of Italy would be very different from what it would be at present."[115] The importance of this point was underscored when Mussolini visited Hitler in late September. London could only guess what transpired at this ominous meeting, but one fact was certain: the European situation was far from reassuring, and Britain would be wise not to involve herself in East Asian difficulties.

Another important reason for the British to avoid a conflict with Japan was Washington's passive policy in the Far East. Secretary of State Hull and President Franklin Roosevelt sympathized with China, but did not want to annoy Japan. Their attitude reflected not only their own strong desire to avoid any risk of war, but also their sensitivity to vocal isolationist opinion in the United States, which held that the only safe stance was a neutral one. The Roosevelt administration especially feared that joint efforts by Washington and London to restrain Japan would provoke her and also irritate the isolationists, who had a definite anti-British bias.[116] It is therefore not surprising that the State Department rebuffed Britain's repeated attempts in July and August to secure American cooperation. By early September there was a widespread feeling in London that the British should, in Sir John Pratt's phrase, "take the hint and in the future act independently."[117] As J. T. Henderson of the Far Eastern Department pointed out: "It is clear that this U.S. attitude will not be altered by talking, and we shall have to accept it. We can obviously not rely on American cooperation so we must go ahead under our own steam."[118] From his vantage point in Tokyo, Sir Robert Craigie added that "any further initiative on our part to secure such cooperation will in present circumstances tend to diminish [the] influence which we can exercise here on our own without any corresponding advantage to our relations with [the] United States."[119] At this juncture, apparently only Eden was convinced that joint Anglo-American action in East Asia was both possible and useful.*

In spite of such compelling reasons for avoiding conflict with Japan, however, there were few, if any, signs that London was willing to consider appeasing the Japanese. Britain's quick decision to terminate her talks with Tokyo after the outbreak of hostilities in East Asia was an early and definite indication of her determination not to be unduly conciliatory. The Foreign Office, though generally conceding that Japan had not instigated the fighting either in North China or in Shanghai, nonetheless regarded the Japanese as aggressors and refused to admit that a reasonable case could be made for their actions. Convinced that Tokyo was, in James Dodds's words, "as a rule incapable of seeing any point of view but [its] own," the British bristled at what they considered Japanese impertinence,[120] and above all at Japan's claim to be the greatest power in Asia. Dodds suggested that Tokyo should be made aware that Britain was in fact "a much greater Asiatic power than Japan." H. H. Thomas of the Far Eastern Department welcomed this suggestion:

The point that we are a much greater Asiatic Power than Japan is one that might well be made to the Japanese when they become over-

---

* Significantly, Britain and America had reversed their positions toward Japan since 1931-32. Joseph Grew reflected on this point in his diary: "Humorists might find humor in the complete turning of the tables between 1931 and 1937. Then it was we who stepped out in front and the British would not follow. Now it is the British who are taking the lead while we are moving slowly and very, very carefully. It has always been thus in Anglo-Japanese relations, but the logic of it is perfectly clear. British material interests were not acutely affected by the Manchurian issue. But the farther south Japanese aggression extends, the more closely are British material interests touched. There's not much sentiment or ethical principle involved in international action nowadays, if there ever was. It's generally a matter of dollars and cents, or of strategic necessity to protect those dollars and cents." See Diary, July 14, 1937, Grew Papers. Neville Chamberlain, for his part, believed that if the United States had cooperated with Britain in July 1937 the two countries might have succeeded in stopping the Sino-Japanese hostilities. See note by Chamberlain on FO memo., Aug. 10, 1937, FO F5708/9/10.

insistent on their claim to a leading role in Asiatic affairs. . . . Consistent firmness and "standing up for one's rights" is unquestionably the policy to adopt in dealing with the Japanese. . . . It is useless to expect that the Japanese will on any occasion come half way to meet you.[121]

Apart from revealing the intensity of Anglo-Japanese rivalry, such comments reflected a deeply held notion that Britain's status as a great world power depended on the maintenance of her predominant position not only in Africa, the Middle East, and India, but also in areas such as East Asia. Britain may have been overextended in the world, but she had little desire to pull back.

It is significant to note that none of the British officials concerned with the Far East during July and August espoused appeasement of Japan. Dodds and Nigel Ronald were rather unsympathetic to China and had hoped that Nanking would conciliate Tokyo in July, but both of them were quite suspicious of Japan's intentions and felt that London should deal firmly with her.[122] Charles Orde and Sir John Pratt, though careful to consider all sides of the situation, were not inclined to favor conciliatory approaches to Tokyo. In fact, Orde scoffed at Japanese attempts to " 'rectify' our attitude" and stressed that Britain "must try to open their eyes and show them we are not intimidated."[123] Both Orde and Pratt were to leave the Far Eastern Department in early 1938, and their replacements proved to be very contemptuous of Japan. Knatchbull-Hugessen, too seriously wounded to continue as ambassador to China, was to be succeeded by Sir Archibald Clark Kerr, an even more fervent advocate of the Chinese cause. The most influential policy-makers, Eden and Sir Alexander Cadogan, strongly supported the pro-Chinese viewpoint. So did Sir Robert Vansittart, permanent under-secretary in the Foreign Office, who declared in late August: "I hope we shall stretch points in favour of the Chinese whenever we can. It is in our interest to help them prolong this struggle as long as possible."[124] Neville Chamberlain, for his part, paid surprisingly little attention to events in East Asia during this period, and, except for his opposition to sanctions, his views were not a major factor in the evolving British policy.

Only Sir Robert Craigie, after his arrival in Tokyo in early September, advocated appeasement. Though he was convinced that the Japanese military was determined to pursue a "policy of aggression," he maintained that there was a large group of civilian moderates in Tokyo who wanted good relations with Britain, America, and China. If the British were conciliatory, Sir Robert believed, the position of these moderates would be strengthened.[125] His opinions, however, were clearly out of line with official thinking in London, and his influence on British policy was to be limited.

One factor underlying Britain's reluctance to appease the Japanese was her cautious optimism about the outcome of the conflict between Tokyo and Nanking. Admiral Little maintained in September that China would very possibly be able to resist until Japan became exhausted.[126] His assessment was shared by many observers in the Foreign Office. As Pratt declared: "There is no doubt that China will never submit and that active resistance may be kept up for 7 years."[127] Eden, though realizing that the possibility of a Chinese collapse could not be ruled out, was far from convinced that Tokyo's war effort would be successful. In August he wrote: "Is a quick victory for Japan in China likely? I should hardly have thought so."[128] He told the Cabinet on September 8 that "in a year's time the whole situation in the Far East might have been profoundly altered, possibly to the detriment of the Japanese, who might then be much more anxious for our friendship than they were at present."[129] London's faith in China's resistance wavered at times later in the year, but by 1938 the British were surprisingly confident that China could outlast Japan.

Britain was also rather sanguine about her own future in East Asia if China did ultimately succeed in wearing down Japan. Sir John Pratt guessed that a victorious Chiang Kai-shek would demand Chinese administrative control over at least Hongkew and Yangtzepoo in Shanghai, but believed that British enterprise would prosper.[130] Little was even more optimistic.

China is our friend for the asking and it has been shown that we are the best qualified to exploit her markets.... Although British trade in

China must have at least a temporary set back as the result of this war there is reason to expect that if China remains united and takes toll of the Japanese forces and resources, we should gain handsomely in the long run if full advantage is taken of the situation in our diplomatic and "military" relations with China and Japan.[131]

Not much thought was given to the possibility that Chiang might try to minimize Britain's economic and political influence in China if and when he ejected the Japanese.

The general direction of British policy in East Asia during 1937-39 was clearly discernible in London's reaction to the outbreak and spread of hostilities in July through September. Very little attempt, however, was made in these three months to formulate a comprehensive, as opposed to a day-to-day, response to Japan's action in China. This task was to be undertaken only in October and November, when Britain was to consider the feasibility of mediation and examine seriously the case for a firmer policy toward the Japanese.

Chapter three

The Brussels Conference

For the Japanese government the fall of 1937 was a period of external success and internal dissension. The Chinese were decisively defeated in the battle for Shanghai by early November even as the Japanese armies to the north were forming local puppet governments in Inner Mongolia and in the Peking-Tientsin area. Meanwhile, Japan's political and military leaders were vigorously debating the future direction of her China policy, especially the question of whether to attack Nanking. Important strategists in the General Staff, fearing that further warfare in China would weaken their preparations to meet the potential threat posed by the Soviet Union, called for a rapid diplomatic settlement of the conflict. But Premier Konoe, Foreign Minister Hirota, and the mainland army commanders felt that Nanking could easily be taken, which would destroy Chiang Kai-shek's will and ability to fight; hence this powerful group pressed for an attack. By the end of autumn the hard-liners held the upper hand.[1]

British public opinion was unfavorable toward the Japanese military victories in China and the threat they posed to British interests there. On August 20 *The Times* warned that "it is time for Japan to learn that the free hand which she desires in Eastern Asia will in no circumstances include licence to play havoc" with British interests.[2] In the *New Statesman and Nation* on September

25, Freda Utley called for sanctions against Japan and, in a letter to *The Times* four days later, John Maynard Keynes claimed there were "at least nine chances in 10" that even the threat of sanctions would halt the Japanese.[3] *The Times* was not prepared to go this far, nor were the *Manchester Guardian*, the *Daily Mail*, and the *Daily Express*, but the *Spectator* and *Time and Tide* both showed interest in economic measures to restrain Japan.[4] And at the Labour Party Conference in early October, party leader Clement Attlee moved a resolution calling for Britain to cooperate with other powers to impose economic pressure on the Japanese.[5] On a more informal level, numerous protest meetings, including one chaired by the Archbishop of Canterbury, sought to mobilize public opinion.

This eruption of feeling, representing the peak of non-governmental interest in the Sino-Japanese war,[6] was not the only pressure exerted upon the Chamberlain government between August and November. Chiang Kai-shek sought to induce Britain and other members of the League of Nations to give both material and moral support to his cause. On August 20 Chinese Ambassador Quo Tai-chi told the Foreign Office that China had decided to bring her case before the League and wanted Britain's full support at Geneva.[7] Ten days later the Chinese delegation to the League gave Secretary-General Joseph Avenol a "Statement on Japanese Aggression in China since the Lukouchiao Incident," and then on September 13 asked the League "to take cognizance of the fact that Japan has invaded China," invoking Articles X, XI, and XVII of the Covenant.[8]

These Chinese moves were not welcomed by the British. The Foreign Office correctly surmised that Nanking hoped to get the League to condemn the Japanese as aggressors and vote economic sanctions against them, and its members to provide munitions and financial assistance to China. The British realized that Chiang desperately needed such support, but they were very wary of taking any action through the League. Measures taken against Japan by the League were likely to provoke retaliation and would not be actively backed by the United States. In a memorandum written on August 22, Charles Orde had stressed that London should not risk a war with the Japanese and suggested that Britain be prepared to obstruct any move toward sanctions at Geneva even if it meant "humiliation for the League and a diminution of its potential power for the future."[9] Though Eden doubted that Japan was in a position to retaliate against the British, Orde's opposition to sanctions was widely supported in the Foreign Office. Indeed, Sir Alexander Cadogan had tried to talk the Chinese out of taking their case to the League by telling Quo that nothing effective could be done at Geneva and that invoking Article XVII would lead to recognition of a state of war, which, by forcing the United States to apply the Neutrality Act, would hurt China.[10] After the formal Chinese appeal to the League on September 13, Eden, Secretary-General Avenol, and French Foreign Minister Yvon Delbos warned Wellington Koo, China's ambassador in Paris and her chief delegate at Geneva, of the dangers of proceeding along the lines proposed. They urged him to agree that the matter should be referred to the Far East Advisory Committee, rather than to the Council or the Assembly.[11] Koo reluctantly acceded to this request and, on September 15, made a speech to the Assembly which opened the way for meetings of the committee.

Just before the first session of the Advisory Committee was held on September 21, Stanley M. Bruce, the Australian High Commissioner in London, suggested to the League Assembly that a conference of Pacific powers be called. Bruce's proposal, aimed at involving the United States actively in deliberations on the Sino-Japanese conflict, was consistent with the desires of the British government, but the Foreign Office feared that too sudden an approach on these lines might embarrass Washington and felt that it was best not to pursue Bruce's proposal until there were signs that the United States was ready to participate in a conference. Britain decided that in the meantime she would work through the Advisory Committee and also establish a working subcommittee that could be viewed, in Sir John Pratt's words, as "the first step towards a Conference of Pacific Powers."[12]

Predictably, China continued to press for immediate and strong action. Wellington Koo repeatedly urged Lord Cranborne, parliamentary under-secretary in the Foreign Office and the leading British representative at Geneva for much of this period, to support economic measures against Tokyo and large-scale aid for China. And Chiang Kai-shek warned that if the League did not help him he would turn to the Soviet Union, which, he implied, would be willing to fight on his side.[13]

Chiang's threat did not frighten the Chamberlain government, presumably because earlier in September the British embassy in Moscow had assured the Foreign Office that the Sino-Soviet Non-Aggression Pact of August 21 "in no way represents a new forward tendency" in Russian policy and that Stalin would not intervene against Japan.[14] Nor did Koo succeed in overcoming London's opposition to moves at the League toward sanctions. Eden told the Cabinet on September 29 that Britain should take no step without full American backing, thus ruling out action by the League alone. Chamberlain added that he hoped "no-one would give any support" to proposals for an economic boycott of Japan. He "was most anxious to avoid the position which had been reached with Italy over Abyssinia."[15] Britain therefore steered the Advisory Committee on a moderate course. In reply to Chinese complaints about British inaction, Cranborne sponsored a resolution condemning Japanese bombing of cities in China, a move approved by the committee on September 27. Koo, however, was not satisfied. When on October 4 he tried to force the issue of sanctions, Cranborne blocked his move by endorsing Bruce's earlier proposal for a conference of Pacific powers. The British naturally hoped that Washington would agree to participate in such a conference.[16]

The Advisory Committee finished its work on October 5, when it presented two reports to the League Assembly. The first declared that Japanese military operations were "out of all proportion to the incident that occasioned the conflict" and were in violation of the Nine-Power Treaty and the Pact of Paris, but it avoided the word *aggression*. The second, after expressing moral support for Nanking, recommended that no action be taken "which might have the effect of weakening China's power of resistance," called for League members to "consider how far they can individually extend aid to China," and proposed a conference of the nine Washington Treaty powers "to seek a method of putting an end to the conflict by agreement."[17] These two reports, adopted by the League Assembly on the following day, represented a tactical triumph for the British, who had succeeded in resisting Koo's demands for condemnation of Japan as an aggressor and for economic sanctions, while giving in only partially to his request for material aid to China.

At this juncture, news of Roosevelt's famous Quarantine Speech reached London and Geneva. In retrospect it seems that the President, in calling for a "quarantine" of nations spreading the "disease" of "world lawlessness," was not hinting at sanctions against Japan.* At the time, however, it seemed to many observers that he did have economic pressure in mind. The speech evoked mixed feelings among the British leaders. They hoped that it would be the forerunner of closer American cooperation with Britain and that it would have a sobering effect in Tokyo, Berlin, and Rome. They doubted, however, that the President would face up to the implications of his statements. This reaction was most clearly expressed by Neville Chamberlain, who had a deep-seated distrust of Washington's initiatives and policy: "It is always best and safest to count on nothing from the Americans but words." He believed that America's extensive trade in scrap metal and oil with Tokyo would keep Roosevelt from taking action against the Japanese.[18]

More important than these hopes and doubts, however, were

* Exactly what Roosevelt was hinting at, however, remains an open question. Dorothy Borg has argued persuasively that he was groping for a non-belligerent mechanism of neutral cooperation to isolate aggressors. John Haight has contended, less persuasively, that Roosevelt was thinking of a naval blockade against Japan. Still other historians have maintained that he had no specific program in mind. See Borg, *The United States and the Far Eastern Crisis of 1933-1938* (Cambridge, Mass.: Harvard University Press, 1964), pp. 380-86; John McVickar Haight, Jr., "Franklin D. Roosevelt and a Naval Quarantine of Japan," *Pacific Historical Review*, 40.2 (May 1971): 203-26; and Arnold A. Offner, *American Appeasement: United States Foreign Policy and Germany, 1933-1938* (Cambridge, Mass.: Harvard University Press, 1969), p. 190.

the apprehensions aroused by Roosevelt's speech. Chamberlain and other British leaders blanched at the thought that the United States might now press for a large-scale economic boycott of Japan. The Prime Minister felt there was "something lacking" in Roosevelt's quarantine analogy, in that "patients suffering from epidemic diseases do not usually go about fully armed."[19] He told the Cabinet on October 6 that effective sanctions could easily lead to war and that he "could not imagine anything more suicidal than to pick a quarrel with Japan at the present moment when the European situation had become so serious. If this country were to become involved in the Far East the temptation to the Dictator States to take action, whether in Eastern Europe or in Spain, might be irresistible." Consequently, he explained, the President's speech "had rather embarrassed the situation." Chamberlain emphasized that the British should not "be manoeuvred into a position in which it could be said that the United States had offered to cooperate in economic sanctions if the United Kingdom would join them and that we were standing in the way of such action."[20] Such an outcome would produce mutual recriminations similar to those that had occurred after Britain's alleged failure to follow Stimson's lead in 1932 and, as a result, would seriously hinder the future development of Anglo-American cooperation. Chamberlain's colleagues in the Cabinet concurred in his analysis, though Eden was inclined more than the others to stress the desirability of American support, rather than the danger of Japanese retaliation.

Thus, whatever he may have intended, Roosevelt had brought the issue of sanctions to the fore. At the same time, his speech paved the way for American participation in the conference of Pacific powers that had been endorsed by the League Advisory Committee. This prospect was very pleasing to the British, who hoped that the conference would bolster Anglo-American solidarity. After some disagreement among the Belgians, Dutch, Americans, and British over the location of the conference and the wording of the invitations, it was resolved that the powers would meet at Brussels in early November. An invitation was sent to Japan, and both the British and the Americans made a special effort to persuade her to attend.

To Ambassador Sir Robert Craigie in Tokyo, the developments of September and October were disconcerting. He firmly opposed both condemnation of Japan by the League and any discussion of sanctions at a nine-power conference, fearing that such moves would only strengthen the position of the Japanese military extremists and push Japan into the arms of Germany and Italy. Instead of contemplating firm action, he argued, Britain should make discreet but persistent efforts to mediate between China and Japan. Sir Robert believed that a large group of civilian moderates in Tokyo wished to end the fighting by agreement and would welcome British help in doing so. In his view, successful mediation by Britain would greatly increase her influence in Tokyo, would enable the moderates there to gain control over the military, and would destroy Moscow's hopes of turning the situation in China to its own advantage.[21]

Very soon after his arrival in Japan, Craigie had begun to act in accordance with his views. On his own initiative, he told Foreign Minister Hirota on September 15 that Nanking would probably consider any reasonable peace terms transmitted by Tokyo. Hirota replied that Japan was willing to offer generous proposals. He also assured Craigie that the Konoe government wanted good relations with Britain and was eager to resume the Anglo-Japanese talks as soon as possible. Two days later Sir Robert received a list of peace proposals from an "absolutely reliable" Japanese source and sent them immediately to London, urging that China be asked to indicate her attitude toward them.[22] The Foreign Office was both unenthusiastic about the idea of mediating and unconvinced of Hirota's professed desire for better relations with Britain. With regard to the latter point, Nigel Ronald flatly stated that "there can be no question of resuming the Yoshida conversations before peace is made with China." Sir Alexander Cadogan agreed, adding that what Hirota "says at the present juncture means nothing." As for Craigie's request that the Japanese terms be transmitted to Nanking, Cadogan feared that Britain might "become inconveniently involved" if she took this action, but said that London might consider such a step later.[23]

After this somewhat inconclusive discussion in the Foreign Office, the question of mediation languished until September 22, when the Chinese Foreign Minister commented that he would be receptive to any suggestions concerning the cessation of hostilities, provided that Tokyo made the first move.[24] Craigie responded to this statement by telling London that immediate British mediation offered the only hope of ending the conflict on satisfactory terms. If negotiations were started at once, he maintained, Japan would agree to "leave Nanking with an authority in [the] Northern Provinces not less and possibly even somewhat greater than that exercised before the present incident occurred," in return for economic concessions by China. Tokyo would also want the Chinese to resist the spread of communism, to grant *de facto* recognition to Manchukuo, and to allow Japan to assist Inner Mongolia in blocking Soviet penetration. Sir Robert warned, however, that if London and Nanking delayed at all, the Japanese terms would harden. He also pointed out that Japan might soon crush Chiang Kai-shek. In his view, it was futile to hope that the Japanese armies would be defeated either by China or by financial difficulties at home. Thus Britain should make the Chinese "face facts" and help them recover by diplomacy what they were "never likely to regain by force of arms."[25]

Sir Robert's urgent appeals for mediation were discussed by Chamberlain and Eden on September 27 and by the full Cabinet two days later. Chamberlain felt that "we ought not to neglect any opportunity of bringing about a cessation of the present horrors if we could do so without undue risks to British interests." He was hopeful that Tokyo and Nanking would welcome peace talks, and he thought that once negotiations were started, Washington could be persuaded to join London in making proposals to both sides. Eden was not so optimistic. He doubted that the United States would want to become involved, and he did not believe that British mediation would be successful.[26] His top advisers in the Foreign Office were suspicious of Japan; the terms

Craigie had reported were, in Orde's words, "vague enough to open a wide door, in the usual manner, to exaggerated Japanese interpretation."[27] Furthermore, Eden and some of his colleagues in the Cabinet apparently thought that Chamberlain was not sufficiently sensitive to the risks run by an intermediary. Eden nonetheless agreed that the British should transmit the Japanese terms to the Chinese.[28] No attempt, however, was to be made to press Nanking to "face facts." London specifically instructed its embassy in China to express no opinion about the terms, "still less of course in any way advocate their acceptance."[29]

Britain's initiative immediately ran into an obstacle. With the enthusiastic approval of his mercurial wife, Chiang indicated to the British on October 4 that Japan's terms were not "worth serious consideration." He emphasized that Nanking would settle for nothing less than complete sovereignty in North China. As Madame Chiang pointed out, the Generalissimo's response meant that there was "no possibility of any mediation."[30]

Even if the Chinese had reacted more favorably, it is very unlikely that London could have brought about a settlement. On October 1, after ten days of heated discussion within the Japanese government, Konoe, Hirota, and the two armed services ministers approved peace terms more severe and less ambiguous than those Craigie had transmitted to London. Among the new conditions was a demand for an indemnity, certain to be unacceptable to China.[31] Also at this time, the Japanese General Staff, which wanted peace but distrusted Britain, was pressing Hirota to use German rather than British good offices. The General Staff was to have its way. Later in the month, Germany was approached and agreed to mediate.[32]

Craigie was disappointed by the failure of Britain's initiative and dismayed by the upsurge of anti-British feeling among the Japanese public in October. Accusations that Britain had encouraged the League to condemn Japan, and charges that British military authorities at Shanghai had actively assisted the Chinese army led him to warn the Foreign Office that Britain and Japan were "approaching the parting of ways."[33] Since Britain's lack of military power, her preoccupation with the European situation, and

her inability to secure Washington's cooperation made it imperative for her to avoid trouble in East Asia, Craigie felt that the
wisest policy would be to seek cooperation with Japan in the hope
of exercising a restraining influence. In Sir Robert's opinion, the
Japanese "would listen to us, as they would listen to no one else."
To achieve this rapport with Japan, the British must demonstrate
that they were "neither irretrievably opposed to every Japanese
ambition nor determined to view in the worst possible light every
Japanese activity." They must also "have the courage to advise
China to make reasonable terms while reasonable terms are still
to be had."[34]

During October and early November, Craigie made recommendations to the Foreign Office that reflected these views. He repeatedly argued the merits of British mediation, suggesting on October 19 that the Brussels Conference be persuaded to nominate
London to serve as an intermediary. Anglo-American good offices,
he believed, would be unacceptable to Japan, and an approach by
the United States alone would be dangerous because the Americans might not show much regard for Britain's interests.[35] Toward
the end of October, Sir Robert assured London that "many of the
most influential and best informed people here [Tokyo] not excluding the army leaders" sincerely desired close Anglo-Japanese
relations. But he warned that if the Brussels Conference took any
action that had the effect of ruling out mediation, the moderates
in Japan would be undermined.[36] On November 3 he again voiced
his concern about the widespread anti-British sentiment in Japan.

Feeling has assumed such proportions that I consider [the] possibility of
some incident in China, perhaps deliberately encouraged by [the] young
officer group in the navy or army, cannot be precluded and that action
rashly directed might immediately gain wide support here. . . . I do not
believe that the agitation is due to official inspiration or that [the]
government desires a quarrel with us. . . . We must I think make up our
minds whether or no we are prepared for trouble with this country. If
not then a concerted effort must be made promptly by both governments
to put the brake on.

Craigie suggested that the Chamberlain government, for its
part, moderate anti-Japanese newspapers in London, stop the
arms traffic to China through Hong Kong, and urge British mili-

tary authorities in Shanghai to improve relations with their Japanese counterparts.[37]

Sir Robert's suggestion that the Brussels Conference appoint Britain to mediate was carefully considered by the Foreign Office, but his other recommendations were rejected rather quickly. Charles Orde said that the British press had been fair and that the military in Shanghai deserved praise. He also insisted that London should not stop the export of munitions from Hong Kong to China. Eden agreed completely, noting that the Japanese might be heading for disaster and that Britain should help them along.[38] When the question of an arms embargo came before the Cabinet Committee on British Shipping in the Far East, Craigie's proposal was unanimously opposed.[39] London's willingness to allow munitions to be shipped through Hong Kong proved invaluable to China's war effort.*

One reason why the Foreign Office rejected Sir Robert's advice was that his warnings about anti-British agitation in Japan were not taken very seriously. H. H. Thomas, who had had long experience in the consular service in Japan, claimed that "the Japanese are a somewhat hysterical people (it is the Malay strain in them) and they are very prone to these unreasoned hatreds." Ronald added, "Their attitude is that of spoilt children and one cannot reason with spoilt children."[40]

Another reason was that the Foreign Office thought concessions to Japan would accomplish nothing. Indeed, Orde asserted that

---

* It has been estimated that from July 1937 to November 1938 an average of 60,000 tons of munitions was shipped each month through Hong Kong to China. F. F. Liu, *A Military History of Modern China, 1924-1949* (Princeton, N. J.: Princeton University Press, 1956), p. 156. Very little, however, was sent by Britain herself. The Chamberlain government did not permit its surplus war matériel to be sold to either side. Private firms could be licensed to export munitions to East Asia, but few such shipments were actually made. With regard to Japan, this was a matter of policy: the Board of Trade was instructed to adopt an attitude of "masterly inactivity" in connection with licenses for shipments to the Japanese. But with regard to China, it was largely a matter of economics: the Chinese had little money to spend and British firms, swamped with government orders, had few arms to spare. See the various memoranda and letters in Premier 1/219. See also Cabinet Conclusions of Oct. 6 and Nov. 17, 1937, and Jan. 26, 1938, in CAB 23/89, 90, and 92.

conciliation had already proved bankrupt: "In the past the western powers, ourselves included, have treated [the Japanese] gently and with marked forbearance, and it is perhaps not astonishing that as a result they have come to believe that a policy of swagger and bluster can sweep all before it. [They are] blinded by an overweening national vanity."[41] Sir Robert Vansittart, for his part, dismissed the notion that the Japanese moderates wanted good relations with London. The most sustained attack on Craigie's views, however, was made by H. H. Thomas.

> I do not like Sir R. Craigie's implied suggestion that we must adopt the humiliating and even immoral role of aiding and abetting Japan in her aggression against China. It is both stupid and unnecessary to be afraid of Japan. She has sufficient preoccupations at present to prevent her from striking at us. . . . In the last resort, we have to decide whether it is more in our interests to court Japanese goodwill by manifesting obvious favouritism for them in the present struggle (for nothing less will satisfy them) and actively to encourage them towards the attainment of their objects in China, or to stand firm in our present attitude and do everything that is legitimate to manifest our disapproval of their actions, even at the slight risk of a showdown. . . . To adopt the former course is only to postpone the evil day. If the present régime in Japan remains in the saddle and is successful in its policy, nothing is more certain than that Japan will eventually come into collision with the British Empire. Our policy must surely be to do everything we can, with reasonable safety anyhow, to hasten the downfall of that régime, whose gospel is the sword and whose economics is spoliation. If there is to be a showdown with Japan, it is surely better that it should come now.[42]

Though it is very doubtful that Eden shared Thomas's apparent equanimity at the prospect of a showdown with Tokyo, he agreed with the main lines of his adviser's argument.[43]

While Craigie was making his policy suggestions, the Chamberlain government was preparing for the Brussels Conference. Publicly, the British leaders declared that they hoped to arrange a settlement of the Sino-Japanese conflict at Brussels, as the conference had been directed to do on October 5 by the Far East Advisory Committee of the League. When, on October 21, the case for sanctions was argued by Clement Attlee in the House of Commons, Chamberlain retorted that Britain was going to the conference to make peace.[44]

Privately, however, the government was at a loss to envisage how the war could be ended. Thomas Jones, once deputy secretary to the Cabinet and still in close contact with many ministers, summarized the situation when he wrote that "no-one here seems to know what it is hoped to get out of the Brussels Conference. 'Peace' says the P. M. But how?"[45] For a while, there was some hope, mainly in the Cabinet, that Japan could be persuaded to participate in the conference. But on October 27 Japan officially refused the invitation, insisting that no fair result could emerge from the deliberations at Brussels and that only direct Sino-Japanese talks could settle the conflict.[46] Clearly, the Japanese government feared that China, following the traditional policy of "playing barbarian against barbarian," would induce Britain and the United States to press Japan to accept an agreement based on the status quo ante. Japan's fear of third-power intervention went back at least as far as the traumatic Triple Intervention of 1895, when Russia, France, and Germany intervened after a Sino-Japanese war to make Japan relinquish her newly won hold on the Liaotung Peninsula.

Japan's refusal to attend the conference increased British pessimism about the possibility of making peace at Brussels. In fact, the Foreign Office gave almost no thought to the lines that a settlement might take. Though Sir Alexander Cadogan remarked in late October that "it could not be denied that since 1931 the principles of the Nine-Power Treaty had been violated and there was nothing practical to be gained by shutting one's eyes to that fact," neither he nor his colleagues followed up this comment by proposing new principles to regulate international relations in East Asia;* Eden, for his part, could only lament that he was

---

* Interestingly enough, though nothing came of it at Brussels, the U.S. State Department did discuss schemes designed to remove the basic causes of tension in East Asia, including what might be defined as economic appeasement. Stanley Hornbeck, the department's political adviser for Far Eastern affairs, pointed out on October 6 (see his memo of this date in the Davis Papers): "Action by the powers toward restoring peace and creating a situation of (comparative) stability in the Far East, if to be in any way effective, will have to go far beyond the mere limits and provisions of the Nine Power Treaty and will need to be conceived in terms of a broad group of commitments comparable to

"more and more in doubt as to what this conference can achieve."[47]

Since the Foreign Office believed that there was little chance of arranging a settlement at the conference, and since Roosevelt's Quarantine Speech appeared to hint at sanctions, the Chamberlain government felt compelled to give considerable attention to the question of economic action against Japan. The usual view of Britain's attitude toward sanctions before and during the Brussels Conference is embodied in Sir John Pratt's later claim that "if the United States had been willing to give a strong lead and to continue to play a leading part, England, although she already had her back to the wall in Europe, would have been prepared to run considerable risks in the Far East."[48] In the light of evidence in the unpublished British records, Pratt's implication that London was ready to support an appeal by Washington for sanctions is open to serious question.

The Foreign Office had first discussed the feasibility of Anglo-American economic action on September 23, when Eden, angry at the Japanese bombing of Chinese cities and conscious of the growing anti-Japanese feeling in Britain, asked his advisers what steps could be taken to restrain Japan. Cadogan suggested that the State Department be queried about joint economic measures against Japan.[49] After discussing this suggestion with Chamberlain, Eden instructed Charles Orde to prepare a message to Washington stating that Britain would consider sanctions if she were convinced that they would work. Before the message was sent on September 30, however, the Prime Minister amended it to read: "At present we are not convinced that the sort of action suggested here would be effective but we should be quite prepared to examine it further ourselves or with the United States Government if the latter considers it worth pursuing."[50] Eden, who was not consulted about this change, was irritated when he learned of it. He regarded the

---

those formulated and entered into at the Washington Conference." Maxwell Hamilton, chief of the Far Eastern Division, elaborated on this theme in a long memorandum of October 12 (*Foreign Relations of the United States, 1937, 3:* 596-600) that stressed the importance of meeting Japan's desire for greater access to raw materials and markets.

amendment as too open an invitation to Washington to reject the idea of a boycott.[51] Indeed, some high officials in the State Department did suspect that Britain was hoping for an unfavorable response and was attempting, in the words of one American observer, "to put the odium of making an unpopular decision on us." Not surprisingly, Washington's reply on October 5 was somewhat evasive.[52]

Meanwhile, on the day before the United States responded to the British inquiry, the Foreign Office received an important letter from the Admiralty, which was alarmed by reports that sanctions were being discussed. The letter warned that economic measures would not restrain Japan and that the Americans would probably not help Britain militarily if the Japanese retaliated. It also pointed out that a conflict in East Asia would tempt Germany and Italy to take action in Europe and that the British were not capable of fighting three major powers at once. The Admiralty's firm recommendation was that London should *consider* sanctions only if the United States gave definite assurances in advance that she would provide "the fullest military support" to the British "throughout the whole period of disturbed conditions in the Far East which might be expected to follow." This letter made a deep impression on the Foreign Office; Orde, expressing the sentiments of many of his colleagues, declared that he hoped the Americans would find "economic measures unlikely to be effective" and that he "should strongly deprecate . . . running any risk of war with Japan at the present time."[53]

It was at this point that Roosevelt made his Quarantine Speech, and, in view of the Admiralty's arguments against sanctions, it is easy to see why the British were fearful that the President was calling for a boycott. But, as Chamberlain told the Cabinet on October 6, Britain did not want to appear to lag behind the Americans. Confused by the apparent discrepancy between Washington's reply of October 5 and Roosevelt's speech, London decided to ask the United States to clarify her attitude. For several days, Eden, Sir Robert Vansittart, and Chamberlain discussed how such a probe of American intentions should be worded.

Eden wanted the inquiry to emphasize the need for frank Anglo-American consultations about "the possibilities and consequences of the present situation," whereas Chamberlain felt the communication should explicitly indicate that Britain had serious misgivings about economic action. The message that emerged from these deliberations embodied Chamberlain's suggestions, albeit in somewhat diluted form, and thus attempted to dampen any enthusiasm that Roosevelt may have had for a boycott; after asking whether the President had fully understood the implications of the word *quarantine*, the communication, transmitted to the State Department on October 12, stressed that economic measures might provoke Japanese retaliation.[54]

No doubt the British armed services would have preferred an even more negative message. In a letter circulated on October 13, the Air Ministry expressed apprehension lest "the changed attitude of the United States" might cause Britain to commit herself "to a course of action of which the full military implications may not be fully realized." The letter emphatically warned that "the Royal Air Force is not in a position today to play its requisite part in the major war, which, as the Admiralty have pointed out, may not inconceivably result from economic action against Japan."[55] At the Cabinet meeting on October 6, Leslie Hore-Belisha, the Secretary of State for War, had also objected strongly to sanctions, warning that the Army General Staff felt neither Hong Kong nor Shanghai could be held against a Japanese attack. The General Staff, Hore-Belisha had added, believed that Japan's actions since July "had not been unjustified."[56]

Impressed by the risks that a boycott would entail, Eden and his advisers were certainly not eager for London to become involved in sanctions. They did, however, wish to avoid a repetition of the Simon-Stimson controversy of 1932, which had strained Anglo-American relations severely in the succeeding years.* Eden and the Far Eastern Department were afraid that if the Brussels Conference gave rise to similar mutual bitterness, the British might

---

* The strain had perhaps reached a height in 1936 when Henry Stimson wrote a book, *The Far Eastern Crisis*, in which he charged that Britain had

have to face future crises in East Asia without any hope of American support. Their fears were heightened on October 13 when Norman Davis, who was to head America's delegation at Brussels, remarked to Eden, "Don't think we are going to drop you a bomb over this!" The Foreign Secretary understood him to mean that Washington was "not going to put potentially dangerous proposals to us."[57] In one sense, Davis's statement was reassuring because it implied the United States was not going to propose sanctions; but, in another sense, it was disturbing because it indicated the State Department was suspicious of the Foreign Office's willingness to follow an American lead. In an effort to disarm any such suspicions, Eden immediately told Washington that Britain was "wholeheartedly" with the United States and had not been "in any way embarrassed by any aspect of United States policy."[58]

The British were by this time formulating in detail their views on sanctions so that they could send a further communication to the Roosevelt administration explaining their position. J. W. Nicholls of the Foreign Office prepared a report on October 8 to the effect that only a joint embargo by the British Empire, the United States, the Soviet Union, France, and several other nations on both Japanese imports and Japanese exports would be effective enough to cripple Japan within six months.[59] A draft telegram based on Nicholls's study was composed. This draft, which stressed that a boycott would probably lead to war, was discussed at an interdepartmental meeting on October 13. Orde and Gladwyn Jebb, representing the Foreign Office, stated that the point of the message was to "obviate any risk that we should subsequently be misrepresented as having lagged behind America in taking practical steps to put an end to the war in China." The representatives of the Treasury, the India Office, the War Office, and the Admiralty

---

rejected positive plans of actions he had proposed as Secretary of State in early 1932. The Foreign Office deeply resented the book. In fact, Orde called it a "travesty of history," and Cadogan complained in September 1937 that "the Stimson poison has spread pretty wide in this country and elsewhere." See minute by Orde on letter from Keynes to Jebb, Sept. 29, 1937, FO F7822/6799/10; and minute by Cadogan on Mallet to Foreign Office, Sept. 15, 1937, FO A6896/448/45.

argued that this consideration should not lead Britain to indicate to the Americans that she would be willing to support a policy of sanctions. These officials contended that economic measures would be both ineffective and dangerous and should be mentioned as little as possible in discussions with the State Department. The Treasury representative was particularly vehement, complaining that he "disagreed with almost every word of the draft telegram."[60]

At a Cabinet meeting on the same day, Chamberlain outlined his views on economic measures. Ineffective sanctions would serve no purpose but to embitter Japan. Effective sanctions might not save China and carried with them the risk that the Japanese—"possibly egged on by Germany and Italy"—might in turn attack Hong Kong, the Philippines, or oil supplies in the East Indies. "If they did so what could we do in present conditions? It would not be safe to send the Fleet to the Far East in the present position in Europe." Britain could not embark upon sanctions, therefore, without a guarantee from the United States that she would "face up to all the consequences that might fall on nations with large interests in the Far East"—and even such a guarantee might soon be voided by American public opinion.[61]

Of those who spoke at the meeting only Foreign Secretary Eden did not wholeheartedly endorse Chamberlain's views. Eden stated that though he generally agreed with the Prime Minister's observations and especially with the necessity of a firm guarantee from Washington, Anglo-American cooperation was so vital that he would "not like to indicate that, in the extremely unlikely event of the American Government being prepared to act on those lines [i.e. offer a guarantee], we should refuse." In spite of all the dangers, he thought the risk should be taken in such an eventuality. The rest of the Cabinet was not prepared to go this far. Secretary of State for Dominion Affairs Malcolm MacDonald, normally a supporter of Eden's views, maintained that "the situation in Europe was too critical to justify our taking any risks in the Far East." Showing the distrust of the United States that was widespread among British Conservatives, Halifax, the Lord President

of the Council, argued that "even if America did take a more bellicose line than we, we should have to think carefully before committing to them the defence of our interests in the Far East." The
meeting ended on a conclusive note when Chamberlain declared
that in dealing with Washington "nothing should be done to suggest the imposition of sanctions."[62]

The Foreign Office fully agreed that the State Department must
not in any way be encouraged to call for a boycott. With regard
to Eden's recommendation that the British should not reject an
American initiative, opinion among his advisers was divided.
Gladwyn Jebb, the American Department, and, to a lesser extent, Alexander Cadogan agreed with Eden. Jebb, who felt that
"the whole question is essentially one of tactics," argued that Britain should "emphasize the great difficulties in the sanctionists'
path," but should indicate that she was ready to follow a lead
by Washington. In his view, the risks involved in this course were
small because "sanctions would almost certainly mean war and
the U.S.A. is not now prepared to fight. Therefore there will in
fact be no sanctions."[63] The Far Eastern Department, however,
felt that this line was, in Charles Orde's words, "altogether too
dangerous." Robert Vansittart agreed, pointing out that Italy
would cause trouble in the Mediterranean if a boycott led to war
in East Asia.[64]

In the days following the Cabinet meeting of October 13, the
Foreign Office wrote two alternative drafts of a message to Washington. The first discussed at some length the difficulties involved
in sanctions and then implied that if the United States wanted a
boycott and offered a military guarantee, Britain would cooperate.
The second was "shorter, vaguer, and less frank" and put less
emphasis on the issue of economic action. Chamberlain, Cadogan,
and Orde all preferred the second draft, and Eden agreed with
their choice.[65]

This communication, which reached the State Department on
October 19, stated that since the Brussels Conference would have
considerable trouble in working out a peace settlement, it would
undoubtedly have to face the question of sanctions. The message

went on to say that economic measures would have to be applied by many nations in order to be effective, would probably not operate in time to help China, and might cause Japan to retaliate. It concluded by stressing that the United States must assure participating countries of military support and guarantee the territorial integrity of third powers if such a course were to be pursued. Eden explained to the British embassy in Washington that this communication was designed to "steer a middle course between [the] two dangers" of seeming eager to adopt sanctions and of appearing to lag behind the Americans.[66]

As the Foreign Office had hoped, the United States was as anxious as the Chamberlain government to avoid boycotting Japan.* The State Department replied on October 19 that the question of sanctions "did not arise in a conference which had for its objective the finding of a solution of the conflict in the Far East by agreement."[67] Nine days later Ambassador Bingham told Eden that Washington did not want the British to take the initiative at Brussels or to push America into the lead. Bingham also said that the Roosevelt administration resented attempts "to pin the United States down to a specific statement as to how far it would go."[68] Indeed, Pierrepont Moffat of the State Department complained in his diary that the British, though expressing their desire for Anglo-American cooperation, "made it clear that in the event of trouble they were so preoccupied with the Spanish and German situations that they could do little east of Singapore."[69]

---

* On October 18 Secretary of State Hull gave Norman Davis formal instructions for the Brussels Conference which stressed that the gathering was to seek a peace settlement and pointed out that "public opinion in the United States has expressed its emphatic determination that the United States keep out of war." These instructions strongly implied that sanctions were not to be considered. See *Foreign Relations of the United States, 1937*, 4: 84-85. Roosevelt, who talked with Davis the next day, also stated clearly that the purpose of the conference was conciliation. The President, though generally showing less aversion than Hull to the idea of action against Japan, was so vague and evasive on the specific subject of a boycott that his comments almost defy accurate generalization. Nonetheless, it can safely be stated he was not eager to go beyond "moral suasion" in dealing with Tokyo. See memo. by Davis, Oct. 20, 1937, Norman Davis Papers. The best account of Washington's attitude toward sanctions is Borg, *Far Eastern Crisis*, pp. 400-414, 538-39.

Predictably, Britain was relieved that Washington seemed to want no part of sanctions. "It was clear now," Chamberlain told the Cabinet on October 20, "that the Government of the United States of America had no intention of taking any decisive action in the Far East. The original apprehensions of the Cabinet lest they should urge sanctions without undertaking responsibility for the consequences, or, alternatively, lay the blame on us for not applying sanctions had not developed."[70] London's anxieties diminished even further in the following days when Australia, Canada, and South Africa sent messages opposing sanctions. Now, even if the United States changed her mind about a boycott, the British would have a good excuse to try to dissuade her. This point was stressed by Jebb: "We seem to have put ourselves in the excellent tactical position of allowing the Dominions to torpedo a 'sanctions' policy in advance, before definitely committing ourselves one way or the other."[71]

Safe in this position, the British felt free in late October to state explicitly that they would go as far as the United States, but no further. Eden and Cranborne emphasized in Parliament that Britain would base her policy at Brussels on Washington's course.[72] At a meeting with Eden on November 2, Norman Davis remarked that he supposed London "had had enough of sanctions." Eden replied that the British were "ready for fullest cooperation" with the United States, adding somewhat disingenuously that London "has been playing down its willingness to assume so strong a position particularly as it could not judge how far America could be willing to go." Davis then reported the suspicion of some Americans that Britain was trying to push the Roosevelt administration into saving British interests in China; Eden assured him that London "would neither attempt to take a lead nor to push America out in front." Davis ended this *pas de deux* by declaring that "sanctions were not ... on our present agenda."[73]

The Brussels Conference opened on November 3. Almost at once it became clear that each delegation had a different view of the purpose of the gathering. The Soviet Union and China pressed for strong action; Italy was opposed to any move that might hurt

Japan; and the smaller nations hoped that the conference would do little and end quickly. France wanted a front of the Western democracies in which the United States would carry the main burden and an Anglo-American guarantee for Indochina.[74] The United States was willing to explore every possibility for a peaceful solution, but was mainly concerned with using the conference to educate her public away from isolationism.[75] Britain was also willing to consider ways of reaching a peace settlement, though her attitude was best reflected by Eden's later comment that the conference was an "exercise" from which he "expected no good" except progress in advancing the cause of Anglo-American solidarity.[76] The Germans and the Japanese were not represented.

At Davis's suggestion, it was decided first to send another invitation to Japan and then to set up a small subcommittee that, if the Japanese were receptive, would hold discussions with them looking toward a settlement of the war. The conference, however, did not expect a favorable response. Not only had Japan already rejected one such appeal; the British, American, and French ambassadors in Tokyo had told their respective governments on October 30 that Japan would definitely not accept Anglo-American or any other collective mediation. The ambassadors had said, however, that she might accept an offer of good offices by a single power. Indeed, Craigie still hoped that Britain herself would be able to mediate in the near future if no anti-Japanese measures were adopted at Brussels,[77] a hope that proved unpopular both with his own government and with Norman Davis, representing the American government. The Foreign Office felt Craigie wanted the Chinese to be urged to surrender, and it believed such a course was out of the question.[78] Davis warned Washington that Craigie had a "pro-Japanese bias" and that British mediation would endanger American interests.[79]

In view of this response to Sir Robert's idea and of the unlikelihood that Tokyo would accept the conference's invitation, it is not surprising that sanctions became the main topic of discussion at Brussels. But in light of Davis's remarks to Eden on November 2 and of the Roosevelt administration's aversion to sanctions, it is surprising that the subject was brought up by Davis.* On November 3 he said that if Japan "continued to be recalcitrant to every suggestion," the Roosevelt administration "might be prepared to consider [the] possibility of action," and two days later he suggested to Eden that Britain and America should boycott Japanese goods. Eden was taken aback, and tried to dampen Davis's enthusiasm by pointing out as before that sanctions might lead to a war in which the United States would necessarily have to do much of the fighting.[80] Eden went to Chamberlain for guidance in handling such proposals by Davis, suggesting that perhaps Britain "should go as far as America would go," only to be told adamantly, "On no account will I impose a sanction!"[81] No doubt Chamberlain's objections to economic measures had been strengthened by a recently circulated report by the Advisory Committee on Trade Questions in Time of War stating that boycott schemes were either impractical or ineffective and would probably result in war.[82] The Prime Minister's comment, together with the deliberations in London in October, is clearly strong evidence that Britain would not have followed an American initiative for sanctions—notwithstanding her public statements to the contrary in late October.

Meanwhile, the British learned that Davis's suggestions were not likely to be supported by the Roosevelt administration. On November 6 Sir Ronald Lindsay reported from Washington that Davis was too sanguine about how far the American government and public were prepared to go, and five days later, on November 11, he added that "sanctions, whether mild or severe, are hardly in the atmosphere at all."[83] Such reports made it easier for the British to criticize Davis's proposals without fear of alienating

---

* Possibly illuminating here is a comment by Craigie recorded in Grew's diary entry for November 14, 1937 (Grew Papers): "Can you imagine Norman Davis being willing to play a secondary role in *any* conference? Why the very word conference is to Norman Davis what the smell of powder is to a war-horse!" Perhaps even more illuminating is Pierrepont Moffat's diary entry for September 15, 1937 (Moffat Papers), describing Davis as convinced both that "the world can best be run by a close cooperative partnership between Britain and the United States" and that Tokyo should be "curbed." Moffat should have added that Davis was not beyond exceeding his instructions and then sending misleading reports to Washington.

the State Department. On November 8, when both Davis and Stanley Hornbeck approached Malcolm MacDonald about economic measures, MacDonald stressed that Britain "was proceeding on the theory of not discussing the problem of 'sanctions' until it develops that we have to." He added that London had had a bad experience with sanctions against Italy in 1935-36 and consequently "the question of any form of economic pressure would have to be studied very carefully."[84] The next day Davis told Eden that if Japan refused to cooperate with the conference, one of three steps might be taken: sell arms to China; declare that the results of Japanese aggression would not be recognized and that no money would be lent to Japan for the development of conquered territory; or boycott Japanese goods. Eden, after asserting that "it was almost impossible to exaggerate the significance of some common Anglo-American decision at this conference," said that he would examine these proposals, but pointed out that all three steps were risky and impractical.[85]

In London, Nigel Ronald noted that Britain appeared "to be in the position of objecting to every American proposal and putting forward no constructive proposal of our own. Of course Mr Davis' suggestions are all equally impracticable, but the mere fact of his having made them and meeting with only destructive criticism from us may be very damaging to us in America."[86] Eden also evidently felt that his response had been too critical. In conversations with Davis on November 10 and 12, he showed more sympathy toward the American's proposals, stating that sanctions "would be none too popular" in Britain, but the Chamberlain government "could none the less carry [them] through" if necessary. Davis, for his part, indicated that he was now thinking primarily in terms of calling for non-recognition of Japan's conquests and for a refusal to lend her money.[87]

At this point, Eden suggested to the Foreign Office (though not to Chamberlain) that the British should be prepared to support Davis's suggestions. He stressed that even though non-recognition and the withholding of loans would be ineffective, Britain should try to lay the foundation for future Anglo-American collaboration in Europe and East Asia by showing a readiness to act jointly with the United States at Brussels.[88] Eden's desire to back Davis's proposals generated a lively discussion in the Foreign Office. The consensus there held that Washington would not authorize Davis to follow through with his ideas. If, however, the Roosevelt administration did decide to approve action against Japan, London would face a very real dilemma. As one official observed:

Unfortunately we are torn between the desire to cooperate in this question as closely as possible with the United States and our fear of complications in the Far East with a possibility of America at the last moment not being able to give us full support, particularly when we ourselves are not ready for a major conflict, public opinion would not support it, and enemies in Europe are just waiting for the moment to make our situation as difficult as possible for us near home.[89]

Vansittart, Orde, and Pratt wanted Britain to take no chances, and thus were unenthusiastic about Davis's proposals. But Cadogan agreed with Eden that if Washington pressed for such measures as non-recognition and the withholding of loans, the Chamberlain government should cooperate.[90]

Before discussions went any further, the State Department informed both Davis and the British that it did not want the Brussels Conference to take any positive steps.[91] Davis, who had obviously misinterpreted the climate of opinion in Washington, was very disappointed. Discussion of sanctions quickly died down, and the conference turned its attention to Japan's refusal of the second invitation. This rejection, which arrived on November 12, contended that Japanese action in China did not come within the purview of the Nine-Power Treaty and that the dispute concerned only the two nations directly involved. In response, on November 15, the conference adopted a resolution refuting these contentions and stating that the powers represented at Brussels would have to consider what was to be their common attitude toward Japan.[92] After making this vague threat, the gathering recessed for a week.

The Japanese government, apparently fearful that the Brussels Conference would take definite steps, intimated to Grew and Craigie on November 15 that it would be disposed to accept an offer of good offices. Ambassador Yoshida in London brought these hints to the attention of the Foreign Office the next day. Though the British, including Craigie, doubted that Japan genuinely desired Anglo-American mediation, they did not ignore the initiative[93]—perhaps largely because reports of a German attempt to mediate had been reaching London with increasing frequency since early November. In fact, Chinese Ambassador Quo Tai-chi had told Malcolm MacDonald on November 15 that if the Brussels Conference ended in failure, China would be compelled to accept Berlin's help in negotiating a settlement.[94] Fearing that mediation by Germany would seriously damage British influence in East Asia, the Foreign Office considered whether it might be able to forestall this eventuality by offering its own good offices.

The threat posed by a German attempt to mediate loomed over the Cabinet as well when it discussed on November 17 the line Britain should take when the conference reconvened. Eden first assured his colleagues that "any tendencies in the direction that the United Kingdom were frustrating a lead by the United States had been stifled." He then said that the conference could take three possible courses: end with a "tepid resolution"; nominate the British and Americans to offer their good offices to the two sides; or condemn the Japanese, decline to give them credits, and refuse to recognize their conquests. The first course, Eden stated, would anger China and cause her to demand that the League reconsider the whole affair, an outcome that would be very embarrassing for London and Washington. The third course, in his view, "might not be futile" in the unlikely event that the Americans subscribed to it. Pointing out that the effect of German mediation "upon our prestige would be very serious," the Foreign Secretary suggested that refusing Japan both credits and recognition of her gains might keep the Chinese from accepting Berlin's good offices. The rest of the Cabinet, however, was very much opposed to this third course because it might provoke a Japanese attack on Britain's vulnerable position in China. The Cabinet decided that if the United States did call for non-recognition and a ban on credits, the British should try to dissuade her. Chamberlain and most of the Cabinet felt that the best line would be to urge the conference to appoint Britain and America to mediate; if it declined to do this—Eden thought it would—London and Washington should "spontaneously, and independently of the Conference" offer good offices.* Such a course, it was thought, might forestall German mediation.[95]

Immediately after this Cabinet discussion, the Foreign Office told the State Department that Britain was prepared to proffer good offices if the United States would do the same. The State Department replied that Japan's attitude must be clarified before any steps could be taken and that it would be averse to transmitting terms inconsistent with the Nine-Power Treaty. When Craigie reported on November 19 that an Anglo-American attempt to mediate was premature, London did not press Washington further on the matter.[96] The British delegation at Brussels, however, tried for the next three days to convince Norman Davis either that the conference should give Britain and the United States a mandate to offer good offices or that the two countries should try to mediate independently of the conference, but Davis was strongly opposed to these suggestions and on November 22 the British ceased to argue with him.[97] At this point, Craigie said that London and Washington could start "the ball . . . rolling" if they were prepared to act as a "post office"—that is to say, a neutral channel for the transmission of terms. The Foreign Office, realizing that this proposal would be unacceptable to the United States, decided not to approach the State Department about it for the time being.[98]

While Davis and the British delegation were debating the merits of mediation, two other points of Anglo-American contention developed. The first arose when Secretary of State Cordell Hull concluded that world and American opinion was blaming Washington for the obvious failure of the Brussels Conference and that British leaks to the press were partially responsible for this devel-

---

* It is interesting to note in passing that the Cabinet also discussed briefly the possibility of Britain's associating herself with any offer of good offices by Berlin. Such a move, it was suggested, would avert the dangers of mediation by Germany alone and might improve Anglo-German relations. Eden said that he had already considered this idea very carefully, but had concluded that it would pose great difficulties, not the least of which would be French and Soviet objections. The hope that a basis for cooperation between London and Berlin could be found in East Asia was to recur in 1938 and 1939.

opment. Fearing that Hull's notions might result in a deterioration of Anglo-American relations, Britain declared herself prepared to share any blame, rather than shift it upon the United States.[99] The second arose when it came time to draft the conference's final reports. Davis and Stanley Hornbeck wanted them to hint at possible future pressure against Japan, but the British felt that it was dangerous to use strong language without being prepared to do anything.[100] Craigie had just warned the Foreign Office that "there is no room whatever for bluff in the situation which has developed and [the] unreliability of American assurances of armed cooperation are too notorious to need emphasis from me."[101] Though Davis and Hornbeck were, according to Malcolm MacDonald, "extremely obstinate" about the wording, the British had their way.[102] The resulting report and declaration, which merely reaffirmed general principles, were adopted on November 24, and the conference ended.*

The Brussels Conference was unmistakable proof, if any were needed, that the Washington Conference treaty order was extinct. In fact, apart from British and American maneuvering with regard to the question of sanctions, the most noteworthy feature of the conference was its unwillingness to reappraise the treaty order in East Asia in light of the momentous developments since the Washington Conference. For all her talk about mediation (and despite her policy of appeasement in Europe), Britain did not even consider proposing a comprehensive settlement similar to that of 1921-22.[103]

The British disagreed among themselves about the value of the conference. Malcolm MacDonald, though conceding that the results of the gathering "had been somewhat inglorious," said the cause of Anglo-American cooperation had been advanced. Eden shared this view, but Chamberlain did not, believing that Brussels "had been a complete waste of time" and that "the main lesson to be drawn was the difficulty of securing effective cooperation

---

* Nicholas R. Clifford, *Retreat from China* (Seattle: University of Washington Press, 1967), p. 43, and Borg, *Far Eastern Crisis*, p. 437, both write that Britain wanted the final declaration to call for non-recognition of Japanese conquests and a ban on loans and credits to Japan. There is no evidence in the British records to support this view.

from the United States of America." Perhaps the shrewdest assessment, however, was Craigie's retrospective view that the conference had further alienated Japan from Britain.[104]

One unmistakable result of the gathering was that, by failing to take action in support of China, it convinced Chiang Kai-shek to accept German mediation. Germany had been displeased by the outbreak of war in East Asia. She not only carried on a profitable trade with China and maintained a military mission there, but also enjoyed a growing political friendship with Japan. The Sino-Japanese conflict made it very difficult for her to maintain both ties. The Nazi Party favored Japan for ideological reasons, but the German Foreign Ministry, as well as the General Staff and business circles, sympathized with the Chinese. There was considerable fear in Berlin that the war would exhaust Japan, making her less valuable as an ally and opening the way for increased communist influence in East Asia.[105] It is therefore not surprising that the Germans responded favorably when in late October Tokyo asked them to mediate. They gave Chiang a list of the Japanese peace terms in early November, but the Generalissimo stated that he would discuss the terms only after Japan agreed to restore the status quo ante July 7. He clearly wanted to see what happened at Brussels before committing himself to peace negotiations.[106] On December 2, eight days after the conference ended, Chiang indicated to the Germans that he was now prepared to open peace talks on the basis of the terms transmitted to him a month before.[107]

The British were deeply disturbed at this turn of events. They feared that if Germany succeeded in reconciling China and Japan, her influence in East Asia would be vastly increased and Britain's position there would become very precarious.[108] This specter, following the failure at Brussels, made painfully apparent to London the necessity of taking action to safeguard Britain's interests and influence in the Far East. Just what measures should be taken was a main topic of discussion in the Chamberlain government from late November to January.

Chapter four

The Growing World Crisis

From the standpoint of British foreign policy, the Brussels Conference was by no means the only noteworthy event of November 1937. Just three days after the conference opened on November 3, the Italians joined the German-Japanese Anti-Comintern Pact. Though the expanded agreement was formally directed against communism, it was also anti-British in spirit. Mussolini believed such an indication of close ties between the three expansionist powers would frighten London into allowing Italy to expand at will.[1] Similarly, Hitler, who was becoming increasingly hostile to Britain, calculated that the pact would make it easier for him to get his way in Central Europe. He may also have viewed the understanding as the prelude to a tripartite military alliance.[2] The Japanese, for their part, were primarily interested in the anti-Soviet dimension of the agreement, though they too surely hoped that it would have a "salutary" effect on British policy.[3]

The Foreign Office perceived that the new "triangle" was highly dangerous for Britain. As Sir Laurence Collier of the Northern Department observed: "I don't believe anything we can do, short of giving the Japanese everything they want at our expense, will prevent this Pact being used as an anti-British alliance. . . . We must make up our minds that Italy, Germany and Japan are definitely leagued against us, because they each want to expand at the expense of British interests."[4] The most obvious implication of the agreement for Britain was the greater likelihood of a future war against three formidable enemies. Understandably alarmed, the Chiefs of Staff declared in an important report of November 12:

The outstanding feature of the present situation is the increasing probability that a war started in any one of these three areas [Europe, the Mediterranean, and the Far East] may extend to one or both of the other two. Without overlooking the assistance which we should hope to obtain from France, and possibly other allies, we cannot foresee the time when our defence forces will be strong enough to safeguard our territory, trade and vital interests against Germany, Italy and Japan simultaneously. We cannot, therefore, exaggerate the importance, from the point of view of Imperial defence, of any political or international action that can be taken to reduce the numbers of our potential enemies and to gain the support of potential allies.[5]

Chamberlain, of course, fully agreed with the idea of reducing the number of Britain's potential enemies, and an opportunity to get on better terms with one of them seemed at hand. Halifax had been invited to visit Germany. Chamberlain, dissatisfied with the cautious attitude and slow methods of the Foreign Office, urged him to go.[6] Eden assented to the visit, but he and his advisers did not want Halifax tacitly to approve German aspirations in Austria and Czechoslovakia.[7] Halifax, however, was "not happy over the F.O. attitude as to Czecho S. or Austria—and personally should like to go further. It is going to be very bad, if we get to talks and they break down. And therefore I think we must see pretty clearly how far we are really prepared to go: and I hope we should not feel bound to . . . oppose 'peaceful evolution'—action liberally interpreted, perhaps."[8] When he talked with Hitler on November 19, he made it clear that Britain would not insist on maintaining the status quo in Central and Eastern Europe so long as changes were brought about peacefully. Hitler, for his part, offered only vague assurances about his policy toward Austria and Czechoslovakia and indicated that a general European settlement was rather impractical, but he nevertheless expressed a desire for African colonies.[9]

In short, Hitler apparently wanted to receive concessions without promising anything in return. Even so, Halifax was not discouraged. On November 24, shortly after his return to London, he told the Cabinet that he "had encountered friendliness and a desire for good relations." The colonial question, he felt, was the key to an understanding with the Germans; if they were given colonies, Hitler might become a "good European."[10] Chamberlain was very pleased with the visit. He, as well as Eden and the French, agreed with Halifax that the question of colonies should be pursued, though they all felt that concessions in Africa should be made only as part of a comprehensive settlement in Europe.[11] The Germans were informed on December 1 that Britain would approach them along these lines after she had had time to examine the colonial issue.[12]

Meanwhile, London had been puzzling over what to do about Italy. Mussolini's behavior in October and November had seemed menacing to many observers. Britain's ambassador in Egypt was particularly alarmed: "In fact, the Italians are on their way to obtaining a pincer-like hold over Egypt, the Sudan and the Red Sea while our policy in Palestine bids fair to facilitate their penetration in the Arab world and thus to provide them with the necessary grip to bring the horns of the pincers together." The roots of the problem, he judged, were Mussolini's "expansionist frame of mind" and the fact that Rome could count on Berlin and Tokyo "to create diversions elsewhere, if not to give active help."[13]

London had sought to alleviate Italy's pressure on the British position in Egypt, the Middle East, and the Mediterranean by proposing Anglo-Italian talks on these points of friction in early October. The Foreign Office had, however, made it clear that such conversations could not start until Mussolini adopted a conciliatory attitude with regard to the problem of foreign intervention in Spain. Since little progress was made on the Spanish question in the following weeks, Eden and his advisers decided in late October that talks were not possible.[14] By this time the Foreign Office was quite concerned that Mussolini might attack Egypt, and thus wanted British defenses there to be strengthened. Chamberlain, Sir

Thomas Inskip, and the Chiefs of Staff held a more optimistic view of Italian intentions and argued that, in any case, Britain could not afford to increase her forces in the Mediterranean substantially. They accordingly pressed for a renewed effort to get on better terms with Mussolini.[15] The Prime Minister had already indicated on September 8 what London's goal should be: "The important thing was to strive for a change of heart and attitude on the part of Italy. Was this too much to hope for?"[16] Annoyed by the Foreign Office's caution, he had in October asked Sir Maurice Hankey, the influential secretary to the Cabinet and to the Committee of Imperial Defence, to "help him w[ith] the F.O. over Italy." Hankey tried without success to convince Eden of the need for a conciliatory policy toward Mussolini. Sir Maurice then wrote to Vansittart on November 3, arguing that "we have our danger in the West and our danger in the Far East, and we simply cannot afford to be on bad terms with a nation which has a stranglehold on our shortest line of communication between the two possible theatres of war." Hankey went on to say that if London recognized Italy's conquest of Abyssinia, Rome would probably be willing to withdraw some troops from Libya and to cease anti-British propaganda. He concluded by stressing that good relations with the Italians were *vital to the existence of the Empire and of the United Kingdom as a first-class Power.*"[17]

The Foreign Office balked at recognizing Italy's takeover of Abyssinia, but it did reconsider its attitude toward Anglo-Italian conversations about North Africa, the Middle East, and the Mediterranean. This reconsideration was due not so much to Hankey's letter as to signs—particularly Italy's entrance into the Anti-Comintern Pact—that the Rome-Berlin axis was growing stronger. One observer in the Southern Department noted that "in the space of a little over a year we have seen Italo-German relations proceed from a rapprochement to an entente. The step from an entente to an alliance is a short one."[18] By late November the consensus in the Foreign Office favored a new effort to open talks with Italy.[19] At an Anglo-French conference on November 29-30 it was agreed that the British should seek conversations with the Italians, but on the new condition that Rome cease its propaganda. Eden informed Italy on December 2 of the decision which London and Paris had reached.[20]

Thus in early December Britain appeared on the verge of a dual effort to get on better terms with two of her antagonists. Eden and his advisers seriously doubted that negotiations would lead to a settlement, and they wanted to move very cautiously. They feared above all that the Cabinet, in its eagerness to reach an understanding with Berlin and Rome, would be excessively conciliatory. The Foreign Office expressed its apprehensions and its aims in an important memorandum of late November dealing with the Chiefs of Staff report of November 12. Eden and his advisers, after agreeing with the military authorities that it was important for Britain to reduce the number of her potential enemies, said London should seek harmonious relations with Berlin, Rome, and Tokyo, "if such is possible." The memorandum warned, however, that it would "be a mistake to try to detach any one member of the German-Italian-Japanese bloc by offers of support or acquiescence in the fulfillment of their aims. The aims of all three are in varying degrees inimical to British interests and a surrender to one might well be the signal for further concerted action on the part of all three Powers." Rather than make significant concessions, it was argued, London should "tolerate, for the time being at any rate, the present state of armed truce." By rearming quickly, gaining the support of potential allies, and exploiting differences within the bloc, Britain could maintain an equilibrium, though she might "have to acquiesce perforce in more than one *fait accompli*." The obvious goal of this "cunctation" policy was to gain time.[21]

This call for a cautious stance was rejected by the ministers. At a meeting of the Committee of Imperial Defence on December 2, Sir Thomas Inskip, Sir John Simon, and Lord Halifax harshly criticized the memorandum. It was evident that they favored a greater effort to conciliate one or more of Britain's potential enemies than was implied by the word *cunctation*. Eden's response to this criticism was somewhat ambiguous. In defense of the idea of playing for time, the Foreign Secretary argued that both Japan and Italy would probably grow weaker in the future. He then contended that in any case the basis of British foreign policy could not be altered. With regard to Japan he "knew of nothing that we could do in the political sphere to remedy the present situation." As for Italy, "no reliance whatsoever could be placed on her promises." Having made these observations, however, he proceeded to blunt some of their force by concluding that Britain "should make every effort to come to terms with each or all of our potential enemies, but not by conduct which would lose us our friends, both actual and potential." In ending on this note, he seemed to put more emphasis on reaching a settlement with London's antagonists than had the memorandum. At any rate, this is how Chamberlain interpreted his comments. The Prime Minister made it clear that he disliked the memorandum. Implying that it was an appeal for a policy of "doing nothing," he asserted that it did not accurately define the course Britain was following. Though he was opposed to attempts to "detach" one or more of the expansionist powers by "methods that would shame us in the eyes of the world," he wanted London to continue to practice "active diplomacy." In Chamberlain's opinion, Eden's remarks—as distinct from the memorandum—"took proper account of the situation."[22]

Whatever differences in outlook existed between Chamberlain and Eden had been papered over, and in the ensuing weeks the way was paved for an attempt to wean Hitler from expansionism. At a Cabinet meeting on December 8, Chamberlain summarized the Committee of Imperial Defence discussions and then declared that "Germany was the real key to the question."[23] Two weeks later the Cabinet decided definitely to follow up as soon as possible the "opening" created by Halifax's talk with Hitler.[24] Eden raised no serious objections to this course, and on January 1 circulated a memorandum outlining in general terms the various forms that a settlement with Berlin might take. Chamberlain pondered this Foreign Office paper for two weeks and then asked for a more detailed report on what "contributions" Hitler might make if he were given colonies.[25]

Though Chamberlain placed first priority on reaching an understanding with Germany, he was still eager to get on better terms with Italy as well. Britain's approach of December 2, linking the opening of talks with the cessation of propaganda, had not appealed to Rome. When the Italians finally replied on December 23, they indicated their willingness to begin conversations, but gave no assurances about propaganda and made it clear that any discussions should include the question of recognition of their rule in Abyssinia.[26] Impatient to start talks, Chamberlain pressed Eden to tackle the recognition issue and, in late December and early January (1938), the Foreign Office did examine the problem.[27] According to Sir Horace Wilson, chief industrial adviser to the government and Chamberlain's "grey eminence," the Prime Minister intended "to move as fast as he possibly can."[28] Chamberlain was optimistic in mid-January: "I am about to enter upon a fresh attempt to reach a reasonable understanding with both Germany and Italy, and I am by no means unhopeful of getting results."[29]

The period from November 1937 to January 1938 clearly represented an important stage in the evolution of the Chamberlain government's appeasement policy in Europe, which stood in marked contrast to its policy toward Japan. Far from seeking to conciliate the Japanese, London searched during these months for ways to restrain them and help the Chinese.

The Chamberlain government's course in East Asia was questioned in late November and December of 1937 by Craigie and Robert Howe, *chargé d'affaires* in China and normally a firm supporter of Chiang Kai-shek. Fearing that a prolonged war would result in vastly increased communist influence on the Asian mainland, Howe intimated that Britain should press Chiang to make a settlement, even if the terms were highly favorable to Japan.[30] Craigie, who was becoming very irritated by the Foreign Office's unwillingness to take his advice, echoed his previous calls for an attempt to improve relations with Tokyo. Convinced that the Japanese would respond to friendly treatment, Sir Robert wanted London at least to assure Japan that it intended to be neutral and was not giving material assistance to Chiang. The embassy in China also proposed such a step.[31]

London was not moved to reconsider its policy. The Foreign

Office felt that Craigie and Howe overrated Japanese power and underrated Chiang's political acumen. As Charles Orde declared, "The chances of wearing down Japan's strength are not negligible and Chiang Kai-shek's insight and foresight not to be lightly impugned."[32] The communist bogey mentioned by Howe did not alarm Eden's advisers, nor did they accept Craigie's view that Tokyo's attitude could be moderated by conciliatory overtures. Nigel Ronald commented that the Japanese were "not very reasonable at the best of times" and were "not likely to listen to reason at the present time," while other observers noted that Ambassador Craigie apparently did not realize the extent to which Japan's policy was determined by the military.[33] As for the proposal that Britain should tell Tokyo that she was not helping China, Eden, Cadogan, and Ronald said such a step was unthinkable because it would involve "taking credit" for not aiding a "victim of aggression" and because Britain might soon decide to give China significant assistance.[34]

Though the British refused to give up encouraging China to resist, they did briefly explore again the possibility of mediation. On December 6, four days after Chiang had told Germany that he would be willing to discuss peace terms with Japan, the Foreign Office decided to ascertain Washington's opinion about Craigie's earlier suggestion that Britain and the United States should offer to act as a "post office" for the two sides. But Sumner Welles of the State Department was unenthusiastic, pointing out that there was little chance of Japan's being receptive to Anglo-American mediation in any event. London agreed, and ceased to bring up the matter.[35]

The possibility of mediation was thus of only very minor concern to the Chamberlain government during this period. The British were instead preoccupied with searching for firm measures that could be taken to protect their interests and influence in East Asia. This search presented great difficulties, since only action that would be effective, yet not likely to cause Japanese retaliation, was deemed appropriate by the Cabinet and the Foreign Office. Britain was acutely aware that Hong Kong was vulnerable; the Air Ministry had already warned in October 1937 that "the problem of the effective defence of Hong Kong against the maximum scale of air attack which Japan could bring to bear against the fortress and base is virtually insoluble."[36]

Not surprisingly, China had her own ideas of what action the British should take. During the last days of the Brussels Conference, she had pressed London to give her munitions and other supplies, and on November 29 this general appeal was translated into specific terms by an *aide-mémoire* asking for 1,000 airplanes, 500,000 rifles, 60,000 machine guns, a large quantity of ammunition and other supplies, and a loan of £100 million to finance the purchase of these items. This request confronted the Foreign Office with a dilemma. Believing that the survival of the Chinese government was in Britain's interest, Eden and his advisers wanted to help. They were, however, opposed to a loan, fearing that it would cause, in Orde's words, "a first-class row with Japan." They were slightly more helpful with regard to the request for munitions. Though the Chamberlain government's own defense requirements precluded assistance on the desired scale, the Foreign Office was able to give China information about "such small quantities of military supplies as might be available for immediate purchase," and Eden pressed the Air Ministry and War Office to find additional arms for her.[37]

The Chinese were far from satisfied, and on January 4 they made another request for a loan, asking this time for £30 million to help maintain their currency.[38] Ten days later they appealed for a credit to finance the construction of a railway from Burma to western China. This proposal was followed by a request that Britain build an all-weather road in Burma along which supplies could be sent to China.[39] The British carefully examined these new appeals. Though their general policy, as reaffirmed by the Foreign Office in January and February, was to give China "every possible encouragement and support,"[40] only the proposal that an all-weather road be constructed in Burma was judged acceptable. At the Foreign Office's urging, the Burma Office convinced the Governor of Burma to undertake this project. The idea of a railway credit was rejected as being too much of a financial risk. With regard to the key question of floating a loan, the Foreign Office, the Treasury, and the War Office agreed in late January that such a step was no more feasible than before.[41]

At this point the discouraged Chinese decided to take their case back to the League of Nations. On January 28 Wellington Koo tried to persuade Britain, France, and the Soviet Union to support a resolution paving the way for sanctions against Japan. The British and French managed to convince Koo to settle for a declaration reaffirming the duty of League members to help China.[42] After this statement was made public on February 2, the British government again reviewed the question of aiding the Chinese. Eden, though averse to a loan, was particularly eager to assist them. Chamberlain authorized him on February 10 to summon an interdepartmental committee to consider how Britain could implement the League resolution. No action, however, resulted from the deliberations of this committee, which met only once.[43]

While the British were examining China's various appeals for assistance in late 1937 and early 1938, they were also exploring the feasibility of a show of naval strength in the western Pacific. In September 1937 the Chief of Naval Staff, Admiral Lord Ernle Chatfield, had pointed out that Japan could be restrained only if she were made to fear British sea power. He believed, however, that any fleet dispatched to the Far East "must be in sufficient strength to defeat the full strength of the Japanese navy"; if only two capital ships were sent, Tokyo would be tempted to attack them, rather than be cowed by them.[44] The problem with sending eight or nine battleships to East Asia was that Britain would be left vulnerable in her home waters and in the Mediterranean. Eden, intrigued by the idea of a naval demonstration, felt that this difficulty could be overcome if the United States agreed to collaborate. At a Cabinet meeting on November 24 he suggested that Britain ask the Americans "if they would send ships to the Far East if we would do the same." Though Chamberlain doubted that the Roosevelt administration would be interested, he had no objections to such an inquiry.[45] Chatfield told the Foreign Office two days later that there would be considerable risks even in joint action, but Eden nevertheless instructed Ambassador Lindsay to approach the State Department. Sumner Welles was not enthusiastic about the idea in his initial reaction on November 27, especially since in any "overwhelming display of naval force" in the western Pacific it seemed that the United States would have to carry the main burden. Three days later Welles confirmed that the Roosevelt administration was opposed to Britain's suggestion.[46]

After this rebuff, discussion in London of naval action died down until December 5, when several British ships were damaged during a Japanese raid on Wuhu. The next day Eden again told Lindsay that Britain was willing to make a show of strength if the United States would cooperate, but he did not want the Ambassador to make another approach to the State Department until a further incident occurred. Admiral Lord Chatfield, for his part, was worried: "I have tried to impress on the Foreign Office the weakness of our Naval position, to try to deter them from doing anything to provoke the Japanese, but I am afraid there is already a considerable feeling against us in Japan."[47]

At this juncture a very serious crisis developed. On December 12 Japanese ground forces shelled HMS *Ladybird* and HMS *Bee*, killing one seaman and wounding several others. British naval authorities protested to Japan's senior officer in the Wuhu area, Colonel Hashimoto Kingoro, who conceded that he had erred in shelling Britain's ships, but said that he had orders to fire on every vessel moving on the Yangtze River. Later that day Japanese naval aircraft sank USS *Panay* and also bombed three Standard Oil tankers.[48]

These attacks enraged the British public and the government. Hashimoto was known to be a fiery ultra-patriot, and *The Times* angrily claimed that the shellings were either a deliberate attempt to drive foreign shipping off the Yangtze or proof "that—save for a small civilized upper class—no Japanese can be trusted to carry firearms, even in the Emperor's service, because he is too ignorant and too irresponsible not to run amok without provocation."[49] Eden, who felt the attacks were deliberate, wanted the British and the Americans to take firm measures against Japan. On the Foreign Secretary's instructions, Lindsay made it clear to the United

States on December 13 that London hoped the two governments would act jointly in response to the incidents, and he also said that Britain was ready to hold naval staff conversations. The State Department nevertheless sent its formal note of protest to Tokyo independently, and expressed no interest in naval action. As Lindsay told Secretary of State Hull on December 14, Washington's refusal to cooperate was very disappointing to the British, who felt that the Japanese could be restrained only by a joint show of "possibilities of force on a large scale."[50]

London puzzled over its next step. At a Cabinet meeting on December 15, Eden proposed that the United States should again be pressed to join Britain in sending a fleet to the western Pacific. Alfred Duff Cooper, the First Lord of the Admiralty, warned that a further approach would only irritate. When at this point a message from Lindsay arrived, stating that the Roosevelt administration was not yet prepared to cooperate in naval action, Chamberlain remarked that there seemed to be no use in asking Washington to send battleships to East Asia. The Prime Minister said, however, that Britain should suggest to the United States a joint mobilization of their respective fleets as a warning to Japan. "That might be sufficient in itself; but if, nevertheless, further outrages should occur, the Americans might then be able to do more." Chamberlain ended by stressing that in any event it would be imprudent for Britain to take unilateral action.[51]

The British doubted that the United States would be willing to mobilize her fleet or make any other menacing move. But indignation over the sinking of the *Panay* was growing in Washington, mainly because fresh reports from China seemed to prove that the Japanese attacks had been deliberate. Admiral William Leahy (the Chief of Naval Operations), Norman Davis, and several members of the Roosevelt Cabinet favored strong action.[52] The President, for his part, told Lindsay on December 16 that he wanted "a systematic exchange of secret information" between representatives of the Admiralty and the Department of the Navy and that the first object of these talks should be to plan for a blockade of Japan in which British and American cruisers would patrol the area between the Aleutian Islands and Hong Kong. The blockade, to be instituted after "the next grave outrage" by the Japanese, would be designed to keep raw materials from reaching Japan. When the surprised Lindsay suggested that action of this kind would lead to war, the President disagreed. Lindsay then mentioned that London had been thinking in terms of either sending battleships to East Asia to make a show of strength or carrying out mobilization measures. Roosevelt indicated that he did not like these ideas, though he did say that he would seriously consider arranging a visit by American cruisers to Singapore.[53]

Britain found the President's blockade proposals naïve and downright bewildering. Even Lindsay, impressed as he was with Roosevelt's eagerness to help, referred to them as "the utterances of a hare-brained statesman or an amateur strategist." But because the British wished to take some action in East Asia and to keep the way open for Anglo-American cooperation, they did not want to make a discouraging response. Ronald expressed the hope that the scheme could be shaped "into something more congruous."[54]

While London was pondering the President's startling initiative, an even more perplexing episode occurred. On December 17 Henry Morgenthau, the United States Secretary of the Treasury, telephoned his British counterpart, Sir John Simon, and outlined a tentative plan for exchange control against the Japanese. Morgenthau, with whom the State Department's passive policy in East Asia rankled, emphasized that he was calling with Roosevelt's approval and then asked Simon whether Britain would cooperate with this plan, which might be implemented if Tokyo gave an unsatisfactory reply to Washington's protest over the sinking of the *Panay*. Taken aback, Simon could only say that Morgenthau should have contacted the Foreign Office first and that it was risky to conduct business over the telephone because serious misunderstandings—such as that with Stimson in 1932—could result. Simon did nonetheless promise to discuss the matter with Chamberlain. The next day Morgenthau cabled Sir John, explaining that his plan was to be discussed during the proposed naval conversations.[55]

From the British point of view, Morgenthau's scheme was open to the same objections as any other kind of economic sanction: if the measure was going to be ineffective, there was no point in adopting it, whereas if the action was going to be effective, it would probably lead to war. Simon and his top advisers in the Treasury wanted no part of the plan. Sir Warren Fisher, the permanent under-secretary, warned: "Over and above the imbecility of economic sanctions, we sh^d find ourselves left in the lurch sooner or later by the U.S.A. (who incidentally have no very special stakes in Asia) & Japan w^d scoop Hongkong. Sh^d we then add the fatal folly of going to war with Japan & so committing suicide in Europe?"[56] After communicating with Chamberlain and Eden, neither of whom showed any interest in the American proposal, Simon made it clear to Morgenthau on December 21 that Britain did not like the plan.[57] The United States never brought the matter up again.

In the meantime, Eden had decided that the best response to the President's proposal of December 16 was "to try to tie Roosevelt down to *present* movement of ships rather than future blockade." Chamberlain agreed, maintaining that "now was the time for a move if it was to be made at all. Our prestige was suffering in the Far East and elsewhere owing to our unavoidably passive attitude. . . . Any simultaneous demonstration of force by the United States and ourselves, whether in the Far East or even at a distance, would have a steadying influence all over the world."[58] The British received word that Roosevelt was sending Captain Royal E. Ingersoll, the director of the Navy's War Plans Division, to London to engage in staff talks with the Admiralty. The Americans also reiterated that they were seriously thinking of sending some cruisers on a visit to Singapore in February 1938 and said that they might advance the date of the Navy's annual maneuvers, which were scheduled for March. But the United States gave no indication that she was interested in immediate naval action of any kind. In fact, the indignation that had developed in Washington after December 15 was dying down. On Christmas Eve the Japanese sent the State Department an apologetic note in which they offered to pay an indemnity for the *Panay* and gave assurances that there would be no recurrence of attacks on American interests. The Roosevelt administration expressed its satisfaction, thus settling the *Panay* incident.[59]

The Japanese note to Britain about the Yangtze shellings was less conciliatory in tone. Unlike Washington, London was not inclined to regard the affair as closed.[60] The Foreign Office hoped that Ingersoll's visit would pave the way for an immediate Anglo-American naval demonstration in the western Pacific. Upon his arrival in London on January 1, Ingersoll told an inquisitive Eden that he did not know whether the Roosevelt administration was ready to take action at this stage. After explaining that in any case "no movement could be made at all in the Pacific unless full preparation had been made for every eventuality, including war," Ingersoll made it clear that he was there primarily to discuss technical problems with the Admiralty and that political decisions could not easily be made until such discussions were held and plans were coordinated.[61] Staying in London less than three weeks, he met next with Admiral Lord Chatfield on January 3 and thereafter with Captain Sir Thomas Phillips, the head of the Plans Division of the Admiralty. The main result of the visit was an informal agreement that in the event of war with Japan, the British and the Americans could use each other's "waters." Contingency plans for a blockade were also made.[62]

Eden had been disappointed by the modest objectives of Ingersoll's mission, and had told Lindsay to press the American government to take a more urgent view of the situation in East Asia. But the Ambassador replied on January 3 that he was reluctant to push too hard about an immediate naval demonstration, because in his opinion the Roosevelt administration was "a horse that will run best when the spur is not used."[63]

Four days later the Foreign Office received a report that Japanese soldiers had assaulted two British police officers in Shanghai. Feeling that she might have to do more than merely protest to Tokyo, Britain asked the Americans whether they would take parallel action if she announced that she was "completing certain

naval preparations." Lindsay doubted that the Roosevelt administration would be receptive to this approach, but on January 10
Washington said the President was about to announce that the
annual American naval maneuvers would be advanced and that
three cruisers would visit Singapore when the dock there was formally opened in February. More important, the United States also
indicated that, if Britain declared the completion of naval preparations, she would publicly state that the vessels of the Pacific Fleet
were being sent to drydock to have their bottoms scraped—a
measure of preparatory action.[64]

This response caught the British between wind and water. On
the one hand, the Americans were showing some disposition to
act, and the Foreign Office felt it might be unwise for London to
vacillate. On the other hand, Britain believed (perhaps somewhat
captiously) that Washington's offer did not, in Sir Alexander Cadogan's words, "indicate any very great alacrity on the part of
the Americans." In particular, Charles Orde maintained, it would
"not commit the U.S. Government politically as much as a statement by us about naval preparations would commit us." Seemingly Britain feared that if she rushed ahead, a situation might
arise in which her fleet went to the western Pacific without the
American navy following suit.[65] Eden, who was on vacation in
France and hence in a poor position to influence deliberations in
London, wrote Chamberlain about the importance "of effectively
asserting white race authority in the Far East." He also wrote
Cadogan that "it looks from here as though the moment was fast
approaching when, if we are to retain our position as a world
power, we shall be compelled to move the larger part of the fleet to
Singapore." If this were done, he argued, the United States would
probably take parallel action, because it was unlikely that she
"would sit with folded hands & watch [the] British Empire in
jeopardy, if it really came to that."[66] Eden's colleagues, however,
were not willing to take this risk. Chatfield suggested that London
should probe the Americans to see how far they would go, but
Chamberlain and Cadogan were opposed to this idea, fearing that
it would arouse suspicion in Washington. Significantly, Chamber-

lain pointed out that in any case it was a bad time for Britain to send her fleet to Singapore. His effort to get on better terms with Mussolini—motivated in part, ironically, by a desire to be in a better position to deal with Japan—would hardly be enhanced by moving capital ships from the Mediterranean to the western Pacific.[67] In addition, as Sir Robert Vansittart noted, "there has of late been considerable expression of *hope* in German military circles that we would send our fleet to the Far East. This is a fact, and it has its significance, which shᵈ not be overlooked."[68]

The British therefore decided not to announce the completion of naval preparations. This episode illuminates the menacing global dimensions of their troubles and especially the interlocking constraints on their freedom of action. But their irresolution at this point should not be allowed to obscure the interesting, if less important, fact that they had shown more enthusiasm in December of 1937 and early January of 1938 for a naval demonstration than they had just weeks earlier for economic measures. This was largely because they believed a show of force was likely to deter a Japanese military attack on British and American interests, whereas sanctions would provoke one.

Apart from its value as a deterrent, a naval show of force could also be used to impose a peace settlement on Japan and China. This idea was first explored in the Foreign Office in December 1937.[69] Then in early January both Sir John Pratt and Sir John Brenan of the Far Eastern Department prepared memoranda suggesting specific peace terms that Britain, presumably in conjunction with the United States, could force the two sides to accept. Pratt, though stating that any imposed settlement should be "generous" to Japan as well as "fair" to China, emphasized that the British should not propose terms "unless our naval forces in the Far East are so strong that Japan will not care to court defeat by opposing any policy that we may adopt in defence of vital British interests." He defined these vital interests as stable political conditions, equal opportunity and an "open door" in China, the security of Hong Kong, the integrity of the Customs Administration, and the denial to Japan of a hold over Shanghai. The Chinese, he argued, should be given control over Shanghai, though foreigners should be allowed to participate in the municipal government. By supporting such a line, Britain would enhance her prestige and prevent Japanese domination of the city and of the Yangtze Valley. In his opinion, if the Shanghai problem could be worked out, most of the other difficulties involved in a peace settlement would fall into place. One important conundrum, however, would remain: North China. Pratt said that "it was no part of our business to drive the Japanese beyond the Great Wall, even if we had the force to do so." Britain should therefore leave China and Japan to negotiate about the five northern provinces, advising the Chinese to make economic concessions in return for a full recognition of their sovereignty over the area. But, as Pratt noted, if Chiang Kai-shek "does not succeed in securing the withdrawal of all Japanese troops from China proper, . . . one of the main objects of British policy—stability—will not have been achieved." He ended by asserting that if Britain were compelled to use force to expel the Japanese from Shanghai, she might then be in a position to take a stronger line in North China.[70]

Brenan, who had moved to the Foreign Office in November 1937 after many years in the consular service in China, reached similar conclusions in his memorandum. On the one hand he warned that "it would be foolish not to adopt a realistic attitude towards Japan's undoubted military power and her firm resolve to secure a stronger economic and strategic position in East Asia. No more than the Germans can the Japanese be indefinitely suppressed." On the other hand he declared that in the long run the Chinese "will be more than a match for the Japanese." He suggested that Britain should concentrate on "saving the main China market for our trade and that of other nations" and on putting China "on her feet as an independent nation." Though Brenan felt that to some extent the northern provinces had to be left to "forces beyond our control," he nonetheless proposed that Britain should press for recognition by Japan "of the sovereignty, the independence and the territorial and administrative integrity of China proper, and the withdrawal of all Japanese forces south of the Great Wall." In return, the Chinese should recognize Manchukuo and make economic concessions to Japan. With regard to Shanghai, he called for "as large a Chinese participation as possible" in a reorganized administration of the city. Finally, Brenan said that the British, while insisting on certain safeguards, should consider giving up extraterritorial privileges, even though such a step would mean the end of their "political pretension" in China.[71]

Both memoranda envisaged that a settlement would be reached through concessions by Japan and China and, to a lesser degree, by the Western powers. From one angle, the two plans might be viewed as a call for appeasement of Japan, because they conceded to her a special economic position in North China and because one of them proposed that the Chinese recognize Manchukuo. A more balanced assessment, however, must emphasize that the two officials were suggesting that Britain and the United States could dictate terms to Japan, thus protecting their vital interests and ensuring the survival of China, if they were able to make a show of naval force. A scheme based on the threat (and possibly the use) of force is hardly compatible with the idea of appeasement.*

Even though the two memoranda should not be regarded as calls for appeasement, Brenan and Pratt did evidently believe that stability in East Asia was very unlikely unless Japan's aspirations for a stronger economic and strategic position were at least partially fulfilled. Yet in its day-to-day response to the situation in China, the Foreign Office was guided by the notion that Japanese expansion had to be halted and Japan's attempts to consolidate her influence over North China should be thwarted. This contradiction between Britain's policy and her view of long-term realities in East Asia was never resolved.

Since Britain decided against sending her fleet to the western

---

* It might in fact be more accurate to label the schemes a "counter-imperialist" version of "gunboat diplomacy" updated by the lessons of the Treaty of Versailles. If the terms were too harsh, Japan would have a very powerful grievance. As Cadogan noted, "If we are strong enough to impose a peace, let us not repeat the errors of Versailles." Nor was this the only consideration against an attempt to return to the status quo. According to Pratt and Brenan, Chinese incompetence had also to be borne in mind: "Moreover the inherent incapacity of the Chinese Government, apart altogether from the effect of recent hostilities, may make a restoration of the status quo unattainable." See FO memo., Dec. 18, 1937, and minute by Cadogan, FO F11749/4880/10.

Pacific, the proposals made by Brenan and Pratt were never carried out. An essay summarizing the main points of the two memoranda was sent on February 14 to Stanley Hornbeck of the State Department, who, at the Brussels Conference, had urged the British to do some thinking about possible solutions to the Sino-Japanese conflict. On April 13 Hornbeck sent a lengthy reply that stressed the desirability of not intervening and thus vividly reflected the difference between the Foreign Office and State Department approaches to East Asia.[72] The American memorandum made one particularly incisive observation about the British scheme: it took for granted that Japan would not react violently to forcible Anglo-American intervention. The Foreign Office had indeed calculated that so long as the demands on Japan were moderate, she would not retaliate. Terms that seemed moderate to London, however—such as granting the Japanese a special economic position in North China but restoring Kuomintang political authority there —might seem harsh and unacceptable to Tokyo.

Leaving aside the important question of "face" that would be raised by a naval show of force, Japan might have accepted such a solution of the North China problem as late as November 1937. But by December the situation had changed. Premier Konoe, Foreign Minister Hirota, and the others in Japan who wanted to crush Chiang Kai-shek had definitely gained the upper hand over the General Staff, which favored an immediate diplomatic resolution of the conflict. One measure of the strength of the hard-line group was that a campaign against Nanking was finally launched on December 1.[73] This Japanese action was no doubt an important reason why Chiang told Germany on December 2 that he was prepared to open talks with Tokyo. On December 7, however, Hirota told the Germans that he doubted whether Japan could negotiate on the basis of the terms she had formulated in early November.[74] Six days later Nanking fell, forcing the Chinese government to withdraw to the interior. Leaving the Foreign Ministry at Hankow, Chiang established a new capital at Chungking. On December 14 Japan's North China Area Army set up a Provisional Government of the Chinese Republic in Peking, and Konoe hinted that this puppet regime might become the nucleus of a future Japanese-sponsored central government.

The victory at Nanking and the establishment of the puppet regime further strengthened the position of the hard-line group in Tokyo. The General Staff was still desperately trying to convince the government to negotiate seriously with the Chinese, but was being outmaneuvered by the Premier. On December 17 the Konoe Cabinet approved new peace terms at once so vague and so severe that there was little chance of China's accepting them. Sure enough, when the Germans transmitted these terms nine days later, the Chinese were shocked.[75]

The General Staff took its case to the Emperor, but were again frustrated by Konoe's political skill. At an Imperial Conference on January 11—the first such gathering in more than three decades—the hard-line policy was sanctioned. Japan told the Germans on the following day that Chiang must approve her demands within seventy-two hours or face the consequences. The Chinese asked for a clarification of the terms, but this plea was ignored, and Hirota informed Germany on January 16 that Japan was cutting off negotiations with China.[76] The same day Konoe publicly announced that the Japanese government would no longer deal with Chiang Kai-shek and was looking forward to the development of a new Chinese regime that would cooperate with Japan. The Premier had committed Japan to a war of annihilation on the mainland, despite the protests of the General Staff that a protracted conflict would leave her vulnerable to the potential threat posed by the Soviet Union. In a speech to the Diet on January 22, Hirota indicated for the first time that the Japanese were seeking a "new order" in East Asia.[77]

The British were bewildered by these rapid changes. Japan's onslaught against Nanking in early December temporarily shook their cautious optimism about Chiang's strength.[78] The Foreign Office feared that the Japanese might attack South China next, threatening Hong Kong.* But Japan paused after capturing Nan-

---

* Warning that "any abandonment of Hong Kong would have the most far-reaching effects, not only on our position in the Far East but throughout the

king, and by the end of December Eden could say that "the Chinese seem to be standing up well now."[79] Craigie suggested on January 9 that China be pressed to continue negotiating with Japan, but the Foreign Office refused, realizing that a settlement could be reached only on the basis of "the more or less complete surrender of the Chinese Government."[80]

Konoe's cutoff of negotiations on January 16 astonished the Far Eastern Department. As one observer noted: "It will take great skill to avoid disputes with third Powers if the Japanese keep up their present arrogant line."[81] In his speech of January 22, Foreign Minister Hirota stated that Japan had no territorial ambitions in China and would respect Western interests there, but the Far Eastern Department, which felt that the Foreign Minister was under the influence of the military, was skeptical.* Sir John Pratt said Hirota's promises were designed to keep London "quiet until Japan was ready to expel British interests from China as she has expelled them from Manchuria," and Charles Orde pointed out that the references to Britain in the speech were distinctly less cordial than those to the United States.[82] The British were quite sensitive to any such attempt to drive a wedge between London and Washington.

---

world," Cadogan asked the Chiefs of Staff on December 18 to consider what could be done to protect the Crown Colony if the Japanese did strike south. The strategists, though conceding that Hong Kong was vulnerable, were not particularly worried. "Japan," they reported, "is notoriously short of money and raw materials; she has already three-quarters of a million men involved in operations on the mainland of China; she has seriously antagonised public opinion in the United States of America; and she cannot but be apprehensive of Soviet Russia. In all these circumstances it seems scarcely conceivable to us that she will deliberately do anything at Hong Kong which is bound to involve her in war with the British Empire." See letter from Cadogan to Hankey, Dec. 18, 1937, and Chiefs of Staff memo., Dec. 21, 1937, CAB 53/35. Looking back on the situation six months later, Sir John Brenan wrote: "We know that the 'Panay' and 'Ladybird' incidents caused the Japanese such alarm that they abandoned the invasion of Kuangtung (Canton) for fear of complications with the Western Powers." Minute by Brenan on Craigie to FO, June 20, 1938, FO F6708/84/10.

* Though the officials in the Far Eastern Department were correct in supposing that Hirota was no moderate, like all British observers they did not realize that one section of the Japanese military—the General Staff—was the leading moderate group in Tokyo.

Eden was apparently less skeptical than his advisers, for he told the Cabinet on January 24 that there had been "some alleviation in the tension in the Far East," and cited Hirota's speech in support of this view.[83] Chamberlain agreed with Eden's assessment. The next day he told a deputation from the National Council of Labour Members that he felt as strongly as Labour did about Japan's behavior. But he brushed aside the deputation's appeals for sanctions, explaining that a naval demonstration would be more effective and that in any case a new situation might be developing within the Japanese government. "There had been an internal struggle and it seemed that the moderates had come out on top." He was hopeful, moreover, that "the Japanese moderates might succeed in stopping this policy of offering insults to foreigners."[84]

Chamberlain was of course correct in saying that there had been an internal struggle in Japan, but quite incorrect in his view of the outcome. Still, there were signs that the Konoe Cabinet hoped to keep its relations with Britain from deteriorating further. Hirota told a committee of the Japanese House of Representatives on February 3 that Japan wished to maintain her traditional friendship with the British. The next day Ambassador Yoshida gave Eden an *aide-mémoire* from Hirota calling for Anglo-Japanese cooperation in reconstructing China. Acting on his own initiative, Yoshida then suggested that Britain should try to mediate. Eden's advisers regarded this approach as unimportant. Cadogan scoffed that the Japanese wanted "to 'eliminate' us 'gradually' in China," and Orde noted that mediation was hopeless, since the Chinese would not accept Japan's terms, "nor do we want them to do so."[85] At a Cabinet meeting on February 9, however, Chamberlain pressed Eden to follow up Yoshida's suggestion that Britain try to mediate. Eden replied that the task would be "one of great difficulty and delicacy, as the Germans had found, and he felt that it could only be carried out hand in hand with the United States of America. On that basis he was prepared to consider making the attempt."[86] Chamberlain, for his part, was hopeful that a British initiative would bring not only peace but also better Anglo-

Japanese relations. At a conference of ministers four days later, he declared that "he would not like it to be thought for a moment that all chances of appeasement with Japan had slipped away.... It was essential that some effort should be made in that direction."[87] Not surprisingly, his hopes proved unrealistic. On February 15 Yoshida admitted to Eden that the Japanese government was not prepared to accept British mediation.[88]

Though Chamberlain's views on the Far Eastern situation after July 1937 are not easy to reconstruct in detail, it can be said that his attitude toward the Japanese was far less conciliatory than his attitude toward Hitler and Mussolini. Even so, he was generally averse to threatening the Japanese, and in early December 1937 he told the Cabinet that Britain should try to keep open the possibility of getting on better terms with Japan after the trouble in East Asia was over.[89] His remarks of February 13, however, were his only explicit mention of an immediate attempt to appease Japan as both feasible and desirable. The British records do not indicate why the Prime Minister suddenly suggested an initiative that could succeed only at China's expense. Presumably, his assessment of the shifting balance of forces in Tokyo was one reason. Another may have been the increasingly dangerous European situation. Hitler was exerting intense pressure on Austria, and Chamberlain might have calculated that it would be very difficult to deal with Germany so long as Britain had to look apprehensively over her shoulder at the Japanese menace.

In early January Chamberlain had no doubt thought that by mid-February he would be well on his way to securing an understanding with both Germany and Italy. His plans, however, met with obstacles. The first came from an unexpected source: the United States. On January 11 the Roosevelt administration sounded the British about a plan to call a conference in Washington to formulate principles of international behavior and to remove the causes of world tension. The American proposal, which stressed economic questions and the problem of treaty revision, was designed to help London reach agreement with Germany and Italy. The originator of the plan, Sumner Welles of the

State Department, felt that if Britain's appeasement policy succeeded in Europe, Japan would probably lose the support of Germany and Italy and would then be compelled to make peace with China on terms consistent with the Nine-Power Treaty.[90]

Far from regarding this initiative as helpful, Chamberlain feared that it would undermine his attempts to appease Hitler and Mussolini. Disdainful of American diplomacy, he had declared at a Cabinet meeting in December 1937 that only a rash man would base his calculations on help from the United States.[91] He surely noticed that, in making their proposal on January 11, the Americans had said their "traditional policy of freedom from political involvement" would be maintained. Thus, even though Lindsay warned that a rebuff would anger Washington, Chamberlain asked Roosevelt on January 13 to defer the initiative until the results of Britain's attempts at appeasement became known. He explained that American intervention might cause the Germans and the Italians to delay negotiations with Britain and even to increase their demands. He made clear that he was quite hopeful of success in his own efforts, and also indicated that he was considering recognizing Italy's conquest of Abyssinia.[92]

Eden was away in France, and Chamberlain did not consult him before sending this reply. He rushed back to London on January 15, very upset at the way the American approach had been handled, and urged Chamberlain to support the President's offer, arguing that any intervention by the United States would certainly steady the situation in Europe.[93] On January 17 Roosevelt agreed to defer proposing the conference for a while, but cautioned Britain against recognizing the Italian hold on Abyssinia, not least because such a step would encourage Japan to press for recognition of her conquests. According to Lindsay, the President's disappointment over Chamberlain's reply "had been distinctly felt."[94] Eden, fearing that London's attitude might jeopardize Anglo-American relations and push Washington further into isolation, promptly told Chamberlain that Britain should drop the idea of recognition and cooperate with the United States. Chamberlain, however, did not want to be diverted from his attempted rapprochement with Mussolini. As Eden noted in his diary on January 18, Chamberlain regarded himself as a man with a mission to make peace with the dictators.[95]

The issue was bitterly debated by the Cabinet Committee on Foreign Policy, and a compromise was finally reached on January 21.[96] Chamberlain informed Roosevelt in somewhat restrained terms that Britain was ready to support the American plan. In another message to the President, he explained that he would recognize Abyssinia's changed status only as part of a general settlement with the Italians. Pointing out that "the Rome-Berlin axis has attained a solidity which no one would have expected twelve months ago" and that "a new relationship is developing between Italy and Japan which twelve months ago was not even foreshadowed," he contended that Britain could not afford to pass up a chance to improve her relations with Italy, "especially at a time when events in the Far East may at any moment make new demands upon our resources."[97]

Roosevelt never launched the conference. Eden felt Britain had discouraged the President, and he, as well as Winston Churchill and others, later wrote that Chamberlain had thrown away a very important opportunity to avert war.[98] These claims are exaggerated. Though it is true that a prompt and cordial British response might have led to closer Anglo-American cooperation in East Asia, it seems very doubtful that Roosevelt's rather vague plan would have had any decisive impact on the European situation. The United States had no specific peace program in mind, nor did she intend to assume any political or military commitment in support of the British. The American initiative would, however, have gained time for Britain. The episode illuminates the important point that whereas Eden was interested in playing for time in Europe, Chamberlain was not. Chamberlain was confident that he could reach a genuine settlement with Italy and Germany.

On January 24—before Roosevelt had made any response to the British messages of January 21—Chamberlain told the Committee on Foreign Policy that it was very desirable to show Berlin "at the earliest possible moment that we are giving serious consideration to the position arising out of Lord Halifax's visit." He proceeded to propose a solution of the colonial problem: a large international zone would be established in Central Africa, and Germany would be allowed to administer (but not hold sovereignty over) part of it. Though prepared to make this concession to the Germans only as part of a general settlement, Chamberlain felt the colonial question should be taken up first, in the hope that Hitler would then be willing to discuss European issues. His colleagues, however, persuaded him that negotiations about colonies should not be separated from talks on the other elements of a settlement.[99]

The committee then discussed what to ask from Germany in return for concessions in Africa, concluding that Britain should press for restrictions on air bombing and for assurances about German policy in Central and Eastern Europe. On February 12 Ambassador Nevile Henderson in Berlin was instructed to open talks with Hitler.[100] But complications developed the same day. Hitler bullied Austrian Chancellor von Schuschnigg into accepting demands that greatly increased Nazi influence in Austria. This ominous event caused the British to delay, though not to cancel, their approach to the Germans. They still hoped that if Hitler were offered concessions in Africa, he might moderate his policy toward Austria and Czechoslovakia. This illusion was shattered when Henderson finally talked to him on March 3, and he showed no interest in colonies. Summarizing this interview six days later, Halifax noted that "the German Government appeared to be set head-on to achieve their *desiderata* in Central Europe and did not want to tie their hands by talks, and still less by undertakings to ourselves. That left us in a rather dangerous position."[101]

As Britain's difficulties with Germany increased, Chamberlain became more eager than ever to improve relations with Italy. On February 18, not long after learning of Hitler's pressure on Schuschnigg, he demanded that Eden open formal conversations with the Italian government. Chamberlain believed that the Italians were apprehensive about the Austrian situation and sincerely wanted cordial relations with Britain. Eden disagreed, arguing that Italy had shown no sign of good will and, moreover, had probably given the Germans a free hand in Austria in return for their support in the Mediterranean. He placed himself squarely in Chamberlain's path by insisting that formal talks should not be held until the Italians withdrew some of their troops from Spain. When the Prime Minister refused to accept this procedure, Eden resigned.[102]

Halifax succeeded Eden as the Foreign Minister. There was no perceptible change in Britain's East Asian policy, nor in her line toward Germany, but the way was finally open for a new attempt to conciliate Italy. On March 1 Chamberlain told the Cabinet Committee on Foreign Policy that an understanding with Rome "should be reached as rapidly as possible." He hoped that if the Italians could be won over, Hitler might behave more circum-spectly toward Austria, and Britain might "find it unnecessary to incur very heavy expenditure on Mediterranean fortifications."[103] Notwithstanding Chamberlain's sense of urgency, no agreement was signed until April 16, 1938. Its provisions included a British promise to ease the way at the League of Nations for *de jure* recognition of Italy's hold on Abyssinia, and an Italian pledge to adhere to a formula for the withdrawal of their troops from Spain. The understanding was not to come into effect until the Spanish question was "settled."

The Anglo-Italian talks did not have the desired restraining effect on Hitler, and when the German army marched into Austria on March 11, Rome refused even to discuss the situation with London. The British gave no thought to challenging Germany. Chamberlain summed up his attitude on March 12 when he declared that at any rate the Austrian question was now "out of the way."[104] He and his colleagues immediately began to consider how to prevent a similar move by Germany against Czechoslo-vakia, where the existence of a discontented Sudeten-German mi-nority gave Hitler convenient grounds for intervention. France was committed by treaty to help Czechoslovakia in the event of an attack; hence the specter of a full-scale European conflict loomed over London's deliberations. After some hesitation,

Chamberlain, Halifax, and their pliant colleagues opted for the course involving the smallest risk of war: no guarantee against German attack should be given to Czechoslovakia or France, and the Czechoslovak government should be pressed to reach a settlement with the Sudeten Germans.[105] From this point, the road to Munich was a short one.*

The ministers' desire to avoid risks was fully shared by the Chiefs of Staff. In a report of March 21, the strategists stressed that the British and the French did not possess the military means to prevent the Germans from overwhelming Czechoslovakia. They also warned that if Britain became involved in a war with Germany, "it is more than probable that both Italy and Japan would seize the opportunity to further their own ends." Thus Britain had to face the possibility of a world war—and in their opinion she lacked the power to cope with it. A comparison of air forces, for example, showed that Britain could mobilize 420 bombers and 378 fighters, whereas Germany appeared to have 1,570 bombers and 540 fighters, and Japan could put 427 bombers and 348 fighters into the air. In addition, if Britain sent part of her fleet to Singapore to counter the Japanese, Italy would gain control of the eastern Mediterranean and would be in a good position to drive the British out of Egypt, Palestine, and the rest of the Middle East.[106]

This report was, in Halifax's words, an "extremely melancholy document."[107] It was also a telling commentary on how slowly British rearmament had been progressing. In June 1937—less than a year after Britain had begun to rearm in earnest—the Treasury had pressed for stringent financial controls on defense spending. Sir John Simon, insisting that expenditure on rearmament must not exceed £1,500 million for the 1937-41 period, called for an intensive review of Service estimates. Such an examination was launched in late October.[108] Sir Thomas Inskip, who conducted the review, circulated an interim report to the Cabinet in mid-December upholding the Treasury view that defense spending

---

* The mainsprings of British policy toward Czechoslovakia will be assessed in Chapter 6.

should be limited to £1,500 million for the next five years. Inskip also declared that "in the long run the provision of adequate defences within the means at our disposal will only be achieved when our long-term foreign policy has succeeded in changing the present assumptions as to the number of our potential enemies." His report met with Chamberlain's approval and was endorsed by the Cabinet on December 22.[109]

Simon, Inskip, and Chamberlain believed that this limitation on defense spending was desirable for economic, strategic, and political reasons. They feared that large expenditures on rearmament would disrupt Britain's economy, particularly her export trade, and might even lead to a financial crisis such as that of 1931. Economic instability would in turn cripple the country's ability to wage war. They therefore considered finance to be the "fourth arm" of British defense. Finally, vastly increased spending would require heavier taxation. This would be politically unpopular, not least in the City.[110] In fact, Simon maintained in April 1938 that Britain could not spend large sums on rearmament "unless we turned ourselves into a different kind of nation."[111]

Predictably, the Chiefs of Staff were quite alarmed that the momentum of rearmament was being slowed down. Admiral Lord Chatfield found this "swing of the pendulum" difficult to understand, especially in light of the "grave world political situation, which appeared almost daily to grow more menacing."[112] He and his colleagues circulated a report on February 11, 1938, warning that "the military situation with which the British Empire is now faced is fraught with greater risk than at any time in living memory, apart from the war years."* They added that "our approved

---

* Eden, though sharing the military's alarm at the pace of rearmament, felt that the Chiefs of Staff were too pessimistic about the world situation and even suspected that they wanted "to clamber on the band wagon with the dictators." He could—surprisingly enough—"well understand" that their "chief anxiety" was the Far East, but believed that they overrated the power and solidarity of the German-Japanese-Italian bloc. Indeed, he thought it very unlikely that the bloc would "hold together so strongly as to come into a war against us." See letter from Eden to Chamberlain, Jan. 31, 1938, Premier 1/276. In retrospect, Eden's optimism seems as remarkable as the pessimism of the Chiefs of Staff.

rearmament programme is falling behind and . . . in our opinion it will fail to give us security in time."[113]

The Services appealed for defense programs that would cost £2,000 million in the 1937-41 period. Inskip maintained that to spend this much might cause economic ruin. He proposed a compromise figure of £1,650 million, to be rationed among the three defense ministries. Though the Services were not at all satisfied with this proposal, the Cabinet approved it on February 16. Chamberlain acknowledged that this compromise meant postponing decisions on important programs, and said that he could accept it only because of "his hope for some improvement on the international side."[114] Germany's absorption of Austria less than a month later made it more difficult to be optimistic. On March 22 the Cabinet abandoned its former formula of not allowing rearmament to interfere with "the normal course of trade," and agreed to accelerate and to some extent expand its Air programs.[115] These decisions by no means represented the beginning of all-out rearmament, but they were a departure from the surprising lack of urgency in 1937 and early 1938.

The Admiralty was disappointed at the priority given to the Air Force. Both Admiral Chatfield and First Lord Duff Cooper were very concerned over the Royal Navy's weakness. From May 1938 to the fall of 1939, three of the fleet's fifteen capital ships would be undergoing modernization. Nine of the ships ready for duty had been built before the Battle of Jutland, and only one of them had been fully modernized. Chatfield had pointed out in January 1938 that if Britain "had to despatch an adequate fleet to the Far East to meet that of Japan, we could leave practically no modern ships at home to deal with the German and Italian fleets which were composed of comparatively new ships."[116] To make matters worse, the base at Singapore, though formally opened in February 1938, would not be able to handle large repairs and other essential wartime functions until 1940. And though Singapore was the linchpin of Britain's strategic position in the East, its defenses against air attack were woefully inadequate.[117] Clearly the British were very vulnerable in the western Pacific.

Since the spring of 1937, the Admiralty had been calling for a new standard of naval strength that would enable the Royal Navy to protect British interests against simultaneous attacks by Germany and Japan.[118] This ambitious proposal was firmly opposed by Sir Thomas Inskip and the Treasury. In his interim report of December 1937, Inskip said that the Admiralty should keep its spending in line with the so-called D.R.C. (Defence Requirements Sub-Committee) standard, which provided for defense against the German navy in Europe, but only for "cover" against the Japanese fleet in East Asia.[119] Duff Cooper retorted in early February 1938 that the D.R.C.-size fleet was "in no way related to the present international situation, or to the barest necessities of Imperial defence." He pointed out that Britain's relations with Japan, "the most important Naval Power with whom we are likely to find ourselves in conflict," had steadily deteriorated, and "we have been compelled to contemplate the despatch of the Fleet to the Far East as a possibility no longer remote."[120] Duff Cooper's arguments did not sway his colleagues. The Cabinet agreed on February 16 to postpone a decision on the new standard.[121]

Undaunted, Duff Cooper called after the German annexation of Austria for an increase in Britain's naval construction plans for 1938, and he asked in April that the modernization program be accelerated. Both appeals were brushed aside by the Cabinet.[122] Meanwhile, Inskip had proposed a ceiling of £360 million on the Admiralty's spending in the 1939-41 period. Duff Cooper complained that this "ration" was insufficient even for the D.R.C. standard, and he prepared a paper in late April contending that "the system of rationing the Service Departments is impossible to defend." Though Simon was able to prevent this memorandum from being circulated to the Cabinet,[123] the debate dragged on, finally coming to a head almost three months later. The outcome was a compromise. On July 20 the Cabinet, following Chamberlain's lead, decided that "in present circumstances we cannot commit ourselves to the standard known as the New Standard Fleet." Shortly after this meeting, however, Simon, Inskip, and Duff Cooper agreed that £410 million would be spent on the Royal Navy in the next three years.[124] This figure represented a sizeable increase over Inskip's original proposal.

Capital ships took time to build; thus this expenditure could not be transformed into actual naval power until the early 1940's. In the meantime, Britain would remain militarily weak in East Asia. This fact, together with the exceedingly dangerous European situation, made it imperative for the British to avoid trouble with the Japanese. Japan was fully aware of London's difficulties. She was therefore emboldened to intensify her pressure on Britain's position in China. The British, however, did not give way. Believing that Japan was getting bogged down on the Asian mainland, they felt that they could outlast her without being forced to fight a war or to make damaging concessions. There was to be no Munich in East Asia.

Chapter five

Crosscurrents in East Asia

JAPAN'S ADVANCE in China naturally brought in its wake a marked increase in Anglo-Japanese tension. As the British embassy in Tokyo noted in its annual report for 1937, the underlying cause of this friction was obvious: "Britain has got what Japan wants, and what no other country has, a dominating position in China."[1] British officials generally assumed that so long as Japan was preoccupied with fighting Chiang Kai-shek (and so long as Europe remained peaceful), she could not afford to provoke a war with Britain. They recognized, however, that in view of the conflict of interest between London and Tokyo the possibility of a Japanese surprise attack could not entirely be ruled out. In fact, Sir John Pratt later wrote that a sudden strike against British possessions in East Asia "was from the beginning a serious danger. On several occasions such an attack seemed imminent."[2] Sir Robert Craigie was particularly sensitive to this possibility. Shortly after the Yangtze shellings, he warned that Japan was rapidly developing a "bitter hatred" against Britain and that, since "a compound of mysticism and nationalism is apt to distort reason even among responsible leaders" in Tokyo, there was a "real and growing danger" in this bitterness.[3] According to a report of late 1937 from the commander of Britain's forces in the Tientsin area, the

Japanese army in North China hated the British more than the Chinese and talked openly of attacking Hong Kong.[4]

Such a direct onslaught did not occur between 1937 and 1939, but Japan did exert steady pressure against British interests in the hope of removing what she regarded as a major obstacle in the way of her success in China. Britain's position at Shanghai and Tientsin was challenged; her stake in the Maritime Customs was threatened; her shipping and railway interests were injured; and her economic activity throughout North China suffered heavily. The Far Eastern Department of the Foreign Office, besieged with appeals for help by British business groups, painstakingly searched for ways to ward off this Japanese pressure.

Britain was especially determined to protect her vast network of interests at Shanghai. Her investments there amounted to three-quarters of her holdings in China. In addition, the city was a very important port, and British shipping firms handled much of the extensive inland trade on the Yangtze River. Underpinning these enormous economic interests was Britain's substantial political influence. Shanghai was divided into three administrative areas: the International Settlement, the French Concession, and the Chinese Municipality. In theory the Settlement was administered internationally, but in practice it was dominated by the British. Of the fourteen members of the Municipal Council, the main governing body, five were British. Though well over twice as many Japanese as British lived in the Settlement, there were only two Japanese on the Council.[5] Most of the officers of the Shanghai Municipal Police were British. As Sir Archibald Clark Kerr, who succeeded Knatchbull-Hugessen as ambassador to China, pointed out: "The Americans and Continental Powers are prepared to accept the fact that institutions which have been built up by us should be administered on Anglo-Saxon lines and largely with British personnel, but if there is to be an injection of an alien element the least welcome of all is the Japanese."[6]

During the battle for Shanghai in 1937, Japan had occupied Hongkew and Yangtzepoo, the main shipping and industrial centers of the Settlement. Britain hoped that normal conditions would be restored after hostilities in the area ended in early November, but the Japanese insisted that "military necessity" made it imperative to keep these two northern districts closed.[7] In late December, after repeated British representations, Japan opened certain parts of Hongkew and Yangtzepoo to non-Chinese, and in February 1938 she allowed Chinese to return to the area. But many restrictions remained, hampering the revival of industry and commerce.[8]

Not only did the Japanese retain control over the most valuable sections of the Settlement, but they also tried to expand their influence and extirpate Kuomintang activity in the areas still under the effective authority of the Municipal Council. Amid threats by the Japanese military to take action if the Settlement officials were uncooperative, Japan's consul-general in Shanghai asked the Council on November 20 to evict Chinese government organizations and to suppress all anti-Japanese subversion. The Council assured him that it would cooperate as far as possible.[9] Two weeks later, during a victory march held by Japan (against British and American wishes), a Chinese terrorist threw a bomb at Japanese soldiers. Pointing to this incident and other instances of terrorism, Japan claimed that the Settlement authorities were unable to maintain order, and on January 4, 1938, she demanded that Japanese be placed in controlling positions in all important organs of the municipal administration, and that the number, rank, and power of her nationals in the police force be increased. Japan also indicated that she desired a larger representation on the Council. The British embassy, with the approval of the Foreign Office, advised the Settlement authorities not to make concessions.[10] The Council accordingly stalled, waiting until mid-March to reply to the Japanese. By this time the Settlement officials felt compelled to give a little ground, and they told Japan that they would make certain changes in the police force if they were allowed to reassert their control over Hongkew and Yangtzepoo. After it became apparent in early April that this proposal did not satisfy Japan, the Council appointed a Japanese Special Deputy Commissioner of

Police in the hope of eliciting a similar indication of good faith from Japan. The Japanese, however, still refused to give up their hold on the two northern districts.[11]

Apart from the questions of increased Japanese influence in the Settlement's administration and of the status of Hongkew and Yangtzepoo, there were other problems. Japan failed to do conservancy work in the Whangpoo River, causing the Shanghai harbor to deteriorate. Even more disturbing, relations between British and Japanese authorities in Shanghai were poor. Britain decided in May 1938 to send Major-General F. S. G. Piggott, her military attaché at Tokyo, to Shanghai in the hope that he could improve them. Some officials in London doubted that Piggott would be effective, because he had too sanguine a view of the Japanese mentality. According to Robert Howe, who had been transferred from China to the Foreign Office, Piggott thought it was "only necessary to throw a few saki or cocktail parties and all our difficulties with the Japanese are solved by the soothing assurances of good will which they elicit from the Japanese." Notwithstanding such reservations, Piggott apparently succeeded in relieving some of the tension in Shanghai,[12] only to have it mount again after a wave of terrorist outrages in the summer. Even though the Municipal Council warned in July that it would expel from the Settlement anyone connected with such incidents, and even though both London and Washington urged Chiang to restrain the Kuomintang underground in Shanghai, terrorism continued to be a vexatious problem.[13]

Disputes also developed at Tientsin, which had no international settlement, but contained four concessions—British, Japanese, French, and Italian—as well as a Chinese city. Britain's total investment in Tientsin and the surrounding area in 1937 was approximately £37 million. In addition, there was a considerable volume of trade into and from the city, which was the leading commercial and industrial center in North China.[14]

Economic issues proved to be a major source of Anglo-Japanese friction in Tientsin. A Federal Reserve Bank was established in Peking under Japan's auspices in February 1938 and in March began issuing a new currency that was supposed to supersede the Chinese national currency, or *fapi*.[15] The new bank, needing silver to back its own currency, wanted to get control of silver stocks worth Ch $40,000-60,000 that were held by Chinese government banks in various vaults in the British and French Concessions. The Provisional Government at Peking announced on July 30 that the Tientsin branch of the Currency Reserve Board, to which the silver had been entrusted by the Chinese central government, was to be replaced by a Peking-Tientsin Silver Custody Committee. This attempt by the puppet regime to gain control of the silver was justified by the Japanese on the grounds that the silver belonged to the people of North China. Believing that the stocks were the property of Chiang's government or of the northern branches of the Chinese banks, the British were not prepared to surrender them. The stocks thus stayed where they were, but remained the source of much Anglo-Japanese friction.[16]

"Subversion" was also a problem in Tientsin. In January 1938 Japan demanded the surrender of a Chinese living in the British Concession who was allegedly involved in anti-Japanese activities. When Britain refused, the Japanese at first threatened to enter the Concession to arrest him, but later moderated their attitude after a warning by British military and consular authorities that such a move would be forcibly resisted.[17] During the summer of 1938 tension increased as Japan claimed that the British and French Concessions were centers of counterfeiting and of communist activities. Then in early September the Japanese reportedly instructed their firms and nationals in the two Concessions to move out. E. G. Jamieson, Britain's consul-general in Tientsin, feared that these instructions presaged an attempt by Japan to take over the Concessions. When London and Paris protested, the Japanese tried to explain away the orders, but their assurances did little to clear the air.[18] The situation in Tientsin was to grow steadily more serious, erupting in a major crisis in 1939.

Another area of British concern was the future of the Maritime Customs. Though the Customs Administration was both an organ of the Chinese government and an international service, its staff was dominated by British citizens. Inspector-General Sir Frederick Maze was responsible to the Chinese Finance Minister, but he also sought to advance the interests of foreign traders and to maintain Britain's influence in the administration and in China.[19]

Though Maze often complained that London gave him insufficient backing, the Foreign Office was eager to safeguard the administration. As Sir John Pratt noted in November 1937: "The maintenance of the Chinese Maritime Customs Administration has always been regarded as an important object of British policy in China (a) because it would be difficult to carry on legitimate trade without an efficient and honest Customs administration and (b) because the Customs revenues have always been the chief prop of Chinese credit in which British bondholders are deeply interested."[20] Since the Customs Administration handled the main source of Chinese revenue securing foreign and domestic loans, the British wanted to ensure that Japan would not seize or disrupt the administration, and to devise an arrangement whereby Customs revenues would continue to be applied to the service of foreign obligations in spite of the war. London felt that such an arrangement would be in China's interest because it would preserve her credit abroad so that she could borrow money to rebuild after the war.[21] Japan, for her part, wanted to gain control of the revenues or, failing that, to prevent them from reaching the Chinese government.[22]

The first dispute over the Maritime Customs sprang up at Tientsin in late August 1937, when the Japanese told Customs Commissioner W. R. Myers that the money he collected should be deposited in their foreign exchange bank, the Yokohama Specie Bank. Quotas to pay the interest on foreign loans would be remitted, the Japanese said, but no remittances could be made for domestic loans.[23] The British, fearing that Japan would take over the Customs Administration in Tientsin if her demands were not met, urged the Chinese to allow Myers to make the best possible deal on the basis of these terms. Chiang, however, understandably did not want the revenues deposited in the Yokohama Specie Bank. London pressed him so hard to moderate his stand that Howe

warned on October 9 that the British had "gone as far as we properly can in exerting pressure on the Chinese Government to give
way on what they regard as a vital matter of principle." But the
Foreign Office replied that preserving the Customs machinery was
"so important that . . . we must risk some resentment if further
pressure is necessary."[24] On October 20 the Chinese Finance Minister privately indicated to Maze that so far as the deposit of the
Tientsin revenue was concerned, Myers should use his own discretion.[25] The way thus seemed open for an agreement based on
Japan's terms of late August. Myers, however, was under heavy
Japanese pressure, and exceeded these "instructions" by concluding an agreement that not only met Japan's original demands but
also held up remittances for loan services pending the settlement
of hostilities. This capitulation both confused and upset the
British.[26]

    Japan next turned her attention to Shanghai, hoping to achieve
a similar success there. On November 22 she made it clear to the
Commissioner of Customs in Shanghai that she wanted control
over the funds he collected. Since more than half of all customs
revenue came from Shanghai, the British were quite alarmed by
this demand. Though the local Japanese authorities opposed "outside" interference in the negotiations, Britain worked her way into
them after making representations to Tokyo. She wanted above
all to ensure that the Customs Administration would continue to
function and that foreign loans would be fully serviced. She also
hoped to convince Japan that the revenues should be deposited in
a neutral bank.[27]

    No progress was made in the negotiations at Shanghai during
December and January. In February 1938 Britain had the talks
moved to Tokyo in the hope that the Foreign Ministry would take
a more moderate line than the Japanese authorities in China.[28] Sir
Robert Craigie's bargaining position was weakened by the attitude
of the United States, which was unwilling to be involved in the
making of any specific arrangement that might have to be forced
on China. Left on their own, the British in late February gave up
trying to persuade Tokyo to put the revenues in a neutral bank,

and the basis of an understanding was then worked out in March.[29] After some final details were settled in April, the agreement was announced on May 3. It specified that the revenues from occupied ports—including sums already deposited in the Hong Kong and Shanghai Bank—be placed in the Yokohama Specie Bank, which would remit full quotas to Maze for the service of foreign obligations. China was to convert these remittances into foreign exchange, and also to release the Boxer indemnity payments to Japan that she had held up since the fall of 1937. Tokyo gave assurances that all remittances would be in China's national currency, rather than in Federal Reserve Bank notes. There was no mention of Chinese domestic loans.[30]

Before the terms were announced, Craigie had shown Joseph Grew drafts of the text, but the United States had declined to comment. The announcement of May 3, however, erroneously indicated that Washington did not object to the agreement. Despite an apology by Craigie for this blunder, the State Department was displeased.[31] China, which had not been consulted by the British during the negotiations, was even more displeased. She told London that the terms of the arrangement impaired her administrative integrity and therefore violated the Nine-Power Treaty.[32] Insisting that she was not bound by the agreement, China refused to authorize Maze to release the Boxer indemnity funds or transfer revenues previously deposited in the Hong Kong and Shanghai Bank; consequently, the arrangement never came into force. Nevertheless, Japan generally took a more restrained attitude toward the Customs question for the rest of the year, mainly because Maze and his commissioners decided to put current revenues in the Yokohama Specie Bank. China, for her part, continued to service foreign loans until January 1939, but ignored British attempts to persuade her to implement the agreement.[33]

The Customs understanding represented the first notable instance of British appeasement of Japan during the Sino-Japanese conflict. London made concessions—at China's expense—in the hope of averting drastic action by Japan and saving interests that were primarily British. Britain maintained that the agreement, by ensuring that the occupied ports paid their share of the foreign-loan quotas, would have helped to maintain Chinese credit.[34] She also argued that it had the virtue of preserving the integrity of the Customs Administration. But as Craigie later noted, the Chinese preferred "to risk the disruption of the Customs service rather than see it become the subject of an agreement, however provisional, with their hated enemies."[35] From the Chinese viewpoint, the arrangement had many damaging aspects. It legalized Japan's control over much of the customs, and the Japanese might even claim that it constituted *de facto* recognition by Britain of the puppet regimes in occupied China. The provisions calling for the Chinese to transfer funds to Japan were of course very distasteful, as was the stipulation that China, whose reserves of exchange were shrinking, would have to supply the foreign and local currency for all debt payments.[36]

Struggles for influence in Shanghai, Tientsin, and the Customs Administration were not the only issues that generated Anglo-Japanese friction. Japan's treatment of British interests in Chinese railways also created bad feeling. At the outbreak of the war, Britain had almost £14 million outstanding in railway loans to China. During the fighting the Japanese took control of many important lines, expropriating revenues and preventing British employees from discharging their duties. London repeatedly pressed the Japanese to pay the money due to British bondholders and to allow the lines to be inspected. These representations, however, generally went unheeded.[37]

Another problem was Japanese restrictions on foreign shipping. In August 1937 the Chinese constructed booms across the Yangtze and Whangpoo rivers to keep Japanese warships from advancing inland. After the fall of Shanghai, Japan cut openings in the booms for her military vessels. Though she admitted the general right of foreign powers to navigate the river, she would not allow merchants to move upstream, arguing that unrestricted shipping would interfere with her military operations and might hit mines in the Yangtze. Early in 1938 the Japanese said they would provide convoys for foreign vessels, but then refused to cooperate when the British tried to make such an arrangement. London believed that Japan's real motive for obstructing navigation was to eliminate British competition with her trade. Britain's protests, however, were to no avail. Even after the fighting moved far upstream in the summer of 1938, Japan continued to insist that military necessity made it impossible to allow unrestricted shipping on the lower section of the Yangtze.[38]

It is not surprising that Britain saw in all this a deliberate Japanese attempt to undermine her position in China. Japan seemed particularly determined to make North China an exclusive Japanese domain. In January 1938 the tariff rates for that area were revised by the Provisional Government at Peking that Japan had set up in the previous month. Though the new rates did not discriminate as to the country of origin or destination of imports and exports, Britain felt that the tariff favored the Japanese by reducing duties on products in which they were interested.[39] More significant was the currency battle that began in March when the Federal Reserve Bank introduced notes that were designed to drive the *fapi* out of North China and to incorporate the region into a yen bloc centered on Tokyo. Both Chinese and Westerners were hostile to the new currency, and its circulation therefore increased very slowly, even though the Provisional Government issued decrees aiming at the devaluation or elimination of the *fapi*.[40] For a while in March, the British feared that Japan might impose exchange control in North China. These fears were slightly premature; widespread controls were not instituted in the northern provinces until 1939, though at Tsingtao and Chefoo, where the Japanese exercised more or less complete authority because of the absence of foreign concessions, the export trade was subject to paralyzing restrictions in 1938.[41]

Potentially as damaging to British enterprise as these measures was Japan's attempt to establish monopolies or quasi-monopolies in North China. In March 1938 the Japanese Diet approved a bill creating a North China Development Company. This organization, which began operations on November 7, was a holding company for investments in subsidiaries engaged in such important enterprises as transportation, communications, electricity, salt mining and manufacture, and iron and coal mining. The Japanese government supplied half of its investment capital, supervised its activities, and reserved the right to give the subsidiaries orders that were necessary for national defense.[42] Also, Japan imposed an embargo on the export of skins and hides from North China in late June and on wool and hemp four months later; and in Meng-chiang (Inner Mongolia) she instituted a system of export and exchange controls and made an abortive effort to establish an oil monopoly.[43]

There were some indications that the Japanese were seeking a predominant economic position in Central China as well. They set up a Reformed Government of the Republic of China in Nanking in late March 1938, and two months later this regime revised Central China's tariff rates.[44] The Japanese also established a Central China Economic Revival Company. More concerned with rehabilitation and reconstruction than with the exploitation of natural resources, this organization was narrower in scope than its counterpart in North China. The new company did nonetheless give Japan control over transportation, communications, and much industry in Central China. The Japanese, however, were less interested in obtaining economic domination of this area than of the north. Their priorities were demonstrated by their currency policy. The Reformed Government did not issue its own currency until the spring of 1939, and even then the use of *fapi* was not prohibited. Japan apparently did not envisage Central China as an integral part of the yen bloc.[45]

Under the impact of the war and of these Japanese measures, British trade declined.[46]

	January-June 1937	July-December 1937	January-June 1938	July-December 1938
Exports to China (thousands of £)	4,118	3,153	2,039	1,858
Imports from China (thousands of £)	2,164	2,637	1,188	2,027

There was a slight rise in Britain's trade with Hong Kong up to late 1938, but this increase was not nearly enough to offset the decline in trade through Chinese ports. It was of course the drastic fall in British exports that concerned London most, because this drop meant the ruin of prewar hopes for a large share in an expanding China market. Britain's shipping interests also suffered. Though her relative share in the shipping for both domestic and foreign trade increased for a while, the tonnage carried showed a steady decline. Almost 13 million tons of foreign trade and over 23 million tons of domestic commerce were transported in British vessels in 1937; the corresponding figures for 1938 were 12.4 million and 16.2 million.[47] Notwithstanding these trade and shipping statistics, by no means all British enterprise in China was crippled. Certain big commercial houses, notably Jardine, Matheson and Company, did very well in 1938. So did some industrial concerns. The Kailan Mining Administration, which represented Britain's largest investment in North China, came to an understanding with the Japanese and greatly increased its sale of coal in 1938. On the whole, however, these cases seem to have been exceptional.[48]

Japan repeatedly promised that she would respect foreign rights and interests in China and would maintain the Open Door, but the British suspected from the start that in fact she wanted to drive out Western economic influence. During 1938, as reports of Japanese economic measures reached London in increasing numbers, the Foreign Office became convinced that Japan intended to make the northern provinces, if not all of China, into another Manchukuo.[49] British businessmen shared this assessment of Tokyo's intentions. The Tientsin branch of the influential China Association warned in April 1938 that the consequences of Japanese schemes would be "firstly, the economic and fiscal bondage of North China; secondly, the payment of Japanese import requirements by North China produce through its purchase by token notes without exchange value; thirdly, the payment indirectly of the costs of the war by the same means; and fourthly, the elimination of all foreign trade and other foreign interests."[50]

This warning envisaged that the Japanese would achieve their ambitions. The Foreign Office, however, thought the Japanese would become financially exhausted before they could consolidate their control over the occupied areas. Since 1934, if not before, the British had believed that Japan's economy was weak and possibly on the verge of a crisis.[51] London calculated that military operations in China might greatly exacerbate Tokyo's economic and financial difficulties, perhaps paralyzing the Japanese war effort. The Foreign Office felt, moreover, that Japan would not have enough capital to exploit resources and run industries in North China. Ambassador Craigie had first called London's attention to Tokyo's shortage of capital in November and December of 1937, asserting that Japan would try to secure economic assistance from the West to develop North China.[52] During the first half of 1938 the Japanese did in fact put out numerous feelers for British cooperation in reconstructing the occupied areas.[53] From these approaches the Foreign Office concluded that Japan's need for funds could be used as a lever to compel her to respect British interests and even end the war on terms acceptable to the Chinese. Clearly this tactic could succeed only if money were withheld until Japan had become very weak; premature aid would enable her to consolidate control over the occupied territory and thus to win the war.*

In a word, Lord Halifax and his advisers felt Britain's position would be strongest when these two related strains—economic exhaustion at home and shortage of capital to rehabilitate North China—were felt sharply in Japan. The Foreign Office therefore believed that the British should play for time.[54] Craigie, however, viewed the situation differently. He expected Japan to win the war and doubted that she would suffer from serious financial exhaustion in the foreseeable future.† He also felt that Britain could

---

* The Foreign Office also believed that until Japan became exhausted, she would not allow British investors to have any control over the schemes in which they invested.

† See Craigie to FO, Apr. 2, 1938, FO F3623/12/10. Sir George Sansom, who was still commercial counsellor to the embassy in Tokyo, agreed. Between 1934 and 1937 Sansom's analyses had done much to foster the British government's belief that the Japanese economy was structurally weak, but in June 1938 he reported that Japan was not even partially exhausted, and that she was likely to defeat the Chinese. See letter from Sansom to FO, June 2, 1938, and minute by Ronald, FO F7532/84/10. Sansom was highly respected in London, and Nigel Ronald called his letter a "very useful corrective," but for the most part Foreign Office opinion remained unchanged.

make only limited use of her financial weapon. If the Japanese were driven too hard, they would try to develop China by themselves. "Japan," Sir Robert warned, "may not be rich enough to develop China on her own resources but she is sufficiently powerful to prevent anyone else from doing so with that sense of confidence and security which would be necessary for the success of the enterprise."[55] Craigie acknowledged that a Japanese success in China would pose problems for Britain, but he argued that a total Japanese collapse would be worse.

There exists a limit to the extent to which Japan can suffer exhaustion without upsetting the whole equilibrium in the Far East and without grave risk to our own future interests. If, for example, Japan's financial and economic exhaustion were to become really serious, the danger of an attack by Soviet Russia could not be disregarded and he would be a brave man who would predict that our interests in China or our prestige in the Far East would benefit from a Russian victory over Japan. Even if matters did not proceed to the length of war, there is little doubt that Japan, under the menace of a Russian attack, would feel obliged to depend for her safety more and more on German aid and Germany, while not in the habit of sponsoring the weak, would nevertheless feel reluctant to lose altogether such advantage as she would still derive from association with Japan as a makeweight to Soviet Russia.[56]

From these assumptions Craigie concluded that Britain should try to end the war rather than play for time. He also believed that she should try to improve relations with Japan at once.[57] In support of this view he offered his interpretation of Japanese politics. According to Sir Robert, there were three elements in Japan's ruling circles: the military extremists, who wanted Japan to expand rapidly; "liberals," who had very little influence; and civilian "moderates" such as Konoe and Hirota who favored a cautious expansion of Japanese power. Whereas the military wanted to control all industrial enterprises and public utilities in China and to exclude all foreign influence, the "moderates" were "a hard-headed realistic group of men" who realized that Japan would need British cooperation in the economic development of China. In Craigie's opinion, those who wanted cautious expansion still held the upper hand, but as the war continued the extremists would gain control of the government, intensify their efforts to dominate China, and move Japan into Germany's camp. The only hope of forestalling this development and protecting British interests was to help the moderates by adopting a more cooperative attitude and, in particular, by arriving at "working arrangements" —Craigie cited the Customs Agreement as an example—with the Konoe government in regard to occupied China. Such an effort by Britain to reduce causes of friction would pave the way for a more general Anglo-Japanese agreement after the war.[58] Craigie informed London in March that Major-General Piggott had been discussing the possibility of working arrangements with General Homma Masaharu of the Japanese General Staff. Homma, whom the embassy regarded as one of the most moderate military leaders, told Piggott that if Britain closed Hong Kong to all foreign munitions, Tokyo could make a reciprocal gesture toward British interests in China. Craigie passed this proposal on to London. He also suggested to the Foreign Office in April that Britain should drop her policy of refusing to recognize Japan's conquests.[59]

Craigie's analyses and recommendations in the first half of 1938 were rejected by the Foreign Office, which felt Sir Robert still greatly overrated Japan's chances of defeating the Chinese. Though in December 1937 London's faith in China's ability to survive had flagged somewhat, in early 1938 the cautious optimism of the previous autumn reemerged.[60] By spring the Foreign Office was more hopeful than ever that the Chinese would withstand Japan's onslaught. Sir John Brenan, whose influence with his colleagues was growing rapidly, asserted in April that the Japanese had reached the peak of their effort in late 1937 and that time was on China's side. Robert Howe shared this sanguine outlook, stressing that Craigie's "whole case rests on the assumption that the Japanese are going to win the war, an assumption which I do not myself believe in; and I think that there is at least an equal possibility, if not of a Chinese victory, then certainly of a stalemate."[61] As for the Ambassador's notion that a total collapse by Tokyo would lead to Soviet intervention and would therefore endanger the British position in East Asia, the Foreign Office viewed the matter from a different perspective. The officials did not want to see Japan ruined; but as Brenan pointed out, since Japan had a strong navy and the Soviet Union did not, the continued growth of Japanese power would be more of a menace to Britain's important possessions in the southern hemisphere than the extension of communist influence in East Asia would be.[62] In fact, according to the Foreign Office, a primary danger of cooperating with Japan was that doing so would help her defeat the Chinese, after which she could turn her attention on British possessions to the south.[63]

London believed there were other drawbacks to Anglo-Japanese cooperation, not least of which was that cooperative arrangements would do little to safeguard the British position in China. The Foreign Office did not accept Craigie's judgment that the so-called moderates in Tokyo would allow Britain to retain her interests in the occupied areas. Howe held particularly strong views on this question: "Though we should not go out of our way to provoke Japan, nothing is to be gained by attempting to placate her. British interests in Japanese-dominated territory would receive no more consideration simply because we had thrown over the central government. The Japanese find us in their way all along the line . . . ; a policy of weak conciliation will not get us anywhere."[64] After Hirota told the Diet in March that "Britain's influence in the Far East must inevitably recede before the advance of Japan," Howe commented sarcastically that "the *anti-British elements* in Japan want to kick us out of China now—our *friends* wish to do it more gently."[65]

Still another important drawback to cooperative arrangements was that Japan would probably not accede to them unless Britain ceased to support the Chinese. Convinced that the preservation of British interests and influence in East Asia was directly linked to China's independence, the Foreign Office regarded abandoning Chiang Kai-shek as out of the question and was completely unreceptive both to Craigie's hint about recognizing Japan's conquests and to Homma's suggestion about closing Hong Kong to munitions. Lord Halifax and his advisers were also opposed to reaching new formal understandings with the Japanese government similar to the Customs Agreement. London did tell Craigie on

May 17 that it would be prepared to negotiate "informal *ad hoc* arrangements" so long as no obvious concessions at China's expense were made. In keeping the door slightly ajar, the Foreign Office was seeking, not to establish the foundations of permanent cooperation with Japan, but merely to placate Craigie and, in Howe's words, "to keep the Japanese in play."[66]

In view of Japan's pressure on Britain's interests in 1937-38, London had good reason to look askance at proposals for Anglo-Japanese cooperation. There was also some basis in the first half of 1938 for the Foreign Office's optimism about Chiang's resistance. After the fall of Nanking in December 1937, Japan eased her military pressure temporarily, and Chinese morale recovered. In early April China won a battle at Taierhchuang, a small town in southern Shantung. Though the Chinese no doubt exaggerated the magnitude of this success, the victory showed that they had, as Brenan noted, "a large reserve of moral and material strength."[67] In fact, Clark Kerr, Cadogan, and other observers believed that the Japanese war effort was producing unprecedented national feeling and unity in China.[68] Even in July, after Chiang's military fortunes had taken a turn for the worse as a result of Japan's capture of Suchow in the late spring, Clark Kerr could report that the Chinese government was "full of life, vigour and determination and that even on the worst hypothesis its complete destruction is beyond the power of the Japanese armed forces."[69] Clearly, Britain's traditional view of the Chinese as incompetent and irresolute had given way to a far more favorable image of their capabilities and spirit.

The British felt that the key to China's new unity and strength was Chiang Kai-shek. As head of the government, leader of the Kuomintang, and supreme military commander, he evidently made all the important decisions. In Clark Kerr's opinion, which was shared by the Foreign Office, Chiang had through his energy and prestige won the unanimous and genuine support of all shades of opinion, including the Communists.[70] It seemed to British policymakers at the time that the growing national sentiment would redound largely to his advantage. In retrospect, however, it is apparent that Britain underestimated China's potential for disunity and Mao Tse-tung's potential for attracting widespread nationalistic support.

This misjudgment no doubt owed much to Britain's inability to obtain reliable information. Clark Kerr, when he was not traveling around the country, spent much of his time in Shanghai, the center of commercial activity but hardly the center of politics in wartime China. There were of course British officials in Hankow and Chungking, but they were unable to establish a close relationship with the uncommunicative Generalissimo. For the most part, therefore, Britain could only speculate about the Kuomintang's intentions, its factional disputes, and the range of its authority.

Even less was known about the Chinese Communists. Both Clark Kerr and the British embassy in Moscow doubted that Stalin was aiding the Communist Party.[71] Howe feared that communism could nonetheless become a vital force in China, but Cadogan disagreed, arguing that it had shown no ability to establish itself in sections of the country where it might be expected to thrive.[72] In August the Foreign Office asked the British consul-general in Peking to report on communist guerrilla activities in North China. He replied that communist organizations were growing steadily, were in control of one-third of the area north of the Lunghai Railway and east of the Yellow River, and were likely to be "a more serious difficulty to the Japanese than positional warfare fought by regular troops in the South." He warned that if Japan were expelled from North China, "the 'Red' areas might prefer to remain semi-independent and thus hold up the work of national unification, which presumably is the only hope for China and for foreign interests here as well." The Foreign Office, though realizing that Japanese imperialism was engendering some support for the Communist Party, felt this report overrated the guerrillas' prospects.[73] Sir John Brenan, for his part, saw little cause for alarm even if communism did spread.

Whatever the spread of the communist elements in China may lead to, one may be fairly sure that the result will be quite different to the regime produced in Russia. The Chinese are racially strong and are tenacious of their own ancient civilisation. Among their more prominent characteristics are their easy going nature, their tolerance, their readiness to compromise and refusal to proceed to extremes. And, above all, they are individualists and keen traders. I find it difficult to believe that they will ever evolve the sort of communist dictatorship which depends on a highly centralised government.[74]

Brenan added that if communist influence did become widespread, Britain's extraterritorial privileges would be abolished, but the China market would still be open to foreign traders. It is clear, however, that neither he nor his colleagues expected Chiang's authority to be challenged seriously, and they only dimly perceived the extent to which the Kuomintang-Communist United Front represented an uneasy truce.

Assessing these swirling currents of communism, Chinese nationalism, and Japanese imperialism was a baffling task. Even more puzzling was the problem of how to protect British interests from buffeting by these forces. The Labour Party and even some Conservatives thought sanctions against Japan were the answer.[75] The Chamberlain government did not agree, though it was drawing up contingency plans for economic pressure. Just after United States Treasury Secretary Morgenthau had approached Chancellor of the Exchequer Simon in December 1937 about instituting exchange control against Japan, the Committee of Imperial Defence had instructed the Advisory Committee on Trade Questions in Time of War to prepare a detailed program for imposing sanctions on Japan. This project was given priority over the preparation of a similar scheme against Germany, and the first planning stage was nearly finished by the end of February,[76] but the Cabinet, obviously still opposed to sanctions, gave no thought to implementing it. The question of economic pressure came up again in April, when the State Department said that it was studying the possibility of commercial reprisals (not full sanctions) against Japan and hinted that Britain should do the same. Far from being encouraged by this indication that the United States was considering a firmer policy in East Asia, Cadogan was skeptical: "I have learned to expect nothing of America." The Foreign Office nonetheless decided that the feasibility of limited reprisals against Japan should be examined.[77] This investigation proceeded slowly and proved inconclusive. The Treasury and the Board of Trade were opposed to economic measures, and an interdepartmental committee that met once in July merely reviewed the possible steps that Britain could take and the unfavorable consequences that might ensue.[78]

Meanwhile, China was again pressing the British for financial assistance. Quo Tai-chi asked on March 15 for a loan of £20 million to be secured by Chinese exports of tungsten and antimony to Britain.[79] China needed the loan to support her currency. There had been a run on her foreign exchange holdings since the outbreak of the war, and she had decided on March 14 to institute exchange rationing, but it was not likely that this measure would stabilize her dollar for long. Realizing this, the British gave careful consideration to Quo's appeal. Sir John Simon thought a government-guaranteed loan undesirable, and without such a guarantee money probably could not be raised for the Chinese on the London market. Simon supposed, however, that tungsten was important enough to Britain on defense grounds that she should try to get control of China's production of it, if only to keep Germany from gaining access to it. He therefore told Prime Minister Chamberlain on April 5 that he favored a commercial credit to China to be repaid from the proceeds of Britain's purchases of tungsten. Such a credit, in his opinion, would strengthen the Chinese currency, whose weakness was causing difficulties for British banks in the Far East. Chamberlain agreed with this proposal.[80]

Further high-level consideration of the matter was delayed at this point, apparently because the Treasury was discussing the idea of a credit with both bankers and strategic planners. In an attempt to goad the British into action, Chiang Kai-shek asked Clark Kerr on April 24 why they were not giving more help to China. He pointed out that the Soviet Union was providing substantial material support and that France had agreed to a £1 million credit for railway equipment.[81] He then put additional pressure on London by taking his case to Geneva for the third time. On May 14 the League passed a resolution calling on its members to consider Chinese requests for aid sympathetically.[82]

Even before the proceedings at Geneva, the Foreign Office had decided to try to convince the Cabinet that China should be given assistance. In an important memorandum of May 4, Robert Howe declared that

given certain conditions, they [the Chinese] are capable of continuing to put up an effective resistance to Japan for an unlimited period, which in the end will wear down the Japanese and so reduce their strength that a good deal of their potentiality for threatening our interests in the Far East may be averted for some time to come. Of the conditions above-mentioned, only one appears to me to be essential and that is financial assistance; and I consider that all considerations of morality and self-interest should urge us to do what we can to provide this for China.[83]

Howe's colleagues shared his view, and five days later Foreign Secretary Halifax sent Simon a letter arguing in favor of aid to the Chinese. He maintained that they were capable of prolonged resistance and that if and when they fought Japan to a stalemate, Britain and America could intervene "with effective results and safeguard our position for another generation."[84]

The Foreign Office's stance was in line with that of Ambassador Clark Kerr. Though he had been despondent in March when China's finances seemed in irreparable disarray, by late April he felt Chiang could frustrate Japan's war effort "provided the financial end can be kept up."[85] On May 7 Clark Kerr told the Foreign Office that China should be helped, because she was "fighting our battle" and because British support "would put the Chinese under an obligation to us which would stand us in good stead when the time comes for reconstruction in which we . . . ought to play a prominent part."[86]

Predictably, Sir Robert Craigie saw things differently. He asserted in early May that British assistance to the Chinese might lead to serious complications with Japan and would in any event end all hopes of protecting Britain's interests in China through cooperation with Tokyo. He also warned that "whereas in a world war or threat of a world war the attitude of China would not be a determining factor, the reverse is true of Japan"; if the British drove Japan into Germany's grasp, this mistake would react upon their defensive position in Europe.[87] Craigie returned to the charge at the end of May, arguing that there were better ways to help

China to her feet than giving her direct assistance in the present struggle and thus driving Japan "irretrievably into the camp of landgrabbers and totalitarians." Foreign Secretary Halifax replied irascibly that Craigie seemed "to imply that we should stand aside until China has been knocked down by Japan. . . . I very much doubt whether a victorious Japan . . . would allow us to cooperate in [China's] rehabilitation on any terms which we could accept. . . . Furthermore is not Japan committed already to the totalitarian triangle?"[88] Halifax and his advisers thought it perverse "to refrain from assisting a valuable potential customer in her hour of need because it would irritate an unscrupulous competitor, whose one idea is to secure that customer for his sole exploitation."[89]

On June 1 the Cabinet Committee on Foreign Policy discussed the question of financial assistance to China. Halifax presented the Foreign Office's case for helping the Chinese, but immediately met an obstacle: Simon no longer favored a credit. Maintaining now that China's tungsten was not important to British rearmament, Sir John stressed Craigie's warnings that aiding Chiang might involve Britain in hostilities with Japan. He concluded that a government loan or credit was out of the question and that, left on their own, financial institutions in the City would at best offer only £1 million, which would hardly help the Chinese at all. Retorting that Craigie's opinion should be largely discounted, Halifax argued that Japan was too bogged down in China to retaliate and that Chiang's resistance might well succeed. Chamberlain said he sympathized with Halifax's point of view and resented "our being singled out by Japan for differential treatment to our great detriment as compared with other countries." He cautioned, however, that "this particular proposition was an inherently bad one" and that Britain's position in East Asia was very vulnerable. Oddly enough, he also warned that any money given to China might be handed over to the Soviet Union, in payment for the supplies that Moscow had sent to Chiang.[90]

The meeting ended without reaching a decision, and the debate became even more intense in the following weeks. After Sir Vandeleur Grayburn of the Hong Kong and Shanghai Bank made it clear on June 2 that no credit could be granted unless the government guaranteed it, the arguments centered on the question of whether or not a guarantee should be given. Sir Frederick Leith-Ross and Cyril Rogers, a British adviser to the Chinese Central Bank, favored such a move, but the Bank of England was opposed to it, and Sir Warren Fisher of the Treasury argued that if Britain aided Chiang, she would incur the "undying hostility of Japan who sooner or later—perhaps at a time when we are at death-grip w[ith] Germany—will take her revenge. Thus to risk our country's security, indeed survival w^d be nothing short of a crime." Chamberlain, Simon, and Halifax discussed the issue at the end of June but reached no consensus.[91]

On July 1 Halifax and Simon circulated papers to the Cabinet summarizing their respective views. Halifax linked the problem of assistance to China with the question of Britain's future in Asia. He said that unless the Chinese were helped, their currency might collapse, damaging foreign interests, undermining the confidence of the Chinese people in Chiang's leadership, and perhaps crippling their resistance. If China did crumble, the Japanese would eliminate all British interests and influence in that country, and then—"flushed with success" and "allied with the 'Have-not' Powers in Europe"—would "pursue her expansionist ambitions in the South Seas and throughout Asia." But if the Chinese war effort could be sustained, Japan might well be worn down, and Britain's interests would be secure. He concluded that British prestige and even the unity of the Empire were at stake and that, accordingly, a loan of £20 million should be granted.[92] Halifax did not ignore the drawbacks of such a move, but Simon argued that he underrated them. In particular, Sir John stressed that helping China would anger Japan at a time when the European situation was menacing and would therefore greatly increase the chances of simultaneous hostilities in Europe and East Asia in the future. "Our military advisers," he noted, "have consistently urged that it should be a prime object of our foreign policy to avoid that possibility." Simon also thought that £20 million would have no immediate impact on the course of the war and that Chiang would soon ask for more.[93]

The Cabinet considered the two papers when it met on July 6. After the opposing viewpoints were thoroughly debated, Chamberlain gave a somewhat confused summary of his thinking. He asserted at one point that £20 million would not necessarily enable China to outlast Japan, but maintained at another point that the Chinese might successfully resist. Though expressing fear that a loan would commit London irrevocably "to a policy based on the supposition that our interests were against a Japanese victory," he conceded that Japan no doubt wanted to drive Britain out of China. After reiterating that any money given to Chiang might end up in the Soviet Union, not in the hands of British bondholders, he finished by warning that if Britain became embroiled in East Asia, "Germany might seize the opportunity to do something in Czechoslovakia, or Italy in Libya." This discursive speech did little to clarify the issue, and the Cabinet agreed to postpone a decision for a week.[94]

Halifax was in a difficult position. On the one hand, his own advisers and the China Association were pressing him to help China, as was Lord Lytton, a prestigious and experienced observer of East Asian affairs who had aired his views in a letter to *The Times* on July 5.[95] Even cautious Australia—when she was finally consulted—favored a loan, though not if it would lead to trouble with Japan.[96] On the other hand, Chamberlain, Simon, and others in the Cabinet were averse to assisting China. They might have been more amenable to a loan had the Americans been willing to collaborate, but the United States was unreceptive to a suggestion by Halifax that she cooperate with the British in helping the Chinese. In fact, Joseph P. Kennedy, who had become the American ambassador to Britain after Robert Bingham's death in late 1937, indicated to Halifax on July 11 that "the British Empire had enough trouble on its hands at the moment without gratuitously taking on more."[97] Halifax himself was more and more impressed by this consideration. He was deeply disturbed by recent developments in Europe. Mussolini had complained bitterly (if perversely) on July 6 that though Italy had carried out her side of the Anglo-Italian agreement of April, Britain had not reciprocated.[98] There were also hints that "Germany was working up for a rapid *coup* [against Czechoslovakia] at the end of August, and that Herr von Ribbentrop [the German Foreign Minister] was in an aggressive mood."[99]

By the time the Cabinet met again on July 13, the growing disquiet in Europe had caused Halifax to revise his views about assisting China. He reluctantly advised his colleagues against taking the risk of an adverse Japanese reaction to a British loan to the Chinese. If Japan attacked Hong Kong, he said, the fleet would have to be sent east. "That would be a grave risk to take in the present European situation with Signor Mussolini in a curious and somewhat inexplicable frame of mind and with a somewhat critical situation in Central Europe." Simon welcomed Halifax's change of mind and tried to cheer up his despondent associate by pointing out that it was unlikely that Japan, "even if successful in the war, could thereafter deal with so vast an area of territory as was involved, to our exclusion. Nor was it certain that China could be forced to collapse." Chamberlain was also pleased by Halifax's about-face, stressing that "it was necessary to bear in mind in these matters that our defensive arrangements were still far from complete." A decision was quickly reached against granting financial assistance to the Chinese.[100]

The Cabinet's fear of becoming involved in hostilities with Japan and then with Germany and Italy had obviously overridden all other considerations. Prime Minister Chamberlain wrote in late July that he had thought "long and anxiously" about aiding Chiang, but was convinced that such action would be a "fatal blunder."[101] Both the British press and China disagreed with Chamberlain's assessment of the situation. The *New Statesman* on the Left and *Finance and Commerce* on the Right, for example, criticized the decision.[102] The Chinese were hurt and puzzled by the rebuff, and Chiang made it clear that he might move closer to the Soviet Union if Britain continued to let him down. The British took his warning seriously.[103] In an attempt to soothe Chiang as well as critics at home, Chamberlain and R. A. Butler (parliamentary under-secretary of the Foreign Office) told the House of Commons in late July that the British government was prepared to consider proposals for assistance submitted by the Chinese to the Export Credits Guarantee Department.[104] China had already requested an export credit of £10 million earlier in the month, but she soon discovered that the Guarantee Department was inclined to impose severe conditions on such applications. By September negotiations on her request had bogged down.[105] Despite efforts by London to dissuade them, the frustrated Chinese then appealed to the League again in the hope that the Council would finally call for economic sanctions against Japan. The League adopted a report on September 30 declaring that its members could individually put sanctions into force, but noting that coordinated economic action was unlikely.[106] Clearly, neither Britain nor any other power would be persuaded by this report to apply sanctions.

In their search for ways to safeguard their interests and to help China, the British virtually ignored one possibility: working in concert with the Soviet Union to thwart Japanese expansion. Stalin had given the Chinese considerable assistance, sending them five air wings of planes and pilots and granting them credits in March and July of 1938 that amounted to U.S. $100 million.[107] In addition, he had formidable military forces in East Asia. According to British intelligence estimates in late 1937, there were 250,000 Soviet troops in the Far East and, perhaps even more important, 870 aircraft east of Lake Baikal, many of which could strike directly at Japanese cities and industries.[108] Not surprisingly, Tokyo was very much concerned over both the air and ground threats. As Craigie pointed out in February 1938, Japan regarded the British and the Soviets as the greatest obstacles to her expansion and desperately wanted to ensure that they would not act together against her.[109] The Chinese, for their part, were quick to see the potential value of Anglo-Soviet cooperation. As early as October 1937, members of the central government tried to persuade the British to guarantee the Soviet Union's European frontier so that Stalin would be more willing to intervene on China's side. In December 1937 Chiang Kai-shek told two British journalists that Moscow would actively support him if London cooperated. Convinced that the Soviet Union was as reluctant as Britain to risk becoming involved in hostilities with Japan, Eden saw no need to respond to Chiang's appeal.[110]

In July 1938, however, fighting between the Soviets and the Japanese did break out at Changkufeng on the Manchukuoan-Korean-Russian border. The origins of this incident are still disputed.[111] At the time the British felt, as Nigel Ronald put it, that "both Russians and Japanese are such accomplished liars and so addicted to all forms of bluff and bluster that one can be sure of nothing in this strange affair." Ronald and Craigie guessed that the Soviet Union provoked the trouble to divert Japan from China and win Chiang's favor, but Howe and the embassy in Moscow suspected that the Japanese were responsible for the fracas. All British officials agreed that in any case London should adopt a detached attitude.[112] In retrospect it would seem that this incident might have provided an appropriate opportunity for Britain to approach the Soviet Union about the possibility of concerted moves that would have a sobering effect on Japan (and perhaps, indirectly, on Germany). The British did not even contemplate such an approach, however, and, in fact, remained indifferent for the rest of the prewar era to the "positive" role that Anglo-Soviet cooperation could play in East Asia.

The reasons for this indifference are fairly clear. First, the Cabinet and most officials in the Foreign Office had a deep-rooted distrust of the Soviet Union. They felt she only wanted to stir up trouble between other powers and within the British Empire and would accordingly be a faithless ally. Second, notwithstanding the size of Moscow's army and air force in the east, the British government held a low opinion of Soviet strength.[113] Between the spring of 1937 and the autumn of 1938, Stalin purged three of five marshals of the Red Army as well as 80 percent of the staff of his Far Eastern forces.[114] The British were convinced that such drastic purges would be militarily crippling. Though the Soviet forces actually did surprisingly well during the Changkufeng Incident—Japan agreed to a truce on August 11 after suffering heavy casualties—a Foreign Office memorandum claimed that the hostilities "demonstrated beyond all doubt that the local Russian General Staff had little or no capacity to take full advantage of their strength in mechanised equipment."[115] Third, the British believed that closer Anglo-Soviet ties would push Japan into a military alliance with Germany. Finally, they apparently feared that cooperation with Moscow would enhance Soviet influence in China and that this greater influence would in turn cause trouble in India and Burma. In short, though the British regarded Japan as a bigger threat than the Soviet Union in the Far East, they nonetheless saw the Soviets as more of a threat than a possible ally.

Since Britain was unwilling to approach Stalin and unable to enlist Roosevelt, there was no basis for "collective security" in East Asia. Even if she had felt able to rely on American and Soviet support, however, it is doubtful that Britain would have challenged Japan during the spring and summer of 1938. Preoccupied with the unsettled European situation and acutely aware of her military weakness, she might well have hesitated to take any risks in East Asia no matter who was at her side. At any rate, left on her own, Britain shied away from firm action. Though she was determined neither to appease the Japanese nor to allow them to keep her "quiet by a technique of promises and intimidation,"[116] sanctions seemed likely to be counterproductive, a government-guaranteed loan or credit to China might provoke Japanese retaliation, and a private loan was too risky for British bankers. Britain felt that for the time being her only weapon was a campaign of verbal pressure. Accordingly, she sought a redress of her grievances from the new Japanese Foreign Minister, General Ugaki Kazushige.

Chapter six

Japan's New Order and Britain's Response

BY THE SPRING of 1938 Premier Konoe had come to doubt the wisdom of his bellicose January announcement that Japan would no longer deal with Chiang Kai-shek. Konoe and many of his advisers at last appreciated the force of the General Staff's warnings that a war of annihilation against China would seriously drain Japan's resources. Konoe accordingly reorganized his Cabinet in late May, replacing Hirota, whom he viewed as a leading advocate of the January statement, with Ugaki Kazushige. Ugaki, a reserve army general and the first Foreign Minister in two decades not from the diplomatic service, accepted his new post on the condition that he be allowed to begin peace negotiations with the Chinese. He also made it clear that he wanted to improve relations with the British. Both of his aims were in line with views held by court circles, the political parties, and the business community, but were regarded unfavorably by the powerful hard-line element in the military. The peace talks, begun in June and apparently kept secret from the Western powers, proved unsuccessful. So did efforts to reduce Anglo-Japanese friction. By October the army, which had blocked Ugaki's appointment as Premier in early 1937, had in effect forced his resignation as Foreign Minister and had greatly increased its influence over Japan's China policy.[1]

Sir Robert Craigie welcomed Ugaki's appointment because he

felt the General was a "forceful" and "liberal-minded" statesman who would stand up to the military and would try to ensure respect for British interests in China.[2] Hopeful that Japan was moderating her policy, Sir Robert wished to hold discussions with Ugaki to settle the questions that were causing trouble between London and Tokyo. The Foreign Office was skeptical. Sir John Brenan remarked that "the procedure is for the Japanese army and navy to destroy our interests while the authorities in Tokyo calm us with promises to protect them," and Sir Alexander Cadogan asserted that "if there is any change, it is a change of tactics. There is no 're-orientation of policy.' Japanese policy is a fixed obsession."[3] But since the Cabinet was unwilling to take a strong line in East Asia, the Foreign Office resigned itself to entering into discussions.

London and Craigie disagreed about the direction these talks should take. Predictably, Sir Robert wanted to conciliate Japan. In particular, he still hoped to reach working arrangements that would safeguard British interests and open the way for friendly Anglo-Japanese relations in the future. The Ambassador continued to argue that cooperation between Britain and Japan in the occupied areas would bolster the position of the "better elements" in Tokyo and would keep the Japanese from collaborating with the Germans and the Italians.[4] Though conceding in June that a policy of compromise would irritate the United States, he maintained that very little would be lost thereby. According to Craigie, Washington's Far Eastern policy was "inconsistent, incalculable and selfish"; American and British interests were not identical; and Britain could never rely on help from the United States.[5] In a long and impassioned message in mid-July, he reminded his government of the dangerous interaction between its problems in East Asia and in Europe, noting that "one of the underlying causes of our anxieties in the field of foreign affairs during the last few years has been the inevitable estrangement of two old friends— Italy and Japan. With Germany growing to unprecedented strength under the present dictatorship, we can afford to give no hostages to fortune." He argued that it was essential for Britain to establish "a nicely calculated relationship between the country's powers of defence and its capacity to make and confront new enemies. So far as Japan is concerned, we are in any case likely to do more constructive work by considering plans for the cure of the disease from which these advocates of expansion suffer rather than by chafing at its unpleasant symptoms." He added that

the prospect of a re-established friendship between the two countries would afford the best hope visible today of weaning Japan from her foolish policy of armed imperialism. Of the cynic who denies that any such hope exists, I would enquire whether the alternative of constant bickering and impotent condemnation is not likely to leave China for years in a state of unrest and economic distress. I maintain that such a hope in fact exists.[6]

The Foreign Office was no more receptive than before to Craigie's appeals for conciliation. Brenan expressed the opinion of his colleagues when he stressed that the Japanese would agree to working arrangements only if Britain recognized their new position on the mainland and abandoned Chiang Kai-shek. Even then, Sir John cautioned, the Japanese would still push the most important British interests out of China. Believing therefore that Britain should persist in playing for a stalemate and the further exhaustion of Japan, Brenan and his associates concluded that the object of the Craigie-Ugaki talks should be not to conciliate the Japanese but to press them to "put the clock back and restore us to the position we occupied before the outbreak of hostilities, or as near thereto as may be possible."[7] The Foreign Office had no illusions that its demands would be met at this stage unless the Chamberlain government was prepared to take forcible action. As Brenan observed:

The truth of the matter is that we acquired our dominant position in China as the result of our wars with that country in the nineteenth century and we can now only keep it by the same or similar methods. We must either use force, or otherwise bring sufficient pressure to bear on the Japanese authorities to compel them to relinquish in our favour what they regard as the spoils of victory. We may, without fighting ourselves, be able to apply that pressure if the Japanese are exhausted by a long war with the Chinese, but it is futile to expect that we shall get what we want for the mere asking, or by protests about the infringements of our "rights," or by a more friendly attitude.[8]

After a few preliminary discussions with Ugaki, Craigie gave him a list of five British desiderata on July 26. Three of them concerned Shanghai—the restoration of normal conditions in the northern district of the Settlement, the removal of restrictions on various British enterprises, and the resumption of work on the Whangpoo River Conservancy—and the other two were the reopening of the Yangtze to navigation and the granting of facilities for the inspection of railways in which Britain had investments. Ugaki said that he could promise an early settlement of outstanding problems, though the question of navigation on the Yangtze presented difficulties.[9]

The cordial atmosphere in which the talks opened was shattered almost immediately. In Parliamentary debates in late July, Prime Minister Chamberlain, Foreign Secretary Halifax, and R. A. Butler spoke of possible action open to Britain if Tokyo did not respect her interests.[10] The Japanese were incensed by these "threats." Craigie decided "to let things simmer" for a while, and postponed his next meeting with Ugaki until the third week in August. The Foreign Office regarded Japan's reaction as "only to be expected" and "perfectly in character," and was quite willing to allow the talks to be postponed.[11] In fact, one official insisted that even if the conversations settled some of the outstanding cases, "there will soon be plenty more, as long as the present anti-British mentality persists:—and it is bound to persist until we are driven out of China, because Japanese ambitions find themselves thwarted by our established interests."[12]

Notwithstanding the statements made to Parliament by Chamberlain, Halifax, and Butler, Chiang Kai-shek was evidently apprehensive that London might turn away from him, and he approached the British in early August about the possibility of an Anglo-American-French offer of good offices. If the Japanese rebuffed this tripartite initiative, Chiang wanted the three powers to give them a "sharp warning."[13] The request of good offices perplexed Britain. Though in May and July she had publicly offered to mediate, Halifax and his officials (if not Chamberlain) had privately been averse to mediation, fearing that until the Japanese became exhausted, peace talks could only take place on the basis of terms highly unsatisfactory to the British and the Chinese.[14] The Foreign Office therefore assumed—not altogether correctly, in Sir Archibald Clark Kerr's opinion—that China's approach meant Chiang was no longer sure of his ability to continue the struggle. London decided to explore the feasibility of proffering good offices, but Craigie and the United States both said the Chinese proposal was unlikely to succeed, and the matter was soon dropped.[15] The lapse of time revealed in any case that Chiang was hardly at the end of his tether.

When Craigie finally saw Ugaki again on August 17, he made no mention of mediation. Instead, the discussion centered on Britain's threats at the end of July. Ugaki maintained that such statements inflamed Japanese public opinion, making it difficult to settle the problems at issue. Discouraged by this attitude, Craigie told London that his negotiations were failing and that the government should examine ways of exerting pressure on Japan.[16] The Foreign Office was surprised, but asked other government departments to reconsider the possible economic measures that Britain could take against Tokyo. Though Halifax realized that such retaliation might hurt certain British interests, he felt that "what is at stake is worth a sacrifice."[17] As before, however, London's investigation of the question of reprisals proceeded slowly.

Meanwhile, Craigie had been heartened by a personal message from Premier Konoe declaring that Japan still wanted to accommodate Britain wherever possible and also hoped to find a basis for future cooperation between the two nations. In talks on August 20, Ugaki complained about the attitude of British officials and the British public, but also asked about the possibility of Anglo-Japanese cooperation in the occupied areas. Seizing on this reference to cooperation, Craigie wanted the Foreign Office to allow him to assure Ugaki that "we are quite prepared to co-operate in the sense in which we understood the word and on the understanding that our collaboration is to be for the benefit and not to the detriment of China." In Sir Robert's opinion, such an assurance would enable Ugaki to demonstrate to his many critics that Britain was not irretrievably hostile.[18] The Foreign Office refused, stressing that the word *co-operate* had dangerous implications and would arouse suspicion in Parliament, China, and the United States. Clark Kerr, for his part, questioned that Anglo-Japanese collaboration could benefit the Chinese.[19] Sir Robert showed his customary persistence in arguing his views, but to no avail. Brenan pointed out at the end of August that Ugaki was angling for a one-sided bargain: the Japanese would remove some of Britain's complaints if Britain agreed to abandon Chiang and cooperate with them. Sir John emphasized that such a bargain would entail "a reversal of our whole attitude towards the Far Eastern conflict in return for minor and problematical advantages of a temporary kind." He concluded that London should merely mark time until the situation in East Asia or in Europe changed for the better. As usual, Sir John's colleagues in the Foreign Office agreed with him.[20]

Craigie met again with Ugaki on September 8. Ugaki made it clear that (as Brenan had warned) there would be no progress in the conversations unless Britain ceased to support Chiang Kai-shek.[21] Though Sir Robert was disappointed by this line, two more meetings were held on September 14 and 22. The first was uneventful. At the second, Ugaki said Japan would allow the Shanghai Municipal Council to reassert its authority over the northern district of the Settlement if the Council cooperated fully with Japanese officials in maintaining order and gave the Japanese greater representation in the Shanghai police force. Craigie told London that acceptance of this scheme might lead to more important agreements. The Foreign Office and Clark Kerr, however, were opposed, pointing out that it would in practice lead to Japanese control of the municipal administration.[22] The conversations therefore remained in deadlock. In any case they had by this time been thrust far into the background by the Czechoslovak crisis. As Cadogan noted, "we shall get nothing out of the Japanese *now*. They are waiting to see what will happen in Europe. If we can surmount the imminent crisis, they may be in a different mood. If we can't, we shall have other things to occupy us than our interests in the Far East."[23]

Britain's refusal to conciliate the Japanese at this stage was in complete contrast to her desperate attempts to appease Germany. Though there is no need to recount here the events leading to Munich, it is appropriate to reassess briefly, in light of the newly opened Cabinet records, the mainsprings of British policy during the European crisis. Above all, the Chamberlain government dreaded war and did not want to risk a large-scale conflict—with all its human, social, and economic upheaval—merely to maintain Czechoslovakia's integrity. The government's attitude might have been different had Hitler's designs on the Sudetenland been seen as a step toward further territorial expansion. But Chamberlain and Halifax, though conceding that it was impossible to be certain about Hitler's intentions, doubted seriously that he wanted to incorporate non-Germans into the Reich and would eventually pick a quarrel with Britain and France. According to this view, an Anglo-German understanding could be reached. After Chamberlain's second (and rather unsuccessful) visit to Hitler in September 1938, for example, the minutes of a Cabinet meeting recorded that:

The Prime Minister was sure that Herr Hitler was extremely anxious to secure the friendship of Great Britain. The crucial question was whether Herr Hitler was speaking the truth when he said that he regarded the Sudeten question as a racial question which must be settled, and that the object of his policy was racial unity and not the domination of Europe. Much depends on the answer to this question. The Prime Minister believed that Herr Hitler was speaking the truth.

Herr Hitler had also said that, once the present question had been settled, he had no more territorial ambitions in Europe. He had also said that if the present question could be settled peaceably, it might be a turning-point in Anglo-German relations. . . .

The Prime Minister said that he thought it would be a great tragedy if we lost this opportunity of reaching an understanding with Germany on all points of difference between the two countries. A peaceful settlement of Europe depended upon an Anglo-German understanding. He thought that he had now established an influence over Herr Hitler, and that the latter trusted him and was willing to work with him. If this was so, it was a wonderful opportunity to put an end to the horrible nightmare of the present armament race. That seemed to him to be the big thing in the present issue.[24]

In addition to believing that Hitler's aims were limited, Chamberlain and Halifax thought the Führer teetered between reasonableness on the one hand and frenzy on the other. They judged that threats would drive him "over the edge," whereas a conciliatory personal approach would influence him to act reasonably.[25]

Such an image of Hitler's intentions and mentality was no doubt wishful thinking. Still, it was a very important consideration shaping London's response to the crisis. Military weakness was certainly another factor in British policy. The Chiefs of Staff stressed, and the ministers readily agreed, that even with Soviet help Britain and France could not prevent Germany from overrunning Czechoslovakia and that Britain was not ready for a general war. It seems, however, that Chamberlain and Halifax feared defeat less than war itself. In fact, Halifax told the Cabinet on September 17 that "he had no doubt that if we were involved in war now we should win it after a long time, but he could not feel we were justified in embarking on action which would result in such untold suffering."[26]

In dealing with the crisis in Europe, Britain also had to keep in mind the situation in East Asia. The interaction between her problems in the two areas was mentioned at a number of Cabinet meetings, and both the Chiefs of Staff and the Foreign Office gave careful thought to the possibility that if the British became involved in hostilities with Hitler, Japan might attack them in the Far East. One cause for alarm was that Japan's relations with Germany had apparently been growing closer since early 1938. Germany had recognized Manchukuo in February and recalled her military advisers from China in May. More important, Japan and Germany were by the summer discussing in earnest the feasibility of converting the Anti-Comintern Pact into a military alliance.[27] Konoe made the first public disclosure of these talks on September 15, just as the European crisis was moving toward its climax. On the previous day, moreover, the Japanese Foreign Ministry had expressed sympathy with Hitler's stand on the Sudeten question, blaming the Comintern for the trouble and declaring that Japan was ready "to join forces with Germany and Italy for fighting against Red operations in accordance with the spirit of [the] Anti-Comintern agreement."[28] Even before these announcements, the British Chiefs of Staff feared that if war started in Europe, it might spread to East Asia.[29] Halifax and his advisers were somewhat less pessimistic. Though conceding that Japan would take advantage of an Anglo-German conflict by stepping up her pressure on the British position in China, they felt that she would be very reluctant to intervene directly on Hitler's side.[30] This estimate was probably accurate. It seems that the Japanese, who were in the middle of an important campaign to take Hankow, were too bogged down in China to consider fighting Britain. The German ambassador in Tokyo later told his government that Japan had not planned any active measures against the British or the Soviets and that even the army had not wanted the European trouble to develop into a world conflict, though it did welcome the crisis "as a source of relief to its own position in China."[31]

The Munich agreement temporarily reduced the tension in Europe. Craigie felt that the settlement had a salutary impact on Japan and that Britain's influence in East Asia would grow stronger.[32] But this sanguine view underrated the importance of changes that took place in Tokyo in late September, when the differences between Ugaki and the Japanese army came to a head. The hard-line military leaders not only criticized Ugaki's talks with Craigie, but also pressed for the establishment of a China Affairs Board, which would largely supplant the Foreign Ministry as the principal formulator and executor of Japan's China policy. Ugaki naturally opposed the creation of this new agency. When Konoe failed to side with him on the issue at the end of September, Ugaki resigned. On October 1 the China Affairs Board was formally created.[33]

Ugaki's resignation was a turning point, signifying that those who favored a strong line toward Britain and Chiang were once again dominant in Tokyo. Craigie nonetheless wanted to resume his talks with the Japanese. Still interested in Ugaki's Shanghai proposals of September 22, he urged the Foreign Office to adopt a conciliatory attitude. The Foreign Office, however, was as averse as ever to making a deal with the Japanese. Howe, for example, complained that what Craigie "thinks are merely concessions of no importance are really matters of principle."[34] This reluctance to compromise was reinforced by Washington's strongest protest yet against Japanese policy in China. It was hoped that the stern note, given to Konoe on October 3, would be the prelude to a firmer American stand in East Asia, and the British did not want to undercut it by showing a readiness to accommodate the Japanese.[35] The Foreign Office did permit Craigie to talk with Konoe on October 12, but this meeting proved rather superficial, and in effect it ended Britain's three-month effort to extract concessions from Tokyo without offering anything in return.

On the same day, the Japanese launched military operations against Canton, the principal city of South China, in a drive to isolate Hong Kong from unoccupied China and cut off the flow of supplies and munitions to Chungking. Though in announcing the operations Tokyo said it would try to respect the interests of third powers, the effect (if not the purpose) of the Japanese drive was to damage Britain's preeminent position in South China. After observing Chamberlain's appeasement of Hitler at Munich, Japan was no doubt confident that Britain would not interfere with her new campaign. By October 21 the Japanese had captured Canton, blocked the railway to Kowloon, and closed the Pearl River to shipping. Four days later they also successfully terminated their operations in Central China by taking Hankow.

Surprisingly, Britain was not particularly concerned about Japan's drive into South China. The Foreign Office conceded that British interests would be hurt, but thought that Tokyo would try to avoid excessive friction with London. Craigie, though suspicious that Germany had inspired the Japanese move, believed that the campaign was a big commitment of Japan's resources and might hasten her exhaustion.[36] Britain was concerned, however, about Chiang Kai-shek's attitude. The Generalissimo seemed to be turning away from the British and moving toward complete dependence on the Soviets. Just prior to the Japanese onslaught against Canton, Howe warned his colleagues that *"we are losing our influence with the Chinese Government . . . , and it is impossible to foretell what the consequences of this loss of influence may be."*[37] Upset by the Munich agreement, China believed, as Clark Kerr pointed out, that the British were "entirely self-seeking" and would invariably let their friends down.[38] London's failure to contest Japan's campaign against Canton served to strengthen these suspicions, and the Chinese openly expressed their disappointment. Chiang warned Britain on October 17 that the Japanese invasion of South China was the beginning of a policy of southward expansion that would challenge all British interests in the East, and he urged immediate action.[39]

In raising the specter of a Japanese move against Britain's possessions to the south of China, Chiang touched a sensitive chord in the Foreign Office. Officials there had long feared that Japan might eventually use China as a base from which to attack the British Empire in Asia. Japan's capture of Canton obviously increased this danger.[40] Even so, Chiang's warning did not stimulate the Chamberlain government to give significant assistance to China in October. When Clark Kerr complained about this inaction, the Foreign Office explained that the Cabinet was "unwilling at this moment to take any chance of provoking an incident with the Japanese which would face us with the choice of climbing down or depleting our forces in European waters."[41] Instead of taking a harder line at this stage, the government was considering the possibility of joint Anglo-German mediation in East Asia.[42] The Foreign Office felt there was some basis for such cooperation between Britain and Germany. In particular, the economic interests of both countries would be served by the restoration of peace in China. There was of course a major obstacle: the Germans attached great importance to their political and ideological ties with Japan and would surely be reluctant to press her to compromise on peace terms. Conceivably, this obstacle could have been surmounted if the Munich agreement had been followed by a general settlement between London and Berlin.* By the end of 1938, however, Anglo-German relations were deteriorating, and the British concluded that there was no hope of cooperating with Hitler in East Asia.[43]

In the meantime, the Japanese had intensified their challenge to Britain's position in China. Encouraged by their military triumphs in October and by Germany's diplomatic success at Munich, they outlined their war aims. On November 2 the Foreign Ministry issued a statement declaring that Japan had occupied all the vital areas of China and calling for "a new order which will ensure the permanent stability of East Asia." The announcement explained that the foundation of the new order was to be "a tripartite relationship of mutual aid and coordination between Japan, Manchukuo , and China in political, economic, cultural, and other fields" and added that Tokyo wanted the Chinese to "share in the task of bringing this new order in East Asia." In a radio speech the next day, Premier Konoe emphasized that if the Kuomintang repudiated its past policy, Japan would be glad to cooperate with it. He also maintained that Tokyo wanted to end the "imperialistic rivalry" that had plagued China, and he urged the powers to adapt their policies to the new conditions.[44]

* A variation on this theme was stressed in a curious letter written by Arnold Toynbee that was brought to Halifax's attention in November 1938. Hitler had told Toynbee in 1936 that if the British returned the former German colonies in Africa and in the Pacific to Berlin's control, "I should make the general interests of Europe overseas my affair. . . . Then, if you had trouble with Japan, I would give you 'two divisions of troops and some warships, at Singapore!' " Toynbee's letter claimed that "there is no reason why this should not all still hold good, and, if you look into Hitler's argument, you will notice that he has put his finger on a fundamental point: Britain can't *both* deny Germany colonies *and* check Japanese aggression in the Far East. We must choose; and to my mind, the choice between a fratricidal European War and a joint European—and American demarche in the Far East is not hard to make!" Toynbee outlined a scenario: once Germany's former colonies were restored, Hitler would agree to a "mutual guarantee of their Pacific area possessions between *all* European colonial Powers. . . . *Then* we could deal with China (where the Japanese are destroying some very valuable German trade) and could rescue her from Japan's clutches." The idea no doubt struck Halifax as rather fanciful. See letter from Noel Brandon to Halifax (and enclosed letter from Toynbee), Nov. 4, 1938, H/XV/108 in Halifax Papers, FO 800/314.

In retrospect it is apparent that Japan's proclamation of a new order did not necessarily mean that she had developed a detailed blueprint for the "rejuvenation" of East Asia. The declaration did reflect, however, her desire to minimize Western and communist influence in China and build a Pan-Asian movement under Japanese leadership. The British regarded the announcements of November 2 and 3 as an important development in Japan's foreign policy and as proof of their suspicions that Japan was systematically trying to monopolize the economic and political life of China. Ambassador Craigie stressed that "the hitherto vague conception of a 'tripartite *bloc*' has now received definite official sanction," and Clark Kerr asserted that the proclamations were "of capital importance in that they should dispel all doubts about the real intentions of [the] Japanese."[45]

Britain's disquiet was not assuaged by Tokyo's attempts to elucidate and justify its plans. Arita Hachiro, a career diplomat who had succeeded Ugaki as Foreign Minister, told Craigie on November 17 that previous Japanese promises to respect British interests "might not be wholly applicable to the new situation which had developed." Arita emphasized that it was unfair for the Western powers to insist on the Open Door in China while their own empires remained closed. Pointing out that Japan—unlike Britain, America, and the Soviet Union—lacked resources and was vulnerable to economic sanctions, he argued that the solution to this problem was for the Japanese to form an economic bloc similar to the British Empire. Arita elaborated on these points in early December, when he informed Craigie that Tokyo's purpose in seeking closer economic relations with China and Manchukuo was to ensure that Japan would have an adequate supply of products essential to her "national existence." He admitted that it would be necessary to establish monopolies in certain fields, but insisted that many economic activities would be kept open to foreign interests and that "as a rule" trade barriers would not be erected against third powers. The British were skeptical that their interests would be allowed to have even this much scope.[46]

Even as the Japanese were challenging Britain in China, Chiang

Kai-shek was threatening to sever his ties with her. He had long been disappointed by the Chamberlain government's reluctance to give him substantial aid, and his disillusionment was increased by a statement made in Parliament by the Prime Minister on November 1. On that day, after Clement Attlee had said that Tokyo was closing one of the largest potential markets in the world, Chamberlain had replied that the Labour leader was taking too gloomy a view, because it was "quite certain that when the war is over and the reconstruction of China begins, she cannot be reconstructed without some help from this country."[47] The Prime Minister may have been trying to brandish Britain's financial "weapon," but to most observers his comment seemed to imply that he was eager to see the conflict end so that London could lend money to the Japanese to enable them to complete the exploitation of China. Chiang was dismayed, and told Clark Kerr on November 6 that the British and the Chinese "were now at the parting of the ways." He stressed that Britain's position in East Asia was tottering and that the traditional Chinese faith in the prestige of the British was being destroyed by Japan's successes. If Britain helped him, she would be "amply recompensed." If not, he "would be obliged to re-orientate his whole policy and to look elsewhere for friends. . . . He would never again concern himself with our policy in the Far East or consult us about China's future policy or anything else." Chiang concluded by hinting that he might even join Japan in a policy of excluding Britain from East Asia.[48]

The British were disturbed by this veiled threat to cooperate with the Japanese. In view of Konoe's appeal on November 3 for Chinese participation in the creation of the new order, such a prospect no longer seemed remote, and Sir Archibald Clark Kerr maintained that it would be far more dangerous even than close Sino-Soviet ties.[49] Britain's apprehensions were heightened in early December when Sir Archibald reported that Japanese agents were trying to persuade T. V. Soong, Chiang's brother-in-law and chairman of the Bank of China, to support a policy of "Asia for the Asiatics." Though Clark Kerr thought it difficult to conceive of cooperation between Chungking and Tokyo at this stage, he warned London not to exclude the possibility that events might move rapidly in this direction.[50] China was soon put to the test. On December 22 Konoe announced terms for "adjusting" Sino-Japanese relations and establishing the basis of the new order. He said that Japan sought neither territory nor reparations, but wanted the Chinese to recognize Manchukuo, sign an anti-Comintern pact, allow Japanese troops to be stationed in Inner Mongolia and at other "specified points," and cooperate with Japan in trade and the development of natural resources. As one observer in the Foreign Office noted, these rather harsh peace terms would give Japan control over China, in which case "Pan-Asianism will not only be a reality but a definite and concrete menace to the British Empire."[51] Predictably, Chiang rejected the terms on December 26. Any vacillation on his part would probably have precipitated a revolt by the Chinese Communists and left-wing elements in the Kuomintang. Not all Chinese leaders, however, favored continued resistance. Wang Ching-wei, long one of Chiang's main rivals in the Kuomintang, defected from Chungking and associated himself with Japan's drive for a new order.[52] But Wang's move did not spark a mass desertion; indeed, the British consul-general in Chungking felt the Chinese government was strengthened by the episode.[53]

As a result of these important developments of November and December, Britain began anxiously to reappraise her policy of benevolent neutrality. The cause of her anxiety was not that China was about to collapse or that the Japanese suddenly seemed able to finance their military and economic programs in China indefinitely. On the contrary, the Foreign Office and Ambassador Clark Kerr were still quite hopeful that Chiang could outlast Japan and that Tokyo's plans would be frustrated by financial difficulties. Even Craigie was coming to accept this view. As 1939 began, he reported that "Japan finds herself in an economic situation which can fairly be described as critical. Her margin of safety is small. The balance of merchandise trade with countries outside the yen *bloc* is against her, her gold reserves are steadily diminishing and her gold production cannot make up the difference." He added that there was "no real sign of the collapse of the Chinese National Government, or of the will to resist of the Chinese people."[54]

What bothered the British in late 1938 was that they were failing to protect their interests effectively and were alienating both Japan and China. Indeed, it seemed that they were losing influence in East Asia so rapidly that they might not be able to benefit from a successful Chinese war effort or Japanese exhaustion. Japan had made very clear her determination to allow foreign interests, in Sir John Brenan's words, "to survive in the conquered areas only under strict Japanese control and only in so far as they do not conflict with the scheme for economic and military self-sufficiency within the tripartite bloc."[55] As Robert Howe stressed, moreover, even though Japan might lack the capital to implement her schemes, her resentment against the British was so intense by this stage that she probably would never come "hat in hand" to London to ask for money.[56] At the same time, Chiang was becoming very irritated with the Chamberlain government, and it appeared that if he succeeded in thwarting Tokyo's ambitions, he might then squeeze any remaining British interests out of his country. As Clark Kerr warned on November 7, Britain's position in China was "fast slipping from under us."[57]

Clark Kerr attributed this deterioration to the "general indecision" of British policy, and emphasized that the time had come to give substantial help to the Chinese. Such action would enable Britain to preserve Chiang's good will, which Sir Archibald considered "to be something of real and lasting value [and] of essential importance to our whole position in this country in [the] future."[58] The Foreign Office was inclined to agree with Clark Kerr's diagnosis and recommendations. To be sure, some officials were a little annoyed at Chiang's attitude, but none of them wanted to abandon the Generalissimo and compromise with Japan. Sir Alexander Cadogan expressed the consensus when he asserted that "we should get nothing in the end by making up to the Japanese. If they win all their points, they will still throw us over—and out."

Britain, he added, would also lose "the last shreds" of American respect and sympathy if she compromised.[59]

The depth of British reluctance to conciliate Japan was clearly revealed in mid-December when Shigemitsu Mamoru, an experienced diplomat who had replaced Yoshida as the Japanese ambassador, suggested an exchange of notes stating in effect that Britain recognized Japan's "unique position" in China and that all questions between the two countries should be explored in friendly conversations. Then a committee would be appointed at Shanghai to discuss outstanding Anglo-Japanese problems. This simple formula, presumably meant to be a Far Eastern Munich declaration, was not well received by the Foreign Office. Howe, for example, was "profoundly suspicious" of the proposal, while Sir George Mounsey, an assistant secretary of state superintending the Far Eastern Department, said it was "preposterous—we are to concede precisely what Japan wants in exchange for mere consultation in regard to all our legitimate grievances." Halifax, though willing to talk to Shigemitsu, indicated that he could not accept the basis of the proposal. The Japanese Ambassador apparently realized that his plan had no chance of success, and he dropped the matter.[60]

The question of whether Britain should conciliate Japan was again raised in an important dispatch from Craigie that reached London at the end of December. Sir Robert argued that "continuing along the present lines of alienating one party to this conflict without assisting the other" would have disastrous results. Claiming that the Foreign Office still tended to view the East Asian situation mostly in terms of safeguarding Britain's interests in China, Craigie said he was concerned with the Far Eastern question primarily as a factor in the general world situation and as part of the problem of defending the British Empire. He stressed that there were two major dangers: Japan might enter into a military alliance with Germany and Italy; and she might persuade or force the Chinese to join a Japan-China-Manchukuo bloc, in which event a Japanese-directed "Yellow Peril" would swamp foreign markets and try to conquer Indochina, Malaya, and even India and Australia. In his opinion, Britain could stave off these dangers only by adopting a positive policy. He suggested two alternatives: cooperation with the Japanese; or a strong line in association with the United States, perhaps involving reprisals and other forcible action. According to Sir Robert, cooperation with Tokyo would not "necessarily involve a complete surrender to the wishes of the Japanese extremists or the abandonment of the cause of China," but it would mean the abandonment of any further scheme to assist Chiang Kai-shek, as well as the recognition of Japan's military and economic predominance in China and "an effort to win back ultimate Chinese independence through co-operation, both with China and Japan, in establishing that assured market and that source of raw materials which represent Japan's primary needs in the economic field." Admitting that this course was "not an attractive policy at first sight," he stressed that it would achieve the important goal of separating Tokyo from Berlin and Rome. He indicated that the other alternative—a strong line—was potentially more effective, especially in forestalling a Yellow Peril, but he feared that Washington would never agree to cooperate with London in any move that might lead to war. Sir Robert concluded by asking permission to make soundings in Tokyo to discover whether a tripartite military alliance could "still be averted and, if so, at what price."[61]

The Foreign Office gave careful consideration to Craigie's dispatch. The officials readily agreed that the East Asian question should be viewed in close relation to the world situation and to the problem of imperial defense. Still, Sir John Brenan felt that the Ambassador's fears of a Yellow Peril might be exaggerated,[62] and other officials doubted that there was any real difference between the existing Anti-Comintern Pact and the military alliance that Craigie dreaded. This last point was forcefully argued by Sir William Strang, an assistant secretary of state and formerly head of the Central Department of the Foreign Office:

The anti-Comintern Pact is of the greatest danger to us even in its present form; and we have some reason to think that Herr Hitler, with his well-known contempt for paper obligations, is not in favour of establishing precise contractual obligations between the parties, since he holds—and rightly so—that in case of a general conflict the three parties concerned will act in the manner best designed to serve their own interests, whatever their obligations may be.

The conclusion would seem to be that we should not stand to gain very much, if anything, by persuading Japan to refrain from entering into an anti-Comintern *alliance*; and that it is therefore not worth paying any substantial price in an attempt to achieve this end.

Strang opposed concessions to Tokyo for other and even weightier reasons:

I do not myself believe (though I am here straying beyond my province) that the Japanese could be bought off by any compromise or concession that we could safely offer them; nor does their present military and economic position seem to be so strong as to warrant our choosing this moment to abandon Chiang Kai-Shek and by so doing nip in the bud a useful form of collaboration with the United States, and thus jeopardize a movement in the United States for collaboration with like-minded Governments in Europe which has already gone far beyond what we could have dared to hope for a few months ago.[63]

Sir William's conclusions were seconded not only by the Southern and Northern Departments, but also by the Far Eastern Department.* Summarizing the discussion, Cadogan stated that "the overriding consideration is the danger of alienating the U.S."[64] Though the officials unanimously agreed that there would be no advantage in appeasing Japan, Halifax did leave Craigie discretion to make the soundings he had asked about in his dispatch. Halifax made it clear, however, that a policy of cooperation with Tokyo was open to very serious objections.[65]

In his message, Craigie had of course also indicated that joint Anglo-American action could be effective, and it was this alternative that the Chamberlain government was exploring most carefully. There were signs that the United States was less reluctant than before to cooperate. On November 3 she told Halifax that she was going to protest the continued closure of the Yangtze

---

* Interestingly enough, for all their desire to reduce the number of Britain's potential enemies, the three armed services shared the Foreign Office's opposition to a policy of cooperation with Japan. See Air Ministry to FO, Feb. 17, 1939, FO F1689/176/23; Admiralty to FO, Mar. 2, 1939, FO F2134/176/23; and War Office to FO, Mar. 15, 1939, FO F2692/176/23.

River and invited him to make similar representations to Tokyo. He eagerly agreed, and Britain, France, and America delivered parallel communications to Foreign Minister Arita on November 7. Though Japan's reply was unsatisfactory, the tripartite protest was significant, since up to this time the State Department's representations had been made independently.[66] Later that winter the three Western powers sent notes to the Japanese government protesting Konoe's call for a new order and a tripartite bloc of Japan, China, and Manchukuo. Though the representations were similar in content and tone, this action was not so well coordinated as the November protests had been. The Americans sent their communication on December 30, without giving the British prior notification. Britain did not give her note to Tokyo until January 14, and the French démarche was not made until January 19.[67] In any case the British fully realized by this stage that representations were not going to restrain Japan and save their position in China. Japan's proclamation of a new order and Chiang's threat to turn away from London had convinced the British that the time had come to assert themselves in East Asia. Two familiar options—sanctions against Tokyo and assistance to China—were reconsidered in late 1938 and early 1939.

In August 1938, when the Craigie-Ugaki talks had reached an impasse, the Foreign Office had given thought to a four-stage program of progressive reprisals against Tokyo, starting with the "institution in British-controlled territories of various petty administrative vexations on [the] Japanese model" and culminating in the denunciation of the Anglo-Japanese Commercial Treaty of 1911. But Clark Kerr indicated in September that such a course of "pin-pricks working up in a crescendo of irritation to denunciation of [the] trade treaty" would be both ineffective and dangerous. He urged that if the British were going to take economic action against Japan, the measures "should be as effective and far-reaching as possible so as to bring quick results."[68] Craigie, for his part, stated in October that there would be no advantage in a program of progressive reprisals, and warned that denouncing the trade treaty might bring on a war with Japan. On November 4 he explained that though he opposed economic measures by Britain alone, he would be in favor of joint Anglo-American sanctions against Japan. But in his opinion "it would be a mistake to count too much on any such move by the United States."[69]

Even as Craigie was expressing these doubts, the State Department was asking the British what could be done if Japan replied unfavorably to the tripartite protest against the continued closure of the Yangtze. Prime Minister Chamberlain was not pleased by this indication that the Americans might be interested in joint economic action. He told the Cabinet on November 7 that the Japanese were "becoming increasingly arrogant and difficult," but that economic retaliation would be ineffective and might cause Japan to attack Hong Kong. The Foreign Office nevertheless launched a new review of the question.[70] This investigation moved no faster than the ones that had preceded it, and the Roosevelt administration soon showed signs of what appeared to be impatience. Assistant Secretary of State Sumner Welles told Ambassador Sir Ronald Lindsay on December 1 that there was "increasing need" for London and Washington to coordinate economic action in defense of their interests, and asked for the British views on this question "within a few weeks."[71]

Craigie, dismayed by Japan's hardened attitude, welcomed America's apparent interest in joint retaliatory measures. On December 5 he urged the Foreign Office to work for parallel action "at the earliest possible moment in order to bring it home to Japan in time that her new China policy will not pay." In his view, Anglo-American economic action would involve no risk of war with the Japanese.[72] Sir Robert added in early January that since Japan's gold reserves were very low, an embargo on her exports to the British Empire, the United States, and France would cripple her economy, and even a refusal by the Western powers to purchase any gold from Japan would have a damaging effect. He also maintained that, in view of Washington's stronger stance and of the economic and political situation in Tokyo, the "present moment is the most favorable for such action since my arrival in

Japan."[73] Clearly, Sir Robert's attitude had changed markedly since October 1938.

Craigie was not alone in urging London to act. British commercial groups were also clamoring for economic pressure.[74] Within the Foreign Office, such a course received strong support from Sir John Brenan, who argued that retaliation would not merely help maintain Britain's interests in China, but would also be "a stroke of high policy that may have a beneficial effect on the whole world situation."[75] The Treasury and the Board of Trade were firmly opposed to economic measures, however,[76] and Foreign Secretary Halifax, for his part, doubted that it was "very feasible to do anything very effective along these lines." Halifax did stress, on the other hand, that it was "of great political importance . . . that the Americans should not again have the fun of saying what they would have done if only we had not stood in the way."[77] Thus, in responding to the State Department, the British wanted to steer the course that they had followed at the time of the Brussels Conference: appearing to be willing to join the United States in retaliatory measures, but gently trying to dissuade her from them. The Foreign Office prepared a draft reply which, as Halifax told Chamberlain, set out "fairly plainly some of the obvious difficulties" and did not "commit us to anything either explicitly or implicitly." The Prime Minister approved the draft, noting that he would "be very much surprised if we draw the badger." Even so, Sir John Simon prevailed on the Foreign Office to put still more emphasis on the dangers of retaliation.[78]

The communication was finally delivered to the State Department on January 25. It mentioned Craigie's view, but on the whole presented an exceedingly conservative picture of what various economic measures might achieve, and pointed out that any effective action would involve a risk of war. The message concluded by indicating that Britain has "hitherto been disposed to think that, in the present state of Europe, the right policy for the present is not to embark on retaliation," but that she was willing to reconsider this conclusion if the Roosevelt administration could show her that the time was appropriate for economic action.[79] Predictably, Craigie was upset by this reply:

What is at stake is not only our commercial investment in China but the whole political and economic future of countries with interests in the Pacific to say nothing of the urgency of ensuring the observance of treaty obligations as a matter of principle. If what we are striving for is to uphold a principle and avert a future danger we are justified in taking greater risks in terms of short-run disadvantage than if our aim were merely to preserve existing interests intact.[80]

Presumably in an effort to soothe Sir Robert, the Foreign Office passed his comments on to the State Department. Washington replied on February 3 that it felt a policy of assistance to China was preferable to one of retaliation against Japan.[81]

The Chamberlain government agreed, and had in fact made some progress along these lines. In November 1938 British and Chinese interests agreed in principle to construct a railway from Burma to Yunnan.[82] In December the famous Burma Road was completed. By the spring of 1939, approximately a thousand tons of supplies were passing over the road into China each month of the dry season. The British had speeded the construction of this route by pressing Burma to finish and improve her section of it.[83] Also during December the Cabinet introduced legislation into Parliament empowering the Board of Trade to guarantee credits for £10 million of exports in cases where such action was financially risky, but justifiable on political grounds. Oliver Stanley, the president of the Board of Trade, had proposed this step on November 30. Sir John Simon objected at first, but Stanley persuaded him to change his mind, and the Cabinet approved the proposal on December 7. China hoped that London would grant her about half of the £10 million. Though the British felt she should have first claim, they did not want to give her a lump sum right away. After discussions among the Foreign Office, the Treasury, and the Board of Trade, it was decided to allot Chiang £500,000 to buy trucks for the Burma Road and then to consider additional credits, up to a total of £3 million, when Chungking made further specific requests for particular consignments of goods.[84]

All these steps helped the Chinese, but the most important move made by the Chamberlain government at this stage was its decision to guarantee what amounted to a loan for the stabilization of China's currency. Following the Cabinet's refusal to help Chiang in July 1938, the question of a loan had been pushed into the background until early November, when Clark Kerr urged that the matter be re-examined. The Foreign Office decided to press the Cabinet to authorize a £3 million grant to help the Chinese establish a currency-stabilization fund. In a memorandum circulated on November 25, Halifax argued the case for such a step, stressing that China had threatened to turn away from Britain and toward either Japan or the Soviet Union, and noting that if Chiang's resistance faltered, Japan would be in a good position to advance south.[85] Not surprisingly, Sir John Simon expressed doubt about the wisdom of guaranteeing a loan. As he had done in July, he emphasized that such a move would "expose us to risks in the Far East which we are not in a position to deal with."[86] At a Cabinet meeting on November 30, Halifax disagreed with Simon's contention that a loan would be dangerous. But Prime Minister Chamberlain, who had recently been involved in a stormy argument with Shigemitsu, felt that Japan was in an angry mood and would retaliate if Britain helped China. He suggested that the Foreign Office should find out whether the United States would participate in a scheme to support the Chinese currency, and that London should not act unless she would.[87]

Throughout December the British tried to elicit a promise of cooperation from the State Department. In the middle of the month the Americans announced that they would give China $25 million in credits. Though the United States had previously helped the Chinese by purchasing silver from them, these credits represented her first significant intervention in the East Asian conflict and reflected a hardening in her attitude toward Japan.[88] Even so, she shied away from cooperating with Britain to support China's currency; in fact, she seemed to feel that it was now Britain's turn to help Chiang.[89] In a message to the State Department in early January, the British acknowledged that they were lagging behind in assistance to China, but once again pressed for a joint loan. Such cooperative action, they argued, "might indeed prove the turning point in the whole struggle and lead to the salvation of United States and British commercial interests."[90] At first it appeared that this approach had succeeded, but the Americans soon drew back, lest the idea of collaboration with Britain excite the isolationists in Congress.[91]

America's caution did not keep the British from going ahead with a currency loan. By January 18 Chamberlain was moving away from his previous view that London should act only in concert with the United States. His change of mind was due both to his realization that the Roosevelt administration would be disappointed if Britain held back and to a message from Craigie indicating that there was little serious risk in unilateral action.[92] The Foreign Office fully agreed that London should act on its own. Sir John Brenan maintained that "the Japanese themselves regard their situation as dangerous and are desperately anxious for peace. . . . It is in the highest degree unlikely that they would do anything to provoke a conflict with Britain over a mere economic measure designed for the protection of British commercial interests."[93] There was, however, one complicating factor: China had announced on January 15 that she was suspending all payments on loans secured by the Maritime Customs. The British felt this decision provided a suitable opportunity to press China to implement the Customs Agreement of May 1938, and for a while consideration of the loan question became entangled with this matter. The Chinese of course resented London's pressure on this point.[94] Accordingly, the Cabinet decided on February 22 that a currency loan should not be made conditional on China's willingness to service foreign debts or implement the Customs Agreement, and Chiang was informed three days later that the Chamberlain government had decided in principle to guarantee a loan.[95] The final scheme, publicly announced on March 8, called for two British banks to contribute £5 million—£2 million more than the figure that the Foreign Office had originally proposed—to a currency-stabilization fund and specified that the Treasury would reimburse these banks for any losses suffered.[96]

Thus Britain had at last given significant assistance to China. By now there were definite signs that Japan was engaged in a major campaign to undermine the Chinese currency in the hope that Chiang's resistance would be crippled and occupied China would be completely absorbed into the yen bloc. In acting to support Chungking's currency, the British had clearly deviated further than ever before from benevolent neutrality. Though the Japanese press complained that Britain was launching a "frontal attack" against the new order, the Japanese government did not react violently.[97] Whether or not the British could continue to assert themselves in East Asia was nonetheless open to serious doubt. Much depended on the European situation. Chamberlain had told the House of Commons in December 1938 that "events in the Far East are intimately connected with affairs in Europe, so that when we consider our position there we must do so in close relation to the position nearer home."[98]

At least until mid-March 1939, however, it was hard to decide precisely what "the position nearer home" was. Uncertainty reigned. Though the absence of any major crisis in late 1938 and early 1939 made it easier for Britain to help China, the lack of any definite progress toward a comprehensive Anglo-German agreement made it increasingly difficult to sustain a policy of appeasement in Europe. In the period immediately after Munich, Prime Minister Chamberlain had thought that a European settlement was within reach. His outlook then was one of hope tempered somewhat by wariness. On October 3 he told the Cabinet that:

Ever since he had been Chancellor of the Exchequer, he had been oppressed with the sense that the burden of armaments might break our backs. This had been one of the factors which had led him to the view that it was necessary to try and resolve the causes which were responsible for the armaments race.

He thought that we were now in a more hopeful position, and that the contacts which had been established with the Dictator Powers opened up the possibility that we might be able to reach some agreement with them which would stop the armament race. It was clear, however, that it would be madness for the country to stop rearming until we were convinced that other countries would act in the same way.[99]

Foreign Secretary Halifax, for his part, was considerably less hopeful than Chamberlain. Still, he felt that London must continue to work for an agreement with Germany,[100] as did his top adviser, Sir Alexander Cadogan. Cadogan believed the British had to "give up any idea of policing Europe such as has come down to us from Versailles and the Covenant of the League. We simply cannot protect our own interests all over the world and at the same time claim a preponderant voice in the ordering of affairs in continental Europe." He grimly recommended in early November that London should have a frank discussion with Berlin. Though conceding that Germany would make impossible demands, he suggested that if most of her "grievances" were redressed, Hitler perhaps could not get the German people to fight for the rest.[101]

No such approach to Berlin was finally made, however, because a brutal pogrom took place in Germany on November 10, 1938, and also because the Foreign Office received a number of confidential reports indicating that Hitler wanted to destroy the British Empire. Concluding that there was no point in talking with the Germans at this stage, Chamberlain and Halifax decided to concentrate on improving relations with Italy.[102] On November 16 London brought into force the Anglo-Italian agreement of April, even though Mussolini had withdrawn only 10,000 troops from Spain. Chamberlain and Halifax also made plans to visit Italy in January 1939. Halifax explained to the Cabinet on December 21 that the purpose of the trip was to weaken the Rome-Berlin axis and that "our main principle should be 'Nothing for nothing.'" Chamberlain thought this too negative a view. He favored "Something for something" and hoped that Mussolini "could be persuaded to prevent Herr Hitler from carrying out some 'mad dog' act."[103] Contrary to Chamberlain's hopes, the visit proved uneventful. No understandings were reached, and Mussolini refused to be drawn into any discussion of his feelings toward Hitler. Upon their return from Rome in mid-January, Chamberlain and Halifax found their attention forced back to Germany by reports reaching the Foreign Office that Berlin was considering an invasion of Holland or even an air attack on Britain. Chamberlain was quite skeptical of these reports, but Halifax was concerned.[104] Britain decided to hold systematic staff conversations with France to prepare joint military plans for fighting both Germany and Italy and also for countering any moves by Japan.* Though Hitler was relatively quiet in February and early March of 1939, Halifax remained wary. Chamberlain was more optimistic about the future than his colleague, but he did not press for any new approach to Berlin. British policy was adrift.

Much of the uncertainty in London vanished after Hitler occupied what remained of independent Czechoslovakia on March 15. This move undermined the assumptions (and the public support) on which the Chamberlain government had based its policy of appeasement. As the Prime Minister explained to the Cabinet on March 18,

Up till a week ago we had proceeded on the assumption that we should be able to continue with our policy of getting on to better terms with the Dictator Powers, and that although those powers had aims, those aims were limited. We had all along had at the back of our minds the reservation that this might not prove to be the case but we had felt that it was right to try out the possibilities of this course. . . .
He had now come definitely to the conclusion that Herr Hitler's attitude made it impossible to continue to negotiate on the old lines with the Nazi regime. This did not mean that negotiations with the German people were impossible. No reliance could be placed on any of the assurances given by the Nazi leaders.[105]

Prodded by Halifax and by public opinion, Chamberlain abruptly changed Britain's European policy by setting out to build a "peace front" that would deter Germany from territorial expansion. The British announced a guarantee of Poland on March 31, and after Italy seized Albania on April 7, they made similar commitments

---

* Desultory and inconclusive staff conversations had been held in 1936 and 1938. They had dealt only with the possibility of war with Germany alone, and no joint plans had been made. The British regarded the talks to be held in 1939 as a big step forward. The Cabinet Committee on Foreign Policy, for example, asserted that the preparation of joint military plans with the French "would constitute a far more binding commitment than has hitherto been contemplated." See meeting of the Cabinet Committee on Foreign Policy, Jan. 26, 1939, CAB 27/624; and Cabinet Conclusions, Feb. 1, 1939, CAB 23/97.

to Greece and Rumania and then reached a provisional agreement with Turkey for cooperation against aggression in the Mediterranean area. London was also trying to get the Soviet Union to declare that in the event of an attack on any of her European neighbors she would provide armed assistance if desired. Stalin, however, pressed for a pact of mutual assistance with the British and French. This proposal did not appeal to the Cabinet and the Foreign Office. Not only did nearly all British policy-makers openly distrust the Soviet Union and hold a low opinion of her military capability, they also felt that an alliance with her would provoke Hitler, offend Poland and Rumania, and antagonize Japan, Italy, and Spain. Accordingly, in late April and early May, Britain merely tried to keep Moscow in play.[106] Under pressure in the House of Commons as well as from the Chiefs of Staff and France, the Chamberlain government adopted a more flexible attitude in late May.[107] By this time, however, the Soviet Union's suspicions, and hence her demands, were growing. The talks remained deadlocked.

With or without Soviet support, Britain was evidently ready to resist any new German thrust. Though she hoped that her firmer line might restrain Hitler and eventually lead to a détente, she was by no means confident that a conflict could be avoided. In any case, she apparently believed herself better prepared to fight a European war now than in 1938, owing to the progress of her rearmament since Munich. If Japan joined Germany and Italy in a conflict against Britain, however, the situation would be very grave; neither existing British forces nor any visualized for the foreseeable future could cope with three major powers simultaneously. Indeed, the Chiefs of Staff warned in early 1939 that such a world war would confront the Chamberlain government "with a position more serious than the Empire has ever faced before. The ultimate outcome of the conflict might well depend upon the intervention of the other Powers, in particular of the United States of America."[108] Even a war against Germany and Japan, with Italy remaining neutral, would be exceedingly dangerous. To be sure, in the summer of 1939 the Admiralty was at last allowed to begin preparations for attaining a new level of naval strength that would in effect be a two-power standard.* Such long-term plans, however, were at this stage merely a "matter of theory."[109] For the immediate future, the Chamberlain government could exercise no more military power than before in East Asia. In fact, during much of 1939 the British would have only ten of their fifteen capital ships immediately available, though two others being refitted could be pressed into action at short notice. In mid-1939 the Japanese had nine capital ships available and the Germans had the equivalent of three; in the Admiralty's view, this meant that Britain needed sixteen to be safe and that she therefore had a deficit of four to six capital ships.[110]

Sir Robert Craigie, who had at one time been the Foreign Office's expert on naval affairs, was quite aware of London's weakness in capital ships. He nonetheless recommended in December 1938 that a squadron of capital ships be stationed at Singapore. "I have no illusions as to the difficulties in the way of despatching such a squadron at this time, but I feel that we must nevertheless be prepared to face a steady deterioration in our prestige and influence throughout the Far East unless we can do something more to sustain in this part of the world our position and responsibilities as the greatest naval Power." According to Sir Robert, sending even three or four capital ships would help achieve the "all-important objective" of deterring the Japanese "from a resort to extreme action."[111] Acting on Craigie's recommendation, the Foreign Office suggested to the Admiralty in February 1939 that five to seven capital ships should be kept at Singapore in peacetime. Foreign Secretary Halifax and his advisers explained that

what appears to be necessary is the consideration from the broadest aspect of vital imperial needs of what measures should, and could most

---

* I.e., a standard designed to enable Britain to confront Japan and Germany simultaneously. Apart from increasing tension in East Asia, the main reason for this decision was Germany's denunciation in April 1939 of the Anglo-German naval agreement of 1935 limiting German naval tonnage to 35 percent of that of the British Commonwealth. This denunciation seemed to foreshadow a considerable expansion of the German fleet.

effectively, be taken permanently to defend British interests in the Far East against the threat inherent in Japan's plans for the setting up of what she calls "a new order in East Asia." The problem would appear to be one of preventing Japan from creating a vast closed area from which she would be able to draw nearly all the raw materials which are essential to her and thereby attaining such strength as might enable her subsequently to absorb into that area other territories producing two at least of the other raw materials of really vital importance to her, oil in the Netherlands East Indies and high-grade iron ore in Malaya. The power thus acquired by Japan would enable her to present, either in combination with Germany and Italy or even alone, a permanent and formidable threat to British interests throughout the Eastern Hemisphere.[112]

The Admiralty, though appreciating the danger inherent in Japan's new order, rejected the Foreign Office's suggestion. In their reply of late March, the naval strategists argued that Britain's limited number of capital ships and her heavy commitments in the Mediterranean made it impossible to send a fleet east in peacetime; the most that could be hoped for was to station one capital ship at Singapore by 1942. The Admiralty pointedly reminded the Foreign Office that there was a close relation between naval strength and foreign policy and that "a reduction in the number of our potential enemies is as definite an accretion to our strength as is an increase in the number of our battleships."[113]

The only consolation the naval strategists could offer was that a fleet would be dispatched to East Asia in the event of war there. Actually, even this axiom was being reappraised because it would mean leaving the Mediterranean empty of British capital ships. At meetings of the *ad hoc* Strategical Appreciation Committee in March and April, the Admiralty maintained that in a war against Berlin, Rome, and Tokyo the best strategy would be to try to "knock out" the Italians before sending a fleet east. Admiral Lord Ernle Chatfield, who had in January replaced Inskip as Minister for the Co-ordination of Defence, did not like the idea of letting the Far East "look after itself" for an indefinite period. In March, for example, he warned his former colleagues at the Admiralty that such a strategy would endanger Britain's Eastern empire.[114] But Italy's seizure of Albania in early April and Britain's subsequent commitments to Greece and Rumania made it difficult to plan on sending a fleet from the Mediterranean to Singapore at the outbreak of world war.* The rather vague consensus that finally emerged among British strategists was "that there are so many variable factors which cannot at present be assessed, that it is not possible to state definitely how soon after Japanese intervention a Fleet could be despatched to the Far East. Neither is it possible to enumerate precisely the size of the Fleet that we could afford to send."[115]

This new formula represented not only a significant shift in Britain's strategic thinking, but also a distinct modification of assurances she had given to Australia and the other Dominions. At the Imperial Conference in 1937 the British had pledged that as soon as possible after the outbreak of hostilities with Japan they would send an "adequate" fleet east—regardless of the situation elsewhere. In November 1938 the Admiralty indicated to Stanley Bruce, the Australian High Commissioner in London, that seven capital ships would be dispatched to Singapore in the event of war. Chamberlain retreated somewhat from these undertakings in a message to Australia on March 20, 1939. Explaining that in 1937 London had not planned for a conflict against Rome as well as against Tokyo and Berlin, he intimated that if Britain had to fight all three powers, she might not be able to send east so many capital ships as previously contemplated.[116] London realized that this message would shock the Australians. Looking for a way to reassure them (and cow the Japanese), Halifax asked the United States on March 21 to move her fleet to the Pacific. Roosevelt did order the American fleet to San Diego on April 15, but Australia's

---

* Britain had also to take into account France's view, expressed during the Anglo-French staff talks in the spring of 1939, that a British fleet should not be sent east. It was agreed at the talks that any weakening of Britain's naval strength in the Mediterranean could not be undertaken lightly. See note by Ismay, June 12, 1939, and enclosed reports, D.P. (P.)56, CAB 16/183. At a conference in June 1939, however, British and French commanders in the Far East warned that Singapore was very vulnerable. In July the Committee of Imperial Defence in London decided to send air and ground reinforcements—but no warships—to Singapore. Cornwall-Jones to Howe, July 13, 1939, FO F7285/2742/61; meeting of Committee of Imperial Defence, July 21, 1939, CAB 2/9.

anxieties were not assuaged.[117] Bruce pressed for specific information about plans in case of war in East Asia. The British replied that no final decision had been reached, but that in any event they would not (in Chatfield's words) "abdicate our position in the Far East without fighting."[118]

This reply was accurate. The shift in London's naval strategy in the spring of 1939 did not reflect an intention to abandon either the antipodean Dominions or British interests in East Asia. Instead, apart from European considerations, it reflected two rather optimistic assumptions. The first one was that if Britain became involved in a conflict with her three antagonists, the United States might help her hold the position in the Pacific. In a review of the political situation circulated in April, the Foreign Office stated that if a European war spread to East Asia, the Americans "might well feel themselves compelled in the opening phases of hostilities to resort to common naval action with Great Britain and France. In particular, any Japanese threat to Australia and New Zealand, whether by way of a direct descent upon them or indirectly in the form of an expedition against Singapore, would be a matter to which the United States could hardly remain for long indifferent."[119] No doubt hoping to elicit a promise of cooperation in some form from the Roosevelt administration, London sent Commander T. C. Hampson of the Admiralty to Washington for naval talks in June 1939. Hampson explained how the situation in Europe had affected Britain's ability to send a fleet east, but found the Americans reluctant to say anything about their intentions and plans. Accordingly, the talks were disappointing from London's point of view.[120]

The second, and more fundamental, assumption underlying Britain's strategic thinking was that she believed war with the Japanese could be avoided. This belief was based on her assessment of the East Asian situation. Unaware that friction between the Kuomintang and the Communist Party was growing apace, the British thought that Chiang Kai-shek's government was still united and that Chinese resistance would remain strong.[121] They also judged that Japan's morale and finances were slipping badly.

Tokyo presumably had to worry, moreover, about American and Soviet reactions to any precipitate Japanese move. In short, it appeared that Japan was close to exhaustion, bogged down in China, and threatened by potentially hostile powers. Prime Minister Chamberlain, the Foreign Office, and British military strategists therefore strongly doubted that she would intervene in a European war.[122] Still less did they envisage hostilities breaking out first in East Asia, rather than in Europe. The events of the summer of 1939, however, were to shake this optimism. During that period Japan exerted her strongest pressure yet against Britain's position in China, and when serious troubles erupted at Tientsin, an Anglo-Japanese war no longer seemed remote. With the prospect of a European conflict also looming over her, Britain was more deeply involved than ever in a world crisis.

Chapter seven

The Crisis at Tientsin

By THE BEGINNING of 1939, the Konoe Cabinet was faltering under the weight of the problems that confronted it. Though Japan had confidently proclaimed a new order in East Asia and though she could claim by this stage to have killed 800,000 Chinese in battle and occupied 1,500,000 square kilometers of Chinese territory,[1] no end to the war was in sight. Chungking seemed far from collapse, and communist guerrillas were harassing Japanese forces in North China. The Japanese government had other troubles as well. In domestic politics, it was torn by a controversy over whether a single-party system should be established. In foreign affairs, it was hopelessly divided over the issue of its relations with Italy and Germany. Premier Konoe and his associates agreed that it was desirable to convert the Anti-Comintern Pact into a tripartite military alliance against Moscow. They believed that such a step would "neutralize" the Soviets and thereby help Japan's war effort in China. Hitler, however, had made it clear as early as the summer of 1938 that he wanted any military alliance to be directed at all other powers, not merely at Moscow, obviously in order to immobilize the British in Europe by giving them increased cause for worry in East Asia and the Mediterranean. The Japanese army wished to accept Hitler's terms, but Konoe, Foreign Minister Arita, and the navy were firmly opposed to any commitment that might involve Tokyo in war with Britain and the United States.[2]

Unable to resolve these major issues, Konoe resigned as Premier on January 4, 1939. He was succeeded by the President of the Privy Council, Baron Hiranuma Kiichiro, a well known albeit mellowing reactionary. The Hiranuma government continued the debate over what commitments Tokyo should make to Berlin and Rome. In fact, during Hiranuma's eight-month tenure this question was discussed more than seventy times by an "inner cabinet" composed of the Premier and the Foreign, War, Navy, and Finance Ministers. The British had reasonably accurate information about the situation in Tokyo, and Craigie frequently tried to dissuade Japan from throwing in her lot with Germany and Italy.[3] Events in Europe, however, made his task difficult. After Germany annexed the rest of Czechoslovakia in mid-March, Japan decided to accept in principle the idea of a general alliance, though she insisted on a secret written understanding that would for the time being relieve her of any obligation to go to war against the Western powers and would also allow her to inform London and Washington that the new agreement was aimed only at the Soviet Union. This concession did not satisfy the Germans and Italians. The Japanese army accordingly stepped up its pressure for an unlimited alliance, but the Foreign Ministry and the navy continued to resist.[4]

Even though this bitter debate demanded much of Japan's attention in the first four months of 1939, she by no means neglected the situation in China. Neither the change of leadership in January nor London's currency loan to Chiang Kai-shek caused Japan to modify either her demands on the Chinese or her pressure on British interests. Hiranuma, like Konoe, worked for the establishment of a new order in East Asia, but not by launching further large-scale military campaigns. Instead, he concentrated on undermining China's currency and tightening Japan's hold on the occupied areas. On March 10, for example, the puppet regime at Peking prohibited the circulation of *fapi* in North China; and on March 11 it instituted trade and exchange controls there. These steps were damaging to British firms, since they now had either to accept the notes of the Japanese-sponsored Federal Reserve Bank and take a loss, or to give up exporting certain goods.[5] Japan also made moves in Central China that seemed to presage a currency war there. On May 1 the Hua Hsing Commercial Bank was opened in Shanghai under the aegis of Japan and the so-called Nanking Reformed Government. Unlike the Federal Reserve Bank, this new bank would issue notes convertible into foreign currency and the Chinese national currency. Japan invited the British to cooperate with the bank, but they refused. They feared that—notwithstanding Japanese assurances to the contrary—the bank had been established to facilitate raids on China's currency stabilization fund and the institution of trade and exchange controls in Central China.[6]

British military circles had as much cause for worry as British business circles. Japan annexed Hainan Island in February and the Spratly Islands in March; she was interested in these islands as "defense" posts against Britain in the event of an Anglo-Japanese conflict.[7] Hainan, which was off the South China coast, could be used to stage air attacks against Indochina, gain control of the Gulf of Tonkin, and sever communications from Singapore to Hong Kong. The Spratly Islands were in the South China Sea, midway between Singapore and Manila and only 375 miles from North Borneo. In a memorandum circulated to the Cabinet on March 30, Halifax and his advisers in the Foreign Office interpreted these annexations as part of a long-range Japanese plan to absorb Borneo and Malaya into a self-sufficient economic bloc. They also suspected that Japan's action had "been undertaken at the instigation of the Germans and Italians, or anyhow in pursuance of some plan concerted with them." The memorandum speculated that if such a plan did exist, it presumably called first for Japan to goad Britain and France into sending their fleets east and then for Germany and Italy to strike in Europe. In any case, "the present time appears to be specially critical in the Far East in the light of what the Japanese are doing in North China and in the islands in the South China Seas."[8]

Having offered this analysis of the situation, Halifax and his advisers recommended that the Chamberlain government make plans—such as consulting all interested governments and obtaining the necessary Parliamentary powers—to put economic pressure on Japan. According to the memorandum of March 30, overt signs of such planning might give Japan a sobering jolt and restrain the Germans and Italians by bringing home to them how little help they could expect from their East Asian associate; but even if overt signs of planning did not work, and if it was then decided to go ahead with retaliatory action, Britain need not fear that the Japanese would have recourse to war.[9] The Board of Trade, however, disagreed with this sanguine assessment and opposed the Foreign Office's proposals. Some officials in the Treasury were also averse to starting down the road toward retaliation against Japan. As a result of such differences of opinion, discussion of plans for economic pressure made little headway during the spring.[10] Not until June, when the crisis at Tientsin developed, did the question receive serious high-level attention.

Another alternative open to Britain in the spring of 1939 was to extend the Anglo-French-Soviet negotiations to the Far East. As the Chiefs of Staff noted in April, the Soviet fleet in East Asia, which included two cruisers, eleven destroyers, and many submarines, could help deter the Japanese from advancing to the south; the Soviet army, with five cavalry and thirty-two infantry divisions in the Far East, could "exercise a containing influence on Japan in Manchukuo and China"; and the Soviet air force, which now numbered 1,000 aircraft east of Lake Baikal, would also have a restraining influence on Japan and could give valuable assistance to China.[11] Even so, the British did not like the idea of an Anglo-Soviet agreement for mutual assistance in East Asia. They feared that such an arrangement would push Japan into an unlimited alliance with the Germans and Italians and hence increase the possibility that she might intervene in a European war.[12] Thus, though Halifax and Chamberlain publicly indicated that the negotiations between London and Moscow might be extended to the Far East, Halifax privately assured Japan in late April that the conversations would not cover East Asia, if Anglo-Japanese relations "developed as I hoped they might."[13] The caveat that Halifax tacked onto his assurance hinted at a bargain: Britain would not ally herself with the Soviet Union in the Far East so long as Japan resisted German pressure for an alliance. In the event, neither Britain nor Russia raised the question of East Asia in their talks; and the Japanese refrained from joining the Pact of Steel that Germany and Italy concluded on May 21.

Though Japan's refusal at this juncture to accept Germany's terms for an alliance did not end the debate in the Hiranuma Cabinet over a tripartite arrangement, it did mean that the "anti-Axis" group still held the upper hand. The British were not surprised Japan refused to make a commitment that might involve her in hostilities with the Western powers. The Foreign Office was surprised, however, to learn in late May that Premier Hiranuma had sent a secret message to Roosevelt suggesting a joint effort to preserve peace in Europe and had also indicated to the Americans that, if a world conference were held, the Japanese would be willing to include the China problem on the agenda.[14] Though Halifax and his advisers had long doubted that Japan would intervene in a European war, they had assumed that she was hoping for a conflict in the West because it would give her a freer hand to expand in East Asia. Now it seemed, as Sir John Brenan noted, that the Japanese were "beginning to think that a war will result in the eventual defeat of their European friends and that Japan will then be menaced on all sides by hostile Powers." Brenan and his colleagues also felt it was clear that the Japanese were "heartily tired of the China campaign and would gladly bring it to an end provided the more essential gains required by their long term programme can be retained."[15] In short, to the Foreign Office Hiranuma's move represented evidence that Japan was worried about the European situation and was tired of fighting the Chinese. Craigie, however, warned that it was not necessarily a sign of economic exhaustion, though he did concede that China's resistance was still strong. To Sir Robert it was above all a clever attempt to drive a wedge between Britain and the United States by putting Japanese-American relations on a better footing.[16] Whatever Hiranuma's motive was, his approach met with a decidedly unfavorable reception in Washington.[17]

Meanwhile, Japan was exerting very strong pressure against the International Settlements at Shanghai and Amoy and the British Concession at Tientsin. Predictably, Brenan maintained that this "more aggressive attitude now being adopted by the Japanese towards our concessions and interests in China is not, I think, based on confidence of victory, but is rather a symptom of growing desperation on the part of the military authorities, who feel that they must show some results."[18] Sir John's assessment was somewhat overstated. The Japanese army was frustrated and irritated, rather than desperate. The military leaders (and surely the civilian "moderates" as well) felt that Britain's moral and material support had encouraged Chiang to continue the struggle. They also believed that the foreign settlements and concessions were important stumbling blocks in the path of Japanese efforts to absorb occupied China into the new order. As the Chief of Staff of Japan's Central China Expeditionary Army emphasized in July:

There is no doubt that the foreign settlements are disturbing the strengthening of discipline and order as well as affecting adversely economics and finance. To take some drastic measures against this state of affairs is the best way . . . to make the Third Powers abandon their pro-Chiang policy and so awaken China and the Chinese people from their ominous dream of "dependence upon Europe and America." . . . The problem of the foreign settlement is one of the most important questions relating to the construction of the New Order in East Asia . . . and it is our belief that the solution of this problem will constitute an important part of the settlement of the Incident.[19]

Clearly, the Japanese hoped that pressure against the strongholds of Britain's position in China would produce a Far Eastern Munich and shatter Chungking's resistance. The "extremists" believed that it also would decisively strengthen their hand in the controversy over an unlimited Japanese alliance with Germany and Italy.

Shanghai, with its great concentration of British wealth, was a particularly inviting target. Throughout 1938 Japan had pressed the Municipal Council to take resolute steps to maintain order and give her greater representation in all branches of the Settlement's administration. In early 1939 the biggest wave of terrorism that Shanghai had ever seen broke out, and even the Reformed Government's Foreign Minister was assassinated. Japan responded to these political crimes with five demands, the most important of which was that the Settlement authorities allow Japanese gendarmerie to take "necessary measures" for the suppression of terrorism. Sir Archibald Clark Kerr feared that Japan might use force in Shanghai, and he asked Chiang to persuade Chinese terrorists to "lay off." The Municipal Council, for its part, was willing to let the Japanese gendarmerie cooperate with the Settlement police, but refused to let them take independent action.[20] A further though much smaller wave of terrorism erupted in April, and on May 2 the Japanese naval authorities in Shanghai declared that the Municipal Council still had not taken adequate measures to suppress crime. The next day the Japanese Foreign Ministry gave Craigie a memorandum calling for a revision of the Land Regulations, which had constituted the legal basis of the Settlement administration since the 1860's, so as to make them less "incongruous with the new situation of today" and give the Japanese "full and fair expression" in the governing of the city. The British reply of May 19 maintained that "the present moment is inopportune for discussions on this subject." The Japanese government found this response unsatisfactory, and a Foreign Ministry spokesman told the Japanese press on May 24 that Japan had every right to resort to force against terrorists in the Settlement.[21] This statement seemed to portend intensified Japanese pressure against Shanghai. By this time, however, both Tokyo and London were preoccupied with the trouble that had arisen in Amoy and Tientsin, and it turned out that Tokyo was not prepared to make further moves in Shanghai before seeing the outcome of the disputes in the other two cities.

At Amoy, where there was a small international settlement on the island of Kulangsu, the pro-Japanese chairman of the local chamber of commerce was murdered on May 11. The next day

200 Japanese marines landed in the Settlement and conducted a search for the assassins. Then on May 15 Japan's consul-general demanded more Japanese representation both on the Kulangsu Municipal Council and on the police force.[22] The British regarded the landing as illegal and registered a strong protest in Tokyo, but received an unsatisfactory reply. Clark Kerr, who had been told by the Chinese government that the Japanese occupation of Kulangsu was in the nature of a test and had a grave bearing on the future of the International Settlement in Shanghai, suggested to the Foreign Office that the British send a naval party to Amoy. Impressed by the notion that acquiescence in Japan's action at Kulangsu would lead to increased Japanese threats at Shanghai, Britain, along with the United States and France, landed sailors on May 17 to "join" the Japanese. When Tokyo asked for an explanation of this step, Ambassador Craigie said that since the Settlement was an international one, any force that went ashore should be international.[23] Negotiations on the Japanese demands for increased representation were held throughout the summer. By October Japan had given way on some major points, and an agreement was reached.

The most serious crisis in Anglo-Japanese relations prior to the outbreak of war in Europe was the one at Tientsin in the summer of 1939. Craigie later likened it to "a volcano whose sudden eruption threw into the political firmament all the pent-up feelings and animosities which had been simmering and boiling beneath the surface since Japan's invasion of China two years earlier."[24] The Japanese had three major grievances against Britain at Tientsin. First, they believed that Chinese guerrillas used the British Concession there as a base and that Britain was lax in suppressing anti-Japanese terrorism and propaganda. Second (and an issue destined to be more important, if less emotional, than terrorism), the Concession authorities did not prohibit the circulation of *fapi,* and British banks were averse to dealing in Federal Reserve Bank notes. Third, the banks had refused to hand over the silver reserves deposited by Chinese government banks. Tokyo wanted this silver to be used as backing for the Federal Reserve Bank currency.[25] Harassed by guerrillas and envious of the wealth tied up in the British and French Concessions, the Japanese felt that they would never be able to consolidate their control over North China until they induced Britain to collaborate with their currency schemes and help suppress Chinese patriots operating out of Tientsin.

In October 1938 the British began to search for a solution to the problem of the silver reserves. Consul-General E. G. Jamieson believed that the Japanese were actually less interested in gaining control of the silver than in preventing it from being shipped out of the city. He and his French counterpart agreed on a scheme to place the silver under seal. The plan was acceptable to the Chinese, who feared that Japan might try to seize the reserves if an agreement was not reached. Japanese officials, though concurring in principle with the scheme, were afraid that allowing the silver to be sealed would prejudice their claim that the final disposal of the reserves should rest with them. And they wanted the sealing to take place, if at all, in the presence of representatives from the Federal Reserve Bank and the Japanese army. Negotiations on these two points dragged on into 1939.[26]

In the meantime, a dispute had developed after the British had refused to turn over to Japan a guerrilla leader, Ssu Ching-wu, who had been arrested in the Concession in late September 1938. Japanese authorities had provided Britain with the intelligence leading to the arrest and then had produced evidence that Ssu had used the British and French Concessions as a base for anti-Japanese activities. But it was Britain's policy to hand over suspects only if there was direct evidence that they had committed a crime; purely political offenders were to be interned. As one observer in the Foreign Office stated, "To do anything more would be repugnant to British ideas of justice and would arouse the hostility of the Chinese Government."[27] Craigie and Jamieson urged London to depart from its policy in this case, but the Foreign Office, backed by Clark Kerr, rejected their advice.[28] Enraged by this decision, Japan erected barriers around the British and French Concessions in December. Non-Japanese who wished to enter or leave the two Concessions were required to have passes. When Craigie complained to Tokyo, the Foreign Ministry replied that these measures would not be relaxed until British authorities at Tientsin suppressed anti-Japanese activities there and assumed "an attitude in conformity with the new situation in North China."[29]

Despite the uncompromising tone of this reply, Japan did take steps to relax the situation. General Homma, who was regarded as sympathetic to Britain, took command of the Japanese troops at Tientsin in January 1939 and removed the barriers for a while during the following month. Friction soon developed again, however, and the British and French Concessions were then encircled with electrified wire.[30] In late March Craigie suggested to London that Major-General Piggott should visit Tientsin and "use his influence with the Japanese military authorities in the same way as he did in Shanghai in June 1938." The Foreign Office approved of this idea, and Piggott arrived in Tientsin on April 3. After several meetings with the Japanese military, he warned Ambassador Clark Kerr and the Foreign Office that the situation was very serious, explaining that there were in fact anti-Japanese organizations operating in the Concession and that the Japanese were bewildered and resentful at not receiving British cooperation. Piggott's observations infuriated the Foreign Offce. Brenan, for example, thought it "unfortunate that we have to go on employing an agent who is so fanatical and undiscriminating in his attachment to the people who are practically our open enemies."[31]

On April 9, as Piggott was leaving Tientsin, an official of the Peking puppet regime was assassinated in the British Concession by a band of Chinese. This incident was especially serious in that it seemed to confirm Japan's accusation that the Concession was a center of terrorist activity. British and Japanese authorities collaborated in apprehending four suspects. The Japanese interrogated the men, two of whom confessed, and then gave all four to the British. Both the Concession's police chief and Britain's superintending consul, convinced that the suspects who had confessed were guilty, assured the Japanese that all four Chinese would be handed over to the Peking regime for trial. While in British custody, however, the men who had confessed retracted their earlier statement, claiming that the Japanese had extracted it from them by torture.[32] Consul-General Jamieson urged Clark Kerr and the Foreign Office to allow the four men to be turned over for trial anyway. Craigie agreed, warning that Japan might use force to get her way. But Clark Kerr, who was under heavy pressure from Madame Chiang Kai-shek to take a firm stand, said that such a move would be repugnant to his conscience and difficult to justify to Chungking.[33] The Foreign Office, unaware of the assurances given by the superintending consul and the police chief, sided with Clark Kerr. Though Halifax had at first favored handing over the suspects, the Far Eastern Department had convinced him that there was insufficient evidence to warrant it.[34]

Had the Foreign Office been aware at this stage of the promises made by Britain's officials on the scene, its attitude might have been different. In any case, Japan concluded that the British were procrastinating and acting in bad faith. She set June 7 as the deadline for turning over the suspects. The British informed Tokyo on June 6 that though they would deal more ruthlessly with terrorists in future cases, they were not prepared to surrender the four Chinese in question. The Foreign Office was inclined to doubt that Japan would react violently to this stand. Halifax, for example, told the Cabinet on June 7 that the Japanese were having difficulties in China and were therefore trying to stir up trouble for Britain, but that there would probably not be any serious developments in the Tientsin situation.[35] Jamieson, however, warned on June 9 that Japan meant business and implored London to reverse its decision. Then, two days later, he told the Foreign Office for the first time that British authorities in Tientsin had agreed to hand over the men, and insisted that Japanese demands were legally and morally justified.[36] Craigie supported Jamieson's appeals, emphasizing that "we are risking our whole position in North China involving ourselves at an inappropriate moment in serious trouble with Japan on account of legal niceties which I frankly find myself unable to appreciate." Clark Kerr objected: "The issue seems to be a nicety of morals rather than of law." Yielding at Tientsin, he added, would mean increased Japanese pressure at Amoy and Shanghai.[37]

Jamieson's message of June 11 made the Foreign Office realize that Britain had stumbled into potentially serious and embarrassing trouble. Halifax's advisers believed, however, that it was too late to change course; if Britain were suddenly to announce that new information had persuaded her to turn over the suspects, this would look to the rest of the world like capitulation.[38] At this juncture, the furthest that London would go to forestall drastic action by Tokyo was to propose the establishment of an advisory committee, consisting of one British, one Japanese, and one neutral member, to decide whether there was a *prima facie* case against the four Chinese. The Americans agreed to permit their consul-general at Tientsin to serve as the neutral, but Japan rejected the scheme and proceeded to blockade the British and French Concessions on June 14. The Foreign Office at first hoped this blockade was merely a "damp squib" and a face-saving measure on Japan's part.[39] Such optimism soon dissolved in the face of a Japanese army announcement that the crisis could no longer be settled by the "mere delivery of criminals"; for the blockade to be lifted, Britain would have to abandon her support of Chungking and cooperate in the building of the new order.[40] In short, Japan wanted to make the crisis a decisive test case. As the Foreign Office asserted on June 16: "We are now faced with a show-down with the Japanese in regard to the whole foreign position in China."[41] Craigie later wrote that young Japanese officers "were determined to exploit the affair to the point of war" and that the British had information "showing that the Japanese General Staff had their plans fully laid for a single-handed war with Great Britain."[42]

From Britain's point of view, the showdown had come at the wrong time and place. In addition to the fact that her side of the argument rested on shaky ground, she could not count on Washington's help. The United States had few economic interests in Tientsin, and American action in support of the British would have aroused the wrath of Congressional isolationists at a time when the Roosevelt administration was trying to secure an important revision of neutrality legislation. To make matters worse for Britain, European affairs—particularly the mounting German-Polish tension over Danzig—were a major source of worry. Anglo-Japanese friction would surely tempt Hitler to move decisively in Europe; in fact the Foreign Office felt "we cannot exclude the possibility that the Japanese are acting in collusion with the German Government."[43]

Acutely aware of all these circumstances, Sir Robert Craigie wanted to open negotiations about Tientsin. In his opinion, unless Britain made some fundamental changes in policy, or at least in tactics, there was serious danger of a conflict with Japan. Clark Kerr took a different view of the matter. He maintained that conciliating Japan would be disastrous to Britain's position in East Asia and might even cause the Chinese to throw their hand in and cooperate with the Japanese. If talks were to be held, he stressed, they should be preceded by "a declaration of an intention to retaliate in respect of all Japanese acts of aggression."[44] Sir Percy Loraine, Britain's ambassador in Rome, also warned against conciliation: "Our future relations with Italy will be deeply affected by [the] degree of determination which His Majesty's Government show in dealing with the direct and symptomatic Japanese threat to specifically British interests in Tientsin."[45] These appeals by Clark Kerr and Loraine for a firm stance were in line with sentiments expressed by public opinion in Britain, which was angered by reports that the Japanese were abusing British nationals at the barricades in Tientsin. *The Times*, for example, warned the Cabinet that "passive submission to the blockade . . . will not satisfy the British public." The *Manchester Guardian* called for reprisals against Tokyo, as did some members of Parliament. Important British commercial groups also pressed for a hard line.[46]

It was in this heated atmosphere that the Chamberlain government tried to formulate an effective response to Japan's actions in North China. At a Cabinet meeting on June 14, Halifax said that if the trouble at Tientsin persisted, Britain should seriously consider economic sanctions. Prime Minister Chamberlain, who felt that the Foreign Office had handled the situation poorly, expressed uneasiness about this suggestion. He stressed that sanctions had not worked in the past and that, owing to the tension in Europe, the British could not safely send a fleet to East Asia. Halifax admitted the force of these considerations, but warned that if Britain yielded at Tientsin, she would come under increasing pressure elsewhere in the Far East. "It was difficult," he concluded, "to hold the balance between action which might involve us in serious difficulties and action which would result in our being subjected to further pressure from the Japanese." The Cabinet decided that the question of reprisals should be examined again.[47]

On June 16 Halifax circulated a memorandum noting that the Tientsin crisis was the culmination of an anti-British offensive conducted by Japan for the past two years. In his view, Britain had three options: to compromise and cooperate with the Japanese; to do nothing; and to adopt retaliatory measures. The memorandum ruled out the first course, "since it would lead to the downfall of China, it would put Japan in a better position to undermine the British Empire in the East, and it would alienate America, whose goodwill is essential to us in the West as well as in the East." The second course was also deemed inappropriate, because a passive policy would only encourage Japan, Germany, and Italy to undermine Britain's "general world position." The third course, the memorandum maintained, provided the only chance of frustrating Japanese ambitions to gain control over East Asia and advance southward against the British Empire.[48]

On the same day that this memorandum was circulated, however, a report prepared by an informal committee—composed of representatives from the Colonial Office and the Board of Trade as well as from the Foreign Office—emphasized the grave dangers involved in any reprisals broad enough to be effective. The committee pointed out that Japan might well retaliate and that, if she did, it was unlikely that America would join Britain in fighting back. The report accordingly concluded that there were "strong arguments for seeking to keep the incident localised if possible and searching for a solution by negotiation."[49] The committee's conclusion was given strong support by a Chiefs of Staff appreciation completed two days later. This paper stated that if Japan took warlike measures in response to British reprisals, a fleet of at least eight capital ships would be required to deal with her. But since Anglo-Japanese hostilities would probably cause Germany and Italy to take action in Europe, Britain could afford to send only two capital ships to the Far East without jeopardizing the security of her home waters and the Mediterranean. A force of two ships (the same number sent east in 1941, with disastrous results) could not prevent the Japanese from investing Singapore. The Chiefs of Staff concluded that unless the active cooperation of the United States could be obtained, "it would not be justifiable, from the military point of view, having regard to the existing international situation, to take any avoidable action which might lead to hostilities with Japan."[50]

The Cabinet Committee on Foreign Policy met on June 19 to consider what the British should do in the light of these three reports. Admiral Lord Ernle Chatfield noted that Britain's recent strategic calculations had been based "on the assumption that we could avoid being involved in hostilities with Japan" and that it was therefore not surprising the Chiefs of Staff thought it most undesirable for London to become embroiled in East Asia. Impressed by these views, Halifax did not urge the committee to approve economic measures. Instead, he brought up Craigie's negotiation proposal, stating that negotiations might place Britain in a "very humiliating position," but that on the whole he favored them. Chamberlain also thought it best "to endeavour to reach some settlement with the Japanese on the most favourable terms obtainable," though this would no doubt expose Britain "to considerable humiliation and criticism." Presumably fearing another Munich, Oliver Stanley objected that Japan might raise her demands "to an extreme limit" and compel Britain to make a "very humiliating surrender," in which case Hitler and Mussolini might take action leading to war in Europe. Chamberlain retorted that he did not see why things need go that far.[51]

The discussion was continued at another meeting the next day. Chatfield reported that he had asked the Chiefs of Staff "whether it might not be advisable to withdraw practically all our Naval forces from the Eastern Mediterranean rather than to leave the Far East open to the Japanese naval forces." The Chiefs of Staff had agreed to reconsider this matter, though the Admiralty did not like the idea of withdrawing forces from the Mediterranean. Commenting on Chatfield's report, Chamberlain said the prospect of losing control of the Mediterranean led him to conclude that Britain should make "every endeavour to reach an early settlement of the dispute at Tientsin" and should consider sending a fleet to the Far East only "if Japan made our position there quite intolerable." Halifax agreed, pointing out that dispatching a fleet to Singapore would not even prevent the Japanese from overrunning Hong Kong and Britain's position in China.[52] His point was reinforced by the Chiefs of Staff in a report made on June 24. This new appreciation also emphasized that sending east a fleet "strong enough to accept action with the Japanese" would have a "bad effect" in Egypt, Turkey, and the Arab world and might encourage Spain to side definitely with the Axis.[53]

Halifax's advisers did not like the gloomy conclusions of all these high-level discussions and reports. Nigel Ronald, for example, complained that "we are too prone to believe that our adversaries are less afraid of us than we are of them." Robert Howe wanted the Cabinet to prepare to take action that would show Japan and the world how seriously Britain took the Tientsin situation.[54] Such views of course were quite out of line with those held by Chamberlain and many of his colleagues. Not only was the Prime Minister reluctant to withdraw British forces from the Mediterranean, but he also felt "it was impossible to believe that if we became involved in the Far East, Germany would not take advantage of the situation."[55]

At a meeting of the Committee of Imperial Defence on June 26, Chamberlain stated more categorically than ever that Britain should not take retaliatory action which might lead to war with Japan. War Minister Leslie Hore-Belisha suggested that the British might be able to take a firm line if the Soviet Union agreed to help. The Soviets were currently engaged in a serious conflict with Japan at Nomonhan, on the Manchurian-Mongolian border, and would presumably be willing to extend the Anglo-Soviet talks to the Far East. But Chamberlain dismissed Hore-Belisha's idea: "Judging by their obstructive attitude in recent negotiations," he had "little hope of getting any help from Russia." Inskip and Chatfield then asked what Britain would do if her talks with Japan failed. The Prime Minister saw no need to make any such decision yet. Sir John Simon agreed, stating that "if Japan did not want war it should be possible to reach agreement," and suggesting that "the Foreign Office should consider what could be done to meet the Japanese point of view. Were we, for instance, prepared to see the end of the concession in Tientsin?" Halifax replied that Japan apparently did not wish to interfere with British authority in the Concession. In his view, the currency question would be the most difficult to solve. In any case, he concluded, "there would have to be some form of bargain with the Japanese, and it did not seem impossible for us to end the dispute, at a price."[56]

Thus, Chamberlain and his associates had decided to rest their hopes on negotiations with Japan, rather than take retaliatory action.* Like Simon and Halifax, the Prime Minister was hopeful that talks with Tokyo could be successful. In his opinion, the Japanese would not "wish to push matters to extremes: they had their 'plate full' in China and did not want war with us."[57] Though he thought it "maddening to have to hold our hand in the face of

---

* This decision, it should be noted in passing, met with Australia's approval. The Australians thought Britain "had gone into this business [at Tientsin] 'on the wrong leg' "; in their opinion, London should have followed Jamieson's advice. Now that trouble had arisen, they wanted the British to explore every possibility of resolving it—"short of accepting intolerable humiliation." See minutes of special meeting, June 28, 1939, CAB 2/9.

such humiliations" as the British had suffered at Tientsin, he believed there was little choice.[58] Sanctions might well lead to war in East Asia, which in turn would encourage Hitler and perhaps Mussolini to move aggressively in Europe. Britain would then be confronted with a situation her defense forces could not handle.

Throughout the British records for June, there are statements implying that the Chamberlain government would have been willing to take risks had it been assured of full American support.[59] If London's previous discussions with Washington about joint naval action and economic sanctions are any indication, such statements were somewhat hollow. In any case, no attempt was made at this stage to gain America's cooperation in a policy of reprisals, presumably because Britain realized that such an effort would be futile. The Foreign Office did try to get American diplomatic backing for the coming negotiations, but the most Secretary of State Hull would do was to state publicly on June 19 that the United States was concerned with the "broader aspects" of the Tientsin crisis. Britain was compelled to go ahead on her own.[60]

On June 23 Foreign Minister Arita accepted Sir Robert Craigie's proposal, authorized by Halifax after the June 19 meeting of the Cabinet Committee on Foreign Policy, that negotiations should be held in Tokyo. Arita assured Craigie that only local issues would be discussed and that the Japanese would ask for nothing incompatible with the maintenance of British authority in the Concession, but he did not explicitly state that the blockade would be lifted before the talks began.[61] Sir Robert was pleased, because the Hiranuma government had been able to overcome the military's insistence that any negotiations should be held at Tientsin. In a letter to Sir Alexander Cadogan, he reported that Hiranuma definitely wanted a settlement and that "for the first time since the Customs Agreement the freedom of decision of the Army in China in relation to important China questions is being curtailed."[62] From his vantage point in London, Ronald expressed a different opinion:

I think there can be little doubt that all Japanese hold remarkably similar opinions as regard the objects at which Japan should aim: the Central Gov. only differ from the wild men of the Army and Navy in the matters of the pace at which Japan should proceed and the tactics she should employ. The fact of the Japanese Gov. agreeing to negotiations in Tokyo instead of at Tientsin does not indicate any divergence of view between the Gov. and the Army in China as to the end to be aimed at— in the present case the disabusing of the Chinese of the idea that they have anything to hope for from the British.

Cadogan, for his part, agreed that the aim of all Japanese was the same, but he felt that "the question of pace is most important. In present circumstances we do want to gain time."[63]

In the following weeks, the British discussed what line to take during the negotiations. Ambassador Craigie, pointing out that the currency question would be the main issue, favored concessions on it if necessary, though he acknowledged that the Americans and the French were interested parties and would have to be consulted before any proposals were made. In his view, a conciliatory British attitude would pave the way for a settlement of the Tientsin crisis, which in turn would enhance the position of the moderates in Japan and might well lead to close Anglo-Japanese relations. Clearly, he believed as strongly as ever that Britain's best interests lay in appeasing Tokyo rather than playing for a Sino-Japanese stalemate.[64] Clark Kerr, by contrast, thought that there was "no real room for compromise about currency" and that the British should be prepared to take strong measures against Japan in the event of a breakdown in the talks. According to Sir Archibald, if Britain took a soft line, both her position in East Asia and China's resistance would be undermined; whereas if she continued to hold her ground, the Japanese "will end by giving up the struggle and China will emerge as an independent nation."[65] Clark Kerr's opposition to conciliation received strong support from Ambassador Lindsay in Washington, who warned London that any surrender of principles would have "a more than unfortunate effect" on the United States.[66]

Halifax and his advisers did not share Craigie's views about the efficacy of conciliation and the good will of the Japanese "moderates." Even though by July the Foreign Office had apparently begun to doubt that Japan was nearing the end of her tether, the officials agreed with Clark Kerr that Britain should continue to work for the failure of Tokyo's venture in China.[67] Halifax and his advisers did want, however, to settle the Tientsin crisis, or at least to prevent the forthcoming negotiations from breaking down. Accordingly, they were prepared to compromise on non-essential issues and perhaps even on the question of the silver reserves. But they (and the Treasury as well) were unwilling to compromise on the currency issue, because any such deal would alienate America and cripple China's resistance.[68] Searching for some way to improve Craigie's bargaining position, London pressed Washington to join any discussions that were held on the currency question. Not surprisingly, Washington refused.[69] London also considered giving Craigie a "weapon" to strengthen his hand in the negotiations. Specifically, the Foreign Office wanted a bill introduced into Parliament empowering the government to place "such restrictions as were deemed appropriate upon the goods of any other country." The Board of Trade and the top officials in the Treasury objected that such a step would lead to increased trouble with Japan, and nothing was done.[70]

Meanwhile, Foreign Minister Arita and Premier Hiranuma were under strong pressure from the Japanese army to demand, as a prerequisite for negotiations, that Britain agree to help establish the new order in China. Thus, when Craigie and Arita held their first "preliminary" meeting on July 15, Arita proposed a formula that would "clear the path" for discussion of all outstanding questions relating to Tientsin.

The British Government fully recognise the actual situation in China, where hostilities on a large scale are in progress and note that, as long as that state of affairs continues to exist, the Japanese forces in China have special requirements for the purpose of safeguarding their own security and maintaining public order in the regions under their control, and they have to take the necessary steps in order to suppress or remove any such acts or causes as will obstruct them or benefit their enemy. The British Government, therefore, will refrain and cause the British authorities in China to refrain from all acts and measures which will interfere with the Japanese forces in attaining their above-mentioned objects.

As Craigie pointed out, there were three grounds for objection to this formula: it related to China as a whole, not just to Tientsin; it asked the British to agree without qualification to any measures the Japanese military authorities deemed necessary; and it implied that Britain had interfered with the maintenance of public order in the past.[71] Nonetheless, Craigie urged London to go "some way" to meet Japan's point of view, warning that a rejection of the formula would abort the talks. Clark Kerr maintained that it would be better to abandon the negotiations than to accept anything like Arita's proposal, but the Foreign Office sided with Craigie: "We should go as far as we prudently can to meet [the] Minister for Foreign Affairs on [the] preliminary formula." Halifax and his advisers told Sir Robert that they particularly wanted the phrase "take the necessary steps" deleted and the last sentence altered. They did want other amendments, but these were not essential.[72]

Left with considerable latitude, Craigie was able to reach an agreement on the text of the formula. The phrase "take the necessary steps" was removed, and the last sentence was amended to read:

His Majesty's Government have no intention of countenancing any act or measures prejudicial to [the] attainment of the above-mentioned objects by Japanese forces and they will take this opportunity to confirm their policy in this respect by making it plain to British authorities and British nationals in China that they should refrain from such acts and measures.

Otherwise, the wording (including the reference to Japan's "special requirements") was virtually unchanged from Arita's original proposal.[73] Craigie later wrote that "the formula, stripped of its verbiage, did no more than recognize a situation of fact and involved no new action or fresh commitment on our part."[74] This contention was somewhat misleading. Britain had adopted a conciliatory stance in order to forestall the potentially disastrous consequences of a breakdown of negotiations. In particular, she had for the moment at least withdrawn her moral support of the Chinese cause—an important step at a time when the morale of the two sides seemed the decisive factor in the war. Hence, her adherence to the formula represented a departure, albeit temporary, from her policy of "benevolent neutrality" toward China and could indeed be interpreted as a tentative first step toward appeasement of Japan. It did not represent, however, a Far Eastern Munich.

The Chamberlain government did not want the Chinese or the British public to get the impression that the formula embodied a betrayal of Chiang Kai-shek or a change in Britain's policy. Consequently, in announcing the agreement to Parliament on July 24, Chamberlain and Halifax said that the Craigie-Arita understanding "had nothing to do with His Majesty's Government's China policy but was a question of fact." A week later the Prime Minister elaborated on this interpretation in the House of Commons:

> The formula was a statement of fact. It did not denote any change of policy. It did not denote the recognition of any belligerent rights on the part of Japan. It did not betray any British interest in China, and it did not purport or intend to surrender any rights belonging to third parties. Let me say once again that this Government will not reverse its policy in the Far East at the request of another Power, and I wish to add that we have not been asked by Japan to do so.[75]

Notwithstanding such attempts to prevent an uproar in Britain and China, opinion of the formula in both countries was for the most part very critical. According to the *North China Star* in Tientsin, Chinese circles feared Britain was abandoning China as she had earlier abandoned Czechoslovakia. In Shanghai the *China Press* called the formula "another Munich agreement," and *Oriental Affairs* thought it lopsided and dangerous. British commercial interests in China were apparently divided in their opinion: *Finance and Commerce* supported the understanding, whereas the China Association and the British Chamber of Commerce in Shanghai strongly opposed it.[76] In Britain, opinion was on the whole unfavorable to the agreement. *The Times* approved of the formula, but the *New Statesman and Nation* denounced it as a surrender to Japanese pressure, and the *Spectator* complained it was "a vague and perplexing document, and least satisfactory where it is most intelligible." Perhaps the most perceptive observation was made by the *Manchester Guardian*: "Either the Government has deceived itself or it has deceived China; it is not likely to deceive Japan for long."[77]

Predictably, the Chinese government was deeply disturbed by the agreement. According to Clark Kerr, there could be no doubt that Chiang and his associates believed "they have had a raw deal and that their suspicions have been well aroused." They were particularly concerned that the formula seemed to infringe China's sovereignty by implying *de facto* recognition of Japan's position in the occupied areas.[78] Testing Britain's willingness to continue to support them, the Chinese urged the Chamberlain government to make a new contribution to the currency-stabilization fund, which had almost disappeared as a result of Tokyo's currency war and the Tientsin crisis. London gave little thought to this proposal.[79] China also pressed for some £2.8 million in credits, the remaining unused part of the £3 million allotted by the Chamberlain government to Chungking in late 1938. Negotiations on the details of this further grant had progressed slowly during the first half of 1939, but an agreement had finally been reached in July. Notwithstanding Chinese pressure, the British decided in early August to postpone the signing of this understanding because it might have a bad effect on the Anglo-Japanese negotiations.[80] This decision scarcely assuaged Chinese suspicions.

Chungking's reaction to the Craigie-Arita agreement was predictable; Washington's was not. As Cordell Hull later wrote, the United States was disturbed that "Japan had won a victory in her never ending quest for recognition of 'special rights,' 'special interests,' or 'special requirements' in China."[81] Hoping to stiffen Britain's attitude (and to satisfy Congressional demands for action against Tokyo), the Roosevelt administration gave Japan notice on July 26 of its intention to terminate the American-Japanese Commercial Treaty of 1911. This meant that in six months the United States would be free to restrict or end her trade with

Japan.[82] The Chamberlain government was disappointed at not being consulted about the move. Foreign Secretary Halifax, for example, told the Committee of Imperial Defence on July 27 that "if we had known of it earlier, it might have led us to take a different line."[83] On the whole, however, the government was quite pleased at the shock that Washington had given Tokyo. Though the British decided not to take "parallel action," they did feel in a better position to adopt a firm line in their formal conversations with Japan.[84]

These formal negotiations had already begun on July 24. At the opening meeting, the Japanese had presented an agenda consisting of twelve points, the first eight of which dealt with the maintenance of order in Tientsin. During the succeeding meetings, provisional agreement on these points was reached rather quickly; even the problem of the four suspects was settled fairly easily when Japan produced new evidence against the men and Britain agreed to hand them over for trial.[85] The final four points on the Japanese agenda consisted of economic issues. Japan particularly insisted that the British must prohibit the circulation of *fapi* in their Concession and turn over the silver reserves. She indicated, moreover, that the Tientsin crisis could not be settled until an economic agreement, as well as an understanding on the maintenance of order, was concluded. Since London was not inclined even to discuss the currency and silver questions, the negotiations soon reached an impasse.[86]

Craigie feared that if the talks broke down, the extremists would gain control over Japanese policy and conclude a military alliance with Germany. Sir Robert accordingly urged London to allow the transfer of the silver reserves to the Federal Reserve Bank or the Yokohama Specie Bank if Japan would agree to keep the silver under seal and to withdraw her demands on the currency question. He felt that Tokyo would accept this compromise, paving the way for an Anglo-Japanese rapprochement.[87] Clark Kerr, however, protested that a compromise would have a disastrous effect in Chungking and Washington and would certainly not divert Japan from her intention of expelling Britain from

China. Sir Archibald saw little to choose between Japanese extremists and Japanese moderates and felt that in any case concessions would strengthen the former, not the latter. It was his opinion that the American abrogation of the commercial treaty had
put the British in a favorable position to take a firm stand against
Japan.[88] Craigie countered these arguments by expressing the view
that Washington's move was probably "just another flash in the
American pan" and by insisting that Hiranuma and Arita wanted
friendship with Britain and would be helped by concessions. Sir
Robert added:

Sir A. Clark Kerr appears to advocate a continuation of [the] present
policy of openly assisting China and obstructing Japan at every turn up
to the point at which in any particular case that obstruction becomes
too dangerous in a particular case or contingency. Time has passed
when such a policy can be pursued with impunity. It must lead either to
successive humiliations or else to application of *solo* sanctions, which
would in turn land us quickly in open hostilities with Japan, perhaps in
a world war. I am not blind to difficulties in the way of [the] alternative
policy I recommend, but at least it is constructive and points towards
peace.[89]

Clearly, the clash between the two ambassadors was sharper than
ever. On the one side, there was Craigie's "realism" and his faith
in the Japanese moderates; on the other side, there was Clark
Kerr's passionate belief in the justice and vitality of the Chinese
cause.

London had a very difficult decision to make. In a Cabinet
meeting on August 2—just as the last stage of the Danzig crisis
was beginning to unfold—Halifax made the interesting comment
that "the position in the Far East was now causing him more
anxiety than the position in any other part of the world."[90] He
and his advisers agreed with Clark Kerr that concessions on the
currency and silver questions would have serious repercussions in
Chungking and Washington and would be of no help to British
economic interests. But the Foreign Office feared that a breakdown of the negotiations would mean increased Anglo-Japanese
trouble, perhaps leading to a dangerous campaign of reprisals and
counter-reprisals. In such an eventuality, active American support

would be problematical. More important, Hitler might be encouraged to use force to "solve" the Danzig dispute. In fact, Ambassador Nevile Henderson in Berlin told London that

nothing would, of course, be more calculated to discourage Herr Hitler from attempting a gamble than an early and satisfactory settlement of our present dispute with Japan.
It may be taken for granted that Britain's difficulties in [the] Far East are [the] principal argument used by extremists to egg Hitler on.

There was much force in Henderson's contention. Still, as one observer in the Foreign Office suggested, might it not be that a firm British stance against Japan would have an even greater deterrent effect on Hitler?[91] In any case, it would seem that the Tientsin crisis played a far more significant part in the origins of the European war than has hitherto been realized.

In addition to worrying about the interaction between East Asian and European developments, Halifax and his advisers puzzled over the accuracy of Craigie's distinction between moderates and extremists in Japan. Sir George Sansom, in London on leave, examined this question in a memorandum of August 3. According to Sansom, Britain did not "have any really useful friends in Japan. All Japanese want a 'new order' in Asia, and a 'new order' involves the ultimate displacement of Great Britain in the Far East." Though acknowledging that there were differences in the methods used by the extremists and the moderates, he maintained that concessions on major issues would not help the British. Even compromises on minor issues would be "of dubious value in a struggle which has so far not developed between extremist and moderate forces in Japan."[92] The Foreign Office shared Sansom's view that the extremists and the moderates had the same goals. The officials thought, however, that since Hiranuma and Arita would be less inclined than the military to subject Britain to drastic methods, London should try to strengthen the position of these two men.[93]

With one eye on Chungking and Washington and the other on Hitler and the Japanese extremists, Halifax defined the line that the British should take:

We must clearly do our best to avoid breakdown: by going as far as we can to meet [the] Japanese—and by avoiding every possible delay in [the] handling of [the] larger issues. . . . There is a point beyond which we cannot go—and the dangers of what would be generally regarded as [a] surrender on vital principles are not less great than [the] danger of [a] breakdown of conversations.[94]

In other words, he evidently hoped to find an acceptable half-way point between making concessions of principle on the economic questions and refusing to advance any compromise proposals. This task was very difficult. Despairing from the outset of discovering any middle ground on the currency issue, the Foreign Office devoted most of its attention to the silver problem.* Halifax and his advisers gave thought to a proposal that the silver should be neutralized and put under seal, but Craigie indicated that the Japanese would not accept this arrangement. As for Sir Robert's own suggestion that Britain should allow the transfer of the reserves, the officials felt that this went too far.[95]

The final decisions on the economic issues were made in mid-August. In an important memorandum of August 12, Sir George Mounsey warned that if the British even entered into bilateral discussions with Japan about the currency and silver questions, China would be alarmed and offended, and the United States and the rest of the world would be suspicious. He therefore maintained that London should agree to discuss the economic issues with Tokyo only if the talks were "enlarged so as to include all

* London did consider one rather curious solution of the currency question. In July Dr. Hjalmar Schacht (the former head of the Reichsbank) suggested to Governor Montagu Norman of the Bank of England that the British and the Japanese ask him to submit recommendations about the currency issue. Norman told Chamberlain that Schacht "could be relied upon not to try to steer matters in a way that was adverse to British interests." Halifax's advisers viewed the plan unfavorably. Vansittart asserted: "This seems to me a fantastic and dangerous idea. . . . How can we possibly trust Dr. Schacht?" Frank Ashton-Gwatkin of the Foreign Office nevertheless discussed the idea further with Schacht, who felt it would help maintain peace both in East Asia and in Europe. Halifax then put the plan to Craigie, but he showed no interest, and nothing came of it. See M. Norman to Wilson, July 9, 1939, and Oliphant to Wilson, July 16, 1939, Premier 1/315; memo. by Wilson, July 13, 1939, and a note in DBFP, 9.317: 271-73 [F7904/75/10]; FO to Craigie, July 25, 1939, DBFP, 9.386: 328-29 [F7906/75/10]; and Craigie to FO, Aug. 8, 1939, DBFP, 9.491: 425-26 [F8581/6457/10].

parties whose interests are affected." In his opinion, Japan would refuse to enlarge the negotiations, but would have no excuse to open hostilities with Britain.[96] Halifax endorsed Mounsey's view that London should stand firm by refusing to discuss the currency and silver problems on a purely Anglo-Japanese basis. As he explained to Chamberlain on August 16, he believed that if the British compromised, "we should be very likely to get very little positive result in exchange for the great worsening of our present position" vis-à-vis Washington and Chungking. Chamberlain, who was particularly impressed by Mounsey's memorandum, approved Halifax's decision. He feared that Japan would react badly, but felt that she "had made things impossible." Chamberlain made this additional comment: "I wish I could believe that by a 'compromise' on silver we could begin a new era of Anglo-Japanese agreement but I can't bring myself to such a belief. I see no practical alternative to that proposed, & we must deal with the consequences as best we can."[97] London's decision was transmitted to Craigie on August 17. He was instructed to tell Japan that if she wished to discuss the economic issues, all other interested powers would have to be consulted. Predictably, Japan was not willing to enlarge the discussions, and the negotiations were adjourned *sine die* on August 20.[98]

Thus, after departing from a policy of benevolent neutrality in July by agreeing to the Craigie-Arita formula, Britain decided in August not to conciliate the Japanese further. She feared that compromising on vital issues would both alienate America and undermine China's resistance, without moderating Japan's behavior and safeguarding British economic interests. In short, London decided that the disadvantages of even limited cooperation with the Japanese outweighed the dangers involved in a breakdown of talks. As soon as the Chamberlain government made its decision, it finally signed the agreement granting the Chinese some £2.8 million in credits. The Foreign Office also considered what steps could be taken to meet the greatly increased Japanese pressure that was expected to follow. In his memorandum of early August, Sir George Sansom had suggested that if and when negotiations broke down, Britain should adopt either a policy of non-resistance and evacuation of her nationals from North China, or a course of economic reprisals against the Japanese. Halifax favored a combination of these two alternatives. Hence, in a paper circulated on August 21, the Foreign Office indicated that in the event of trouble with Japan, the British should first denounce the Anglo-Japanese Commercial Treaty, then evacuate their nationals from North China, and, finally, take economic steps against Tokyo and give further financial assistance to the Chinese. Halifax and his officials thought this progressive program would alarm Japan and win America's sympathy. According to the memorandum, when the Japanese military came to realize that its policy of force was not succeeding, the way would be open for multilateral conversations possibly leading to a comprehensive East Asian settlement.[99]

The reaction expected by the Foreign Office never came. Before Japan had a chance to intensify her pressure against the British, she was stunned by the announcement of the German-Soviet Non-Aggression Pact of August 23. Frustrated in his efforts to secure an alliance with Tokyo, Hitler had turned to Moscow. This about-face was, as Craigie later wrote, "one of the worst jolts ever suffered by Japanese diplomacy."* Since May, Japan and the Soviet Union had been fighting at Nomonhan on the Manchurian-Mongolian border, and Tokyo presumably feared that the Non-Aggression Pact would enable the Soviets to concentrate on the East Asian situation without having to worry about their European flank. Not surprisingly, a wave of revulsion toward Germany swept Japan. Humiliated by the unexpected rapprochement, the Hiranuma government announced on August 25 that it would pursue an independent foreign policy "based on morality and irrespective of the international situation."[100] Three days later the

* See Robert L. Craigie, *Behind the Japanese Mask* (London: Hutchinson, 1946), p. 71. The German-Soviet pact was also a severe jolt to British diplomacy. One observer in the Foreign Office perceptively noted that the weakness London showed toward Japan in July "may perhaps have contributed to the Russian decision to make an agreement with the Germans rather than ourselves." Minute by Ashley Clarke on Coverly Price to FO, Aug. 16, 1939, FO F9229/87/10.

Cabinet fell and was succeeded by a new government under General Abe Nobuyuki, a retired soldier with little political experience.

The German-Soviet pact was the prelude to war in Europe, but it removed the possibility of an Anglo-Japanese conflict in East Asia. Japan was isolated and her foreign policy seemed adrift. It appeared that the way was now clear for Britain to get on better terms with Tokyo. London, however, was somewhat wary of "running after" the Japanese, not least because it was afraid of pushing China into the arms of the Soviet Union and Germany.[101] Ambassador Craigie, for his part, saw need for haste. On August 25 he urged the Foreign Office to "strike while the iron is hot and make [a] determined effort to detach Japan from the totalitarians before the Germans have explained away everything, if they can, to the satisfaction of [the] Japanese Government and people." Specifically, he wanted Britain to try to reach a settlement of the Tientsin crisis on the basis of sealing the silver reserves where they were. Once this was done, he added, the British could work for a peace settlement in East Asia "by which we might have to recognize Japanese preponderance in a nominally autonomous North China . . . but by which the economic position in Central China might be saved from further deterioration."[102]

On the day after Craigie sent this message, the Japanese embassy in London suggested on its own authority a formula to settle the Tientsin crisis: the silver would be sealed; and Tokyo would drop its demand about the suppression of *fapi* if Britain stated that she had no intention of obstructing the use of Federal Reserve Bank notes in her Concession. Foreign Secretary Halifax and his advisers told Craigie on August 29 that an agreement along these lines would be acceptable. If Tokyo would also accept such a formula, then Britain, America, France, and Japan could proceed to discuss wider economic questions informally. These discussions might in turn lead to negotiations for a comprehensive settlement. The Foreign Office agreed with Craigie that such a settlement would "probably have to include recognition in some form of Japan's special interests at least in North China." But they warned Sir Robert that, because of the danger of alienating the United States, Britain should not "initiate any proposals of that sort or even . . . take a leading part in mediation between the belligerents."[103] When the British told the Americans on September 1 about their ideas for solving the Tientsin crisis and reaching a general settlement in East Asia, Stanley Hornbeck of the State Department replied that "any policy of giving way to or even compromising with Japan would be worse than useless." This attitude brought London up short.[104]

By this time Hitler was invading Poland. Britain and France declared war on Germany on September 3. Japan stood aloof from the European conflict; hence the Chamberlain government saw no reason to consider sending a fleet to Singapore. In fact, it began withdrawing the major units of the China Squadron for service in the Indian Ocean and the Mediterranean. The British were now quite unable to exercise any significant military power in East Asia. This meant that they could afford less than ever to become embroiled with Tokyo. But it also meant, as one observer pointed out, that Britain was "really dependent on the United States for security in the Pacific . . . and if we decided to come to terms with Japan at the expense of China, American opinion will certainly turn against us, and leave us to fend for ourselves."[105] Thus, the British had to steer a middle course: one that was firm enough to satisfy Washington, yet not so rigid as to involve London in hostilities with the Japanese.[106] In practice, this middle course turned out to differ very little from the policy that Britain had pursued prior to September 1939, though it was marked perhaps by a somewhat stronger inclination than before to try to stay on friendly terms with Tokyo. But if the coming of war in Europe produced no major changes in British policy, it did cause Britain to assess her concerns in East Asia differently. Before the war, she was as preoccupied with saving her position in China as with safeguarding the Dominions and her formal empire in Asia. Now she was mainly interested in the latter problem. Nonetheless, she hoped that when the trouble in Europe was over, she could rebuild her influence and interests in China. This hope was to prove illusory.

Chapter eight

Conclusion

In this age of broken faith—and Treaties—there has been
nothing so blatant as Japan's aggression in China. It would
go sorely against the grain to compromise with it in
any circumstances.
　　　　　—Sir Alexander Cadogan, December 1938

If the European Powers would apply to the Far East even
a tenth of the flexibility of attitude which they display in
dealing with the problems of their own continent, the
attainment of stability in this part of the world would be
very simple indeed.
　　　　　—Prince Konoe, January 1938

BY LATE 1937 Britain could not but realize she was in the grip
of a global crisis that might lead to a world war and her ruin as
a first-class power. Though Italy's ambitions could by no means
be ignored, Germany was of course the storm-center in Europe.
Japan, the first Asian nation to threaten Britain's Eastern empire,
was the principal disruptive force in East Asia. For British policy-
makers, the German challenge was more immediate than the Japanese question, but both problems posed similar and agonizing
dilemmas. Should Britain take a stand against Japan and Germany? Should she play for time—refusing to make significant
concessions yet grudgingly acquiescing in faits accomplis—in the
hope that she would grow relatively stronger and events would
turn in her favor? Or should she try to take the steam out of
Japanese and German expansion by an active policy of conciliation? In a grim assessment of Britain's conundrum, Sir Alexander
Cadogan pointed out in October 1938: "The fact is that we are
faced, at the other side of the world [East Asia], with a situation
not unlike the one that confronts us here (though the structure of
Japan is probably not so solid as that of Nazi Germany)." After
briefly noting some of the courses of action open to the British,
Cadogan felt compelled to conclude that "it is as difficult to find

the answer to the Far Eastern problem as it is to the European one."[1]

Though Britain saw some similarity in the dilemmas confronting her in East Asia and Europe, her response to the Far Eastern situation was quite different from her response to the European question. This contrast constitutes the most notable feature of her East Asian policy from 1937 to 1939. Though the British sedulously tried to moderate German (and Italian) behavior by conciliation, they made no such systematic attempt to wean Japan from forcible expansion. The Customs Agreement of May 1938 and the Craigie-Arita formula of July 1939 were the only two significant instances during this period when London made concessions to Tokyo, but neither of these understandings was followed by a concerted British effort to "appease" the Japanese. In fact, Britain's attitude stiffened noticeably in the negotiations held after the conclusion of the Craigie-Arita understanding. As for the abortive Craigie-Ugaki talks of July-September 1938, it should be emphasized that they were not an attempt by London to conciliate Tokyo. Britain pressed the Japanese at this juncture to restore her to the position she had held before the outbreak of war in China, but the Foreign Office refused to offer any concessions in return. The Chamberlain government did say later, in its reply of January 14, 1939, to Tokyo's proclamation of a new order, that it was prepared to consider constructive Japanese proposals for the modification of the Nine-Power Treaty. There is no evidence, however, to indicate that this was anything more than a pro forma gesture; if Britain had been at all intent on appeasing Tokyo, she would surely have advanced some concrete suggestions herself, rather than leave the initiative with Japan.[2]

Sir Robert Craigie frequently criticized London's reluctance to propitiate the Japanese. The unpublished Cabinet and Foreign Office records reveal that, notwithstanding Craigie's appeals for a conciliatory line, the Chamberlain government gave surprisingly little sustained consideration during the 1937-39 period to a policy of appeasement in East Asia. Even before the Brussels Conference, when Chamberlain was publicly stating that the gathering would be an exercise in peace-making, Whitehall was not seriously pondering how a settlement could be arranged and how the basic causes of friction in the Far East could be removed. In January 1938 both Pratt and Brenan wrote memoranda outlining possible Sino-Japanese peace terms. But though the two papers conceded to Japan a special economic position in North China (Brenan's envisaged Chinese recognition of Manchukuo as well), they should not be viewed as an endorsement of a conciliatory stance. On the contrary, the crucial premise of both memoranda was that Britain could impose a settlement on the Japanese if she were able to make a show of naval force. To describe such a scheme as "appeasement through strength" would be going too far. Not until late August 1939 did the Foreign Office again discuss in any detail how peace could be restored in China and what contributions Britain could make to a comprehensive East Asian agreement. There was even mention at this stage of the possibility that London might offer "at a suitable opportunity" to satisfy Japan's "alleged grievances" regarding her "exclusion from the markets of the British Empire."[3] The discussion along these lines was brief, however, and nothing came of it.

Rather than devote its attention to determining the mainsprings of Japanese imperialism and to formulating proposals that might meet Tokyo's "needs," London concentrated on examining whether a firm stand against Japan was feasible. The Foreign Office was inclined to favor a hard line. The officials regarded Britain as the greatest power in Asia and perceived Japanese expansion as a definite challenge to her position and prestige. They realized that Britain's predominance in the East had been built up largely by force and assumed that the maintenance of her interests and influence there rested ultimately on her ability and willingness to use force, or at least to threaten to use it. But as Chamberlain, Sir John Simon, and the Chiefs of Staff invariably pointed out, the European situation and British military weakness made it extremely risky for London to take provocative steps against Tokyo. Another though less weighty factor militating against strong measures was Washington's attitude. The Roosevelt administration shied away from joint action with Britain against Japan, insisting instead on "parallel but independent" moves (if any at all). Its reluctance to act in concert with the Chamberlain government reflected partly its sensitivity to isolationist and nationalist sentiment in the United States and partly its own fear that Anglo-American efforts to restrain Tokyo might lead to a war in which the United States would have to do much of the fighting.

Except for Eden, the British were soon quite aware of Washington's desire to preserve its independence of action and to avoid antagonizing Japan. London's main concern vis-à-vis the Americans was what their attitude would be in the event of a dire emergency in the Far East, not to mention Europe. Chamberlain and Cadogan tended to feel that Britain could never rely on the Roosevelt administration to support her actively. Eden, in contrast, thought the United States would intervene if the British Empire were in jeopardy. Halifax and most officials in the Foreign Office stood on middle ground on this question. Their view was perhaps best embodied in a remark made by Frank Ashton-Gwatkin in the middle of 1938: "Anglo-American concord will one day save the world, but that day has not yet arrived. There is still suspicion and hesitation on both sides."[4] All British policymakers, whatever their opinion about the direction America's policy would follow, thought it important to try to gain her cooperation in East Asia. But—again except for Eden, whose attempts in late 1937 to draw Washington into an informal alliance were somewhat heavy-handed—they realized that the way to succeed in this endeavor was not to press the Roosevelt administration too hard. Consequently, in 1938 and 1939 at any rate, London's approaches to Washington for support were on the whole tactful in tone and limited in number. As one British observer noted: "There is much in the American attitude which strikes us as unfair, illogical [and] even perverse. But the rules of American conduct of foreign affairs are fairly well known to us now; and our need of American support is such that we are bound to shape our own action according to those rules."[5]

Conceivably, Britain could have looked for help from three other sources: France, the League of Nations, and the Soviet Union. The French, however, were weaker militarily than Britain in East Asia and were not at all anxious to take a hard line against Japan, particularly since Washington would not guarantee the security of their possessions in Southeast Asia. As for the League of Nations, Britain regarded it as more of a hindrance than a help in her attempts to deal with the problems arising from the Sino-Japanese War. As the Chiefs of Staff pointed out in early 1937, the League members could not "be relied upon to take collective military action against an aggressor State when such action conflicts with their interests or even when no interest of theirs is vitally affected."[6] Even if the members did agree to take action against Japan, Britain would bear the brunt of any Japanese retaliation and could not expect American support in fighting back. Accordingly, the Chamberlain government repeatedly tried to forestall Chinese efforts to induce the League to impose sanctions on Japan. The question of cooperating with the Soviet Union presented different difficulties for Britain. The Soviets had large military forces in East Asia, were giving significant material assistance to China, and were twice involved in major border conflicts with Japan. In retrospect it seems that there was a basis for collaboration between London and Moscow, and that such cooperation would have had a restraining effect on Tokyo. But the British never approached Stalin along these lines. In addition to doubting Moscow's trustworthiness and military capabilities, they feared that Anglo-Soviet joint action would push Japan into a military alliance with Hitler and would enhance Stalin's influence in the Far East. London, with bitter memories of the 1920's, when the Soviets had inspired the Chinese Nationalists to attack Britain's position in China, was apprehensive that a revival of strong Russian influence in China would lead to a renewal of such attacks and would also cause trouble for the British in India and Burma. In short, the Chamberlain government was more inclined to regard the Soviet Union as part of its East Asian predicament than as a solution to its problems.

In searching for ways to protect her interests against Japanese encroachments, Britain explored carefully three possibilities: economic sanctions against Japan, a naval show of force, and financial assistance to China. Of these options, sanctions were the least attractive to London. The idea of taking economic action against Japan was first considered before the Brussels Conference. The consensus within the Chamberlain government was that Britain should definitely not press for sanctions at the conference and, without appearing to lag behind, should subtly discourage Washington from calling for economic pressure. The unpublished British records indicate that the Cabinet would have been extremely reluctant to follow an American initiative. London's strong aversion to a policy of sanctions arose in its conviction that ineffective methods of economic pressure were useless and even counterproductive, and that effective measures might well lead to a conflict in East Asia which could easily spread to Europe. Even if Washington had assured the British of its full military support, Whitehall would have regarded with trepidation a war against Japan, Germany, and Italy. Britain reconsidered the possibility of adopting sanctions on a number of occasions in 1938 and 1939 but showed no greater inclination than in 1937 to accept the risks involved in such a course. In fact, when she seemed to be confronted during the Tientsin crisis with a choice of taking economic action or facing possible humiliation, she still refused to resort to sanctions.

The Chamberlain government's deliberations before the Brussels Conference demonstrate that Washington's reluctance to support London was not necessarily the main factor in specific British decisions against taking a strong line. The same can be said, though with less emphasis, about Britain's investigation in late 1937 and early 1938 of the feasibility of a naval show of force in the western Pacific. Eden was particularly attracted to the idea. With Chamberlain's approval, he made a sustained attempt to convince the United States that an immediate and joint naval demonstration was desirable. In December 1937 the most that Roosevelt would offer was an Anglo-American blockade of Japan after the next Japanese outrage. In January 1938, however, the President indicated that if Whitehall would declare the completion of naval preparations, he would announce that the vessels of the U.S. Pacific Fleet were having their hulls scraped. Though Washington thus was showing some willingness to act, the British drew back. With Eden away on vacation, London decided that the situation in Europe and the Mediterranean was too precarious, and seemingly that American steadfastness was too doubtful, for Britain to start down the road toward intervention in East Asia.

Having shied away from economic and naval action against Japan, the British ultimately concluded that granting financial assistance to China was the least dangerous way of asserting themselves in the Far East. To be sure, when the possibility of aiding China was first seriously examined in the summer of 1938, London decided not to guarantee a loan. Chamberlain and Simon stressed that if Britain helped the Chinese, she might become involved in hostilities with Japan, in which case Hitler and Mussolini would move aggressively in Europe. Halifax at first favored a loan, but in the end his anxiety about the European situation caused him to change his mind. Washington's refusal to associate itself with the scheme was a contributing, but not a crucial factor in London's decision. When the question was reconsidered in early 1939, the Chamberlain government reversed its stand and guaranteed a currency stabilization loan, even though the Roosevelt administration still declined to act in concert with Whitehall. The main reason for Britain's change of mind was that the Cabinet now thought Japan was too bogged down in China to retaliate. London also felt that action had to be taken both to keep Chiang's good will and to combat Japan's "currency war," and that if it made no move the Americans would be disappointed.

The Chamberlain government's guarantee of a loan followed a decision in late 1938 to grant export credits to the Chinese. These two moves represented the only significant instances of firm British action against the Japanese from 1937 to 1939, and hence cannot be viewed as characteristic of Britain's policy any more than the Craigie-Arita formula and the Customs Agreement can. Rather, London adhered quite consistently during this period to a middle course of benevolent neutrality that favored China by giving her moral support and limited material aid but nonetheless aimed to prevent a breakdown in Anglo-Japanese relations. In pursuing this policy, the British were playing for time. The passage of time, they thought, might well bring a Sino-Japanese stalemate, since Chiang appeared to be in a position to sustain his resistance until Tokyo became exhausted. In the meantime, London could concentrate on settling its differences with Berlin and Rome. If and when the tension in Europe subsided and a stalemate developed in China, Britain could assert herself in East Asia to safeguard her position there (and end the war on terms favorable to Chiang) by taking decisive advantage of Japan's presumed need for British capital and, perhaps, by making a naval show of force.*

As Craigie often pointed out, there were flaws in this thinking. To begin with, it embodied what Sir Robert felt was an unrealistic estimate of Japanese power. Furthermore, London's policy of benevolent neutrality was not effectively maintaining British interests and influence in China and meanwhile was causing dangerous resentment in Japan. Finally, so long as serious Anglo-Japanese friction persisted, the Chamberlain government's efforts to deal with Germany and Italy would be severely hampered. These points raise the question that Craigie repeatedly asked: why did Britain not try to appease Japan? In examining this problem, it is important to consider another question: why did Britain attempt to conciliate Germany? The question of appeasement should not be explored in an East Asian context alone; by correlating the evidence on Britain's line in Europe and the Far East the main-

---

* Though neither the Cabinet nor the Foreign Office formulated this "scenario" with such precision, it is quite clear that the British were thinking along these lines. See, for example, memo. by Cadogan, Nov. 29, 1937, FO F10284/9/10. In this connection, it should be noted there was some hope in London that if Anglo-German relations in Europe were put on a better footing, Britain and Germany could cooperate to save Western interests in East Asia.

springs of her policy in both areas can perhaps be shown in their proper light.*

Horror of war was a major factor propelling the Chamberlain government's appeasement of Hitler. It should be stressed in this connection that the British felt they were far less likely to become involved in a conflict with Tokyo than with Berlin. Though by no means dismissing the possibility of a "mad-dog act" by Japan, they tended to believe that so long as she was fighting the Chinese, she would be reluctant to initiate hostilities with Britain. There was, moreover, never a situation in East Asia similar to that in Europe in 1938, where Britain stood a good chance of being dragged into war because of France's treaty obligation to defend Czechoslovakia against aggression.[7] True, there was a possibility Japan might make an alliance with the Germans that would commit her to fight the British if a full-scale European war broke out. But the Foreign Office judged that she was unlikely to make such a commitment, and that even if she did she might well refrain from honoring it in the event of an Anglo-German conflict. London therefore saw little need to appease the Japanese just to keep them from entering an unlimited military alliance with Berlin.

The Chamberlain government's foreign policy was also influenced by British military weakness in relation to the threats posed by Germany, Italy, and Japan. Certainly Britain's relative lack of power severely circumscribed her options in East Asia and Europe. It did not, however, push her into conciliating Tokyo. As for her line toward Germany, it is difficult to determine even from the unpublished British records how far military weakness was a motive, as distinct from an ex post facto justification, for

---

* It is beyond the compass of this study, however, to analyze in detail the reasons for the Chamberlain government's attempts to appease Mussolini. Suffice it to say that most British policy-makers were convinced that Britain could not deal with either the German or the Japanese problem unless she stayed on friendly terms with Italy. Chamberlain and many of his colleagues thought that Anglo-Italian differences reflected merely misunderstandings, not fundamental conflicts of interest, and that in any event Britain could not afford the cost of building up her defenses in the Mediterranean.

specific decisions to try to appease Berlin; there is in any case some evidence that fear of defeat was less important than fear of war. Almost as difficult to evaluate is the influence on British foreign policy of the Chamberlain government's anti-communist feeling. The Cabinet felt compelled to regard Hitler as a greater menace than Stalin, at least in the short run. Still, the ministers evidently embraced appeasement in the hope not only of alleviating the German threat, but also of minimizing Soviet influence in Europe. It was believed that a peaceful yet strong Germany would be a bulwark against communism.[8] In theory, Japan could also serve as a counterweight to the Soviets, and the Foreign Office accordingly had no desire to "ruin" her. In practice, however, the threat of communism seemed on the whole less dangerous in East Asia than in Europe. Furthermore, the British realized that the Japanese presence on the Asian mainland only stimulated communist influence in China. Hence Japan's claim that she was a barrier against communism did not induce London to cooperate with her.

These three factors—dread of war, military weakness, and fear of communism—are necessary elements in any account of the Chamberlain government's appeasement of Germany. But even taken together they do not provide a sufficient explanation for that action. Nor do they fully illuminate the contrast between Britain's East Asian and European policies. To add to the analysis, it is essential to examine British images of both Japanese and German behavior. From London's point of view, there seemed little room for doubt about Japan's intentions. The British believed that she wanted to consolidate her hold on North China, dominate the political and economic life of the rest of China, and then extend her control over the rich resources of Southeast Asia. Many observers in London suspected, moreover, that Tokyo also had long-range designs on Australia and even India. In fact, the Foreign Office apparently came to believe that Japan had formulated detailed plans for expansion. One memorandum circulated to the Cabinet, for example, spoke of "adventures scheduled in her programme for, say, 1950."[9] The Foreign Office also believed that, difficult though it was to assess what was sometimes called the "Japanese mentality" or "the Oriental mind," Japan's leaders would probably exercise "a cold and calculating caution in their aggressive moves." According to this view, the Japanese were "hard-headed" and would not be driven to undertake foolish risks by gusts of passion or nationalist hysteria, though they would try to take advantage of the Western tendency to assume they had a "volcanic temperament."[10]

In view of Britain's estimate of Japanese aims, it is not surprising that she dismissed Tokyo's attempts to justify its expansion. In London's eyes, Japan's quest for "self-sufficiency" seemed to be nothing more than a drive to establish hegemony over the East. Though in the early 1930's the British had taken very seriously the notion that Japanese expansion was the inevitable consequence of overpopulation and economic pressures (exacerbated by Britain's restrictions on Japanese exports), by the end of the decade they were inclined to believe that a "will to power" was the mainspring of Japan's foreign policy. Even Craigie said on one occasion that " 'Japan's destiny,' 'stabilise' China, etc. are phrases that cloak Japanese thirst for power, and pleas by Japanese apologists of economic pressure, overpopulation, fear of communism, etc., though not entirely unfounded, are not the real motives of their conduct but rather attempts to 'rationalize' it."[11]

British observers offered, both at the time and retrospectively, various explanations of Japan's obsession with power. One official remarked that "Japan has fed on success for nearly half a century and her achievements in recent years have done nothing to lessen her arrogance and self-esteem."[12] Sir John Pratt, critical of the "almost pathological intensity of the feeling in Japan" with regard to prestige, national status, and racial inferiority, later explained the Japanese fascination with power in these terms: "Japan values wealth and power chiefly as a means of securing from other countries the deference due to an acknowledged leader. Economic factors, such as access to markets and raw materials, played only a subsidiary part in turning Japan away from collaboration with the democratic powers."[13] Craigie, for his part, tended to think that race and feelings of inferiority were at the root of the Japanese "problem": "The relationship of master and pupil can, of course, be a mutually pleasant and happy one; but when the pupil becomes a rival and begins to detect his former mentor's failings, his feelings may well be exacerbated by a most irritating sense of his former intellectual inferiority. This example typifies much in the attitude of the Japanese towards the white race as a whole."[14]

When London's perceptions of Berlin and Tokyo are contrasted, certain significant differences become apparent. Perhaps most important, Chamberlain and his leading colleagues, though certainly aware of the possibility that Hitler might want to dominate Europe, were inclined until 1939 to regard German objectives as limited. In making this assessment, they chose to take at face value Hitler's assurances that he wished to bring into the Reich merely those neighboring areas with substantial German population. To British leaders this aspiration—unlike Japan's declared goal of a new order in East Asia—seemed unobjectionable. They evidently still felt guilty over the Treaty of Versailles; but they definitely had no such qualms about the Nine-Power Treaty.

In addition to the contrast in the British policy-makers' estimates of the extent and "legitimacy" of German and Japanese aims, there was an important difference in their view of Hitler's personality and their image of the Japanese mentality. Whereas they saw Japan's leaders as careful and calculating, they saw Hitler as uninterested in long-range planning, a man who wavered between a mood of reasonableness and fits of wild excitement. Chamberlain and his close associates were surprisingly hopeful that friendly treatment and rational arguments would keep Hitler's behavior on its moderate side and thus open the way for a general European settlement. At the same time, the British strongly doubted that conciliatory approaches would divert Tokyo from its expansionist ambitions. On the contrary, they feared that concessions would only help Japan overcome the Chinese and thereby leave her free to strike south and west against the British Empire.

London feared that conciliating the Japanese would have another drastic consequence: the estrangement of the Roosevelt administration. The Americans sympathized with the Chamberlain government's efforts to appease Germany, but they made it clear that they would view with extreme disfavor any British concessions to Japan. Britain realized of course that in the event of a war on either or both fronts, she would need all the American help she could get. Accordingly, especially in 1939, she did not want to make any move in the Far East that might jeopardize the future support of the United States. It was a truism in the Foreign Office that America would consider helping only those "who helped themselves."

Britain's view that concessions would not wean Tokyo from forcible expansion and her fear that a policy of conciliation in East Asia would alienate Washington were her major reasons for not appeasing Japan. Another factor was the Foreign Office's hope —it is not clear to what extent Chamberlain shared it—that if London did not cooperate with Tokyo, the Sino-Japanese War would end in a manner favorable to the maintenance of British interests and influence in China. This cautiously optimistic outlook was largely based on three assumptions: that Japan's economic plans for the occupied areas would fail because she lacked capital; that the Chinese had the will and the ability to keep up their resistance until Tokyo became financially exhausted;* and that when Japan was no longer able to sustain her campaign in China, Britain could intervene to protect her own position and help Chiang obtain a favorable settlement. According to this

---

* Even as late as the autumn of 1939, the British were hopeful that China could outlast the Japanese. On September 25 the War Cabinet expressed the opinion that "it might well be that, given time, he [Chiang] might defeat the Japanese." War Cabinet Conclusions, Sept. 25, 1939, CAB 65/1. The Chiefs of Staff took a slightly more cautious view: "There are at *present* no grounds for believing that Chinese military resistance is likely to collapse." Memo. by Chiefs of Staff, Sept. 28, 1939, W.P. (G)(39) 56, CAB 66/2.

rather hopeful view of the future, the Chinese would then welcome Britain to play a prominent role in the reconstruction of
their country, though they would no doubt press her to relinquish
the bulk of her extraterritorial privileges.

Two remarks by Clark Kerr, one at the end of 1938 and the
other in August 1939, sum up this British outlook. First: "Big
political issues are now taking shape in the Far East. . . . But these
issues are not such as we should not in the long run be able effectively to deal with." And second: "Our interests in China have
been ravaged but while [the] branches of the tree have been ruthlessly lopped off its roots remain and, if China is saved, it will
flourish again."[15] In retrospect it appears that he and most other
British observers not only were unjustifiably sanguine about the
outcome of the Sino-Japanese conflict, but were also unable to
perceive the depth of Chiang's bitterness at Whitehall for failing
to give the Chinese substantial assistance. It seems likely that if
the Generalissimo had emerged from the war in a strong position,
he would have systematically tried to minimize Britain's influence
in China.*

One final point needs to be examined: decision-making in London on foreign affairs from 1937 to 1939. Chamberlain's "intervention" in the conduct of Britain's diplomacy in Europe was of
course a central feature of her policy of appeasement there. The
Foreign Office, which had earlier made two sustained though unsuccessful efforts to negotiate a comprehensive settlement with
Germany, was skeptical that the Prime Minister's initiatives to
Berlin and Rome in 1937-38 would succeed. Many officials also

---

* Indeed, in 1929 Chiang had predicted that the "imperialists" (presumably Britain, Japan, and the United States) would fight each other in China
during the 1940's and had declared that the Chinese should take advantage
of this war to free themselves entirely from imperialist control. See Akira
Iriye, *Across the Pacific* (New York: Harcourt, Brace, 1967), p. 162. Moreover, after World War II, Chiang restricted the operations of Western banks,
tried to push foreign investors out of Chinese enterprises, banned foreign
shipping in China's domestic trade, and generally pursued a policy of cutting
down "outside" influence in China. See A. G. Donnithorne, *Economic Developments Since 1937 in Eastern and Southeastern Asia and Their Effects on
the United Kingdom* (Lucknow, India: Eleventh Conference, Institute of Pacific Relations, 1950), pp. 2-8.

feared he might be inclined to make imprudent concessions. Still, it must be emphasized that the consensus in the Foreign Office was by no means averse to Chamberlain's efforts to conciliate the dictators. Cadogan's views, in particular, seem to have been very close to those of the Prime Minister.[16] As for the two Foreign Secretaries during this period, Halifax stayed closely in step with Chamberlain, at least until late 1938; and though Eden strongly disagreed with the Prime Minister about the tactics and timing of negotiations with Italy, he felt an agreement with Germany "might have a chance of a reasonable life."[17] Only on one occasion in 1937-38 did the Foreign Office formally and explicitly argue for an alternative to appeasement. This was in late 1937, when Eden and his advisers called for "cunctation." Such a stance would not necessarily have precluded negotiations, but it would have meant making no significant concessions and acquiescing perforce in faits accomplis. The goal of the policy would be to play for time until British rearmament was complete. Chamberlain, Halifax, and Simon did not like this idea; they clearly did not want time to rearm nearly as much as they wanted an agreement that would make rearmament unnecessary.

Though the Prime Minister played a dominant part in making Britain's European policy, he did not assume a leading role in the formulation of her course in the Far East. To a surprising degree, the shaping of the Chamberlain government's response to the East Asian crisis was left to the permanent officials of the Foreign Office, who were sympathetic to the Chinese and quite unsympathetic to the Japanese. The most influential figures were Cadogan, the ubiquitous under-secretary, and Sir John Brenan, whose advice frequently initiated a line of action. Both men had served in China and were extremely reluctant to countenance any concessions to Tokyo. Their views were usually supported not only by their colleagues, but also by Eden, who was if anything more "anti-Japanese" than the Foreign Office staff, and later by Halifax, who was temperamentally inclined to accept the dominant opinion among his top advisers.

The fact that Chamberlain did not intervene in Britain's Far

Eastern policy as decisively as he did in her European diplomacy would at first glance seem to help explain why she did not conciliate Japan. On closer examination, however, this hypothesis proves somewhat misleading. The Cabinet (or its Committee on Foreign Policy) gave sustained consideration to the East Asian situation at four stages: September to December 1937, at which time the course to be followed at the Brussels Conference was the main subject of discussion; June and July 1938, when China's request for a loan was rejected; November 1938 to February 1939, when a decision was made to assist the Chinese; and in the summer of 1939, during the Tientsin crisis. It is important to note that these high-level discussions gave Chamberlain a suitable opportunity to push for an actively conciliatory line toward Japan *if* he had favored such a policy. At Cabinet meetings and especially at meetings of the Committee on Foreign Policy, he was almost always able to exercise a very strong influence on the course of the debates, and if he had desired to effect a "reorientation" of London's relations with Tokyo, it is likely that he could have persuaded his colleagues to agree to such a step. The presumption must be that whereas Chamberlain had wanted Britain to make conciliatory approaches to Japan in 1934, by 1937 or so he was no longer thinking seriously in these terms. After the outbreak of the Sino-Japanese War only once, in February 1938, did he explicitly speak of an immediate attempt to appease Tokyo— and even then he did little to follow through on this remark. Thus, though there was much talk at high-level meetings in the late 1930's about the necessity of avoiding a conflict with the Japanese, and though Chamberlain and Simon generally opposed the Foreign Office's periodic calls for a harder line, neither the Prime Minister nor his colleagues pressed for a policy of appeasement in East Asia. In short, it would seem that Chamberlain's failure to intervene in the conduct of London's Far Eastern diplomacy was not a "cause" of Britain's unwillingness to conciliate Japan so much as a reflection of his view that Tokyo could (or should) not be appeased.

In any case, Britain's policy of appeasement failed to stave off war in Europe, and her line of benevolent neutrality in East Asia failed to protect her position there. In fact, the very contrast between London's stances in the two regions undermined their effectiveness. Watching Chamberlain's attempts to appease Hitler and Mussolini, Japan concluded that she would receive similar treatment if she exerted heavy pressure on British interests; the Germans and Italians assumed, for their part, that so long as serious Anglo-Japanese friction persisted, they need not fear British military intervention in Europe. Perhaps even more important, Britain's policies in both regions rested on erroneous premises. In Europe, her main error was to underrate Hitler's intentions (though she also overrated Italian and possibly German strength). Meanwhile, in East Asia, she not only greatly underestimated Japan's power and tenacity, but also overlooked signs of disunity in China and mistakenly assumed that the flourishing national sentiment among the Chinese would redound to the advantage of Chiang Kai-shek rather than Mao Tse-tung.

But would policies other than those Britain followed in 1937-39 have been any more successful? Her military weakness no doubt ruled out a hard line in either Europe or East Asia during this period and also made a stance based on bluff and warnings extremely dangerous. A line of "cunctation" vis-à-vis Hitler would not have kept him from making conquests that would have added to Germany's strength and hence further increased her recklessness. As for a policy of appeasement in East Asia, it is conceivable, though highly unlikely, that such a course might have succeeded until late 1937. After that time, concessions that were not backed by overwhelming military power would almost certainly not have moderated Japanese policy. Thus, without full American or perhaps Soviet support, Britain's global predicament in the late 1930's was probably insoluble; even with such support, she might still have been unable both to maintain peace and to prevent the erosion of her leading position in the world.

Notes

Notes

Chapter one

1. For important discussions of Britain's views on the advantages and disadvantages of renewing the Anglo-Japanese alliance, see William Roger Louis, *British Strategy in the Far East, 1919-1939* (London: Oxford University Press, 1971), chaps. 1 and 2; and Ian Nish, *Alliance in Decline: A Study in Anglo-Japanese Relations, 1908-1923* (London: Athlone, 1972).

2. Foreign Office memorandum, Jan. 8, 1930, in Great Britain, Foreign Office, *Documents on British Foreign Policy, 1919-1939*, ed., E. L. Woodward, J. P. T. Bury, Rohan Butler, et al. (London: H.M. Stationery Office, 1946-), ser. 2, vol. 8, no. 1, p. 5. This collection will hereinafter be cited as DBFP. Except where otherwise indicated (as in this note), all references are to the third series and will appear as, e.g., DBFP 5.1: 6. References to series other than the third will appear as, e.g., DBFP/2, 8.1: 5. Foreign Office will hereinafter be given as FO; and memorandum as memo.

3. *Ibid.*, p. 19.

4. Winston S. Churchill, *The Gathering Storm* (Boston: Houghton Mifflin, 1948), p. 14; and Robert L. Craigie, *Behind the Japanese Mask* (London: Hutchinson, 1946), p. 13. See also Malcolm D. Kennedy, *The Estrangement of Great Britain and Japan, 1917-1935* (Manchester: Manchester University Press, 1969), pp. 1, 56. Craigie became British ambassador to Japan in 1937 after long service in the Foreign Office.

5. Stephen Roskill, *Naval Policy Between the Wars*, vol. 1: *The Period of Anglo-American Antagonism, 1919-1929* (London: Collins, 1968), p. 450.

6. FO memo., Jan. 8, 1930, DBFP/2, 8.1: 4, 25.

7. See James Crowley, *Japan's Quest for Autonomy: National Se-*

curity and Foreign Policy, 1930-1938 (Princeton, N.J.: Princeton University Press, 1966), pp. 30, 34-80, 187.

8. See the perceptive analysis in Christopher Thorne, "The Shanghai Crisis of 1932: The Basis of British Policy," *American Historical Review*, 75.6 (Oct. 1970): 1616-39.

9. *Ibid.*, p. 1616.

10. Crowley, *Japan's Quest*, pp. 191-96, 390.

11. Cabinet Conclusions, Mar. 29, 1933, Cabinet 23/75. References to Cabinet records will hereinafter be abbreviated CAB; the number preceding the slash is a file number, and that following it is a volume number (see the Bibliographical Note below, pp. 281-82).

12. On Britain's response to Japanese trade competition, see Cabinet Conclusions, Apr. 18, 1934, CAB 23/79; and the records in CAB 27/568. See also Louis, *British Strategy*, chap. 7. Justice Pal of the International Military Tribunal for the Far East (hereinafter IMTFE) and Sir Victor Wellesley of the Foreign Office later maintained that Britain's economic nationalism alienated the Japanese from the "Anglo-American economic world order" and intensified their push for hegemony in East Asia. R. B. Pal, *International Military Tribunal for the Far East: Dissentient Judgment* (Calcutta: Sanyal, 1953), pp. 292, 354; and Victor Wellesley, *Diplomacy in Fetters* (London: Hutchinson, 1944), pp. 171-73.

13. See meeting of Cabinet Committee on Disarmament, May 3, 1934, CAB 16/110; Cabinet Conclusions, Sept. 25, 1934, CAB 23/79; memo. by Chamberlain and Simon, Oct. 16, 1934, CAB 27/596; and Keith Feiling, *The Life of Neville Chamberlain* (London: Macmillan, 1946), pp. 253-54.

14. Memo. by Runciman, Jan. 4, 1935, and letter from Locock to Wilson, Dec. 10, 1934, CAB 27/596. See also Irving S. Friedman, *British Relations with China, 1931-1939* (New York: International Secretariat, Institute of Pacific Relations, 1940), pp. 58-59; and John T. Pratt, *War and Politics in China* (London: Jonathan Cape, 1943), pp. 232-33.

15. On the American and naval obstacles to an Anglo-Japanese rapprochement, see Cabinet Conclusions, Mar. 14, 1934, CAB 23/78; Cabinet Conclusions, Oct. 31, Nov. 7 and 14, 1934, CAB 23/80; letters from Davis to Roosevelt, Nov. 6 and 27, 1934, Norman Davis Papers (Library of Congress; hereinafter Davis Papers); and D. C. Watt, *Personalities and Policies: Studies in the Formulation of British Foreign Policy in the Twentieth Century* (London: Longmans, 1965), pp. 83-99.

16. Memo. by Simon, Jan. 11, 1935, and memo. by Sansom, Oct. 29, 1934, CAB 27/596; Cabinet Conclusions, Jan. 16, 1935, CAB 23/81; Louis, *British Strategy*, chap. 7. Charles W. Orde of the Foreign Office also warned the Cabinet not to make a deal with Japan. He argued that "there can be no doubt about the generally aggressive spirit of Japanese policy," and that it would be neither moral nor expedient "to put ourselves in the same camp with an exponent of such policies." Memo. by Orde, Jan. 7, 1935, CAB 27/596.

17. W. N. Medlicott, *Britain and Germany: The Search for Agree-*

ment, 1930-1937 (London: Athlone, 1969), pp. 9-18. The proposed air, Danubian, and Eastern pacts consisted respectively of a convention against unprovoked aggression from the air, an agreement against intervention in Central Europe, and mutual-assistance agreements covering Eastern Europe. The Anglo-German naval agreement limited Germany's naval tonnage to 35 percent of the British Commonwealth's. France was indignant at Britain for signing this agreement, both because it condoned Hitler's violation of the Versailles Treaty and because she had not been consulted.

18. Viscount Templewood (Sir Samuel Hoare), *Nine Troubled Years* (London: Collins, 1954), pp. 153-77. See also Earl of Avon, *The Memoirs of Anthony Eden, Earl of Avon*, vol. 1: *Facing the Dictators, 1923-1938* (London: Cassell, 1962), pp. 191-311, 387; and Arthur Marder, "The Royal Navy and the Ethiopian Crisis of 1935-36," *American Historical Review*, 75.5 (June 1970): 1327-56.

19. Medlicott, *Britain and Germany*, pp. 18-31. See also Avon, *Dictators*, pp. 323-24, 345, 369.

20. Meeting of Cabinet Committee on Political and Economic Relations with Japan, May 14, 1935, CAB 27/596. This objective reflected pressure exerted on Neville Chamberlain and Sir Walter Runciman by British businessmen who feared that their interests in China were being undermined by Japan. See memo. by Chamberlain and Runciman, May 3, 1935, and report by British companies, May 13, 1935, CAB 27/596.

21. Pratt, *War and Politics*, pp. 235-36.

22. *The Times* (London), June 23, 1936. See also report by Leith-Ross, Sept. 4, 1936, CAB 27/596. There is a retrospective account of the mission in Sir Frederick Leith-Ross, *Money Talks: Fifty Years of International Finance* (London: Hutchinson, 1968), pp. 195-226.

23. See minute by Ashton-Gwatkin on Craigie to FO, Dec. 8, 1937, FO 371 F10655/28/23. (Since the overwhelming majority of FO references are to the 371 group, a number will hereinafter appear in this position only when it differs from 371. Citations to the 371 group will be compressed to, e.g., FO F10655/28/23. The F immediately preceding the first number refers to the Far Eastern Department; a C in the same position stands for the Central Department, etc. The three numbers found in FO citations are, left to right, the cable or document number, the file number, and the code number for the country or area of the world concerned. When the second number is the same as the first, the document referred to is the first in the file.) See also record of interview with the governor of the Bank of England on June 28, 1937, and memo. by Maze, in Confidential Letters (vol. 13), Sir Frederick Maze Papers (Library of the School of Oriental and African Studies, London University); hereinafter Maze Papers.

24. Memo. by Vansittart, Dec. 31, 1936, FO C8998/8998/18. A copy of this memorandum can also be found in the Vansittart Papers (Churchill College Library, Cambridge University).

25. Crowley, *Japan's Quest*, pp. 305-6.

26. See, for example, Rowan (Treasury) to Harvey, Oct. 26, 1936, FO F6511/89/23; memo. by Eden, Nov. 6, 1936, FO F6826/89/23; and memo. by Cadogan, Jan. 7, 1937, FO F214/28/23.

27. See memo. by Eden, Nov. 3, 1936, CAB 27/596; and Avon, *Dictators*, pp. 529-30. See also letter from Knatchbull-Hugessen to Kirkpatrick, Mar. 2, 1937, 37/5 in Knatchbull-Hugessen Papers, FO 800/297 (Public Record Office); and Clive to FO, Mar. 17, 1937, FO F2117/414/23.

28. A summary of these developments can be found in Craigie to FO, Jan. 1, 1938 (received Feb. 28), FO F2286/2286/23. For interesting details, see memos. by Cadogan, Jan. 21 and 25 and Feb. 17, 1937, FO F417, 546, 1001/28/23.

29. Cabinet Conclusions, Nov. 4, 11, and 18, 1936, CAB 23/86; Avon, *Dictators*, pp. 421-22, 425-30.

30. Meeting of Defence Plans (Policy) Committee, Apr. 19, 1937, CAB 16/181; draft memo. by O. St.C. O'Malley, May 25, 1937, CAB 21/558.

31. A. J. P. Taylor, *English History, 1914-1945* (London: Oxford University Press, 1965), p. 380.

32. Letter from Chamberlain to Morgenthau, Mar. 1937, and reply by U.S. State Department, June 1, 1937, Premier 1/261 (the records of the Prime Minister's office; the slash separates file and volume numbers). In April, Chamberlain explained to Norman Davis, an adviser to the Roosevelt administration, that notwithstanding his desire for better Anglo-American–Japanese relations, he was opposed to making any agreement of fundamental importance with Tokyo so long as the military controlled Japan's policy. Memo. of conversation between Davis and Chamberlain, Apr. 26, 1937, Davis Papers. In June, Chamberlain told the Dominions that Japan had recently become more reasonable, and he stressed the need for improving relations with her. Meetings of Imperial Conference, June 2 and 8, 1937, CAB 32/128.

33. Great Britain, Parliament, *Parliamentary (Command) Papers*, Cmd. 5482: *Imperial Conference, 1937: Summary of Proceedings*, pp. 14-16, 53; Paul Hasluck, *The Government and the People, 1939-1941* (Canberra: Australian War Memorial, 1952), vol. 1 in the fourth (civil) series of *Australia in the War of 1939-1945*, pp. 56-58, 69-70; Gwendolen Carter, *The British Commonwealth and International Security: The Role of the Dominions, 1919-1939* (Toronto: Ryerson, 1947), pp. 272-73; memo. by Australian government, May 1937, and minute by Craigie, FO F3281/597/61; memo. by Cadogan, June 16, 1937, FO F3516/597/61. Chamberlain thought the difficulties in the way of a Pacific pact could be surmounted; but he believed much delicate groundwork would be required—especially since in his opinion any pact should include Chinese recognition of Manchukuo and a Japanese pledge of non-interference in China. The outbreak of the Sino-Japanese War ruined the prospects for such an agreement. Meeting of Imperial Conference, June 8, 1937, CAB 32/128.

34. James B. Crowley, "A Reconsideration of the Marco Polo Bridge Incident," *Journal of Asian Studies*, 22.3 (May 1963): 280-81; and Akira Iriye, "Japanese Imperialism and Aggression: Reconsiderations, II," *ibid.*, 23.1 (Nov. 1963): 108.

35. Meeting of Defence Plans (Policy) Committee, May 11, 1937, CAB 16/181.

36. At Sian, Chiang was "kidnaped" by warlords who wanted him to abandon the civil war in favor of resistance to Japan. On this incident and on the subsequent evolution of collaboration between the Kuomintang and the Communists, see the excellent account in Lyman P. Van Slyke, *Enemies and Friends: The United Front in Chinese Communist History* (Stanford, Calif.: Stanford University Press, 1967), pp. 48-90. See also Charles B. McLane, *Soviet Policy and the Chinese Communists, 1931-1946* (New York: Columbia University Press, 1958), pp. 79-97.

37. For evidence of Chiang's shift in policy, see Knatchbull-Hugessen to FO, Mar. 2, 1937 (received Apr. 14), FO F2170/35/10; and Knatchbull-Hugessen to FO, Apr. 30, 1937 (received June 9), FO F3371/1383/10. These two dispatches will be discussed in chap. 2.

38. Compiled from Great Britain, Board of Trade, *Foreign Trade and Commerce Accounts: Relating to the Trade and Commerce of Certain Foreign Countries and British Countries Overseas During the Period Ended June 30, 1938* (London: H.M. Stationery Office, 1938), p. 41.

39. Memo. by Chamberlain and Runciman, May 3, 1935, CAB 27/596.

40. *The Times* (London), Aug. 19 and 20, 1937. Of the £250 million, £50 million were in Chinese government obligations and £180 million were in Shanghai.

41. Craigie to Halifax, Aug. 26, 1938, DBFP, 8.52: 46.

42. Minute by Coghill on War Office summary, Oct. 4, 1937, FO F7361/9/10.

43. Great Britain, Department of Overseas Trade, *Report on Economic and Commercial Conditions in China, April 1935–March 1937* (London: H.M. Stationery Office, 1937).

44. See Douglas S. Paauw, "The Kuomintang and Economic Stagnation, 1928-1937," *Journal of Asian Studies*, 16.2 (Feb. 1957): 213-20. See also James C. Thomson, Jr., *While China Faced West* (Cambridge, Mass.: Harvard University Press, 1969), pp. 15-17; and Albert Feuerwerker, *The Chinese Economy, 1912-1949* (Ann Arbor: University of Michigan, Center for Chinese Studies, 1968). For a different view, see John K. Chang, "Industrial Development of Mainland China, 1912-1947," *Journal of Economic History*, 27.1 (March 1967): 56-81.

45. See, for example, Knatchbull-Hugessen to FO, June 5, 1937, FO F5483/1597/10; and the evidence in Department of Overseas Trade, *Report*.

46. See the interesting discussion in Cabinet Conclusions, June 16, 1937, CAB 23/88.

47. Appreciation by the Chiefs of Staff, June 14, 1937, FO F4772/ 9/10.

48. Memo. by U.S. State Department, June 1, 1937, Premier 1/261. See also Cordell Hull, *The Memoirs of Cordell Hull* (New York: Macmillan, 1948), 1: 532-33; and Feis to Hull, Apr. 15, 1937, Box 41 in Cordell Hull Papers (Library of Congress), hereinafter Hull Papers.

49. On Inskip, see Avon, *Dictators*, p. 479; and letter from Duff Cooper to Hoare, July 19, 1938, Section X.3 in Templewood Papers (Cambridge University Library).

50. Report by Inskip, Dec. 15, 1937, Cabinet Paper (hereinafter C.P.) 316 (37), CAB 24/273; historical note by Chatfield, June 23, 1939, Premier 1/314; M. M. Postan, *British War Production* (London: H.M. Stationery Office, 1952), pp. 23-24, in W. K. Hancock, ed., *History of the Second World War: U.K. Civil Series.*

51. Memo. by Hoare, Apr. 29, 1937 (enclosed in interim report by Inskip, Dec. 15, 1937), C.P. 316(37), CAB 24/273; and meeting of the Defence Plans (Policy) Committee, May 11, 1937, CAB 16/181. See also notes by Hoare, n.d., Section IX.2 in Templewood Papers.

52. Review of Imperial Defence by the Chiefs of Staff, Feb. 26, 1937, C.P. 73(37), CAB 24/268.

53. Appreciation by the Chiefs of Staff, June 14, 1937, FO F4772/ 9/10.

54. *Ibid.*

Chapter two

1. These events in North China from July 7 to July 11 are covered in IMTFE Documents 1750 and 1790 and Defense Documents 973, 1134, and 1169.

2. By far the best account of the origins of the Lukouchiao Incident and its development into an undeclared war is James B. Crowley, "A Reconsideration of the Marco Polo Bridge Incident," *Journal of Asian Studies*, 22.3 (May 1963): 277-91. For different, but less satisfactory, interpretations, see Richard Storry, *The Double Patriots: A Study of Japanese Nationalism* (Boston: Houghton Mifflin, 1957), pp. 215-23; and Yale C. Maxon, *Control of Japanese Foreign Policy* (Berkeley: University of California Press, 1957), pp. 120-24. Perhaps the least satisfactory thesis is advanced by Kimitada I. Miwa, "The Chinese Communists' Role in the Spread of the Marco Polo Bridge Incident into a Full-Scale War," *Monumenta Nipponica*, 18 (1963): 313-28, who suggests, without presenting convincing evidence, that the Chinese Communists may have provoked the incident and were largely responsible for the escalation of the conflict into a major war.

3. FO to Dodds, July 14, 1937, FO F4071/9/10.

4. See the exchange of July 12-14 between Dodds and FO, in FO F4035, 4108/9/10; and Diary, July 14, 1937, Joseph C. Grew Papers (hereinafter Grew Papers).

5. See the exchange of July 13-15, 1937, between Lindsay and FO, in FO F4086, 4087, 4160/9/10; and United States, Department of State, *Foreign Relations of the United States: Diplomatic Papers, 1937* (Washington, D.C.: Government Printing Office, 1954; hereinafter FRUS/ 1937), 3: 158-60.

6. FO to Dodds and Knatchbull-Hugessen, July 14, 1937, FO F4087/ 9/10.

7. Dodds to FO, July 14, 1937, FO F4108/9/10. See also Dodds to FO, July 13, 1937, FO F4088/9/10.

8. Dodds to FO, July 14, 1937, FO F4108/9/10.

9. Knatchbull-Hugessen to FO, Mar. 2, 1937 (received Apr. 14), FO F2170/35/10.

10. Knatchbull-Hugessen to FO, Apr. 30, 1937 (received June 9), FO F3371/1383/10.

11. Knatchbull-Hugessen to FO, July 15, 1937 (received July 16), FO F4159/9/10. The Ems telegram, an edited version of which was published by Bismarck to provoke France, helped bring on the Franco-Prussian War in 1870.

12. Cabinet Conclusions, July 14, 1937, CAB 23/89.

13. Minute by Cadogan on Cowan to FO, July 14, 1937, FO F4130/ 9/10.

14. Knatchbull-Hugessen to FO, July 16, 1937, FO F4190/9/10.

15. Cowan (Peking) to FO, Aug. 2, 1937, FO F4792/9/10.

16. Crowley, "A Reconsideration," pp. 286-87; Knatchbull-Hugessen to FO, Aug. 5, 1937, FO F6115/9/10.

17. Crowley, "A Reconsideration," pp. 285-86; Knatchbull-Hugessen to FO, July 18, 1937, FO F4203/9/10; Dodds to FO, July 31, 1937, FO F5498/9/10.

18. Royal Institute of International Affairs (RIIA), *Survey of International Affairs, 1937*, ed., A. J. Toynbee and V. M. Butler (London: Oxford University Press, 1938), 1: 187-88; FRUS/1937, 3: 216.

19. See the discussion of this point in Crowley, "A Reconsideration," p. 286.

20. Memo. by Cadogan, July 13, 1937, FO F4074/9/10. See also memo. by Eden, July 13, 1937, FO F4085/9/10.

21. FO to Dodds, July 14, 1937, FO F4087/9/10; Dodds to FO, July 13, 1937, FO F4070/9/10; Dodds to FO, July 31, 1937, FO F5498/9/10.

22. Knatchbull-Hugessen to FO, July 16, 1937, FO F4142/9/10.

23. See the exchange of July 16, 18, 19, 1937, between Dodds and FO, in FO F4159, 4192, 4208/9/10; and Diary, July 16 and 19, 1937, Grew Papers. Dodds's action was subsequently approved by the Foreign Office.

24. Minute by Eden on Knatchbull-Hugessen to FO, July 18, 1937, FO F4203/9/10; Great Britain, *Parliamentary Debates: Official Report (House of Commons)*, ser. 5, vol. 326, col. 2182. References to these debates will hereinafter be abbreviated *Parl. Deb.* (Commons) and will

bear no series number (all are to series 5). See also memo. by Eden, July 21, 1937, FO F4389/9/10.

25. FO to Lindsay, July 20, 1937, FO F4302/9/10; Cabinet Conclusions, July 21, 1937, CAB 23/89.

26. FO to Lindsay, July 21, 1937, FO F4301/9/10; Earl of Avon, *The Memoirs of Anthony Eden, Earl of Avon*, vol. 1: *Facing the Dictators, 1923-1938* (London: Cassell, 1962), p. 532.

27. Avon, *Dictators*, p. 532.

28. For the American reply, see Lindsay to FO, July 21, 1937, FO F4352/9/10. See also Cordell Hull, *The Memoirs of Cordell Hull* (New York: Macmillan, 1948), 1: 538-39.

29. Lindsay to FO, July 23, 1937, FO F4463/9/10.

30. Cowan to FO, July 23, 1937, FO F4476/9/10.

31. See Knatchbull-Hugessen to FO, Aug. 5, 1937, FO F6115/9/10; and FRUS/1937, 3: 256.

32. See Dodds to FO, July 21, 1937, FO F4326/9/10; and Dodds to FO, July 23, 1937, FO F4426/9/10.

33. IMTFE, Exhibit 248; Crowley, "A Reconsideration," p. 288.

34. Crowley, "A Reconsideration," pp. 288-89. See also F. C. Jones, *Japan's New Order in East Asia: Its Rise and Fall, 1937-45* (London: Oxford University Press, 1954), pp. 38, 42-44.

35. Dodds to FO, July 27, 1937, FO F4585/9/10. See also the comments on Dodds's views in Diary, July 27 and 29, 1937, Grew Papers.

36. Knatchbull-Hugessen to FO, Aug. 5, 1937, FO F6115/9/10. See also Sir Hughe Knatchbull-Hugessen, *Diplomat in Peace and War* (London: John Murray, 1949), pp. 115-16.

37. Knatchbull-Hugessen to FO, July 21, 1937, FO F4320/9/10.

38. Knatchbull-Hugessen to FO, Aug. 8, 1937, FO F4988/9/10.

39. For example, see Affleck to FO, July 19, 1937, FO F4274/9/10; memo. by Orde, July 27, 1937, FO F4575/9/10; Knatchbull-Hugessen to FO, Aug. 5, 1937, FO F6115/9/10; and Knatchbull-Hugessen to FO, July 27, 1937, FO F4590/9/10.

40. Memo. by Ronald, Aug. 12, 1937, FO F5393/9/10.

41. See *ibid.*; and minutes by Ronald on Cowan to FO, July 15 and Aug. 2, 1937, FO F4156, 4792/9/10.

42. Memo. by Ronald, Aug. 12, 1937, FO F5393/9/10.

43. Minute by Orde on *ibid.*; minute by Orde on Knatchbull-Hugessen to FO, July 26, 1937, FO F4562/9/10.

44. *Aide-mémoire* by Pratt for the American ambassador, July 30, 1937, FO F4890/9/10.

45. Minute by Cadogan on Knatchbull-Hugessen to FO, Aug. 5, 1937, FO F6115/9/10. See also minute by Cadogan on Knatchbull-Hugessen to FO, July 18, 1937, FO F4203/9/10.

46. Minute by Cadogan on Dodds to FO, July 21, 1937, FO F4325/9/10.

47. See, for example, Avon, *Dictators*, p. 531.

48. *Aide-mémoire* by Pratt, July 30, 1937, FO F4890/9/10.

49. United States, Department of State, *Documents on German Foreign Policy, 1918-1945* (Washington, D.C.: Government Printing Office, 1948-), ser. D, vol. 1, no. 468 (hereinafter, e.g., DGFP, 1.468; all references are to ser. D).

50. Memo. by Eden, July 28, 1937, FO F4619/9/10.

51. Minute by Ronald on Dodds to FO, July 28, 1937, FO F4603/9/10. See also memo. by Eden, July 27, 1937, FO F4642/9/10.

52. For example, see minute by Ronald on Guy Wint to Cadogan, Aug. 6, 1937, FO F4993/9/10.

53. Chilston (Moscow) to FO and minute by Ronald, Aug. 7, 1937, FO F4977/9/10.

54. Memo. by Eden, July 28, 1937, FO F4620/9/10; memo. by Vansittart, July 30, 1937, FO F4890/9/10; FRUS/1937, 3: 289-90.

55. *Aide-mémoire* from Britain to the United States, Aug. 3, 1937, FO F4891/9/10.

56. For Grew's views on British policy, see FRUS/1937, 3: 345-48, 529. See also Waldo H. Heinrichs, Jr., *American Ambassador: Joseph C. Grew and the Development of the United States Diplomatic Tradition* (Boston: Little, Brown, 1966), pp. 242-44.

57. FRUS/1937, 3: 349-50, 368-69, 372-73, 384-85; Diary, Aug. 6 and 10, 1937, Grew Papers. See also Dorothy Borg, *The United States and the Far Eastern Crisis of 1933-1938* (Cambridge, Mass.: Harvard University Press, 1964), pp. 297-99.

58. Knatchbull-Hugessen to FO, Aug. 5, 1937, FO F4919/9/10. See also Knatchbull-Hugessen to FO, Aug. 3, 1937, FO F4828/9/10.

59. Memo. prepared by the Far Eastern Department, Aug. 10, 1937, FO F5078/9/10.

60. Report by Davidson (Shanghai) to FO, Aug. 25, 1937 (received Oct. 12), FO F7746/9/10. The War Office made similar observations in its summary of Oct. 4, 1937, FO F7361/9/10.

61. Knatchbull-Hugessen, *Diplomat*, p. 118.

62. *Ibid.*, pp. 118-19. See also Knatchbull-Hugessen to FO, Aug. 8, 1937, FO F4960/9/10.

63. Memo. by Col. Dennys (War Office), Aug. 9, 1937, FO F4990/9/10.

64. See Crowley, "A Reconsideration," p. 289; and John H. Boyle, "Japan's Puppet Regimes in China, 1937-1940" (Ph.D. dissertation, Stanford University, 1968), p. 130. A much-revised form of this dissertation has been published as *China and Japan at War, 1937-1945: The Politics of Collaboration* (Stanford, Calif.: Stanford University Press, 1972).

65. Knatchbull-Hugessen to FO, Aug. 9, 1937, FO F5045/9/10.

66. FRUS/1937, 3: 366.

67. War Office summary, Oct. 4, 1937, FO F7361/9/10; Davidson to FO, Aug. 25, 1937 (received Oct. 12), FO F7746/9/10.

68. Memo. by Orde, Aug. 12, 1937, FO F5164/9/10.

69. Commander-in-chief, China, to FO, Aug. 2, 1937, FO F4776/9/10.

70. War Office summary, Oct. 4, 1937, FO F7361/9/10; FRUS/1937, 3: 386-87.

71. Dodds to FO, Aug. 13, 1937, FO F5167/9/10. See also Diary, Aug. 13, 1937, Grew Papers.

72. FRUS/1937, 3: 417-18.

73. RIIA, *Documents on International Affairs, 1937*, ed., Stephen Heald (London: Oxford University Press, 1939), pp. 658-60; Dodds to FO, Aug. 16, 1937, FO F5215/9/10; IMTFE, Exhibit 3498.

74. FRUS/1937, 3: 426; FO to Dodds, Aug. 15, 1937, FO F5229/9/10.

75. FO to Dodds, Aug. 20, 1937, FO F5428/9/10.

76. Drafted in London on Aug. 14. See FRUS/1937, 3: 409-10.

77. *Ibid.*, p. 397. See also Grew's comments in his Diary, Aug. 14, 1937, Grew Papers.

78. FRUS/1937, 3: 394, 397-98, 414-15; United States, Department of State, *Papers Relating to the Foreign Relations of the United States: Japan, 1931-1941*, hereinafter FRUS/Japan (Washington, D.C.: Government Printing Office, 1943), 1: 346, 353.

79. Knatchbull-Hugessen to FO, Aug. 16, 1937, FO F5292/9/10; FRUS/1937, 3: 419.

80. Dodds to FO, Aug. 19, 1937, FO F5428/9/10.

81. Lindsay to FO, Aug. 19, 1937, FO F5452/9/10; and FRUS/1937, 3: 450. Grew felt that the British plan was "ridiculous" and reflected "muddled thinking." See his Diary, Aug. 20, 1937, Grew Papers.

82. Lindsay to FO, Aug. 21, 1937, FO F5540/9/10.

83. For discussions of the Sino-Soviet Non-Aggression Pact and Russian assistance to China in the fall of 1937, see Aitchen K. Wu, *China and the Soviet Union: A Study of Sino-Soviet Relations* (London: Methuen, 1950), pp. 264-65; F. F. Liu, *A Military History of Modern China, 1924-1949* (Princeton, N.J.: Princeton University Press, 1956), pp. 166-68; Charles B. McLane, *Soviet Policy and the Chinese Communists, 1931-1946* (New York: Columbia University Press, 1958), pp. 98-99; and Arthur N. Young, *China and the Helping Hand, 1937-1945* (Cambridge, Mass.: Harvard University Press, 1963), pp. 20-22, 26, 206.

84. Knatchbull-Hugessen to FO and minute by Ronald, Aug. 23, 1937, FO F5690/1098/10.

85. See James B. Crowley, *Japan's Quest for Autonomy: National Security and Foreign Policy, 1930-1938* (Princeton, N.J.: Princeton University Press, 1966), p. 347.

86. Commander-in-chief, China, to Admiralty, Sept. 14, 1937, FO F8240/9/10.

87. Memo. by Pratt and minute by Orde, Aug. 23, 1937, FO F5642/9/10.

88. Minute by Ronald on memo. by Pratt, Dec. 13, 1937, FO F10934/9/10.

89. Minutes by Orde and Pratt on Davidson to FO, Aug. 25, 1937 (received Oct. 12), FO F7746/9/10; memo. by Pratt and minute by Orde, Dec. 13, 1937, FO F10934/9/10.

90. Sir Hughe's account of the incident is given in Knatchbull-Hugessen, *Diplomat*, pp. 121-22.

91. Memo. by Eden, Aug. 27, 1937, FO F5806/9/10; memo. by Vansittart, Aug. 27, 1937, FO F5838/9/10.

92. Craigie to FO, Oct. 13, 1937, FO F7959/9/10.

93. Dodds to FO, Aug. 31, 1937, FO F5926/5727/10.

94. Craigie to FO, Sept. 6, 1937, FO F6182/5727/10.

95. Cabinet Conclusions, Sept. 8, 1937, CAB 23/89.

96. Craigie to FO and minutes by Cadogan and Eden, Sept. 20, 1937, FO F6685/5727/10.

97. Dodds to FO, Aug. 16, 1937, FO F5223/9/10.

98. Dodds to FO, Aug. 26 and 31, 1937, FO F5735, 5936/9/10; Craigie to FO, Sept. 5, 1937, FO F6145/130/10.

99. Memo. by Eden, Aug. 31, 1937, FO F5981/9/10; minute by Fitzmaurice on commander-in-chief, China, to Admiralty, Sept. 2, 1937, FO F6044/9/10; memo. by Fitzmaurice, Sept. 2, 1937, FO F6092/130/10; meeting of ministers, Sept. 2, 1937, C.P. 208(37), CAB 24/271; memo. by Eden, Sept. 7, 1937, C.P. 212(37), CAB 24/271. Britain's desire to avoid trouble over shipping in East Asia was reinforced by the friction that had recently developed in the Mediterranean, where merchant shipping was being attacked by what were believed to be Italian planes and submarines.

100. Cabinet Conclusions, Sept. 8, 1937, CAB 23/89. See also FO to Craigie, Sept. 10, 1937, FO F6354/130/10.

101. FO to Lindsay, Aug. 30, 1937, FO F5769/9/10; Mallet to FO, Aug. 31, 1937, FO F6303/9/10.

102. Mallet to FO, Sept. 15, 1937, FO F6557/130/10; Borg, *Far Eastern Crisis*, pp. 348-49; Harold L. Ickes, *The Secret Diary of Harold L. Ickes*, vol. 2: *The Inside Struggle, 1936-1939* (New York: Simon and Schuster, 1954), p. 209.

103. Minutes by Ronald and Cadogan on Mallet to FO, Sept. 15, 1937, FO F6557/130/10.

104. Cabinet Conclusions, Sept. 8, 1937, CAB 23/89; meeting of Cabinet Committee on British Shipping in the Far East, Sept. 8, 1937, CAB 27/634; memo. by Far Eastern Department, Sept. 14, 1937, CAB 27/634.

105. Dodds to FO, Aug. 26, 1937, FO F6897/9/10.

106. Note by Eden and enclosures, July 29, 1937, in the Foreign Policy Committee records, hereinafter F.P., (36)36, CAB 27/626.

107. Drummond to Eden, May 20, 1937, FO R3542/1902/22; minutes of a conference, July 15, 1937, in the records of the Defence Plans

(Policy) Committee, hereinafter D.P.(P.), 9, CAB 16/182; Avon, *Dictators*, pp. 448-50; Major-General I. S. O. Playfair, *The Mediterranean and Middle East*, vol. 1: *The Early Successes against Italy (to May 1941)* (London: H.M. Stationery Office, 1954), p. 8, in J. R. M. Butler, ed., *History of the Second World War: U.K. Military Series.*

108. Memo. by Eden, June 15, 1937, CAB 4/26. See also the draft by O. St.C. O'Malley (FO), May 25, 1937, CAB 21/558.

109. Meetings of the Committee of Imperial Defence (C.I.D.), July 1 and 5, 1937, CAB 2/6; Cabinet Conclusions, July 14, 1937, CAB 23/89. See also an important memo. by Sir Maurice Hankey for Chamberlain and Sir Thomas Inskip, July 2, 1937, CAB 21/558. Hankey, who was secretary to the C.I.D. as well as to the Cabinet, argued that Britain, already concentrating on strengthening her home defenses and Singapore, should not divert any of her limited resources to the Mediterranean.

110. Cabinet Conclusions, Sept. 8, 1937, CAB 23/89; also memo. by Hankey, July 19, 1937, CAB 21/558.

111. See the letters and memoranda in Premier 1/276. See also FO to Drummond, July 21, 1937, FO R4985/1/22; Keith Feiling, *The Life of Neville Chamberlain* (London: Macmillan, 1946), pp. 330-31; and Avon, *Dictators*, pp. 450-52.

112. Chamberlain to Halifax, Aug. 7, 1937, Premier 1/276. See also Avon, *Dictators*, p. 456.

113. Annex to memo. by Eden, Sept. 2, 1937, C.P. 210(37), CAB 24/271. See also Cabinet Conclusions, Sept. 8, 1937, CAB 23/89; and Avon, *Dictators*, pp. 457-58, 460.

114. Feiling, *Chamberlain*, p. 331.

115. Cabinet Conclusions, Sept. 8, 1937, CAB 23/89. See also Feiling, *Chamberlain*, p. 332.

116. For a perceptive summary of American policy during this period, see Borg, *Far Eastern Crisis*, pp. 533-39, 544.

117. Minute by Pratt on Mallet to FO, Sept. 1, 1937, FO F6030/9/10.

118. Minute by Henderson on Mallet to Orde, Aug. 31, 1937, FO F6303/9/10.

119. Craigie to FO, Sept. 6, 1937, FO F6169/9/10.

120. Dodds to FO, Aug. 26, 1937, FO F6897/9/10. See also minute by Thomas on Japanese Embassy (London) to FO, Sept. 7, 1937, FO F6200/9/10.

121. Letter from Dodds to Orde and minute by Thomas, Aug. 26, 1937 (received Sept. 25), FO F6926/9/10.

122. Dodds wrote in late August: "Just as the Japanese respect force more than anything else so they despise anyone who does not stand up for his rights." Though in July he had agreed with Joseph Grew that protests and threats would only provoke the Japanese, by August he had rejected the notion that it "is dangerous and useless even to say 'Boo' to them." See *ibid.*

123. Letter from Orde to Dodds, Oct. 1, 1937, FO F6926/9/10.

124. Minute by Vansittart on Lloyd Thomas (Paris) to FO, Aug. 28, 1937, FO F5843/130/10.

125. Robert L. Craigie, *Behind the Japanese Mask* (London: Hutchinson, 1946), pp. 39-40, 49-50. See also FRUS/1937, 3: 401-4.

126. Letter from Admiral Little to Admiralty and FO, and minutes by Henderson and Pratt, Sept. 14, 1937 (received in FO Oct. 20), FO F8240/9/10.

127. Minute by Pratt on Howe to FO, Oct. 10, 1937, FO F7692/9/10.

128. Minute by Eden on letter from F. Walters (League of Nations) to Makins, Aug. 14, 1937, FO F5300/9/10.

129. Cabinet Conclusions, Sept. 8, 1937, CAB 23/89.

130. Memo. by Pratt, Aug. 23, 1937, FO F5642/9/10.

131. Letter from Admiral Little to Admiralty and FO, Sept. 14, 1937, FO F8240/9/10.

Chapter three

1. This important debate is analyzed in detail by John H. Boyle, "Japan's Puppet Regimes in China, 1937-1940," (Ph.D. dissertation, Stanford University, 1968), pp. 41-57; and by James B. Crowley, *Japan's Quest for Autonomy: National Security and Foreign Policy, 1930-1938* (Princeton, N.J.: Princeton University Press, 1966), pp. 348-60.

2. *The Times* (London), Aug. 20, 1937.

3. *Ibid.*, Sept. 29, 1937; and *New Statesman and Nation*, Sept. 25, 1937. Keynes made a similar appeal to Gladwyn Jebb of the Foreign Office. See letter from Keynes to Jebb, Sept. 29, 1937, FO F7822/6799/10. In 1936 Freda Utley had written a popular book, *Japan's Feet of Clay*, which stressed Japan's vulnerability to economic pressure.

4. See *The Times*, Oct. 5, 1937; *Daily Mail*, Oct. 6, 1937; *Daily Express*, Oct. 5, 1937; *Manchester Guardian*, Oct. 5, 1937; *Spectator*, Oct. 1, 1937; and *Time and Tide*, Sept. 4 and Oct. 2, 1937.

5. *The Times*, Oct. 5, 1937. See also John F. Naylor, *Labour's International Policy: The Labour Party in the 1930's* (Boston: Houghton Mifflin, 1969), pp. 207-10.

6. This point is also made in Nicholas R. Clifford, *Retreat from China: British Policy in the Far East, 1937-1941* (Seattle: University of Washington Press, 1967), p. 33. Only in the summers of 1938 and 1939 did the press and the public again give any sustained attention to the crisis in East Asia.

7. Memo. by Vansittart, Aug. 20, 1937, FO F5613/9/10.

8. League of Nations, *Official Journal*, Aug.-Sept. 1937, pp. 653-55, and Dec. 1937, Annex, 1670, p. 100. See also F. P. Walters, *A History of the League of Nations* (London: Oxford University Press, 1952), 2: 734.

9. Memo. by Orde, Aug. 22, 1937, FO F5720/9/10.

10. Memo. by Cadogan, Sept. 7, 1937, FO F6356/9/10.

11. UK Delegation (Geneva) to FO, Sept. 17, 1937, FO F6691/9/10. On Wellington Koo, see Pao-chin Chu, "V. K. Wellington Koo: A Study of the Diplomat and Diplomacy of Warlord China, During His Early Career, 1919-1924" (Unpublished Ph.D. dissertation, University of Pennsylvania, 1970).

12. Pratt (UK Delegation) to Orde, Sept. 22, 1937, FO F6908/6799/10; UK Delegation to FO, Sept. 23, 1937, FO F6830/6799/10; and FRUS/1937, 4: 29-30.

13. Howe to FO, Oct. 1, 1937, FO F7343/9/10; UK Delegation to FO, Sept. 17, 1937, FO F6634/9/10; UK Delegation to FO, Sept. 29 and 30, 1937, FO F7228, 7235/6799/10.

14. Minutes by J. P. Coghill, J. T. Henderson, and Orde on Howe to FO, Oct. 1, 1937, FO F7343/9/10; Viscount Chilston (Moscow) to FO, Sept. 7, 1937, FO F6347/1098/10.

15. Cabinet Conclusions, Sept. 29, 1937, CAB 23/89.

16. UK Delegation to FO, Sept. 27 and Oct. 2 and 5, 1937, FO F7068, 7307, 7444/6799/10. See also Dorothy Borg, *The United States and the Far Eastern Crisis of 1933-1938* (Cambridge, Mass.: Harvard University Press, 1964), pp. 362-63.

17. IMTFE, Document 1691; UK Delegation to FO, Oct. 6, 1937, FO F7457, 7578/6799/10.

18. Keith Feiling, *The Life of Neville Chamberlain* (London: Macmillan, 1946), p. 325.

19. *Ibid.*

20. Cabinet Conclusions, Oct. 6, 1937, CAB 23/89.

21. For Craigie's views, see Robert L. Craigie, *Behind the Japanese Mask* (London: Hutchinson, 1946), pp. 49-51; Craigie to FO, Sept. 25 and 27 and Oct. 29, 1937, FO F6972/9/10, F7020/6799/10, and F8754/44/23.

22. Craigie to FO, Sept. 15 and 17, 1937, FO F6540, 6619/9/10.

23. Minutes by Ronald and Cadogan on Craigie to FO, Sept. 15, 1937, FO F6540/9/10; minute by Cadogan on Craigie to FO, Sept. 17, 1937, FO F6619/9/10.

24. Howe (Nanking) to FO, Sept. 22, 1937, FO F6916/9/10.

25. Craigie to FO, Sept. 25 (two communications) and 29, 1937, FO F6972, 6973, and 7121/9/10.

26. Memo. by Chamberlain, Sept. 27, 1937, Premier 1/314. See also Cabinet Conclusions, Sept. 29, 1937, CAB 23/89.

27. Minutes by Orde, Cadogan, and Vansittart on Craigie to FO, Sept. 29, 1937, FO F7121/9/10.

28. See Cabinet Conclusions, Sept. 29, 1937, CAB 23/89.

29. FO to Howe, Sept. 29, 1937, FO F7121/9/10.

30. Howe to FO, Oct. 4, 1937, FO F7479/9/10. "What cheek!" was Madame Chiang's personal reaction to the Japanese terms.

31. See IMTFE, *Proceedings*, p. 29,864, and Defense Document 1362; Crowley, *Japan's Quest*, pp. 352-53; and Borg, *Far Eastern Crisis*, p. 450.

32. IMTFE, *Proceedings*, pp. 29,696-700, and Exhibit 3286; DGFP 1.501, 506, 514, 515; Crowley, *Japan's Quest*, pp. 354-55.

33. Craigie to FO, Oct. 2 and 3 and Nov. 3, 1937, FO F7317, 7318, 8982/9/10; Craigie, *Japanese Mask*, p. 52; and F. S. G. Piggott, *Broken Thread: An Autobiography* (Aldershot: Gale & Polden, 1950), pp. 295-96.

34. Letter from Craigie to Cadogan, Nov. 4, 1937, FO F10443/28/23. This letter did not reach London until December 3 and thus did not have any influence on British policy at the Brussels Conference (or, for that matter, at any later time). It nonetheless is the most comprehensive exposition of Craigie's thinking in the fall of 1937.

35. Craigie to FO, Oct. 8 and 19, 1937, FO F7600/9/10 and F8130/6799/10; letter from Craigie to Cadogan, Nov. 4, 1937, FO F10443/28/23.

36. Craigie to FO, Oct. 29 and 30, 1937, FO F8754/414/23 and F8783/6799/10.

37. Craigie to FO, Nov. 3, 1937, FO F8982/9/10.

38. Minutes by Orde and Eden on *ibid*.

39. Memo. by Eden, Nov. 5, 1937, and meeting of Cabinet Committee on British Shipping in the Far East, Nov. 9, 1937, CAB 27/634. At a Cabinet meeting on November 17, Chamberlain did, however, express some concern about the export of munitions from Hong Kong, but the Cabinet firmly endorsed the committee's opposition to Craigie's suggestion.

40. Minute by Thomas on Craigie to FO, Oct. 13, 1937, FO F7959/9/10; minute by Ronald on Craigie to FO, Nov. 2, 1937, FO F8942/9/10.

41. Letter from Orde to Dodds, Oct. 1, 1937, FO F6926/9/10.

42. Minute by Thomas on Craigie to FO, Nov. 3, 1937, FO F8982/9/10.

43. See the marks by Eden on *ibid*.

44. *Parl. Deb.* (Commons), vol. 327, cols. 44, 75-77, 144.

45. Thomas Jones, *A Diary with Letters, 1931-1950* (London: Oxford University Press, 1954), p. 370.

46. IMTFE, Document 854-c. See also Document 1683; and Craigie to FO, Oct. 27, 1937, FO F8606, 8622/6799/10.

47. Memo. by Cadogan and minute by Eden, Oct. 26, 1937, FO F8630/6799/10.

48. Sir John Pratt, *War and Politics in China* (London: Jonathan Cape, 1943), p. 244. See also W. N. Medlicott, *British Foreign Policy Since Versailles, 1919-1963*, rev. ed. (London: Methuen, 1968), pp. 162-63.

49. Memo. by Cadogan, Sept. 23, 1937, FO F7014/9/10. Cadogan did warn that if sanctions were imposed on Japan, she would retaliate. He also stated that Washington would probably "recoil with horror from the bare idea" of economic action.

50. Memo. by Orde, Sept. 30, 1937, FO F7240/7240/10.

51. Earl of Avon, *The Memoirs of Anthony Eden, Earl of Avon*, vol. 1: *Facing the Dictators* (London: Cassell, 1962), p. 534; John Harvey, ed., *The Diplomatic Diaries of Oliver Harvey, 1937-1940* (London: Collins, 1970), pp. 48-49. On October 2 Eden tried to counteract the implications of Chamberlain's amendment by instructing the embassy in Washington to tell the State Department that "the question of whether or not the kind of action suggested here would in fact prove effective clearly requires further examination. We should be very glad to undertake such an examination with the United States Government if the latter felt able to join with us in doing so." It is pertinent to note that Eden's formulation and Chamberlain's phraseology differed in degree, not in kind. See memo. by Orde, Sept. 30, 1937, FO F7240/7240/10.

52. The observer was Jay Pierrepont Moffat, chief of the Division of Western European Affairs in the State Department. See his diary, Oct. 2-4, 1937, Jay Pierrepont Moffat Papers (hereinafter, Moffat Papers). See also Nancy H. Hooker, ed., *The Moffat Papers: Selections from the Diplomatic Journals of Jay Pierrepont Moffat* (Cambridge, Mass.: Harvard University Press, 1956), p. 153; and FRUS/1937, 3: 582-83.

53. Letter from Admiralty to FO and minute by Orde, Oct. 4, 1937, FO F7372/6799/10.

54. See the various draft telegrams, letters, and notes of Oct. 8-11, 1937, in Premier 1/314; note for Eden and letter from Vansittart to Eden, Oct. 11, 1937, and FO to Mallet (Washington), Oct. 12, 1937, FO F7477/7240/10; and FRUS/1937, 3: 600-602. Roosevelt was scheduled to speak on radio on October 12. Chamberlain feared that the President might unequivocally call for sanctions and thus wanted the British message to reach Washington before the broadcast.

55. Letter from Air Ministry to FO, Oct. 13, 1937, FO F7835/6799/10.

56. Cabinet Conclusions, Oct. 6, 1937, CAB 23/89.

57. Memo. by Eden, Oct. 13, 1937, FO F7860/6799/10. See also memo. of telephone conversation between Eden and Davis, Oct. 13, 1937, Davis Papers.

58. FO to Mallet, Oct. 13, 1937, FO F7860/6799/10.

59. Memo. by J. W. Nicholls and note by Vansittart to Eden, Oct. 8, 1937, FO F8142/6799/10.

60. FO memo.: record of interdepartmental meeting, Oct. 13, 1937, FO F8143/6799/10.

61. Cabinet Conclusions, Oct. 13, 1937, CAB 23/89.

62. *Ibid.*

63. Minutes by Jebb and Cadogan on FO memo., Oct. 13, 1937, FO F8143/6799/10.

64. Note by Orde and minute by Vansittart on *ibid*. See also minutes by Thomas and Ronald on letter from Air Ministry to FO, Oct. 13, 1937, FO F7835/6799/10.

65. Minute by Jebb and further minutes by Orde, Cadogan, and Van-

sittart on FO memo., Oct. 13, 1937, FO F8143/6799/10. Eden's preference for the second draft may have represented a retreat from the views
he expounded to the Cabinet on October 13 (or a reluctance to press
his opinions on his colleagues). The evidence on this point, however,
is fragmentary.

66. FO to Mallet, Oct. 18, 1937, FO F8013/6799/10; FRUS/1937, 4:
89-92. It should be noted at this point that Eden's account in his memoirs of Britain's attitude toward sanctions is somewhat misleading. See
Avon, *Dictators*, pp. 534-37.

67. Mallet to FO, Oct. 19, 1937, FO F8191/6799/10; FRUS/1937, 4:
92.

68. FRUS/1937, 4: 115.

69. Hooker, *Moffat Papers*, p. 158. Moffat, who wished "to prevent
at any costs the involvement of the United States in hostilities anywhere," was constantly suspicious that Britain wanted Washington "to
fight her battles for her." His views were shared, at least to some extent, by many American officials, including Joseph Grew (who was
Moffat's father-in-law). See *ibid.*, pp. 154, 183; and Diary, Oct. 14, 1937,
Grew Papers.

70. Cabinet Conclusions, Oct. 20, 1937, CAB 23/89.

71. Dominions Office to FO and minute by Jebb, Oct. 28, 1937, FO
F8615/6799/10; Dominions Office to FO, Oct. 28, 1937, FO F8614/
6799/10.

72. See *Parl. Deb.* (Commons), vol. 328, cols. 298, 583.

73. Clive to FO, Nov. 2, 1937, FO F9046/6799/10; FRUS/1937, 4:
145-47. See also Avon, *Dictators*, pp. 536-37; Harvey, *Diplomatic Diaries*, pp. 54-55; and Hooker, *Moffat Papers*, pp. 163-65.

74. See the report by Davis on the Brussels Conference, Dec. 16, 1937,
Davis Papers. In mid-October Japan had persuaded France to halt the
passage of munitions to China through Indochina, angering the British
and the Americans. France indicated at Brussels that she would reverse
this decision only if the United States and Britain would protect French
territories against Japanese retaliation, but neither London nor Washington wanted to give such a guarantee. See memo. by Heppel, Oct. 28,
1937, FO F8698/6799/10; Hooker, *Moffat Papers*, pp. 168-69; FRUS/
1937, 4: 162-63; and Borg, *Far Eastern Crisis*, pp. 415, 420-22, 634-35.
The serially published collection of French records, *Documents Diplo-
matiques Français, 1932-1939*, has not yet reached the autumn of 1937.

75. Hooker, *Moffat Papers*, pp. 165, 169.

76. Avon, *Dictators*, p. 536.

77. Craigie to FO, Oct. 30 and Nov. 6, 1937, FO F8783, 9147/6799/
10; FRUS/1937, 4: 124-25.

78. Minutes by Vansittart, Ronald, and Orde on Craigie to FO, Nov.
6, 1937, FO F9147/6799/10.

79. Hooker, *Moffat Papers*, p. 160; Davis to Hull, Nov. 1, 1937, Davis
Papers. See also FRUS/1937, 4: 131-32.

80. Clive to FO, Nov. 3, 1937, FO F9072/6799/10; FO to Lindsay, Nov. 6, 1937, FO F9234/7240/10; Avon, *Dictators*, p. 538; Harvey, *Diplomatic Diaries*, pp. 55-57. Oliver Harvey was Eden's private secretary.

81. Avon, *Dictators*, p. 539; Harvey, *Diplomatic Diaries*, p. 58.

82. Report by Advisory Committee on Trade Questions in Time of War, Nov. 5, 1937, CAB 47/5. See also meeting of the Advisory Committee, Nov. 4, 1937, CAB 47/1; meeting of the Committee of Imperial Defence (C.I.D.), Nov. 18, 1937, CAB 2/7; and W. N. Medlicott, *The Economic Blockade* (London: H.M. Stationery Office, 1952), 1: 384, in W. K. Hancock, ed., *History of the Second World War: U.K. Civil Series*. The Cabinet had decided on October 20 that the Advisory Committee should examine the feasibility of sanctions against Japan. See Cabinet Conclusions, Oct. 20, 1937, CAB 23/89.

83. Lindsay to FO, Nov. 6 and 11, 1937, FO F9185, 9682/6799/10.

84. Memo. of meeting between MacDonald and Hornbeck, and memo. of meeting between MacDonald and Davis, Nov. 8, 1937, Davis Papers; UK Delegation (Brussels) to FO, Nov. 8, 1937, FO F9293/6799/10; Clive to FO, Nov. 8, 1937, FO F9271/6799/10.

85. Clive to FO, Nov. 9, 1937, FO F9385/6799/10.

86. Minute by Ronald on *ibid.*

87. Hooker, *Moffat Papers*, pp. 176-77; Eden to Lindsay, Nov. 10, 1937, FO F9736/6799/10; Clive to FO, Nov. 10 and 12, 1937, FO F9473, 9474/6799/10.

88. Eden to Lindsay, Nov. 10, 1937, FO F9736/6799/10; Clive to FO, Nov. 12, 1937, FO F9474/6799/10.

89. Minute by Holman on Clive to FO, Nov. 9, 1937, FO F9385/6799/10.

90. Minutes by Vansittart and Orde on *ibid.*, and on Clive to FO, Nov. 12, 1937, FO F9474/6799/10; minutes by Pratt and Cadogan on UK Delegation (Brussels) to FO, Nov. 13, 1937, FO F9572/6799/10. Cadogan, however, warned that Davis's non-recognition scheme "*might* be the thin end of the wedge, and there might be an American attempt to drag us, or push us, further along a dangerous road." This warning reflected the Foreign Office's fear that Washington might decide after all to call for sanctions but at the same time decline to offer a reliable guarantee of full military support to Britain.

91. FRUS/1937, 4: 152-54, 180-81, 187-88; Hooker, *Moffat Papers*, p. 182; Lindsay to FO, Nov. 13 (two communications) and 16, 1937, FO F9683, 9684, 9655/6799/10.

92. UK Delegation (Brussels) to FO, Nov. 13-15, 1937, FO F9547, 9573, 9631/6799/10. See also United States, Department of State, *The Conference of Brussels: November 3-24, 1937* (Washington, D.C.: Government Printing Office, 1938), pp. 53-54, 65-68.

93. FO to Craigie, Nov. 17 and 18, 1937, FO F9704, 9705, 9708/9/10; FRUS/1937, 3: 687-89 and 4: 189-93.

94. Clive to FO, Nov. 15, 1937, FO F9621/6799/10. See also Embassy

Offices (Shanghai) to FO, Nov. 9, 1937, FO F9307, 9322/9/10; FO to Craigie and Howe, Nov. 14, 1937, FO F9539/9/10; and Craigie to FO, Nov. 15, 1937, FO F9578/9/10.

95. Cabinet Conclusions, Nov. 17, 1937, CAB 23/90.

96. See the exchange between FO and Lindsay, Nov. 17 and 19, FO F9704, 9835, 9836, 9837/9/10; and Craigie to FO, Nov. 19, 1937, FO F9798/9/10. See also FRUS/1937, 3: 697-701.

97. Clive to FO, Nov. 22, 1937, FO F9950/6799/10; Diary, Nov. 19, 1937, Moffat Papers; Hooker, *Moffat Papers*, pp. 185-86; FRUS/1937, 4: 219-21.

98. Craigie to FO, Nov. 22, 1937, FO F9883/9/10. Craigie had mentioned his "post office" idea to the Foreign Office three days earlier, but had said that the Japanese were not yet prepared to accept this procedure. See Craigie to FO, Nov. 19, 1937, FO F9798/9/10.

99. Clive to FO, Nov. 22, 1937, FO F9952/6799/10; FRUS/1937, 4: 197-98, 203-4, 212-14, 217-18; Cordell Hull, *The Memoirs of Cordell Hull* (New York: Macmillan, 1948), 1: 554-55; Hooker, *Moffat Papers*, p. 184; report by Davis, Dec. 16, 1937, Davis Papers.

100. Clive to FO, Nov. 22, 1937, FO F9950/6799/10; Diary, Nov. 21, 1937, Moffat Papers.

101. Craigie to FO, Nov. 20, 1937, FO F9854/6799/10.

102. Clive to FO, Nov. 22, 1937, FO F9950/6799/10.

103. Notwithstanding the State Department's sustained discussion in October of the possibility of a comprehensive settlement, the American delegation paid as little attention as the British to the concrete situation in East Asia. See the interesting and perceptive comments in Borg, *Far Eastern Crisis*, pp. 440-41.

104. Cabinet Conclusions, Nov. 24, 1937, CAB 23/90; Avon, *Dictators*, p. 512; Craigie, *Japanese Mask*, p. 51.

105. DGFP, 1.463, 472; E. M. Robertson, *Hitler's Pre-War Policy and Military Plans, 1933-1939* (London: Longmans, 1963), pp. 99-100; Ernst L. Presseisen, *Germany and Japan: A Study in Totalitarian Diplomacy, 1933-1941* (The Hague: Martinus Nijhoff, 1958), pp. 92, 127-29; Frank W. Iklé, *German-Japanese Relations, 1936-1940* (New York: Bookman Associates, 1956), pp. 54-55, 58-59; Ernst von Weizsäcker, *Memoirs of Ernst von Weizsäcker*, tr. John Andrews (London: Gollancz, 1951), pp. 116-17; and Herbert von Dirksen, *Moscow, Tokyo, London: Twenty Years of German Foreign Policy* (London: Hutchinson, 1951), pp. 189-90.

106. DGFP, 1.501, 506, 508, 514, 515, and 516; IMTFE, *Saionji-Harada Memoirs*, p. 1,928.

107. DGFP, 1.528; James T. C. Liu, "German Mediation in the Sino-Japanese War, 1937-1938," *Far Eastern Quarterly*, 8 (Feb. 1949): 160-61; *China Weekly Review*, Apr. 8, 1939, pp. 155-56.

108. Embassy Offices (Shanghai) to FO and minutes by Henderson and Eden, Dec. 5, 1937, FO F10536/9/10.

Chapter four

1. Count G. Ciano, *Ciano's Diary, 1937-1938*, tr. Andreas Mayor (London: Methuen, 1952), p. 27; Ciano, *Ciano's Diplomatic Papers*, ed. Malcolm Muggeridge and tr. Stuart Hood (London: Odhams, 1948), p. 142.

2. E. M. Robertson, *Hitler's Pre-War Policy and Military Plans, 1933-1939* (London: Longmans, 1963), p. 102.

3. See an interesting memo. by H. H. Thomas, Nov. 2, 1937, FO F10344/26/23. See also Ernst L. Presseisen, *Germany and Japan: A Study in Totalitarian Diplomacy, 1933-1941* (The Hague: Martinus Nijhoff, 1958), p. 186.

4. Minute by L. Collier on Craigie to FO, Nov. 5, 1937, FO F9104/26/23. See also Eden's remarks in Earl of Avon, *The Memoirs of Anthony Eden, Earl of Avon*, vol. 1: *Facing the Dictators, 1923-1938* (London: Cassell, 1962), p. 494.

5. Report by Chiefs of Staff, Nov. 12, 1937, CAB, 4/26. See also meeting of Chiefs of Staff, Nov. 4, 1937, CAB 53/8.

6. Letter from Halifax to Eden, Oct. 27, 1937, Premier 1/330. On Chamberlain's feelings toward the Foreign Office, see Sir Samuel Hoare's notes on Neville Chamberlain's letters, Section XIX(B).5, Templewood Papers.

7. Memo. by Strang for Halifax, Nov. 13, 1937, FO C7932/270/18; minute by Eden on Halifax to FO, Oct. 21, 1937, FO C7324/7324/18. See also Avon, *Dictators*, pp. 509-10, 513; and John Harvey, ed., *The Diplomatic Diaries of Oliver Harvey, 1937-1940* (London: Collins, 1970), pp. 59-60.

8. Letter from Halifax to Chamberlain, Nov. 8, 1937, Premier 1/330. See also Earl of Birkenhead, *Halifax: The Life of Lord Halifax* (London: Hamish Hamilton, 1965), pp. 365-66.

9. Halifax's account of his visit can be found in his report, Nov. 26, 1937, F.P.(36)39, CAB 27/626. In addition, see Earl of Halifax, *The Fulness of Days* (London: Collins, 1957), pp. 183-91; and Birkenhead, *Halifax*, pp. 365-74. Also of interest are an incisive minute by Sargent on memo. by Halifax, Nov. 26, 1937, FO C8161/270/18; and Avon, *Dictators*, pp. 513-16.

10. Cabinet Conclusions, Nov. 24, 1937, CAB 23/90; Birkenhead, *Halifax*, p. 372; and Halifax, *Fulness*, p. 190. Halifax's report of the visit was not circulated to the Cabinet. On this point, see CAB 21/542.

11. Cabinet Conclusions, Nov. 24 and Dec. 1, 1937, CAB 23/90; Keith Feiling, *The Life of Neville Chamberlain* (London: Macmillan, 1946), pp. 332-33. On France's attitude, see the record of the meetings between the British and French ministers on Nov. 29-30, 1937, F.P.(36) 40, CAB 27/626. Eden's advisers also thought that Britain should try to use colonial concessions as a lever to obtain a European settlement, but they seriously doubted whether Hitler would respond to such an ap-

proach. Minutes by Sargent and Vansittart on memo. by Halifax, Nov. 26, 1937, FO C8161/270/18.

12. Memo. by Eden, Dec. 1, 1937, FO C8280/270/18. See also DGFP, 1.50.

13. Lampson to FO, Nov. 27, 1937, FO R8100/1/22. Lampson also expressed the view that the "detachment of Berlin rather than the attachment of Rome is the key to our present troubles. . . . I do not believe that Germany, properly treated, is necessarily a real international danger. I reluctantly record my opinion that Italy is."

14. FO memo., Sept. 28-30, 1937, and draft messages to Perth, Oct. 1, 1937, FO R6577/1/22; Perth to FO and minutes by P. B. B. Nichols and Vansittart, Oct. 22, 1937, FO R7059/1/22; Cabinet Conclusions, Sept. 29 and Oct. 13, 1937, CAB 23/89.

15. Memo. by Inskip and report by Chiefs of Staff, Oct. 19, 1937, C.P. 248(37), CAB 24/271; Cabinet Conclusions, Oct. 20 and Nov. 3 and 24, 1937, CAB 23/89 and 90; memo. by Inskip, Nov. 19, 1937, C.P. 283 (37), CAB 24/273; memo. by P. B. B. Nichols, Nov. 3, 1937, FO R7339/1/22; report by Chiefs of Staff, Nov. 24, 1937, CAB 4/27; meeting of the Committee of Imperial Defence, Dec. 2, 1937, CAB 2/7.

16. Cabinet Conclusions, Sept. 8, 1937, CAB 23/89.

17. Note from Hankey to Inskip, Oct. 26, 1937, and letter from Hankey to Vansittart, Nov. 3, 1937, CAB 21/558.

18. Minute by Ingram (and also minutes by Sargent, Vansittart, Cranborne, and Eden) on Perth to FO, Nov. 10, 1937, FO R7536/1/22.

19. Memo. by Southern Department and minutes by Vansittart and Cranborne, Nov. 23, 1937, FO R7776/1/22; memo. by Ingram and minute by Eden, Nov. 27, 1937, FO R8106/1/22; memo. by Southern Department for Eden, Nov. 29, 1937, FO R7975/1/22.

20. See the records of the meetings, Nov. 29-30, 1937, F.P.(36)40, CAB 27/626. See also Cabinet Conclusions, Dec. 1, 1937, CAB 23/90; and memo. by Eden, Dec. 2, 1937, FO R7999/1/22.

21. Memo. by Eden, Nov. 26, 1937, CAB 4/27. On the preparation of this paper, see memo. and minute by Collier, Nov. 10, 1937, FO C8961/2524/62; and memos. and minutes by Collier, Strang, and Sargent, FO C7851/205/62. On the word *cunctation*, see minute by Sargent on Henderson to Sargent, July 20, 1937, FO C5316/270/18.

22. The record of this meeting has been removed from its place in CAB 2/7, but a copy of the minutes can be found in FO C8704/205/62.

23. Cabinet Conclusions, Dec. 8, 1937, CAB 23/90.

24. Cabinet Conclusions, Dec. 22, 1937, CAB 23/90.

25. FO memo., Dec. 31, 1937, and note by Eden, Jan. 1, 1938, F.P. (36)41, CAB 27/626; note from Sir Horace Wilson to Cadogan, Jan. 14, 1938, Premier 1/330. See also memo. by Strang, Jan. 10, 1938, FO C189/42/18.

26. Italian embassy to FO and FO to Perth, Dec. 23, 1937, FO R8568/1/22; Perth to FO and minute by Sargent, Dec. 25, 1937, FO

R8585/1/22. See also Perth to FO and minutes by Ingram and Eden, Dec. 12, 1937, FO R8298/1/22.

27. Feiling, *Chamberlain*, p. 335; Birkenhead, *Halifax*, p. 375; Harvey, *Diplomatic Diaries*, pp. 65-67; FO minutes, Dec. 27-30, 1937, FO R8794/135/22; letter from Eden to Chamberlain, Jan. 1, 1938, and letter from Chamberlain to Eden, Jan. 7, 1938, Premier 1/276.

28. Wilson to Hankey, Jan. 7, 1938, CAB 21/558. Chamberlain told Eden that moving fast with Italy was especially important because of "the way that things are developing elsewhere"—by which he meant events in the Far East discussed later in this chapter. See letter from Chamberlain to Eden, Jan. 13, 1938, Premier 1/276.

29. Feiling, *Chamberlain*, p. 324.

30. Howe to FO, Nov. 19, 1937, FO F9888/9/10.

31. Craigie to FO, Dec. 8, 14, and 17, 1937, FO F10655/28/23, F11035/2595/10, and F11203/4/10; letter from Craigie to Cadogan, Dec. 2, 1937, FO F71/71/23; Howe to FO, Dec. 12 and 23, 1937, FO F10959, 11462/4/10.

32. Minute by Orde, and also minutes by Vansittart and Sir John Brenan, on Howe to FO, Nov. 19, 1937, FO F9888/9/10.

33. *Ibid.*; minute by Ronald on Howe to FO, Dec. 12, 1937, FO F10959/4/10; minutes by Henderson, Thomas, Ronald, Davies, Orde, and Cadogan on letter from Craigie to Cadogan, Nov. 4, 1937 (received Dec. 3), FO F10443/28/23. J. T. Henderson's minute claimed that friendship with Japan was undesirable because it would involve "an economic infiltration which our economic organisation in the outlying parts of the Empire is too weak to withstand."

34. Minutes by Ronald, Cadogan, and Eden on Howe to FO, Dec. 12, 1937, and FO to Craigie, Dec. 21, 1937, FO F10959/4/10.

35. Howe to FO and minutes by Cadogan and Vansittart, Dec. 6, 1937, FO F10615/9/10; Lindsay to FO, Dec. 8, 1937, FO F10702/9/10; Lindsay to FO and minute by Henderson, Dec. 13, 1937, FO F11311/9/10; FRUS/1937, 3: 775-76, 799-801.

36. Memo. by Air Staff, Oct. 12, 1937, in report by Inskip, Dec. 15, 1937, C.P. 316(37), CAB 24/273. See also meeting of Chiefs of Staff, Oct. 11, 1937, CAB 53/8.

37. Memo. by Eden, Nov. 19, 1937, FO F9799/9/10; UK Delegation (Brussels) to FO, Nov. 22, 1937, FO F9952/6799/10 and F9981/9/10; memo. by Cadogan, Nov. 29, 1937, FO to Howe, Dec. 10, 1937, draft memo. for the Cabinet, and minutes by Orde and Cadogan, FO F10659/6799/10; minute by Eden on Gage to FO, Dec. 22, 1937, FO F11773/9/10.

38. Memos. by Cadogan, Jan. 1 and 4, 1938, FO F78, 199/78/10; memo. by Leith-Ross, Jan. 4, 1938, Premier 1/303; memos. by Eden, Dec. 31, 1937, FO F11777/9/10 and F11778/6799/10.

39. Howe to FO, Jan. 14 and 21, 1938, FO F616, 662/279/10 and F892/79/10; FO to Howe, Jan. 18, 1938, FO F761/84/10.

40. See memo. by Pratt, Jan. 24, 1938, and Cadogan to Leith-Ross, Feb. 9, 1938, FO F1023/78/10.

41. FO memo., Jan. 28, 1938, and minutes by Orde and Cadogan, FO F1098/78/10; FO to Howe, Feb. 2, 1938, FO F1339/279/10; minutes by Talbot and Cadogan on Howe to FO, Feb. 3, 1938, FO F1452/84/10; exchange between Burma Office and FO, Feb. 24 and 28 and Mar. 23, 1938, FO F2214, 3130/79/10.

42. UK Delegation (Geneva) to FO, Jan. 28, 1938, FO F1215/78/10; memo. by Cadogan, Jan. 28, 1938, FO F1260/78/10; FRUS/1938, 3: 491-503. Koo also pressed for a reconvocation of the Brussels Conference, but won no support for this move. Memo. by Cranborne, Feb. 11, 1938, Lord Cranborne Papers, FO 800/296.

43. Orde to Leith-Ross, Jan. 26, 1938, FO F912/78/10; minutes by Cadogan and Eden on Howe to FO, Feb. 3, 1938, FO F1452/84/10; FO memos., Feb. 10 and 11, 1938, FO F1784, 1788/78/10.

44. Memo. by Chatfield, Sept. 23, 1937, and report by the Cabinet Committee on British Shipping in the Far East, Nov. 12, 1937, CAB 27/634. Chatfield's conclusion was based on the premise that an Anglo-Japanese conflict "would be, in the main, a war at sea to which Japan could apply her full naval strength unhampered to any real extent by her Chinese adventure."

45. Cabinet Conclusions, Nov. 24, 1937, CAB 23/90.

46. Minute by Cadogan and FO to Lindsay, Nov. 26, 1937, FO F10024/9/10; Lindsay to FO, Nov. 27 and 30, 1937, FO F10138, 10285/9/10; Avon, *Dictators*, pp. 540-41; FRUS/1937, 3: 724-25.

47. Admiralty to FO, Dec. 6, 1937, FO F10553/4880/10; FO to Lindsay, Dec. 6, 1937, FO F10024/9/10; letter from Chatfield to Hankey, Dec. 7, 1937, CAB 21/579.

48. Admiralty to FO, Dec. 12, 1937, FO F10816/10816/10; War Office intelligence summary, Dec. 16, 1937, FO F11331/9/10. For details of these attacks, see Manny T. Koginos, *The Panay Incident: Prelude to War* (Lafayette, Ind.: Purdue University Studies, 1967), pp. 26-30; and Masatake Okumiya, "How the Panay Was Sunk," *United States Naval Institute Proceedings*, 79 (June 1953): 587-96.

49. *The Times* (London), Dec. 16, 1937.

50. Exchange between FO and Lindsay, Dec. 13-14, 1937, FO F10961, 10976, 10978, 11048/10816/10; FRUS/1937, 3: 798-800; FRUS/1937, 4: 490-91, 494-95, 497, 499-500; Avon, *Dictators*, pp. 541-44; Cordell Hull, *The Memoirs of Cordell Hull* (New York: Macmillan, 1948), 1: 561.

51. Cabinet Conclusions, Dec. 15, 1937, CAB 23/90.

52. Dorothy Borg, *The United States and the Far Eastern Crisis of 1933-1938* (Cambridge, Mass.: Harvard University Press, 1964), pp. 491-93; Diary, Dec. 14 and 16, 1937, William D. Leahy Papers; Harold L. Ickes, *The Secret Diary of Harold L. Ickes*, vol. 2: *The Inside Struggle, 1936-1939* (New York: Simon and Schuster, 1954), pp. 274-76; John M.

Blum, *From the Morgenthau Diaries*, vol. 1: *Years of Crisis, 1928-1938* (Boston: Houghton Mifflin, 1959), pp. 487, 489.

53. Lindsay to FO, Dec. 17, 1937, FO F11201/9/10. See also Avon, *Dictators*, pp. 544-45; and Lawrence Pratt, "The Anglo-American Naval Conversations on the Far East of January 1938," *International Affairs*, 47.4 (Oct. 1971): 751-53.

54. Lindsay to FO, Dec. 17, 1937, and minutes by Ronald, Orde, and Cadogan, FO F11201/9/10.

55. Memo. by Simon, Dec. 17, 1937, Treasury 160, F15255/01; Blum, *Morgenthau Diaries*, 1: 489-91; Borg, *Far Eastern Crisis*, pp. 493-95.

56. Memos. by Fisher and F. Phillips, and letter from Simon to Chamberlain, Dec. 18, 1937, Treasury 160, F15255/01. Simon and Phillips emphasized that Morgenthau's scheme would not appeal to India and Australia and would require the Chamberlain government to stretch its existing powers or push for special legislation in Parliament.

57. Letter from Simon to Chamberlain, Dec. 18, 1937, and letter from Eden to Chamberlain, Dec. 19, 1937, Treasury 160, F15255/01; letter from Simon to Chamberlain, Dec. 21, 1937, Premier 1/314; Blum, *Morgenthau Diaries*, 1: 491; Borg, *Far Eastern Crisis*, pp. 495-96.

58. Letter from Eden to Chamberlain, Dec. 19, 1937, Treasury 160, F15255/01; annex to Cabinet Conclusions, Dec. 22, 1937, CAB 23/90; minute by Cadogan on Lindsay to FO, and FO to Lindsay, Dec. 17, 1937, FO F11201/9/10; Avon, *Dictators*, p. 545.

59. FRUS/Japan, 1: 549-52; Joseph C. Grew, *Ten Years in Japan* (New York: Simon and Schuster, 1944), pp. 239-40.

60. Craigie to FO, Dec. 28, 1937, and minute by Cadogan, FO F11646, 11647, 11669, 11673/10816/10; Craigie to FO, Dec. 30, 1937, and minute by Henderson, FO F11697/10816/10.

61. Letter from Eden to Chamberlain, Dec. 31, 1937, Premier 1/314; FO memo. and FO to Lindsay, Jan. 1, 1938, FO F95/84/10; letter from Cadogan to Craigie, Jan. 3, 1938, FO F71/71/13; Avon, *Dictators*, pp. 545-46; Harvey, *Diplomatic Diaries*, pp. 65-66.

62. Markham (Admiralty) to Harvey, Jan. 17, 1938, FO F716/84/10; Pratt, "Naval Conversations," pp. 760-63; Mark S. Watson, *Chief of Staff: Prewar Plans and Preparations* (Washington, D.C.: Historical Division, Department of the Army, 1950), pp. 92-93, in the series *United States Army in World War II: The War Department*.

63. FO to Lindsay, Jan. 1, 1938, FO F95/84/10; Lindsay to FO, Jan. 3, 1938, FO F96/84/10.

64. FO to Lindsay, and letter from Cadogan to Chatfield, Jan. 7, 1938, FO F96/84/10; Lindsay to FO, Jan. 7 and 10, 1938, FO F313, 407/84/10; David Dilks, ed., *The Diaries of Sir Alexander Cadogan, 1938-1945* (London: Cassell, 1971), pp. 33-34. Following London's lead, Craigie was at this time pressing Joseph Grew to urge Washington to cooperate with Britain in naval action. See memos., Jan. 7 and 10, 1938, Grew Papers.

65. Minute by Orde on Lindsay to FO, Jan. 10, 1938, and note from Cadogan to Chamberlain, Jan. 11, 1938, FO F407/84/10.

66. Letters from Eden to Chamberlain and Cadogan, Jan. 9, 1938, Premier 1/276 and FO F407/84/10.

67. Letter from Chatfield to Cadogan, notes from Cadogan to Chamberlain, and note by Chamberlain, Jan. 11, 1938, FO F407/84/10; Cadogan (Dilks), *Diaries*, pp. 34-35. Sir John Simon was not involved in this discussion because the Foreign Office purposely did not circulate the relevant papers to him.

68. Minute by Vansittart on Perth to FO, Jan. 5, 1938, FO R329/23/22. Cadogan had by this time replaced Vansittart as permanent under-secretary of the Foreign Office. Though Sir Robert was made chief diplomatic adviser to the government, he was no longer in the mainstream of policy-making.

69. See FO memo., Dec. 18, 1937, and minutes by Orde, Cadogan, and Eden, FO F11479/4880/10.

70. Memo. by Pratt, Jan. 5, 1938, FO F335/16/10.

71. Memo. by Brenan, Jan. 5, 1938, FO F335/16/10.

72. Minutes by Cadogan and Eden on memos. by Pratt and Brenan, Jan. 5, 1938, and letter from Cadogan to Hornbeck, Feb. 14, 1938, FO F335/16/10; letter from Hornbeck to Cadogan, Apr. 13, 1938, FO F4463/16/10. See also FRUS/1938, 3: 89-93, 141-53.

73. On the decision to attack Nanking, see James B. Crowley, *Japan's Quest for Autonomy: National Security and Foreign Policy, 1930-1938* (Princeton, N.J.: Princeton University Press, 1965), pp. 357-58; and John H. Boyle, "Japan's Puppet Regimes in China, 1937-1940" (Ph.D. dissertation, Stanford University, 1968), pp. 65-66.

74. DGFP, 1.528, 536.

75. Crowley, *Japan's Quest*, pp. 358-66; Boyle, "Puppet Regimes," pp. 63-64; and DGFP, 1.540, 542, 544. Crowley provides an illuminating account of Konoe's adroitness in manipulating the decision-making process in Tokyo.

76. Crowley, *Japan's Quest*, pp. 367-75; DGFP, 1.550-53, 556, 558; IMTFE, *Saionji-Harada Memoirs*, Jan. 8 and 19, 1938. The terms approved by the Imperial Conference on January 11 had been formulated by the Cabinet earlier on the same day and represented an expansion of the demands given to China in late December. Hirota, however, never bothered to transmit these expanded stipulations to Chiang Kai-shek.

77. The announcement of January 16 can be found in Japan, *Archives of the Ministry of Foreign Affairs* (Library of Congress microfilm), IMT 357, reel WT 46. For Hirota's speech, see Craigie to FO, Jan. 22, 1938, FO F900/152/23; also RIIA, *Documents on International Affairs, 1938*, ed., Monica Curtis (London: Oxford University Press, 1942), 1: 342-45.

78. See, for example, Eden's remarks in Cabinet Conclusions, Dec. 8, 1937, CAB 23/90.

79. Minute by Eden on Gage to FO, Dec. 27, 1937, FO F11524/9/10.
80. Craigie to FO, and FO to Craigie, Jan. 9, 1938, FO F340/16/10; memo. by Ronald, Jan. 18, 1938, FO F7148/12/10. The British were aware of the Japanese demands that the Germans had transmitted to the Chinese in late December.
81. Minute by J. T. Henderson on Craigie to FO, Jan. 18, 1938, FO F744/84/10; minute by Ronald on Craigie to FO, Jan. 16, 1938, FO F623/84/10.
82. Memo. by Pratt, Jan. 24, 1938, FO F1023/78/10; minutes by Orde and Davies on Craigie to FO, Jan. 22, 1938, FO F900/152/23. According to Craigie, Hirota had at first planned to refer to Britain in friendly terms, but had later toned down the passage. Craigie to FO, Jan. 21 and 22, 1938, FO F819, 901/71/23. For the Far Eastern Department's assessment of Hirota's views, see FO to Craigie, Dec. 31, 1937, FO F68/68/23.
83. Cabinet Conclusions, Jan. 24, 1938, CAB 23/92.
84. Memo., Jan. 25, 1938, Premier 1/278.
85. Memo. by Eden, Feb. 4, 1938, and minutes by Orde and Cadogan, FO F1472/84/10. For Hirota's remarks on February 3, see Craigie to FO, Feb. 4, 1938, FO F1448/71/23.
86. Cabinet Conclusions, Feb. 9, 1938, CAB 23/92.
87. Conference of ministers, Feb. 14, 1938, Premier 1/308.
88. Memo. by Eden, Feb. 15, 1938, FO F1883/84/10. Interestingly enough, Cadogan thought Sir Horace Wilson had pressed Yoshida to made the mediation proposal. See Cadogan (Dilks), *Diaries*, pp. 42, 46.
89. Cabinet Conclusions, Dec. 8, 1937, CAB 23/90.
90. Lindsay to FO, Jan. 12, 1938, FO A2127/64/45; FRUS/1938, 1: 115-17. For perceptive remarks on the American proposal, see Arnold Offner, *American Appeasement: United States Foreign Policy and Germany, 1933-1938* (Cambridge, Mass.: Harvard University Press, 1969), pp. 190-94, 217-19; and William L. Langer and S. Everett Gleason, *The Challenge to Isolation* (New York: Harper, 1952), pp. 19-26. Sumner Welles's account of the background of the plan can be found in his two books: *The Time for Decision* (New York: Harper, 1944), pp. 64-66; and *Seven Decisions That Shaped History* (New York: Harper, 1950), pp. 14-27.
91. Cabinet Conclusions, Dec. 8, 1937, CAB 23/90.
92. Lindsay to FO, and memo. by Cadogan for Chamberlain, Jan. 12, 1938, and letter from Cadogan to Eden, and FO to Lindsay, Jan. 13, 1938, FO A2127/64/45; Iain Macleod, *Neville Chamberlain* (London: Frederick Muller, 1961), p. 212; Cadogan (Dilks), *Diaries*, p. 36. The British response to Roosevelt's initiative can be followed in Premier 1/259 as well as in the FO files.
93. FO to Lindsay, Jan. 16, 1938, and letter from Eden to Chamberlain, Jan. 17, 1938, FO A2127/64/45; Avon, *Dictators*, pp. 551-56; Harvey, *Diplomatic Diaries*, pp. 68-72.

94. Lindsay to FO, Jan. 18, 1938, FO A2127/64/45. See also FRUS/ 1938, 1: 120-22, 133-34.

95. Avon, *Dictators*, pp. 557-60; letter from Eden to Chamberlain, Jan. 18, 1938, FO A2127/64/45; Harvey, *Diplomatic Diaries*, p. 73; and Cadogan (Dilks), *Diaries*, pp. 37-38.

96. The minutes of the four meetings of the Foreign Policy Committee from January 19 to 21 are missing from the records (CAB 27/622) in London. Accounts of the meetings can be found in Avon, *Dictators*, pp. 560-65; and Harvey, *Diplomatic Diaries*, pp. 74-77. There is a brief summary by Eden in Cabinet Conclusions, Jan. 24, 1938, CAB 23/92.

97. FO to Lindsay, Jan. 21, 1938, FO A2127/64/45.

98. Minute by Eden on Lindsay to FO, Feb. 6, 1938, FO A2127/64/45; Avon, *Dictators*, pp. 567-68; Winston Churchill, *The Gathering Storm* (Boston: Houghton Mifflin, 1948), pp. 254-55. For a different view of the episode, see Viscount Templewood (Sir Samuel Hoare), *Nine Troubled Years* (London: Collins, 1954), pp. 271-75.

99. Minutes of the Cabinet Committee on Foreign Policy, Jan. 24, 1938, CAB 27/623.

100. See FO to Henderson, Feb. 12, 1938, FO C1650/42/18; minutes of the Cabinet Committee on Foreign Policy, Jan. 24 and Feb. 3, 1938, CAB 27/623; and various memos. by Eden and draft instructions to Henderson, Jan. 25-Feb. 10, 1938, F.P.(36)43, 47, 48, and 51, CAB 27/626.

101. Cabinet Conclusions, Mar. 9, 1938, CAB 23/93; FO to Henderson, Feb. 27, 1938, and Henderson to FO, Mar. 5, 1938, FO C1650/42/18.

102. Cabinet Conclusions, Feb. 19 and 20, 1938, CAB 23/92; Avon, *Dictators*, pp. 577-98; memo. by Halifax ("A Record of Events Connected with Anthony Eden's Resignation, February 19th-20th, 1938"), Section X.3, Templewood Papers.

103. Meeting of the Cabinet Committee on Foreign Policy, Mar. 1, 1938, CAB 27/623. See also Halifax's comments in Cabinet Conclusions, Mar. 9, 1938, CAB 23/93.

104. Cabinet Conclusions, Mar. 12, 1938, CAB 23/93. Eden, while still Foreign Secretary, had told the Cabinet that "he did not want to put himself in a position of suggesting a resistance [to Hitler's designs against Austria] which we could not, in fact, furnish." Cabinet Conclusions, Feb. 16, 1938, CAB 23/92.

105. Meetings of the Cabinet Committee on Foreign Policy, Mar. 18 and 21, 1938, CAB 27/623; Cabinet Conclusions, Mar. 22, 1938, CAB 23/93; Cadogan (Dilks), *Diaries*, pp. 61-65.

106. Report by the Chiefs of Staff, Mar. 21, 1938, F.P. (36)57, CAB 27/627. This document was noticeably more pessimistic than a similar report for Nov. 12, 1937, CAB 4/26. And its estimate of Japanese intentions ignores the points made in the Chiefs of Staff memo. of Dec. 21, 1937, CAB 53/35, quoted earlier in this chapter.

107. Cabinet Conclusions, Mar. 22, 1938, CAB 23/93.

108. Memos. by Simon, June 25 and Oct. 22, 1937, C.P. 165 and 257 (37), CAB 24/270 and 272; letters from Chamberlain to Simon, Oct. 22 and 25, 1937, Premier 1/250; Cabinet Conclusions, Oct. 27, 1937, CAB 23/90. Simon's call for a review of defense spending grew out of a study undertaken by Chamberlain just before he became Prime Minister.

109. Interim report by Inskip, Dec. 15, 1937, C.P. 316(37), CAB 24/273; Cabinet Conclusions, Dec. 22, 1937, CAB 23/90.

110. See, for example, interim report by Inskip, Dec. 15, 1937, C.P. 316(37), CAB 24/273; Cabinet Conclusions, Dec. 22, 1937, CAB 23/90; report by Inskip, Feb. 8, 1938, C.P. 24(38), CAB 24/274; Cabinet Conclusions, Feb. 16, 1938, CAB 23/92.

111. Cabinet Conclusions, Apr. 6, 1938, CAB 23/93.

112. Meeting of the Chiefs of Staff, Jan. 19, 1938, CAB 53/8.

113. Memo. by the Chiefs of Staff, Feb. 11, 1938, D.P.(P.)18, CAB 16/182.

114. Report by Inskip, Feb. 8, 1938, C.P. 24(38), CAB 24/274; Cabinet Conclusions, Feb. 16, 1938, CAB 23/92.

115. See Cabinet Conclusions, Mar. 12, 14, and 22, 1938, CAB 23/93.

116. Meeting of the Chiefs of Staff, Jan. 19, 1938, CAB 53/8. See also report by the Chiefs of Staff, Nov. 12, 1937, CAB 4/26; and letter from Eden to Chamberlain, Dec. 31, 1937, Premier 1/210.

117. Report by the Chiefs of Staff, Nov. 12, 1937, CAB 4/26; Markham (Admiralty) to Harvey (FO), Jan. 17, 1938, FO F716/84/10; meetings of the Committee of Imperial Defence, Dec. 16, 1937, and July 27, 1938, CAB 2/7.

118. Memo. by Sir Samuel Hoare, Apr. 29, 1937 (enclosed in interim report by Inskip, Dec. 15, 1937), C.P. 316(37), CAB 24/273; meeting of the Defence Plans (Policy) Sub-Committee of the C.I.D., May 11, 1937, CAB 16/181.

119. Interim report by Inskip, Dec. 15, 1937, C.P. 316(37), CAB 24/273.

120. Letter from Duff Cooper to Inskip, Feb. 3, 1938, CAB 21/531; memo. by Duff Cooper, Feb. 11, 1938, C.P. 29(38), CAB 24/274.

121. Cabinet Conclusions, Feb. 16, 1938, CAB 23/92. See also report by Inskip, Feb. 8, 1938, C.P. 24(38), CAB 24/274.

122. Cabinet Conclusions, Mar. 12 and 14 and Apr. 13, 1938, CAB 23/93; letters from Inskip to Duff Cooper, Mar. 29, 1938, and Duff Cooper to Inskip, Apr. 8, 1938, CAB 21/531; memo. by Duff Cooper, Apr. 8, 1938, C.P. 92(38), CAB 24/276.

123. Letter from Inskip to Duff Cooper, Mar. 11, 1938; letter from Duff Cooper to Inskip, Mar. 29, 1938; memo. by Duff Cooper, Apr. 28, 1938, C.P. 104(38) (withdrawn); letter from Inskip to Simon, May 2, 1938; and letter from Simon to Chamberlain, June 24, 1938, all in CAB 21/531. See also Alfred Duff Cooper, *Old Men Forget* (London: Hart-Davis, 1953), pp. 216-17, 219-20.

124. Cabinet Conclusions, July 20 and 27, 1938, CAB 23/94. See also memo. by Inskip, July 12, 1938, C.P. 170(38), CAB 24/278; letters from Duff Cooper to Inskip and from Inskip to Duff Cooper, July 21, 1938, CAB 21/531; Duff Cooper, *Old Men Forget*, p. 222; and Lord Chatfield, *It Might Happen Again* (London: William Heinemann, 1947), pp. 118-20.

Chapter five

1. Craigie to FO, Jan. 1, 1938 (received Feb. 28), FO F2286/2286/23.
2. John T. Pratt, *War and Politics in China* (London: Jonathan Cape, 1943), p. 245.
3. Craigie to FO, Jan. 5, 1938, FO F291/84/10.
4. War Office to FO and minute by Henderson, Jan. 1, 1938, FO F12/12/10.
5. F. C. Jones, *Shanghai and Tientsin, with Special Reference to Foreign Interests* (London: Oxford University Press, 1940), p. 37.
6. Clark Kerr to FO, Sept. 30, 1938, DBFP, 8.121: 112 [F11324/59/10].
7. Phillips (Shanghai) to FO, Oct. 29 and Nov. 11, 1937, FO F8787, 9477/4880/10; Craigie to FO, Oct. 31, 1937, FO F8785/4880/10.
8. Phillips to FO, Dec. 18, 1937, and FO to Craigie, Dec. 23, 1937, FO F11263/4880/10; Phillips to FO, Dec. 30, 1937, and Feb. 7 and Mar. 2, 1938, FO F11770/4880/10, F1601/59/10, and F2504/62/10; memo. by Ronald, Jan. 18, 1938, FO F7148/12/10; Jones, *Shanghai and Tientsin,* pp. 65-66.
9. Howe to FO, Nov. 12, 1937, FO F9480, 9485/4880/10; Phillips to FO, Nov. 22, 1937, FO F9910/9535/10; War Office intelligence summary, Nov. 29, 1937, FO F10204/9/10. Premier Konoe himself reportedly told a journalist on November 28 that "in the event of [the] settlement authorities being unable to take adequate steps to control anti-Japanese movements in the settlement Japanese military authorities may be compelled to use force." As quoted by Craigie to FO, Dec. 1, 1937, FO F10260/9535/10.
10. Phillips to FO, Dec. 3, 1937, and Jan. 4, 1938, FO F10458/9535/10 and F227/59/10; Howe to FO, Jan. 6, 1938, and FO to Howe, Jan. 8, 1938, FO F290/59/10; memo. by Harvey, Jan. 10, 1938, FO F473/59/10; memo. by Ronald, Jan. 18, 1938, FO F7148/12/10; Phillips to FO and minute by Brenan, Jan. 22, 1938, FO F924/59/10.
11. Howe to FO, Feb. 7, 1938, FO F1585/59/10; Phillips to FO, Mar. 21 and Apr. 8, 1938, FO F3735, 3871/59/10; FRUS/1938, 4: 126-31.
12. Craigie to FO, May 18, 1938, FO F5412/12/10; letters from Howe to Clark Kerr, May 24 and July 19, 1938, 38/21 and 38/31 in Clark Kerr Papers, FO 800/299; Clark Kerr to Howe, June 7, 1938, FO F7673/12/10. For Piggott's account of his visit, see F. S. G. Piggott, *Broken Thread: An Autobiography* (Aldershot: Gale & Polden, 1950), pp. 300-308.

13. Phillips to FO, July 8 and 24, 1938, FO F7331, 7901/35/10; FRUS/1938, 3: 215-17.

14. Jones, *Shanghai and Tientsin*, pp. 135-37, 149-50.

15. Affleck (Tientsin) to FO, Mar. 10, 1938, FO 436/2, F2478/25/10. Unfortunately, the original FO 371 files dealing with currency problems in 1938 have not been preserved, and thus it is necessary to use FO 436 (the Confidential Print), which contains copies of the most important telegrams. See also Jones, *Shanghai and Tientsin*, pp. 163-65.

16. Clark Kerr to FO, May 14, 1938, FO 436/2, F5329/25/10; memo. by Brenan, Nov. 2, 1939, DBFP, 9, Appendix 3: 536-38 [F11381/6457/10].

17. Commander (Tientsin Area) to FO, Jan. 19, 1938, FO F717/717/10; Howe to FO, Jan. 19, 1938, and note by Cadogan for Eden, Jan. 21, 1938, FO F764/717/10; Young (Peking) to FO, Jan. 26, 1938, FO F1048/717/10. See also Jones, *Shanghai and Tientsin*, p. 173.

18. Jamieson (Tientsin) to British Embassy (Shanghai), Sept. 1 and 7, 1938, DBFP, 8.68 and 81: 60-61, 71-73 [F9557, 9654/717/10]; Craigie to FO, Sept. 2, 1938, FO F9477/717/10; Craigie to FO, Sept. 8, 1938, DBFP, 8.83: 73 [F9655/717/10].

19. For Maze's views, see letter from Maze to W. O. Law, Oct. 17, 1938, in Personal Correspondence (July-Dec. 1938) and letter from Maze to Lord Lytton, Jan. 31, 1940, in Confidential Letters (vol. 20), Maze Papers. The best commentary on the Customs Administration is Nicholas R. Clifford, "Sir Frederick Maze and the Chinese Maritime Customs, 1937-1941," *Journal of Modern History*, 37.1 (Mar. 1965): 18-34.

20. Minute by Pratt on Embassy Offices (Shanghai) to FO, Nov. 17, 1937, FO F9713/220/10.

21. *Ibid.*; Young (Treasury) to Chaplin, transmitting a draft letter from Leith-Ross to Kung, Oct. 21, 1937, FO F8466/4/10.

22. Minute by Pratt, Nov. 17, 1937, FO F9713/220/10. The Japanese army believed that since the Customs Administration was an organ of Chiang's regime, it should be seized and its revenue should be diverted to the puppet governments. See John H. Boyle, "Japan's Puppet Regimes in China, 1937-1940" (Ph.D. dissertation, Stanford University, 1968), pp. 107, 138.

23. Myers to Maze, Aug. 30, 1937, in Personal Correspondence (Sept.-Dec. 1937), Maze Papers; Affleck (Tientsin) to FO, Sept. 1, 1937, FO F6032, 6041/220/10.

24. Howe to FO and FO to Howe, Oct. 9, 1937, FO F7636/220/10; Howe to FO, Sept. 16 and 28, and Oct. 8, 1937, FO F6642, 7192, 7691/220/10; Maze to Myers, Sept. 27, 1937, in Personal Correspondence (Mar.-Dec. 1937), Maze Papers.

25. Maze to Lawford, Nov. 30, 1937, enclosing Maze to Myers, Oct. 13 and 19, 1937, in Personal Correspondence (Mar.-Dec. 1937), Maze Papers; Embassy Offices (Shanghai) to FO, Oct. 20, 1937, FO F8283/220/10.

26. Craigie to FO and minute by Chaplin, Nov. 5, 1937, FO F9144/220/10; Affleck to FO and minute by Chaplin, Nov. 6, 1937, FO F9207/220/10; Myers to Maze and Maze to Myers, Oct. 29, 1937, and extract from Myers to Japanese consul-general (Tientsin), Oct. 22, 1937, in Personal Correspondence (Sept.-Dec. 1937), Maze Papers. See also Arthur N. Young, *China's Wartime Finance and Inflation, 1937-1945* (Cambridge, Mass.: Harvard University Press, 1965), p. 41.

27. Lawford to Maze, Nov. 29 and Dec. 1, 1937, in Personal Correspondence (Mar.-Dec. 1937), Maze Papers; Embassy Offices (Shanghai) to FO and FO to Craigie, Nov. 23, 1937, FO F9976/220/10; Cabinet Conclusions, Nov. 24, 1937, CAB 23/90; letter from Barnes (Hong Kong and Shanghai Banking Corporation) to Orde, Dec. 1, 1937, and letter from Orde to Barnes, Dec. 3, 1937, FO F10468/4/10; FRUS/1937, 3: 879-90, 894-98.

28. The FO 371 files about the Customs negotiations in 1938—like the files dealing with currency problems—have not been retained. The high points of the negotiations can be followed in the Confidential Print. On the early stages of the discussions, see Howe to FO, Jan. 6 and 23, 1938, FO 436/2, F316, 923/15/10; and FO to Howe, Feb. 10, 1938, FO 436/2, F1729/15/10. See also Arthur N. Young, *China and the Helping Hand, 1937-1945* (Cambridge, Mass.: Harvard University Press, 1963), pp. 88-89; Clifford, "Sir Frederick Maze," pp. 23-25; and FRUS/1938, 3: 635-36.

29. Craigie to FO, Jan. 6 and Feb. 18, 1938, and FO to Craigie, Feb. 24, 1938, FO 436/2, F261, 2065/15/10; FRUS/1937, 3: 910-15; FRUS/1938, 3: 626-27, 630, 645-46, 655-58, 661-63, 671-74.

30. Craigie to FO, Apr. 29 and May 4, 1938, and FO to Craigie, May 1, 1938, FO 436/2, F4570, 6072, 4571/15/10; FRUS/1938, 3: 676-81.

31. Craigie to FO, Apr. 30 and May 4, 1938, FO 436/2, F4564, 4730/15/10; Diary, late May 1938 (pp. 3739-40), Grew Papers; FRUS/1938, 3: 684-98.

32. Cadogan to Clark Kerr, May 11, 1938, FO 436/2, F4938/15/10; FRUS/1938, 3: 681, 687, 695-97, 702, 704-5; Young, *Helping Hand*, pp. 90, 92.

33. Clark Kerr to FO, May 23, 27, and 31, 1938, and FO to Clark Kerr, June 9, 1938, FO 436/2, F5588, 5731, 5870, 5759/15/10. See also Young, *Helping Hand*, pp. 92, 95; and Clifford, "Sir Frederick Maze," pp. 27-28.

34. Craigie to FO and minute by Brenan, Apr. 26, 1938, FO F4462/71/23. Craigie hoped the Customs Agreement would be the prelude to Anglo-Japanese understandings on other issues, but the Foreign Office was definitely averse to any further conciliation of Tokyo. See *ibid.*; Craigie to FO, Mar. 19, 1938, FO F3042/68/23; and FO to Craigie, May 17, 1938, FO F4462/71/23.

35. Robert L. Craigie, *Behind the Japanese Mask* (London: Hutchinson, 1946), p. 53.

36. For incisive criticism of the Customs Agreement, see Young,

Helping Hand, pp. 93-96. Young was financial adviser to the Chinese government at this time. See also Kung to Clark Kerr, July 9, 1938, in Personal Correspondence (July-Dec. 1938), Maze Papers. Clifford, "Sir Frederick Maze," pp. 26-27, and *Retreat from China: British Policy in the Far East, 1937-1941* (Seattle: University of Washington Press, 1967), pp. 60-61, is less critical than Young of the arrangement.

37. Howe to FO, Jan. 21, 1938, FO F893/62/10; Clark Kerr to FO, Mar. 18, 1938, FO F4683/279/10; Craigie to FO, Apr. 23, 1938, FO F4391/279/10; E. M. Gull, *British Economic Interests in the Far East* (New York: International Secretariat, Institute of Pacific Relations, 1943), pp. 191-95.

38. Howe to FO, Jan. 5 and 15, 1938, FO F208, 633/158/10; Craigie to FO, Jan. 12 and Apr. 11, 1938, FO F471/158/10 and F4000/12/10; FO to Craigie, Jan. 17, 1938, FO F594/158/10; memo. by Ronald, Jan. 18, 1938, FO F7148/12/10; *Parl. Deb.* (Commons), vol. 337, col. 683.

39. Young to FO, Jan. 28, 1938, FO 436/2, F1845/15/10; China Liaison Committee to FO, Mar. 1, 1938, FO F2480/62/10; *Parl. Deb.* (Commons), vol. 333, col. 1386; Jones, *Shanghai and Tientsin,* p. 161.

40. Young to FO, May 7, 1938, FO 436/2, F4978/25/10; Boyle, "Puppet Regimes," pp. 108-9; Young, *Helping Hand,* pp. 66-68.

41. Clark Kerr to FO, Mar. 18, 1938, FO 436/2, F3036/25/10; Craigie to FO, Mar. 26, 1938, FO 436/2, F3306/25/10; Jones, *Shanghai and Tientsin,* p. 168; Clifford, *Retreat,* p. 62.

42. Jones, *Shanghai and Tientsin,* pp. 168-69. The Foreign Office had no doubt that Japan intended the Development Company to monopolize the economic life of North China. See FO to Craigie, May 17, 1938, FO F4462/71/23.

43. Chancery (Tokyo) to FO, Apr. 20, 1938, FO F5131/62/10; Affleck to FO, July 18, 1938, FO F7752/7290/10; Greenway (Peking) to FO, June 27, 1938, FO F8513/62/10; FRUS/1938, 4: 13-14, 29-30, 38-39, 41-42, 46-53; Jones, *Shanghai and Tientsin,* pp. 167-68.

44. Jones, *Shanghai and Tientsin,* p. 162; Irving S. Friedman, *British Relations with China, 1931-1939* (New York: International Secretariat, Institute of Pacific Relations, 1940), pp. 122-23.

45. Boyle, "Puppet Regimes," pp. 140-45.

46. Compiled from Great Britain, *Foreign Trade and Commerce Accounts: Relating to the Trade and Commerce of Certain Foreign Countries During the Period Ended June 30, 1938* and . . . *During the Period Ended December 31, 1938* (London: H.M. Stationery Office, 1938-39). These figures are adjusted to take account of the depreciation of the Chinese dollar, and they do not include trade with Hong Kong. For figures on trade with Hong Kong, see Gull, *British Economic Interests,* p. 179, and Clifford, *Retreat,* p. 65.

47. China Maritime Customs, *The Trade of China, 1937-1938* (Shanghai: 1938-39). See also Clifford, *Retreat,* p. 66.

48. See minutes by Brenan and Ronald on Craigie to FO, May 26,

1939, FO F5037/1236/23; and Gull, *British Economic Interests*, pp. 190, 197.

49. See, for example, FO to Craigie, May 17, 1938, FO F4462/71/23; and memo. by Brenan, May 23, 1938, FO F5554/62/10. See also memo. by Department of Overseas Trade, May 18, 1938, FO F5392/62/10.

50. Affleck to FO, Apr. 14, 1938, FO F4135/12/10.

51. See, for example, the comments in note by G. L. M. Clauson, Nov. 1937, CAB 47/5.

52. Craigie to FO, Nov. 18, 1937, FO F9768/9/10; Craigie to FO, Dec. 6, 1937, and minutes by Eden, Orde, and Vansittart, FO F10574/6799/10.

53. Memo. by Eden, Feb. 4, 1938, FO F1472/84/10; Kirkpatrick to Cranborne, Feb. 14, 1938, FO F2202/103/23; Craigie to FO, Apr. 3, 1938, FO F3647/12/10; Clark Kerr to FO, Apr. 15, 1938, FO F4131/12/10.

54. A full exposition of the Foreign Office's thinking can be found in FO to Craigie, May 17, 1938, FO F4462/71/23. See also minute by Brenan on Hankey to Cadogan, Apr. 5, 1938, FO F3754/16/10; and minutes by Ronald and Brenan on Craigie to FO, June 20, 1938, FO F6708/84/10.

55. Craigie to FO, July 14, 1938, FO F8491/12/10.

56. *Ibid.*

57. Craigie to FO, Apr. 11, 19, and 26, 1938, FO F3994, 4154, 4462/71/23.

58. Craigie to FO, Feb. 28 and Apr. 26, 1938, FO F3359, 4462/71/23.

59. Craigie to FO, Mar. 30 and Apr. 26, 1938, FO F3468, 4462/71/23.

60. See, for example, minutes by Henderson, Orde, and Cadogan on Craigie to FO, Feb. 9, 1938, FO F1679/84/10.

61. Minute by Brenan (and minute by Cadogan) on Hankey to Cadogan, Apr. 5, 1938, FO F3754/16/10; minute by Howe (and minutes by Brenan, Ronald, and Cadogan) on Craigie to FO, Apr. 26, 1938, FO F4462/71/23. Clark Kerr was also optimistic that China's resistance might succeed. See Clark Kerr to FO, Apr. 28, 1938, and minute by Brenan, FO F4551/84/10.

62. Minute by Brenan on Craigie to FO, July 14, 1938, FO F8491/12/10.

63. Minute by Brenan on Craigie to FO, Apr. 26, 1938, and FO to Craigie, May 17, 1938, FO F4462/71/23; minute by J. T. Henderson on Lindsay to FO, Apr. 15, 1938, FO F4129/16/10.

64. Howe to FO, Feb. 3, 1938, FO F1452/84/10.

65. Minute by Howe on Craigie to FO, Mar. 24, 1938, FO F4206/71/23.

66. Minutes by Brenan and Howe on Craigie to FO, Apr. 26, 1938, and FO to Craigie, May 17, 1938, FO F4462/71/23. See also minutes by Ronald, Brenan, Orde, and Cadogan on Craigie to FO, Mar. 30, 1938, and FO to Craigie, Apr. 6, 1938, FO F3468/71/23.

67. Minute by Brenan on Craigie to FO, Apr. 26, 1938, FO F4462/
71/23. For various estimates of the magnitude and importance of the
Chinese victory at Taierhchuang, see MacKillop (Hankow) to FO, Apr.
9, 1938, FO F3824/2/10; Diary, late May 1938, Grew Papers; F. F. Liu,
A Military History of Modern China, 1924-1949 (Princeton, N.J.:
Princeton University Press, 1956), p. 200; O. Edmund Clubb, *Twentieth
Century China* (New York: Columbia University Press, 1964), p. 224;
and Chalmers A. Johnson, *Peasant Nationalism and Communist Power:
The Emergence of Revolutionary China, 1937-1945* (Stanford, Calif.:
Stanford University Press, 1962), pp. 35-36.

68. Clark Kerr to FO, Apr. 28, 1938, FO F4551/84/10; minute by
Cadogan on Howe to FO, Feb. 3, 1938, FO F1452/84/10. See also T. H.
White and A. Jacoby, *Thunder Out of China* (New York: Sloane, 1946),
p. 53.

69. Clark Kerr to FO, July 19, 1938, FO F7853/2/10.

70. Clark Kerr to FO, July 19, 1938, FO F7032/53/10. See also minute by Scott on MacKillop to FO, Feb. 9, 1938, FO F1695/53/10; and
minute by Brenan on Clark Kerr to FO, Mar. 14, 1938, FO F2944/53/10.

71. Clark Kerr to FO, Mar. 14, 1938, FO F2908/53/10; Chilston to
FO, Jan. 17, 1938, FO F952/84/10.

72. Minutes by Howe and Cadogan on letter from Ashton-Gwatkin
to Stirling, May 16, 1938, FO F5989/84/10.

73. Young (Peking) to FO, Aug. 19, 1938, and minute by Ronald, FO
F10791/2/10. See also minute by Ronald on Craigie to FO, June 29,
1938, and letter from Ronald to Craigie, Aug. 26, 1938, FO F8027/152/
23; and minute by Brenan on Craigie to FO, Apr. 2, 1938, FO F3622/
53/10.

74. Minute by Brenan on Clark Kerr to FO, Aug. 24, 1938, FO F9188/
9157/10.

75. Memo., Jan. 25, 1938, Premier 1/278; *Parl. Deb.* (Lords), vol. 107,
cols. 653-73; *Parl. Deb.* (Commons), vol. 332, cols. 367-70.

76. Note by C. N. Ryan, Dec. 31, 1937, CAB 47/5; Annual Report by
Advisory Committee on Trade Questions in Time of War, Feb. 9, 1938,
CAB 47/1; meeting of the Committee of Imperial Defence, Feb. 17, 1938,
CAB 2/7; meeting of the Advisory Committee, Mar. 10, 1938, CAB
47/12; W. N. Medlicott, *The Economic Blockade* (London: H.M. Stationery Office, 1952), 1: 384, in W. K. Hancock, ed., *History of the Second World War: U.K. Civil Series.*

77. Letter from Hornbeck to Cadogan, Apr. 13, 1938, and minutes by
Cadogan and by Brenan, Nicholls, and Howe, FO F4463/16/10. See also
memo. by Brenan, May 23, 1938, and minute by Nicholls, FO F5554/
62/10; Clark Kerr to FO, June 27, 1938, FO F7001/62/10; and Craigie
to FO, June 29, 1938, and minute by Brenan, FO F7031/62/10.

78. Board of Trade to FO, July 8, 1938, FO F7316/62/10; Waley to
Ronald, July 8, 1938, FO F7518/62/10; memo. by Heppel, July 27, 1938,
FO F7991/62/10.

79. FO to Clark Kerr, Mar. 15, 1938, FO 436/2, F2921/25/10. See also Clark Kerr to FO, Mar. 3, 1938, FO 436/2, F2519/25/10; and Mac-Killop to FO, Mar. 10, 1938, FO 436/2, F2746/25/10.

80. Letter from Simon to Chamberlain, Apr. 5, 1938, and letter from Chamberlain to Simon, Apr. 6, 1938, Premier 1/303. See also FO to Greenway, Apr. 5, 1938, FO 436/2, F3704/25/10.

81. Clark Kerr to FO, Apr. 28, 1938, FO F4582, 4642/84/10.

82. UK Delegation (Geneva) to FO, May 10 and 14, 1938, FO F4984, 5234/78/10; Cabinet Conclusions, May 18, 1938, CAB 23/93; League of Nations, *Official Journal*, Jan.-June 1938, p. 378.

83. Memo. by Howe, May 4, 1938, and minutes by Brenan and Cadogan, FO F4774/78/10.

84. Letter from Halifax to Simon, May 9, 1938, FO F4582/84/10.

85. Clark Kerr to FO, Apr. 28, 1938, FO F4551/84/10; Clark Kerr to FO, Mar. 28, 1938, FO 436/2, F3433/25/10.

86. Clark Kerr to FO, May 7, 1938, FO F4969/84/10.

87. Craigie to FO, May 10, 1938, FO 436/2, F5039/25/10. See also Craigie to FO, May 6, 1938, FO F4865/84/10.

88. Craigie to FO, May 31, 1938, and FO to Craigie, June 3, 1938, FO F5850/71/23.

89. See Appendix I to minutes of meeting of the Cabinet Committee on Foreign Policy, June 1, 1938, CAB 27/623.

90. Minutes, *ibid.*

91. Woods to Phillips, June 2, 1938; Phillips to Leith-Ross and Fisher, June 17, 1938; Leith-Ross to Fisher, June 18, 1938, and note by Fisher; Simon to Chamberlain, June 21, 1938; and record of meeting of Chamberlain, Simon, and Halifax, June 28, 1938, all in Premier 1/303.

92. Memo. by Halifax, July 1, 1938, C.P. 152(38), CAB 24/277.

93. Memo. by Simon, July 1, 1938, C.P. 157(38), CAB, 24/277.

94. Cabinet Conclusions, July 6, 1938, CAB 23/94. See also John Harvey, ed., *The Diplomatic Diaries of Oliver Harvey, 1937-1940* (London: Collins, 1970), pp. 160-61.

95. On attempts by the China Association to persuade the government to help China, see Fraser to Brenan, July 13, 1938, FO F7687/62/10; and Cabinet Conclusions, July 6, 1938, CAB 23/94. For Lord Lytton's letter, see *The Times* (London), July 5, 1938. See also letter from Lytton to Halifax, June 10, 1938, Halifax Papers, FO 800. Lytton had headed the League of Nations inquiry into the Manchuria affair of 1931-32.

96. On Australia, see Cabinet Conclusions, July 6 and 13, 1938, CAB 23/94.

97. FO to Lindsay, July 11, 1938, FO 436/2, F7454/25/10. See also FO to Clark Kerr, July 10, 1938, FO 436/2, F7284/25/10; FRUS/1938, 3: 535-37; and Young, *Helping Hand*, p. 74.

98. Cabinet Conclusions, July 6, 1938, CAB 23/94.

99. Cabinet Conclusions, July 13, 1938, CAB 23/94.

100. *Ibid.* See also David Dilks, ed., *The Diaries of Sir Alexander Cadogan, 1938-1945* (London: Cassell, 1971), p. 86.

101. Keith Feiling, *The Life of Neville Chamberlain* (London: Macmillan, 1946), p. 354. See also Alfred Duff Cooper, *Old Men Forget* (London: Hart-Davis, 1953), p. 222.

102. *New Statesman*, July 16, 1938; *Finance and Commerce*, July 20, 1938.

103. Blackburn (Shanghai) to FO, Aug. 5, 1938, DBFP, 8.7: 6-8 [F8451/84/10]; Greenway (Hankow) to FO, Aug. 24, 1938, and minute by Henderson, FO F9157/9157/10. See also minute by Scott on Clark Kerr to FO, July 19, 1938, FO F7853/2/10.

104. *Parl. Deb.* (Commons), vol. 338, cols. 2961-62, 3035-36, 3501.

105. FO to Clark Kerr, July 14, 1938, FO F7545/25/10; FO to Clark Kerr, Sept. 1, 1938, DBFP, 8.67: 58-60 [F9369/78/10].

106. FO to Clark Kerr, Sept. 1, 1938, DBFP, 8.67: 58-60 [F9369/78/10]; FO to Campbell (Paris), Sept. 5, 1938, DBFP, 8.77: 67-69 [F9369/78/10]; UK Delegation (Geneva) to FO, Sept. 12, 1938, FO F9778/78/10; UK Delegation (Geneva) to FO, Sept. 30, 1938, DBFP, 8.120: 110-11 [F10348/78/10].

107. Young, *Helping Hand*, pp. 26, 57, 206-7; Aitchen K. Wu, *China and the Soviet Union: A Study of Sino-Soviet Relations* (London: Methuen, 1950), pp. 268, 270; Charles B. McLane, *Soviet Policy and the Chinese Communists, 1931-1946* (New York: Columbia University Press, 1958), p. 129; Liu, *Military History*, pp. 167-68.

108. See Colonel Dennys (War Office) to Orde, Dec. 22, 1937, FO F11429/9/10; and Air Staff Intelligence report, Dec. 23, 1937, CAB 4/27.

109. Craigie to FO, Feb. 12, 1938, FO F2844/152/23. Japanese strategists did not perceive any fundamental conflict of interests between Japan and the United States in East Asia and even hoped that an agreement for "Pacific defense" or for economic cooperation could be reached with Washington. See Akira Iriye, "Japan's Foreign Policies Between World Wars—Sources and Interpretations," *Journal of Asian Studies*, 26.4 (Aug. 1967): 680-81.

110. Howe to FO, Oct. 21, 1937, FO F8393/9/10; Gage (Hankow) to FO, Dec. 19, 1937, and minute by Eden, FO F11343/9/10. See also memo. by Pratt, Dec. 20, 1937, and minute by Henderson, FO F11289/9/10; Gage to FO, Dec. 26, 1937, FO F11492/9/10; and Earl of Avon, *The Memoirs of Anthony Eden, Earl of Avon*, vol. 1: *Facing the Dictators, 1923-1938* (London: Cassell, 1962), pp. 519-20.

111. For conflicting accounts of the Changkufeng Incident, see Katsu H. Young, "The Nomonhan Incident: Imperial Japan and the Soviet Union," *Monumenta Nipponica*, 22 (1967): 83-86; Martin Blumenson, "The Soviet Power Play at Changkufeng," *World Politics*, 12.2 (Jan. 1960): 249-63; and John Erickson, *The Soviet High Command: A Military-Political History, 1918-1941* (London: Macmillan, 1962), pp. 494-95, 498-99.

112. Viscount Chilston (Moscow) to FO, Aug. 3, 1938, and minute by Ronald, FO F8354/607/10; memo. by Ronald, Aug. 9, 1938, FO F8685/607/10; memo. by Oliphant, Aug. 6, 1938, and minute by Halifax, FO F8703/607/10; Chilston to FO, Aug. 12, 1938, and FO to Chilston and Craigie, Aug. 19, 1938, FO F8732/607/10; Craigie to FO, Oct. 4, 1938, and minute by Howe, FO F11357/607/10.

113. On Britain's distrust of the Soviets and her depreciatory estimate of their military strength, see, for example, Feiling, *Chamberlain*, pp. 325, 347, 403, 408; Viscount Templewood, *Nine Troubled Years* (London: Collins, 1954), pp. 302, 341-43, 350; and Avon, *Dictators*, p. 520.

114. Erickson, *Soviet High Command*, pp. 457-65, 470, 493-94, 505.

115. FO memo., Nov. 16, 1938, FO F12923/4727/61. See also Chilston to FO, Aug. 23, 1938, FO F9213/607/10; minutes by Russell and Lascelles on White (Mukden) to FO, Aug. 20, 1938, FO F10253/607/10; and Craigie to FO, Sept. 12, 1938, FO F10759/607/10. The British view of the fighting at Changkufeng should be contrasted with the assessments in Erickson, *Soviet High Command*, pp. 488-99; and Young, "Nomonhan Incident," pp. 84-86.

116. See minute by Brenan on Craigie to FO, June 20, 1938, FO F6708/84/10.

Chapter six

1. John H. Boyle, "Japan's Puppet Regimes in China, 1937-1940" (Ph.D. dissertation, Stanford University, 1968), pp. 78, 147-49, 188-206. See also Ugaki Kazushige, "Sino-Japanese Peace Talks, June-September, 1938," tr. E. H. M. Colegrave, *St. Antony's Papers, No. II: Far Eastern Affairs, No. I*, ed. G. F. Hudson (London: Oxford University Press, 1957), pp. 94-104.

2. Craigie to FO, May 31 and June 20, 1938, FO F5849, 5850/71/23 and F6708/84/10; Craigie to FO, July 7, 1938, FO 436/3, F7273/25/10; Robert L. Craigie, *Behind the Japanese Mask* (London: Hutchinson, 1946), pp. 60-61.

3. Minute by Brenan on Craigie to FO, June 25, 1938, FO F6898/12/10; minute by Cadogan on Craigie to FO, May 31, 1938 (received July 2), FO F7090/68/23. See also FO to Craigie, July 13, 1938, FO 436/3, F7273/25/10; minutes by Henderson and Brenan on Craigie to FO, July 8, 1938, FO F7307/12/10; and Clark Kerr to FO, July 9, 1938, FO F7479/12/10.

4. Craigie to FO, July 2, 1938, FO F7146/71/23. See also Craigie to FO, July 14, 1938, FO F8491/12/10.

5. Craigie to FO, June 18, 1938 (received July 11), FO F7418/62/10.

6. Craigie to FO, July 14, 1938, FO F8491/12/10.

7. Minute by Brenan (and minutes by Ronald and Mounsey) on Craigie to FO, July 27, 1938, and letter from Cadogan to Craigie, Sept. 15, 1938, FO F8961/71/23. See also minute by Brenan on Craigie to FO, July 14, 1938, FO F8491/12/10.

8. Minute by Brenan on Craigie to FO, July 27, 1938, FO F8961/71/23.

9. Craigie to FO, July 26, 1938, FO F8151/62/10. See also Craigie to FO, July 21, 1938, and FO to Craigie, July 23, 1938, FO F7834/62/10.

10. *Parl. Deb.* (Commons), vol. 338, cols. 2728, 2961-62; *Parl. Deb.* (Lords), vol. 110, col. 1274.

11. Craigie to FO, Aug. 4, 1938, and FO to Craigie, Aug. 5, 1938, DBFP, 8.1 and 6: 1, 5 [F8367/12/10]. See also Craigie to FO, Aug. 10, 1938, FO F9434/12/10.

12. Minute by Henderson on Clark Kerr to FO, Aug. 10, 1938, FO F8695/12/10.

13. Clark Kerr to FO, Aug. 4, 1938, DBFP, 8.2 and 4: 2, 4 [F8403, 8414/16/10].

14. For the Foreign Office's attitude toward mediation, see, for example, minutes by Brenan and Cadogan on Hankey to Cadogan, Apr. 5, 1938, FO F3754/16/10. See also minute by Ronald on Craigie to FO, Nov. 1, 1938, FO F11601/16/10; and FO memo., Nov. 16, 1938, FO F12923/4727/61.

15. FO to Craigie, Aug. 10, 1938, DBFP, 8.11: 11 [F8378/16/10]; Clark Kerr to FO, Aug. 16, 1938, DBFP, 8.24: 21 [F8857/16/10]; minutes by Scott, Ronald, and Mounsey on memo. by Halifax, Aug. 4, 1938, FO F8378/16/10; Craigie to FO, Aug. 12, 1938, DBFP, 8.12: 13 [F8751/16/10]; FO to Clark Kerr, Aug. 15, 1938, DBFP, 8.21: 19 [F8795/16/10].

16. Craigie to FO, Aug. 18, 1938, DBFP, 8.31 and 32: 26, 29 [F8915/62/10 and F9019/12/10].

17. FO to Treasury, Board of Trade, India Office, Colonial Office, and Dominions Office, Aug. 23, 1938, FO F7991/62/10. See also FO to Clark Kerr, Aug. 29, 1938, DBFP, 8.57: 50-51 [F9019/12/10].

18. Craigie to FO, Aug. 20 and 22, 1938, DBFP, 8.38, 39, and 41: 34, 36 [F9106, 9090, 9124/12/10].

19. Minutes by Ronald and Mounsey on Craigie to FO, Aug. 22, 1938, and FO to Craigie, Aug. 24, 1938, FO F9124/12/10; Clark Kerr to FO, Aug. 24, 1938, DBFP, 8.46: 41 [F9194/12/10].

20. Craigie to FO, Aug. 27, 1938, minute by Brenan (and minutes by Ronald and Mounsey), and FO to Craigie, Sept. 1, 1938, FO F9256/12/10. See also Craigie to FO, Sept. 2, 1938, minutes by Ronald and Cadogan, and FO to Craigie, Sept. 7, 1938, FO F9476/12/10.

21. Craigie to FO, Sept. 9, 1938, DBFP, 8.85 and 86: 74-77 [F9696/12/10 and F9684/62/10].

22. Craigie to FO, Sept. 22, 1938, DBFP, 8.107 and 108: 96-101 [F10125, 10829/62/10]; Clark Kerr to FO, Sept. 26, 1938, DBFP, 8.111: 103 [F10187/62/10]; FO to Craigie, Sept. 30, 1938, DBFP, 8.118: 109 [F10200/62/10].

23. Minute by Cadogan on Craigie to FO, Aug. 31, 1938, FO F9455/12/10.

24. Cabinet Conclusions, Sept. 24, 1938, CAB 23/95. See also minutes of the Cabinet Committee on Foreign Policy, Mar. 18, 1938, CAB 27/623; meetings of ministers, Sept. 16 and 24, 1938, CAB 27/646; and Cabinet Conclusions, Sept. 17, 1938, CAB 23/95.

25. See the comments in Cabinet Conclusions, Aug. 30, 1938, CAB 23/94; Cabinet Conclusions, Sept. 12 and 17, 1938, CAB 23/95; and meeting of ministers, Sept. 24, 1938, CAB 27/646. See also W. N. Medlicott, *British Foreign Policy Since Versailles, 1919-1963*, rev. ed. (London: Methuen, 1968), pp. 201, 231.

26. Cabinet Conclusions, Sept. 17, 1938, CAB 23/95.

27. IMTFE, Exhibits 497, 776A, 3508; IMTFE, *Saionji-Harada Memoirs*, pp. 2553, 2555; DGFP, 1.564, 569; Ernst L. Presseisen, *Germany and Japan: A Study in Totalitarian Diplomacy, 1933-1941* (The Hague: Martinus Nijhoff, 1958), pp. 143-46, 189-95; Frank W. Iklé, *German-Japanese Relations, 1936-1940* (New York: Bookman Associates, 1956), pp. 68-69, 78-82. According to British Ambassador Henderson in Berlin, however, when Japan asked Germany for help during the Russo-Japanese border conflict in the summer of 1938, she received only an offer of moral support. Henderson to FO, Aug. 11, 1938, FO F8750/4330/23.

28. Craigie to FO, Sept. 14 and 15, 1938, DBFP, 8.95 and 99: 85-86, 88-91 [F9885/152/23 and F10780/12/10].

29. Report by the Chiefs of Staff, Mar. 21, 1938, F.P. (36)57, CAB 27/627; meeting of the Chiefs of Staff, Sept. 13, 1938, CAB 53/9; report by the Chiefs of Staff, Sept. 14, 1938, C.P. 199(38), CAB 24/278.

30. Minutes by Howe and Mounsey on Craigie to FO, Sept. 28, 1938, FO F10233/152/23. See also FO to Clark Kerr, Oct. 3, 1938, DBFP, 8.123: 114-15 [F10463/13/10].

31. DGFP, 4.535. See also Craigie to FO, Sept. 19, 1938, DBFP, 8.102: 91-92 [F10034/152/23]; and Craigie to FO, Sept. 28, 1938, FO F10233/152/23.

32. Craigie to FO, Oct. 13, 1938, DBFP, 8.148: 134 [F10726/152/23].

33. Ugaki, "Peace Talks," pp. 102-3; Boyle, "Puppet Regimes," pp. 147-49; Craigie, *Japanese Mask*, pp. 61-62.

34. Craigie to FO, Oct. 4, 1938, DBFP, 8.127: 117-18 [F10512/59/10]; Craigie to FO, Oct. 8, 1938, and minute by Howe (and minutes by Ronald and Scott), FO F10611/71/23.

35. FRUS/Japan, 1: 781-90; minutes by Ronald and Howe on Craigie to FO, Oct. 8, 1938, FO F10611/71/23.

36. FO to Clark Kerr, Oct. 19, 1938, DBFP, 8.161: 150 [F10850/2/10]; Craigie to FO, Oct. 23, 1938, DBFP, 8.175: 161 [F11599/62/10]; conversations between Craigie and Grew, Oct. 4, 1938, in Diary, Grew Papers.

37. Memo. by Howe, Oct. 10, 1938, FO F10649/84/10. See also Greenway (Hankow) to FO, Oct. 3, 1938, and minutes by Scott and Brenan, FO F10540/10540/10.

38. Clark Kerr to FO, Oct. 14, 1938, DBFP, 8.152: 137-38 [F10827/13/10].

39. FO to Clark Kerr, Oct. 17, 1938, DBFP, 8.160: 145-49 [F10937/78/10].

40. See, for example, minute by Brenan on Craigie to FO, Sept. 9, 1938 (received Sept. 30), FO F10299/152/23; and minute by Scott on letter from a Chinese student at Camberidge University to Chamberlain, Oct. 31, 1938, FO F11572/71/23. See also Fitzmaurice (Batavia) to FO, Nov. 12, 1937 (received Dec. 20), and minutes by Ashton-Gwatkin and Balfour, FO F11265/615/23; and Fitzmaurice to FO, Jan. 15, 1938 (received Feb. 22), FO F2140/2140/23.

41. FO to Clark Kerr, Oct. 17, 1938, DBFP, 8.158: 142-43 [F10720/78/10]. See also memo. by Howe, Oct. 10, 1938, and minutes by Mounsey, Cadogan, and Halifax, FO F10649/84/10.

42. See minutes by Howe and Mounsey on Clark Kerr to FO, Oct. 12, 1938, FO F10731/16/10; Craigie to FO, Oct. 25, 1938, and FO to Craigie, Oct. 26, 1938, DBFP, 8.176 and 177: 162-63 [F11208/16/10]; and Craigie to FO, Nov. 3, 1938, and minutes by Howe, Mounsey, Ronald, and Cadogan, FO F11672/152/23.

43. FO memo., Nov. 16, 1938, FO F12923/4727/61; letter from Howe to Craigie, Nov. 25, 1938, DBFP, 8.288: 267-68 [F11672/152/23]; letter from Ogilvie Forbes (Berlin) to Howe, Dec. 16, 1938, FO F13740/13740/10; letter from Craigie to Howe, Dec. 29, 1938 (received Jan. 24, 1939), and minute by Ashley Clarke, FO F780/87/10; DGFP, 4.292.

44. For the texts of these statements, see FRUS/Japan, 1: 477-81; and IMTFE, Document 1504C.

45. Craigie to FO, Nov. 10, 1938, DBFP, 8.232: 214-16 [F12433/11783/10]; Clark Kerr to FO, Nov. 22, 1938, DBFP, 8.266: 251-52 [F12366/84/10]. See also FO to Craigie, Nov. 15, 1938, DBFP, 8.242: 229 [F11909/62/10]; and memo. by Brenan, Nov. 29, 1938, FO F13096/84/10.

46. Craigie to FO, Nov. 17, 1938, DBFP, 8.249: 234-36 [F12133/11783/10];Craigie to FO, Dec. 8, 1938, and minutes by Dening, Ronald, and Howe, FO F13116/11783/10; memo. by Brenan, Nov. 29, 1938, FO F13096/84/10.

47. *Parl. Deb.* (Commons), vol. 340, cols. 69, 82.

48. Clark Kerr to FO, Nov. 11, 1938, DBFP, 8.233: 216-18 [F11989/84/10]. See also Clark Kerr to FO, Nov. 7, 1938, DBFP, 8.211: 195-96 [F11990/84/10].

49. Clark Kerr to FO, Nov. 11, 1938, DBFP, 8.234: 218-19 [F11991/84/10]. See also Craigie to FO, Nov. 14, 1938, DBFP, 8.237: 224-25 [F12036/84/10]; and minute by Brenan on Clark Kerr to FO, Nov. 8, 1938, FO F12079/84/10.

50. Clark Kerr to FO, Dec. 2, 1938, DBFP, 8.305: 283-84 [F12825/84/10]. See also Craigie to FO, Dec. 4, 1938, and minute by Brenan, FO F12820/39/10.

51. Japanese Embassy to FO, Dec. 23, 1938, and minute by Dening, FO F13735/84/10. See also IMTFE, Documents 854-T and 2178C; Boyle, "Puppet Regimes," pp. 207-11, 277-84; and David J. Lu, *From the Marco Polo Bridge to Pearl Harbor: Japan's Entry into World War II* (Washington, D.C.: Public Affairs Press, 1961), pp. 80-81.

52. See Boyle, "Puppet Regimes," pp. 242-45, 276-84, 297-303; and Lu, *Marco Polo Bridge*, pp. 80-83.

53. Greenway (Chungking) to British Embassy (Shanghai), Jan. 2, 1939, DBFP, 8.387: 364-65 [F73/69/10]. See also Clark Kerr to FO, Jan. 2, 1939, DBFP, 8.385: 363 [F69/69/10].

54. Craigie to FO, Jan. 1, 1939, FO F2031/2031/23. See also minute by Brenan on Craigie to FO, Nov. 4, 1938, (received Dec. 6), FO F12972/71/23; minute by Howe on memo. by Brenan, Nov. 29, 1938, FO F13096/84/10; Clark Kerr to FO, Nov. 22, 1938, DBFP, 8.266: 251-52 [F12366/84/10]; and Clark Kerr to FO, Dec. 31, 1938, FO F1402/176/23.

55. Memo. by Brenan, Nov. 29, 1938, FO F13096/84/10.

56. Minute by Howe on *ibid*. See also Clark Kerr to FO, Dec. 12, 1938, and minutes by Howe and Mounsey, FO F13269/11783/10.

57. Clark Kerr to FO, Nov. 7, 1938, DBFP, 8.211: 195-96 [F11990/84/10].

58. *Ibid.*

59. Minutes by Cadogan, Howe, and Mounsey, and memo. by Brenan, Nov. 29, 1938, FO F13096/84/10. See also minutes by Brenan, Howe, Mounsey, Cadogan, and Halifax on Clark Kerr to FO, Nov. 8, 1938, FO F12079/84/10.

60. Memo. by Howe, Dec. 19, 1938, and minutes by Mounsey, Cadogan, and Halifax, and letter from Shigemitsu to Halifax, Dec. 21, 1938, FO F13642/12/10. There is no mention of this episode in Shigemitsu Mamoru, *Japan and Her Destiny: My Struggle for Peace*, ed. F. S. G. Piggott, tr. O. White (London: Hutchinson, 1958).

61. Craigie to FO, Dec. 2, 1938, DBFP, 8.308: 290-94 [F13894/71/23].

62. Minute by Brenan on Craigie to FO, Dec. 2, 1938, FO F13894/71/23.

63. Minute by Strang, Jan. 11, 1939, *ibid*.

64. Minutes by Cadogan, Southern Department, Collier, and Dening, *ibid*.

65. Minute by Ronald, Jan. 18, 1939, *ibid*.; FO to Craigie, Jan. 18, 1939, DBFP, 8.433: 407 [F13894/71/23].

66. Cabinet Conclusions, Nov. 9, 1938, CAB 23/96; FO to Craigie, Nov. 5, 1938, DBFP, 8.210: 194-95 [F11778/158/10]; Craigie to FO, Nov. 8 and 15, 1938, DBFP, 8.215 and 239: 201, 226-27 [F11830, 12051/158/10]; FRUS/1938, 4: 194-98.

67. FRUS/Japan, 1: 820-26; FO to Craigie, Jan. 5, 1939, DBFP, 8.395: 370-71 [F183/87/10]; Craigie to FO, Jan. 14 and 17, 1939, DBFP, 8.420 and 431: 393, 403-5 [F439, 2042/87/10].

68. FO to Clark Kerr, Aug. 29, 1938, DBFP, 8.57: 50-51 [F9019/12/10]; Clark Kerr to FO, Sept. 12, 1938, FO F9889/12/10.

69. Craigie to FO, Oct. 23 and Nov. 4, 1938, DBFP, 8.175 and 208: 161-62, 190-93 [F11599, 12895/62/10].

70. FRUS/1938, 4: 194; Cabinet Conclusions, Nov. 9, 1938, CAB 23/96; memo. by Cadogan, Nov. 3, 1938, and FO to Treasury, Board of Trade, India Office, Colonial Office, Dominions Office, and Burma Office, Nov. 11, 1938, FO F11778/158/10.

71. Lindsay to FO, Dec. 1, 1938, and minute by Ronald, FO F12771/62/10.

72. Craigie to FO, Dec. 5, 1938, DBFP, 8.315: 299 [F12896/62/10]. See also Craigie to FO, Dec. 4, 1938, DBFP, 8.311: 295-96 [F12819/25/10]; and Diary, late Jan. 1939, Grew Papers.

73. Craigie to FO, Jan. 1, 1939, DBFP, 8.382 and 384: 359-60, 362-63 [F44, 45/44/10]. See also Craigie to FO, Dec. 30, 1938, FO F875/456/23.

74. See, for example, London Chamber of Commerce to FO, Oct. 28, 1938, and minute by Howe, FO F11432/62/10; Swire (China Association) to FO, Nov. 4, 1938, FO F11730/62/10; and Clark Kerr to FO, Dec. 12, 1938, FO F13212/62/10.

75. Memo. by Brenan, Jan. 7, 1939, FO F285/44/10. See also minute by Brenan on Craigie to FO, Jan. 4, 1939, FO F143/1/10.

76. Board of Trade to FO, Dec. 13, 1938, FO F13291/62/10; Treasury to FO, Dec. 21, 1938, FO F13603/62/10; Wills (Board of Trade) to Howe, Jan. 9, 1939, FO F331/44/10.

77. Letter from Halifax to Chamberlain, Jan. 9, 1939, Premier 1/314. See also minutes by Ronald and Cadogan, Jan. 4, 1939, FO F418/44/10.

78. Letter from Halifax to Chamberlain, Jan. 9, 1939, and note by Chamberlain, Premier 1/314; minutes by Ronald, Jan. 6 and 20, 1939, and letter from Simon to Halifax, Jan. 19, 1939, FO F418/44/10.

79. Foreign Office to Mallet (Washington), Jan. 23, 1939, DBFP, 8.440: 411-14 [F418/44/10]; FRUS/1939, 3: 490-93. London apparently did not inform the Dominions until January 26 that reprisals were being considered. See Dominions Office to FO, Jan. 27, 1939, FO F933/44/10.

80. Craigie to FO, Jan. 28, 1939, DBFP, 8.453: 425-27 [F943/44/10].

81. FO to Mallet, Feb. 1, 1939, DBFP, 8.462: 433-34 [F943/44/10]; Mallet to FO, Feb. 3, 1939, DBFP, 8.465: 435-36 [F1172/44/10]. For the discussion within the State Department about the efficacy of retaliation, see FRUS/1938, 3: 406-9, 425-27; and FRUS/1939, 3: 483-85, 489-90, 496-97, 507-12.

82. See FO to Clark Kerr, Oct. 17, 1938, DBFP, 8.158: 142-43 [F10720-/78/10]; meeting of the Chiefs of Staff, Oct. 19, 1938, CAB 53/9; W. N. Medlicott, *The Economic Blockade* (London: H.M. Stationery Office, 1952), 1: 386, in W. K. Hancock, ed., *History of the Second World War: U.K. Civil Series*; and Nicholas R. Clifford, *Retreat from China: British Policy in the Far East, 1937-1941* (Seattle: Univer-

sity of Washington Press, 1967), p. 95. The later history of this railway project can be followed in CAB 21/1011.

83. See, for example, memo. by Ronald, Nov. 3, 1938, and Secretary of State for Burma to Governor of Burma, Nov. 4, 1938, FO F11719/78/10. See also John T. Pratt, *War and Politics in China* (London: Jonathan Cape, 1943), p. 249; and FRUS/1939, 3: 753-55.

84. Cabinet Conclusions, Nov. 30 and Dec. 7 and 21, 1938, CAB 23/96; memo. by W. B. Brown, Dec. 1, 1938, CAB 21/679; memo. by Stanley, Dec. 5, 1938, C.P. 277(38), CAB 24/281; FO to Clark Kerr, Dec. 19, 1938, DBFP, 8.355; 336-37 [F13505/78/10]; Nixon (Export Credits Guarantee Department) to Howe, Jan. 5, 1939, FO F203/203/10.

85. Clark Kerr to FO, Nov. 7, 1938, DBFP, 8.211: 195-96 [F11990/84/10]; minutes by Brenan, Howe, Mounsey, Cadogan, and Halifax on Clark Kerr to FO, Nov. 8, 1938, FO F12079/84/10; memo. by Halifax, Nov. 25, 1938, C.P. 266(38), CAB 24/280.

86. Memo. by Simon, Nov. 25, 1938, C.P. 268(38), CAB 24/280.

87. Cabinet Conclusions, Nov. 30, 1938, CAB 23/96. For Chamberlain's argument with Shigemitsu, see memo. by Chamberlain, Nov. 22, 1938, Premier 1/277.

88. FRUS/1938, 3: 566-77, 586-87; John M. Blum, *From the Morgenthau Diaries*, vol. 1: *Years of Crisis, 1928-1938* (Boston: Houghton Mifflin, 1959), pp. 505, 509-13, 527; Blum, *From the Morgenthau Diaries*, vol. 2: *Years of Urgency, 1938-1941* (Boston: Houghton Mifflin, 1965), pp. 58-60; William L. Langer and S. Everett Gleason, *The Challenge to Isolation, 1937-1940* (New York: Harper, 1952), pp. 44-45; Frederick C. Adams, "The Road to Pearl Harbor: A Reexamination of American Far Eastern Policy, July 1937-December 1938," *Journal of American History*, 58.1 (June 1971): 73-92.

89. Mallet to FO, Dec. 19 and 21, 1938, and Jan. 4, 1939, DBFP, 8.354, 362, and 390: 335-36, 341, 367 [F13518, 13611/25/10 and F144/11/10]; FRUS/1938, 3: 590-91.

90. FO to Mallet, Jan. 6, 1939, DBFP, 8.397: 373-74 [F184/11/10]. See also memo. by Ronald, Jan. 6, 1939, FO F184/11/10; Cabinet Conclusions, Dec. 21, 1938, CAB 23/96; and letter from Halifax to Chamberlain, Jan. 3, 1939, and note by Chamberlain, Premier 1/303.

91. Mallet to FO, Jan. 11, 1939, DBFP, 8.409: 384-85 [F348/11/10]; Mallet to FO, Jan. 28, 1939, and minutes by Ronald, Balfour, and Howe, FO F938/11/10. See also Cabinet Conclusions, Jan. 18 and Feb. 1, 1939, CAB 23/97; and note from Simon to Chamberlain and Halifax, Jan. 23, 1939, FO F671/11/10.

92. Cabinet Conclusions, Jan. 18, 1939, CAB 23/97. See also Craigie to FO, Jan. 17, 1939, DBFP, 8.427: 399-400 [F539/11/10].

93. Minutes by Brenan, Howe, Cadogan, and Halifax on Mallet to FO, Jan. 28, 1939, FO F938/11/10.

94. Chinese Ambassador to Halifax, Jan. 15, 1939, DBFP, 8.423: 396-97 [F458/24/10]; Clark Kerr to FO, Jan. 17, 1939, DBFP, 8.426: 399 [F541/24/10]; FO to Clark Kerr, Jan. 17, 1939, DBFP, 8.428: 401 [F479/24/10]; Greenway to FO, Jan. 22 and Feb. 5, 1939, DBFP, 8.438 and 472: 410-11, 441-42 [F712, 1250/24/10].

95. Cabinet Conclusions, Feb. 8 and 22, 1939, CAB 23/97; Greenway to FO, Feb. 28, 1939, 8.517: 477-78 [F2067/24/10]. See also Young (Treasury) to Howe, Feb. 13, 1939, FO F1469/11/10; memo. by Simon, Feb. 17, 1939, C.P. 47(39), CAB 24/283; Rowe-Dutton to Howe, Feb. 24, 1939, and notes for Halifax, Feb. 20, 1939, FO F1876/11/10.

96. *Parl. Deb.* (Commons), vol. 344, col. 2147. See also FO to Clark Kerr, Mar. 3, 1939, DBFP, 8.528: 486-87 [F2183/11/10]; and *Parliamentary (Command) Papers*, Cmd. 5963: *Chinese Currency: Arrangements Proposed in Regard to the Chinese Currency Stabilization Fund.*

97. See Craigie to FO, Mar. 14, 1939, DBFP, 8.565: 518-19 [F3601/11/10]. See also Craigie to FO, Mar. 8, 1939, DBFP, 8.547: 503-4 [F2327/11/10].

98. *Parl. Deb.* (Commons), vol. 342, cols. 2524-25.

99. Cabinet Conclusions, Oct. 3, 1938, CAB 23/95. See also Earl of Swinton, *Sixty Years of Power* (London: Hutchinson, 1966), p. 120; Keith Feiling, *The Life of Neville Chamberlain* (London: Macmillan, 1946), pp. 375, 385-86.

100. Cabinet Conclusions, Nov. 7, 1938, CAB 23/96. Just before Munich, Halifax apparently had (in the words of his private secretary) "lost all his delusions about Hitler." See John Harvey, ed., *The Diplomatic Diaries of Oliver Harvey, 1937-1940* (London: Collins, 1970), pp. 198, 202; and Cabinet Conclusions, Sept. 25, 1938, CAB 23/95. After Munich, however, Halifax evidently saw no feasible alternative to working for a settlement with Berlin.

101. Memos. by Cadogan, Oct. 14 and Nov. 8, 1938, FO C14471/42/18. Sir Alexander strongly disagreed with an assertion by Sir Laurence Collier that Germany and Italy were not normal states but represented "a predatory movement which merely gains momentum with each concession made to it." See memo. by Collier, Oct. 29, 1938, and minute by Cadogan, *ibid.* See also David Dilks, ed., *The Diaries of Sir Alexander Cadogan, 1938-1945* (London: Cassell, 1971), pp. 114, 116-19, 122-24.

102. Meeting of the Cabinet Committee on Foreign Policy, Nov. 14, 1938, CAB 27/624; Cabinet Conclusions, Nov. 16 and 30, 1938, CAB 23/96.

103. Cabinet Conclusions, Dec. 21, 1938, CAB 23/96; Harvey, *Diplomatic Diaries*, p. 231.

104. Memos. by Halifax, Jan. 19 and 21, 1939, and enclosures, F.P. (36)74 and 75, CAB 27/627; meeting of the Cabinet Committee on Foreign Policy, Jan. 23, 1939, CAB 27/624; Cabinet Conclusions, Jan. 25, 1939, and appendix, CAB 23/97; Harvey, *Diplomatic Diaries*, p. 245.

105. Cabinet Conclusions, Mar. 18, 1939, CAB 23/98. See also Feiling, *Chamberlain*, pp. 400-401.

106. Cabinet Conclusions, Apr. 5, 1939, CAB 23/98; Cabinet Conclusions, Apr. 26 and May 10, 1939, CAB 23/99; meetings of the Cabinet Committee on Foreign Policy, Apr. 19 and 25, 1939, CAB 27/624; notes by Hoare on Chamberlain's letters, Section XIX(B).5, Templewood Papers.

107. Cabinet Conclusions, May 17 and 24, CAB 23/99; meetings of the Cabinet Committee on Foreign Policy, May 16 and 19, 1939, CAB 27/625; Cadogan (Dilks), *Diaries*, pp. 180-84.

108. Note by Bridges, Jan. 25, 1939, and report by Chiefs of Staff, F.P. (36)77, CAB 27/627.

109. See M. M. Postan, *British War Production* (London: H.M. Stationery Office, 1952), p. 58, in W. K. Hancock, ed., *History of the Second World War: U.K. Civil Series.* See also memo. by Earl Stanhope (First Lord of Admiralty), June 27, 1939, D.P.(P.)63, CAB 16/183A; and Committee of Imperial Defence meeting, July 6, 1939, CAB 2/9.

110. Germany actually had two battle-cruisers and three armored ships (known as pocket battleships), but the British counted the three armored ships as equivalent only to one capital ship. Italy, it should be noted, had two capital ships in service in mid-1939; France had five available. These figures are taken from enclosure no. 2 in annex no. 1 to report by the Chiefs of Staff, June 18, 1939, F.P.(36)96, CAB 27/627. On the Admiralty's view of what Britain needed to be safe, see J. R. M. Butler, *Grand Strategy*, vol. 2: *September, 1939-June, 1941* (London: H.M. Stationery Office, 1957), p. 24, in J. R. M. Butler, ed., *History of the Second World War: U.K. Military Series.*

111. Craigie to Halifax, Dec. 14, 1938, DBFP, 8.338: 320-22 [F471/471/61].

112. FO to Admiralty, Feb. 13, 1939, and memo. by Fitzmaurice, Jan. 27, 1939, DBFP, 8, Appendix 1: 542-48 [F478/471/61].

113. Admiralty to FO, Mar. 29, 1939, *ibid.*, pp. 549-50 [F3147/471/61]. For the Admiralty's minutes on the Foreign Office's suggestion, see Admiralty 1/9909.

114. Meetings of Strategical Appreciation Committee, Mar. 1 and 13, Apr. 6 and 17, 1939, CAB 16/209. See also meeting of the Committee of Imperial Defence, Feb. 24, 1939, CAB 2/8.

115. Memos. by Chatfield, Apr. 19, 1939, and T. S. V. Phillips (Deputy Chief of Naval Staff), Apr. 5, 1939, D.P.(P.)48, CAB 16/183A; meeting of Strategical Appreciation Committee, Apr. 17, 1939, CAB 16/209; meeting of the Committee of Imperial Defence, May 2, 1939, CAB 2/8; Historical Note by Chatfield, June 23, 1939, D.P.(P.)60, CAB 16/183A.

116. See the letters and drafts in Premier 1/309. See also meeting of the Defence Plans (Policy) Committee, July 13, 1937, CAB 16/181; meeting of Strategical Appreciation Committee, Mar. 13, 1939, CAB

16/209; minutes of special meetings of June 28 and July 11, 1939, CAB 2/9; and Butler, *Grand Strategy*, pp. 325-26.

117. Lindsay to FO, Mar. 24, 1939, FO F2942/456/23; memo. by Halifax, Mar. 24, 1939, FO F2963/456/23; FO to Lindsay, Apr. 11, 1939, DBFP, 5.130: 169 [R2820/2613/67]; Cordell Hull, *The Memoirs of Cordell Hull* (New York: Macmillan, 1948), 1: 630; Langer and Gleason, *Challenge*, p. 104.

118. Minutes of special meeting, July 11, 1939, CAB 2/9.

119. Annex to minutes of meeting of Strategical Appreciation Committee, Apr. 17, 1939, CAB 16/209.

120. FO to Lindsay, Mar. 19, 1939, FO F2879/456/23; minutes by Ronald and Ashley Clarke on Lindsay to FO, Mar. 24, 1939, FO F2943/456/23; Danckwerts (Admiralty) to Ronald, May 24, 1939, FO F4962/456/23; Seal (Admiralty) to Harvey, July 3, 1939, FO F7010/456/23.

121. For the situation in China, see Lyman P. Van Slyke, *Enemies and Friends: The United Front in Chinese Communist History* (Stanford, Calif.: Stanford University Press, 1967), pp. 93-94, 169. For the British view of the situation, see annex to minutes of meeting of Strategical Appreciation Committee, Apr. 17, 1939, CAB 16/209; and Clark Kerr to FO, May 20, 1939, DBFP, 8.95: 92-93 [F4965/69/10].

122. See meeting of Cabinet Committee on Foreign Policy, Jan. 26, 1939, CAB 27/624; memo. by Earl Stanhope, n.d. but early April 1939, Premier 1/309; annex to minutes of meeting of Strategical Appreciation Committee, Apr. 17, 1939, CAB 16/209; and meeting of Committee of Imperial Defence, May 2, 1939, CAB 2/8. See also minute by Ronald on Wills (Board of Trade) to FO, Apr. 14, 1939, FO F3696/456/23.

Chapter seven

1. See O. Edmund Clubb, *Twentieth Century China* (New York: Columbia University Press, 1964), p. 226.

2. F. C. Jones, *Japan's New Order in East Asia: Its Rise and Fall, 1937-45* (London: Oxford University Press, 1954), pp. 102, 107-9; Ernst L. Presseisen, *Germany and Japan: A Study in Totalitarian Diplomacy, 1933-1941* (The Hague: Martinus Nijhoff, 1958), pp. 193, 197-200; Frank W. Iklé, *German-Japanese Relations, 1936-1940* (New York: Bookman Associates, 1956), pp. 78-80, 84-89.

3. See, for example, FO to Mallet, Feb. 4, 1939, DBFP, 8.467: 437-39 [C1500/421/62]; Craigie to FO, Feb. 5 and 18 and Mar. 30, 1939, DBFP, 8.473, 491, and 586: 442-44, 460-61, 536 [F1582, 1621/176/23 and C4445/421/62]; letter from Ronald to Mallet, Feb. 16, 1939, DBFP, 8.488: 456-58 [C1612/421/62]; and Mario Toscano, *The Origins of the Pact of Steel* (Baltimore, Md.: Johns Hopkins University Press, 1967), pp. 131-52.

4. Jones, *Japan's New Order*, pp. 113-15; Presseisen, *Germany and*

Japan, pp. 204-8; Iklé, *German-Japanese Relations*, pp. 94-100; DGFP, 6.270.

5. F. C. Jones, *Shanghai and Tientsin, with Special Reference to Foreign Interests* (London: Oxford University Press, 1940), pp. 165-67; Nicholas R. Clifford, *Retreat from China: British Policy in the Far East, 1937-1941* (Seattle: University of Washington Press, 1967), pp. 103-4; Arthur N. Young, *China's Wartime Finance and Inflation, 1937-1945* (Cambridge, Mass.: Harvard University Press, 1965), pp. 167, 170.

6. Broadmead (Shanghai) to FO, Apr. 28, 1939, DBFP, 9.27: 30-31 [F4085/75/10]; FO to Craigie, May 4, 1939, DBFP, 9.42: 45-46 [F4153/75/10]; FO to Clark Kerr, June 2, 1939, DBFP, 9.141: 125 [F5284/75/10]; Clifford, *Retreat*, pp. 104-5; Young, *Finance and Inflation*, p. 213.

7. Akira Iriye, "Japanese Imperialism and Aggression: Reconsiderations, II," *Journal of Asian Studies*, 23.1 (Nov. 1963): 112.

8. Memo. by Halifax, Mar. 30, 1939, C.P. 76(39), CAB 24/284. On the preparation of this memorandum, see FO memo., Feb. 28, 1939, and minutes by Howe, Strang, Cadogan, and Halifax, FO F3478/456/23. See also minute by Ronald on Clark Kerr to FO, Feb. 23, 1939, FO F1833/1/10; and Craigie to FO, Feb. 11, 1939, DBFP, 8.481: 451 [F1376/186/10].

9. Memo. by Halifax, Mar. 30, 1939, C.P. 76(39), CAB 24/284. See also minute by Ronald on Wills (Board of Trade) to FO, Apr. 14, 1939, and letter from Ronald to Wills, Apr. 19, 1939, FO F3696/456/23.

10. Wills to FO, Apr. 14, 1939; minute by Ronald, and letters from Ronald to Wills, Apr. 19 and 26, 1939, all in FO F3696/456/23; letter from Shackle (Board of Trade) to Ronald, Apr. 29, 1939, and letter from Howe to Shackle, May 8, 1939, FO F4119/456/23.

11. Report by Chiefs of Staff, Apr. 24, 1939, C.P. 95(39), CAB 24/285.

12. See, for example, minute by Howe on Craigie to FO, Mar. 23, 1939, FO F2876/456/23; meeting of the Cabinet Committee on Foreign Policy, Mar. 27, 1939, CAB 27/624; and Cabinet Conclusions, May 17, 1939, CAB 23/99.

13. FO to Craigie, Apr. 27, 1939, DBFP, 9.25: 27-29 [F4055/456/23]; *Parl. Deb.* (Lords), vol. 112, cols. 692-93; *Parl. Deb.* (Commons), vol. 346, col. 338.

14. Craigie to FO, May 26, 1939, DBFP, 9.116 and 118: 107-9 [F5037, 5038/1236/23]; Craigie to FO, June 2, 1939, FO F5299/1236/23. Hiranuma's message can be found in FRUS/Japan, 2: 1. See also Jones, *Japan's New Order*, pp. 122-23; and Waldo H. Heinrichs, Jr., *American Ambassador: Joseph C. Grew and the Development of the United States Diplomatic Tradition* (Boston: Little, Brown, 1966), pp. 285-86.

15. See minutes by Brenan, Mounsey, Cadogan, Ronald, Howe, and Halifax on Craigie to FO, May 26, 1939, FO F5037/1236/23; and min-

utes by Dening and Howe on Craigie to FO, June 2, 1939, FO F5299/1236/23.

16. Craigie to FO, May 26 and June 5, 1939, DBFP, 9.116 and 150: 107-8, 134-35 [F5037, 5387/1236/23]; Craigie to FO, June 14, 1939, FO F5867/456/23.

17. For Washington's attitude, see William L. Langer and S. Everett Gleason, *The Challenge to Isolation, 1937-1940* (New York: Harper, 1952), pp. 151-52; and Cordell Hull, *The Memoirs of Cordell Hull* (New York: Macmillan, 1948), 1: 631-32.

18. Minute by Brenan on memo. by R. A. Butler, May 9, 1939, FO F4419/176/23.

19. "Situation Estimate of Central China Expeditionary Army," July 24, 1939, in IMTFE, Document 605.

20. Phillips (Shanghai) to FO, Feb. 22 and 25, 1939, DBFP, 8.496 and 507: 464-65, 471-72 [F1739, 1869/84/10]; Clark Kerr to FO, Feb. 22 and Mar. 14, 1939, DBFP, 8.497 and 561: 466, 514-15 [F1743, 2560/84/10].

21. Craigie to FO, May 4, 19, and 26, 1939, DBFP, 9.44, 92, and 117: 49-52, 88-90, 108-9 [F5165, 6890, 5043/84/10].

22. Broadmead (Shanghai) to FO, May 13, 1939, DBFP, 9.63: 66 [F4525/4522/10]; Fitzmaurice (Amoy) to FO, May 15, 1939, DBFP, 9.69: 70 [4605/4522/10].

23. Clark Kerr to FO, May 16, 1939, DBFP, 9.79: 78 [F4658/4522/10]; Craigie to FO, May 16 and 18, 1939, DBFP, 9.80 and 83: 79-81 [F4663, 4721/4522/10].

24. Robert L. Craigie, *Behind the Japanese Mask* (London: Hutchinson, 1946), p. 72.

25. On these grievances, see Craigie to FO, Sept. 22, 1938, DBFP, 8.108: 97-101 [F10829/62/10].

26. Jamieson (Tientsin) to FO, Oct. 7 and Nov. 15, 1938, DBFP, 8.129 and 244: 119-20, 230-31 [F10624, 12194/25/10]; Allen (Shanghai) to FO, Nov. 23, 1938, DBFP, 8.273: 256 [F12438/25/10]; Clark Kerr to FO, Jan. 11, 1939, DBFP, 8.413: 388-89 [F907/75/10].

27. Minute by Scott on Craigie to FO, Oct. 8, 1938, FO F10611/71/23.

28. See the telegrams in DBFP, 8, Appendix 2: 551-60.

29. Jamieson to FO, Dec. 13 and 17, 1938, DBFP, 8.334 and 346: 314, 328-29 [F13266, 13449/717/10]; Craigie to FO, Jan. 6, 1939, DBFP, 8.401: 377-78 [F2035/1/10].

30. F. S. G. Piggott, *Broken Thread: An Autobiography* (Aldershot: Gale & Polden, 1950), p. 313; Jamieson to FO, Jan. 28 and Feb. 8, 1939, DBFP, 8.454 and 477: 427, 447 [F988, 1295/1/10]; Herbert (Tientsin) to FO, Mar. 6, 1939, DBFP, 8.535: 491-92 [F2252/1/10].

31. Piggott, *Broken Thread*, pp. 314-17; Craigie to FO, Mar. 23, 1939, DBFP, 8.579: 532 [F2867/1/10]; Jamieson to FO, Apr. 11, 1939,

DBFP, 9.2: 1-3 [F3633/1/10]; minutes by Brenan, Howe, and Scott on Craigie to FO, Apr. 19, 1939 (received June 1), FO F5167/1/10.

32. Further details about these events can be found in RIIA, *Survey of International Affairs, 1939-1946: The Eve of the War*, ed. A. J. and V. M. Toynbee (London: Oxford University Press, 1958), pp. 639-41. See also Jamieson to FO, June 11 and 22, 1939, DBFP, 9.180 and 249: 159-61, 216 [F5621, 6239/1/10]; and the telegrams in Japan, *Archives of the Ministry of Foreign Affairs* (Library of Congress microfilm), IMT 459, reel WT 60.

33. Jamieson to FO, May 13, 1939, DBFP, 9.64: 66-67 [F4531/1/10]; Craigie to FO, May 19 and 26, 1939, DBFP, 9.89 and 114: 85, 106 [F4781, 5039/1/10]; Clark Kerr to FO, May 19, 1939, DBFP, 9.86: 82-84 [F4808/1/10].

34. Minutes by Brenan, Howe, and Mounsey on Clark Kerr to FO, May 19, 1939, FO F4808/1/10; FO to Clark Kerr, June 1, 1939, DBFP, 9.139: 123-24 [F5162/1/10]; Cabinet Conclusions, June 7, 1939, CAB 23/99.

35. Jamieson to FO, June 1, 1939, DBFP, 9.137: 121 [F5274/1/10]; Craigie to FO, June 7, 1939, DBFP, 9.158: 142-43 [F5432/1/10]; Cabinet Conclusions, June 7, 1939, CAB 23/99.

36. Jamieson to FO, June 9 and 11, 1939, DBFP, 9.169 and 180: 151, 159-61 [F5581, 5621/1/10].

37. Craigie to FO, June 14, 1939, DBFP, 9.197: 170 [F5785/1/10]; Clark Kerr to FO, June 15, 1939, DBFP, 9.203: 177-78 [F5881/1/10].

38. See minute by Brenan on Jamieson to FO, June 14, 1939, FO F5871/1/10; also Cadogan (Dilks), *Diaries*, p. 187.

39. Cabinet Conclusions, June 14, 1939, CAB 23/99. On the proposal to establish an advisory committee, see the exchange between Clark Kerr and FO, June 10, 12, and 14, 1939, DBFP, 9.176, 182, and 195: 156, 162, 169 [F5593, 5709/1/10].

40. Clark Kerr to FO, June 14, 1939, DBFP, 9.196: 169 [F5784/1/10]; Craigie to FO, June 21, 1939, DBFP, 9.242: 211-12 [F6130/1/10]. Arita shared the military's view that issues other than the case of the four suspects would have to be settled. He also told Craigie that the Japanese army in China had a free hand on "defence questions." See Craigie to FO, June 14, 1939, DBFP, 9.198: 170-71 [F5790/1/10].

41. FO to Phipps (Paris), June 16, 1939, DBFP, 9.221: 191-92 [F5980/44/10].

42. Craigie, *Japanese Mask*, pp. 73-74.

43. FO to Lindsay, June 15, 1939, DBFP, 9.210: 183-84 [F5893/1/10]; minute by Dening on Loraine (Rome) to FO, June 21, 1939, FO F6176/1/10. See also letter from Holman (Berlin) to Kirkpatrick, June 29, 1939, DBFP, 6.180: 208 [C9245/54/18]; and Henderson to Halifax, June 24 and 29, 1939, H/XV/190 and H/XV/208 in Halifax Papers, FO 800/315.

44. Craigie to FO, June 18, 1939, DBFP, 9.227: 196-98 [F6017/1/10]; Clark Kerr to FO, June 19, 1939, DBFP, 9.231: 200-202 [F6074/1/10]. Presumably, Clark Kerr's feelings toward Japan were exacerbated when he learned on June 12 that some Japanese military officers were planning an attempt on his life. See Clark Kerr to FO, June 12, 1939, and letter from Clark Kerr to Howe, June 19, 1939, 39/6 and 39/20 in Clark Kerr Papers, FO 800/299.

45. Loraine to FO, June 21, 1939, DBFP, 9.244: 213 [F6176/1/10].

46. *The Times* (London), June 20, 1939; *Manchester Guardian*, June 20, 1939; *Parl. Deb.* (Commons), vol. 348, cols. 1279, 1509, 1995, 2611; *Parl. Deb.* (Lords), vol. 113, col. 411; London Chamber of Commerce to FO, June 14, 1939, FO F5852/1/10; China Association to FO, June 16, 1939, FO F6317, 6318/1/10.

47. Cabinet Conclusions, June 14, 1939, CAB 23/99. On Halifax's decision to raise the question of retaliation, see memo. by Howe, June 9, 1939, and minute by Cadogan, FO F5801/1/10.

48. Memo. by Halifax, June 16, 1939, F.P. (36)95, CAB 27/627.

49. Report by an Informal Committee of Representatives of the Foreign Office, Colonial Office, and Board of Trade, June 16, 1939, F.P. (36)94, CAB 27/627. See also Percival (Board of Trade) to Howe, June 19, 1939, FO F6111/1/10.

50. Report by the Chiefs of Staff, June 18, 1939, F.P. (36)96, CAB 27/627.

51. Meeting of the Cabinet Committee on Foreign Policy, June 19, 1939, CAB 27/625.

52. Meeting of the Cabinet Committee on Foreign Policy, June 20, 1939, *ibid.*

53. Report by the Chiefs of Staff, June 24, 1939, D.P.(P.)61, CAB 16/183A.

54. Minute by Ronald on Admiralty to FO, June 20, 1939, FO F6081/1/10; minute by Howe on Craigie to FO, June 22, 1939, FO F6198/1/10.

55. Cabinet Conclusions, June 21, 1939, CAB 23/100.

56. Meeting of the C.I.D., June 26, 1939, CAB 2/9.

57. Minutes of special meeting, June 28, 1939, CAB 2/9.

58. Keith Feiling, *The Life of Neville Chamberlain* (London: Macmillan, 1946), p. 413.

59. See, for example, letter from Runciman to Chamberlain, June 19, 1939, Premier 1/316; Cabinet Conclusions, June 21, 1939, CAB 23/100; and report by Chiefs of Staff, June 18, 1939, F.P. (36)96, CAB 27/627.

60. FO to Lindsay, June 15, 1939, DBFP, 9.210: 183-84 [F5893/1/10]; letter from Halifax to Chamberlain, June 19, 1939, FO F6182/1/10; FO to Craigie, June 19, 1939, DBFP, 9.230 and 232: 200, 202-3 [F6017/1/10]; meetings of the Cabinet Committee on Foreign Policy, June 19 and 20, 1939, CAB 27/625; Langer and Gleason, *Challenge*, pp. 152-55; FRUS/Japan, 1: 652.

61. Craigie to FO, June 20 and 24, 1939, DBFP, 9.238, 254, and 255: 207-8, 219-21 [F6102, 6337, 6338/1/10].

62. Letter from Craigie to Cadogan, June 30, 1939, FO F8061/1/10. See also Craigie to FO, June 20, 24, and 27, 1939, DBFP, 9.240, 257, and 269: 209, 222, 233 [F6115, 6339, 6449/1/10].

63. Minutes by Ronald and Cadogan on Craigie to FO, June 28, 1939, FO F6467/6457/10.

64. Craigie to FO, June 24, 1939, DBFP, 9.259: 223-24 [F6340/1/10]; Craigie to FO, July 7 and 17, 1939, DBFP, 9.290 and 332: 249-50, 285-87 [F6945, 7402/6457/10].

65. Clark Kerr to FO, June 26, 1939, DBFP, 9.265 and 267: 228-32 [F6378/1/10 and F6428/87/10]; Clark Kerr to FO, July 7, 1939, DBFP, 9.291: 250-51 [F7017/6457/10].

66. Lindsay to FO, June 26, 1939, DBFP, 9.264: 227-28 [F6423/1/10].

67. Minutes by Howe and Ronald on Clark Kerr to FO, June 26, 1939, FO F6428/87/10; FO to Craigie, July 12, 1939, DBFP, 9.307: 264-65 [F6706/456/23]; minutes by Ashley Clarke and Dening on Craigie to FO, July 17, 1939, FO F7402/6457/10.

68. Waley (Treasury) to Howe, June 27, 1939, and FO to Craigie, July 4, 1939, FO F6470/6457/10; Bewley (Treasury) to Howe, July 3, 1939, minutes by Brenan and Howe, and FO to Clark Kerr, July 6, 1939, FO F6783/6457/10; notes by Brenan and Ronald, July 11, 1939, FO F7723/6457/10; Howe to Waley, July 19, 1939, FO F7183/6457/10.

69. FO to Lindsay, July 11, 1939, DBFP, 9.297: 258 [F7017/6457/10]; Lindsay to FO, July 15, 1939, DBFP, 9.329: 283 [F7392/6457/10].

70. FO to Craigie, June 30, 1939, DBFP, 9.276: 239 [F6716/44/10]; letter from Brown (Board of Trade) to Cadogan, July 6, 1939, and Treasury minutes on letter from Halifax to Simon, July 13, 1939, Premier 1/314; FO to Craigie, July 25, 1939, DBFP, 9.385: 327-28 [F7839/44/10].

71. Craigie to FO, July 15, 1939, DBFP, 9.325: 278-80 [F7347/6457/10]. See also Craigie to FO, July 15, 1939, DBFP, 9.328: 282-83 [F7346/6457/10].

72. Craigie to FO, July 15, 1939, DBFP, 9.327: 281-82 [F7348/6457/10]; Clark Kerr to FO, July 16, 1939, DBFP, 9.331: 285 [F7359/6457/10]; minutes by Ashley Clarke and Howe on Craigie to FO, July 17, 1939, FO F7445/6457/10; FO to Craigie, July 17 and 20, 1939, DBFP, 9.337 and 352: 289-90, 303-4 [F7348, 7601/6457/10].

73. For the final text, see Craigie to FO, July 23, 1939, DBFP, 9.365: 313 [F7701/6457/10].

74. Craigie, *Japanese Mask*, p. 75.

75. *Parl. Deb.* (Commons), vol. 350, cols. 994, 2025-2026; *Parl. Deb.* (Lords), vol. 114, col. 368.

76. *North China Star*, July 23, 1939; *China Press*, July 25, 1939;

Oriental Affairs, Aug. 1939, p. 60; *Finance and Commerce*, Aug. 2, 1939; *The Times* (London), July 26, 1939.

77. *The Times* (London), July 25, 1939; *New Statesman and Nation*, July 29, 1939; *Spectator*, July 28, 1939; *Manchester Guardian*, July 25, 1939. On August 4 the *Manchester Guardian* added: "Lord Halifax seems to think that everyone in this country ought quietly to accept the 'plain terms of the formula' and the interpretation that the Government itself has placed on it. But surely that is impossible."

78. FO to Clark Kerr, July 25, 1939, DBFP, 9.389: 332-34 [F7902/6457/10]; Clark Kerr to FO, July 26 and 27, 1939, DBFP, 9.395 and 401: 340, 343-44 [F7943, 8049/6457/10]; memo. by Quo Tai-chi, July 31, 1939, DBFP, 9.436: 374-75 [F8432/6457/10].

79. Clark Kerr to FO, Aug. 2, 1939, DBFP, 9.449: 386 [F8307/6457/10]; FO to Clark Kerr, Aug. 2, 1939, DBFP, 9.453: 389-92 [F8310/11/10]; memo. by Quo Tai-chi, July 18, 1939, and Halifax to Simon, Aug. 3, 1939, FO F7524/11/10; Simon to Halifax, Aug. 17, 1939, and Halifax to Quo Tai-chi, Aug. 29, 1939, FO F9205/11/10.

80. FO to Clark Kerr, July 25 and Aug. 25, 1939, DBFP, 9.389 and 453: 332-34 [F7902/6457/10 and F8310/11/10]; Cabinet Conclusions, Aug. 2, 1939, CAB 23/100; FO minute, Aug. 8, 1939, FO F8528/6457/10.

81. Hull, *Memoirs*, 1: 635.

82. See *ibid.*, pp. 636-37; Langer and Gleason, *Challenge*, pp. 157-58; and Diary, July 26 and 27, 1939, Jay Pierrepont Moffat Papers.

83. Meeting of C.I.D., July 27, 1939, CAB 2/9.

84. *Ibid.*; minutes by Ashley Clarke, Vansittart, and Halifax on Clark Kerr to FO, July 31, 1939, FO F8151/6457/10; minutes by Balfour and Ronald on Craigie to FO, Aug. 1, 1939, FO F8245/6457/10; Cabinet Conclusions, Aug. 2, 1939, and minutes by Ronald, Mounsey, and Halifax, FO F8393/6457/10.

85. Craigie to FO, July 24 and 30 and Aug. 1, 1939, DBFP, 9.376, 419, and 438: 321, 361-63, 376-78 [F7746, 8244/6457/10 and F8171/1/10]; FO to Craigie, Aug. 8, 1939, DBFP, 9.494: 427-28 [F8535/6457/10]; Piggott, *Broken Thread*, p. 323.

86. Craigie to FO, July 28 and Aug. 1, 1939, DBFP, 9.403 and 442: 346-47, 379-80 [F8071, 8303/6457/10]; Japan, *Archives*, IMT 459, Reel WT 60, pp. 357, 377.

87. Craigie to FO, Aug. 1, 5, and 8, 1939, DBFP, 9.442, 473, and 491: 379-80, 411-13, 425-26 [F8303, 8478, 8581/6457/10].

88. Clark Kerr to FO, July 27 and 31 and Aug. 8, 1939, DBFP, 9.401, 424, and 495: 343-44, 366-67, 428-30 [F8049, 8151, 8656/6457/10].

89. Craigie to FO, Aug. 1 and 10, 1939, DBFP, 9.444 and 505: 381-82, 436-37 [F8245, 8947/6457/10].

90. Cabinet Conclusions, Aug. 2, 1939, CAB 23/100.

91. Henderson to FO, Aug. 10, 1939, and minute by Ashley Clarke, FO F8778/6457/10.

92. Memo. by Sansom, Aug. 3, 1939, DBFP, 9, Appendix 1: 528-32 [F8502/6457/10].

93. Minute by Dening on Craigie to FO, Aug. 5, 1939, FO F8525/6457/10; minute by Ronald on Clark Kerr to FO, Aug. 8, 1939, FO F8656/6457/10; FO to Clark Kerr, Aug. 14, 1939, DBFP, 9.528: 458-59 [F8656/6457/10].

94. Notes by Halifax, Aug. 11, 1939, FO F8502/6457/10. See also minutes by Dening and Ronald on Craigie to FO, Aug. 5, 1939, FO F8525/6457/10; and Cadogan (Dilks), *Diaries*, p. 194.

95. Minute by Dening on Craigie to FO, Aug. 8, 1939, FO F8533/6457/10; Campbell (Paris) to FO, Aug. 11, 1939, DBFP, 9.516: 446-50 [F8792/6457/10]; memo. by Ashley Clarke, Aug. 13, 1939, Premier 1/316; Craigie to FO, Aug. 14, 1939, DBFP, 9.527: 457 [F8912/6457/10]; FO to Craigie, Aug. 15, 1939, DBFP, 9.531: 460 [F8855/6457/10].

96. Memo. by Mounsey, Aug. 12, 1939, Premier 1/316.

97. Letter and note from Halifax to Chamberlain, Aug. 16, 1939, and note by Chamberlain, Premier 1/316. See also minute by Simon, Aug. 17, 1939, FO F9097/6457/10; and Cadogan (Dilks), *Diaries*, p. 195.

98. FO to Craigie, Aug. 17, 1939, DBFP, 9.535 and 537: 463-65 [F9097/6457/10]; Craigie to FO, Aug. 18, 1939, DBFP, 9.550: 473-74 [F9146/6457/10].

99. FO memo., Aug. 21, 1939, DBFP, 9.568: 483-87 [F9297/87/10]. See also memo. by Sansom, Aug. 3, 1939, DBFP, 9, Appendix 1; and notes by Halifax, Aug. 11, 1939, FO F8502/6457/10.

100. *Far Eastern Digest*, 2 (Sept. 1939): 498-99.

101. Minutes by Ronald, Mounsey, and Cadogan on Craigie to FO, Aug. 21, 1939, FO F9258/6457/10; memo. by Ashley Clarke, Aug. 22, 1939, FO F9369/87/10; minutes by Ronald and Mounsey on Phipps to FO, Aug. 25, 1939, FO F9450/456/23.

102. Craigie to FO, Aug. 25, 1939, DBFP, 9.584: 495-97 [F9421/87/10].

103. FO minute by Butler, Aug. 26, 1939, FO F9583/6457/10; FO to Craigie, Aug. 29, 1939, DBFP, 9.599 and 600: 509-11 [F9421/87/10 and F9583/6457/10].

104. Lothian (Washington) to FO, Sept. 1, 1939, and minute by Ashley Clarke, FO F9938/6457/10; FRUS/1939, 4: 242-43; minute by Brenan on Craigie to FO, Sept. 4, 1939, FO F9854/87/10.

105. Letter from Lothian to Halifax, Nov. 3, 1939, H/XV/336 in Halifax Papers, FO 800/317.

106. See, for example, War Cabinet Conclusions, Nov. 27, 1939, CAB 65/2.

Chapter eight

1. Minute by Cadogan, Oct. 10, 1938, on Craigie to FO, Sept. 9, 1938 (received Sept. 30), FO F10299/152/23.

2. Craigie to FO, Jan. 17, 1939, DBFP, 8.431. See also Nicholas R.

Clifford, *Retreat from China: British Policy in the Far East, 1937-1941* (Seattle: University of Washington Press, 1967), pp. 165-66.

3. See, for example, FO memo., Aug. 21, 1939, DBFP, 9.568.

4. Note by Halifax and memo. by Ashton-Gwatkin, July 7, 1938, C.P. 161(38), CAB 24/277.

5. Minute by Ashley Clarke on Campbell to FO, Aug. 11, 1939, FO F8930/6457/10.

6. Review of Imperial Defence by the Chiefs of Staff, Feb. 26, 1937, C.P. 73(37), CAB 24/268.

7. This point is made in a note by G. F. Hudson in William Roger Louis, *British Strategy in the Far East, 1919-1939* (London: Oxford University Press, 1971), p. 266.

8. This is not to imply that the Chamberlain government tried to turn the Germans east against the Soviets. Indeed, despite Britain's intense desire to conciliate Hitler, she was never willing to give him a "free hand" in Europe.

9. Memo. by Halifax, Mar. 30, 1939, C.P. 76(39) CAB 24/284.

10. *Ibid.* See also minute by Brenan on Craigie to FO, Nov. 4, 1938 (received Dec. 6), FO F12972/71/23.

11. Craigie to FO, Feb. 28, 1938 (received Mar. 28), FO F3359/71/23.

12. Memo. by Dening, Dec. 29, 1939, CAB 21/570.

13. John T. Pratt, *War and Politics in China* (London: Jonathan Cape, 1943), p. 188. Farther on in his book, Pratt offered a more simplistic view: "The ferocity of the primitive savage . . . is never far below the surface in Japan" (p. 242). In fairness to Sir John, it must be said that his book was written during World War II.

14. Robert L. Craigie, *Behind the Japanese Mask* (London: Hutchinson, 1946), p. 162.

15. See, respectively, Clark Kerr to FO, Dec. 31, 1938 (received Feb. 13, 1939), FO F1402/176/23; and Clark Kerr to FO, Aug. 8, 1939, DBFP, 9.495: 428-30 [F8656/6457/10].

16. David Dilks, ed., *The Diaries of Sir Alexander Cadogan, 1938-1945* (London: Cassell, 1971), pp. 13, 15, 29, 30, 54, 93.

17. Eden to Chamberlain, Jan. 9, 1938, Premier 1/276.

Bibliographical Note

Bibliographical Note

A. UNPUBLISHED OFFICIAL SOURCES

The principal sources of this study were the British Foreign Office (FO 371) and Cabinet records (CAB) for the 1930's, now open under a "thirty-year rule." The Japanese, Chinese, and general Far Eastern correspondence of the Foreign Office was particularly valuable. The correspondence relating to the United States, the Soviet Union, Italy, Germany, and France was also used. Since well over a hundred files (of one to twelve volumes each) of the FO 371 group were consulted, it would be pointless to list them here. The most important files are cited in the Notes (see note 23, chap. 1, above, for the form of citation used). Where there were gaps in the Foreign Office records, I used the papers of the Treasury and the Admiralty.

The following Cabinet records were of special interest (see note 11, chap. 1, above, for the citation form used in the Notes):

CAB 2 (minutes of the Committee of Imperial Defence, 1933-39), vols. 6-9;

CAB 4 (papers submitted to the Committee of Imperial Defence, late 1932-39), vols. 22-30;

CAB 16 (records of various important committees concerned with defense problems), vols. 109-12, 153, 181-83, 209;

CAB 21 (important material about the Tientsin crisis of 1939 and many interesting letters to and from Sir Maurice Hankey), vols. 569-70 and various other volumes as cited in the Notes;

CAB 23 (minutes of Cabinet meetings from late 1932 to Sept. 1939), vols. 73-101; vols. 74 and 101 are indexes;

CAB 24 (papers circulated to the Cabinet by various departments and committees from late 1932 to Sept. 1939), vols. 233-88;

CAB 27 (records of the important Cabinet Committee on Foreign Policy, 1936-39), vols. 622-27;

CAB 27 (records of other committees concerned with various questions of foreign policy and defense); on East Asian problems, in particular, vols. 482, 568, 596, 634;

CAB 29 (records of the Anglo-French staff talks, 1939), vols. 159-61;

CAB 32 (records of the Imperial Conference, 1937), vols. 127-30;

CAB 47 (records of the Advisory Committee on Trade Questions in Time of War), various volumes as cited in the Notes;

CAB 53 (records of the Chiefs of Staff subcommittee), vols. 8-11, 32-54;

CAB 65, 66, 67 (minutes and papers of the War Cabinet, formed in Sept. 1939), vols. 1-2, 1-2, 1-3, respectively.

Finally, material of considerable importance, particularly with regard to the Tientsin crisis and the decision not to grant a loan to China in the summer of 1938, can be found in the records of the Prime Minister's office, Premier File 1 (see note 32, chap. 1, above, for the citation form used in the Notes). For this study, the following volumes were valuable: 152, 175, 210, 215, 219, 229, 247, 250, 259, 261, 266, 276-78, 303, 308-10, 314-16, 327, 330, 339, 345-47, 366, 367.

Documents and testimony relating to Japanese foreign policy in the 1930's are collected in the voluminous records of the International Military Tribunal for the Far East (IMTFE) convened at Tokyo, 1946-48, which are housed in the Library of Congress and at the University of California, Berkeley. Useful sections of this collection include: *Analyses of Documentary Evidence*; *Chronological Summary*; *Decisions of Conferences*; *Exhibits (Documents)*; *Judgment*; *Proceedings*; and *Saionji-Harada Memoirs*. A helpful guide to this material is Paul S. Dull and Michael T. Umemura, *The Tokyo Trials: A Functional Index to the Proceedings of the International Military Tribunal for the Far East* (Ann Arbor: University of Michigan Press, 1957). The records of the IMTFE must be used cautiously. Both the prosecution and the defense were trying to prove points, not reconstruct a balanced picture of Japan's foreign policy. On the larger issues posed by the trial, see Justice R. B. Pal, *International Military Tribunal for the Far East: Dissentient Judgment* (Calcutta: Sanyal, 1953).

Though it contains much material that is also to be found in the IMTFE exhibits, another useful source for Japanese policy is the English sections of Japan, *Archives of the Ministry of Foreign Affairs*. These records are available in microfilm at the Library of Congress and at the University of California, Berkeley. For this study I used the following reels (in each case the first number should properly be preceded by "IMT" and the second by the word "Reels," e.g., IMT 1, Reels WT1-WT5): 1, WT1-WT5; 2, WT5; 3, WT6; 74, WT19; 84, WT20; 110, WT23; 145, WT27; 175, WT29, WT30; 224, WT34; 253, WT37; 261, WT37, WT38; 317, WT43; 324, WT44; 325, WT44; 350, WT46; 357, WT46; 417, WT55; 423, WT55; 459, WT59, WT60; 509, WT64; 515, WT64. An invaluable guide to these archives is Cecil Uyehara, comp., *Checklist of Archives in the Japanese Ministry of Foreign Affairs, Tokyo, Japan, 1868-1945* (Washington, D.C.: Photoduplication Service, Library of Congress, 1954).

B. PUBLISHED OFFICIAL SOURCES

The most important official publications I relied on were volumes 8 and 9 of the third series of Great Britain, Foreign Office, *Documents on British Foreign Policy, 1919-1939*, ed. E. L. Woodward, J. P. T. Bury, Rohan Butler, et al. (London: H.M. Stationery Office, 1949-70). (See note 2, chap. 1, above, for the form of citation used in the Notes.) These two volumes contain Foreign Office correspondence pertaining to East Asia for the period August 1938 to September 1939. This collection suffers from some major shortcomings: minutes by the Foreign Secretary and his advisers are generally omitted, as are records of the Cabinet, the Committee on Foreign Policy, and the Committee of Imperial Defence. Thus, one must consult the unpublished records to learn how policy was made and what the views of various individuals and departments were. The first seven volumes of the third series cover British policy in Europe from March 1938 to September 1939; vols. 8-11 of the second series deal with Britain's policy in East Asia around the time of the Manchurian crisis. Her course in East Asia from September 1939 to December 1941 is traced in Llewellyn Woodward, *British Foreign Policy in the Second World War*, vol. 2 (London: H.M. Stationery Office, 1971), an official history based on Foreign Office records. Four works in the *History of the Second World War: U.K. Military Series*, ed. J. R. M. Butler (London, 1952-), contain information about Britain's military problems and policies in the late 1930's. For this study, I found the most useful of the four to be S. Woodburn Kirby et al., *The War Against Japan*, vol. 1: *The Loss of Singapore* (1957). The other three are J. R. M. Butler, *Grand Strategy*, vol. 2: *September, 1939-June, 1941* (1957); I. S. O. Playfair, *The Mediterranean and the Middle East*, vol. 1: *The Early Successes Against Italy (to May 1941)* (1954); and S. W. Roskill, *The War at Sea, 1939-1945*, vol. 1: *The Defensive* (1954). Two works in the *History of the Second World War: U.K. Civil Series*, ed.

W. K. Hancock (London, 1949-71), were also helpful. The first one—
M. M. Postan, *British War Production* (1952)—includes material about
Britain's effort to rearm. The second—W. N. Medlicott, *The Economic
Blockade*, 2 vols. (1952, 1959)—discusses the deliberations within the
Chamberlain government on the efficacy of imposing sanctions against
Japan.

Though published American documents constitute a very important
source for information on the policies pursued by Washington and London, it should be emphasized that the Roosevelt administration's perceptions of Britain's policies were not always accurate, and the American records should therefore be correlated with the corresponding British sources. The most valuable collection of American documents is
U.S. Department of State, *Foreign Relations of the United States: Diplomatic Papers, 1937-1939* (Washington, D.C.: Government Printing Office, 1954-55). For each of the three years cited, vols. 3 and 4 deal specifically with the crisis in East Asia (see note 5, chap. 2, above, for the
form of citation used in the Notes). Additional documents can be found
in U.S. Department of State, *Papers Relating to the Foreign Relations
of the United States: Japan, 1931-1941*, 2 vols. (Washington, D.C.,
1943). On problems of strategy and Anglo-American military cooperation, three official histories are valuable: Samuel Eliot Morison, *History
of the United States Naval Operations in World War II*, vol. 3: *The
Rising Sun in the Pacific, 1931 to April, 1942* (Boston: Little, Brown,
1948); Mark S. Watson, *Chief of Staff: Prewar Plans and Preparations*
(1950); and Louis Morton, *Strategy and Command: The First Two
Years* (1962). The last two are part of *The United States Army in World
War II: The War Department* (Washington, D.C., 1950-68).

Further material on various political, economic, and military aspects
of the East Asian situation can be gleaned from the following official
publications:

China, The Maritime Customs. *The Trade of China, 1936-1939* (Shang-
hai, 1937-40).
Germany, Auswärtiges Amt. *Documents on German Foreign Policy,
1918-1945*, ed., U.S. Department of State, Series D, vols. 1, 4-13
(Washington, D.C., 1949-64).
————. *Nazi-Soviet Relations, 1939-1941: Documents from the Ar-
chives of the German Foreign Ministry*, ed., R. J. Sontag and J. S.
Beddie (Washington, D.C., 1948).
Gill, G. Hermon. *Royal Australian Navy, 1939-1942* (Canberra, 1957).
Australia in the War of 1939-1945, Series 2: *Navy*, vol. 1.
Great Britain. Board of Trade. *Foreign Trade and Commerce Accounts:*

Relating to the Trade and Commerce of Certain Foreign Countries and British Countries Overseas During the Period Ended June 30, 1938; and . . . *During the Period Ended December 31, 1938* (London, 1938-39).

————. Department of Overseas Trade. *Report on Economic and Commercial Conditions in China, April 1935-March 1937* (London, 1937).

————. Foreign Office. *Foreign Office List and Diplomatic and Consular Yearbook, 1936-1939* (London, 1937-40).

————. Parliament. *Parliamentary Debates: Official Report (House of Commons)*, Fifth Series (London, 1937-39).

————. *Parliamentary Debates: Official Report (House of Lords)*, Fifth Series (London, 1937-39).

————. *Parliamentary (Command) Papers*: Cmd. 5482: *Imperial Conference, 1937. Summary of Proceedings* (London, 1937); and Cmd. 5963: *Chinese Currency. Arrangements proposed in regard to the Chinese Currency Stabilization Fund* (London, 1939).

Hasluck, Paul. *The Government and the People, 1939-1941* (Canberra, 1952). *Australia in the War of 1939-1945*, Series 4: *Civil*, vol. 1.

League of Nations. *Official Journal* (Geneva, 1937-39). This official record should be read hand in hand with F. P. A. Walters, *A History of the League of Nations*, vol. 2 (London: Oxford University Press, 1952). Walters was formerly Deputy Secretary-General of the League.

United States, Department of State. *The Conference of Brussels, November 3-24, 1937* (Washington, D.C., 1938).

Wood, F. L. W. *The New Zealand People at War: Political and External Affairs* (Wellington, 1958), in *Official History of New Zealand in the Second World War, 1939-1945*.

C. NEWSPAPERS AND PERIODICALS

China Press (Shanghai), 1937-39
China Weekly Review, 1939
Daily Express, 1937-39
Daily Herald, 1937-39
Daily Mail, 1937-39
Daily Telegraph, 1937-39
Far Eastern Digest, 1939
Finance and Commerce, 1937-39
Japan Weekly Chronicle, 1937-39
Manchester Guardian, 1937-39
New Statesman and Nation, 1937-39
North China Herald, 1937-39
North China Star (Tientsin), 1937-39
Observer, 1937-39
Oriental Affairs, 1937-39
People's Tribune, 1938-39
Round Table, 1934-39
Spectator, 1937-39
Time and Tide, 1937-39
The Times (London), 1935-39

D. PAPERS, MEMOIRS, AND BIOGRAPHIES

The private papers of many British policy-makers in the 1930's are still unavailable. Consequently, only the following collections were used for this book: Baldwin Papers (Cambridge University Library); Caldecote (Sir Thomas Inskip) Papers (Churchill College Library, Cambridge University); Templewood (Sir Samuel Hoare) Papers (Cambridge University Library); Vansittart Papers (Churchill College Library, Cambridge University). The Inskip and Vansittart collections were not of much value, but the Baldwin Papers were useful for the early 1930's and the Templewood Papers contained some points of interest for the 1937-39 period.

I also used the Sir Frederick Maze Papers (Library of the School of Oriental and African Studies, London University). Maze was the Inspector-General of the Chinese Maritime Customs, and his papers shed considerable light on the Anglo-Japanese dispute over the Customs Administration.

Some collections of what might be called the "official" papers of various British diplomats have been opened. These papers are on file in the FO 800 series at the Public Record Office. Though these collections include some new material, they mostly contain duplicates of documents that can be found in the FO 371 group. The papers I consulted in the FO 800 series are those of Sir Alexander Cadogan, Lord Cranborne, the Earl of Halifax, Baron Inverchapel (Sir Archibald Clark Kerr), and Sir Hughe Knatchbull-Hugessen.

Nearly every important British minister in the 1930's has written memoirs or has been the subject of a biography. Many of these works, however, are desultory, and surprisingly few of them mention the Sino-Japanese conflict. Perhaps the best of the lot is Earl of Avon, *The Memoirs of Anthony Eden, Earl of Avon*, vol. 1: *Facing the Dictators, 1923-1938* (London: Cassell, 1962), though the picture that emerges is not identical with the impression one gets from a close study of the Foreign Office and Cabinet records. The second volume of Eden's memoirs, *The Reckoning* (London: Cassell, 1965), covers the period after his resignation as Foreign Secretary. Halifax's memoirs, *The Fulness of Days* (London: Collins, 1957), are, as A. J. P. Taylor has noted, "best passed over in silence." Earl of Birkenhead, *Halifax: The Life of Lord Halifax* (London: Hamish Hamilton, 1965) is more helpful, though it ignores East Asia. Alan Campbell Johnson, *Viscount Halifax: A Biography* (London: Robert Hale, 1941) is out of date. For interesting comments on Eden and Halifax by a man who served as private secretary to both, see Oliver Harvey, *The Diplomatic Diaries of*

Oliver Harvey, 1937-1940, ed., John Harvey (London: Collins, 1970). On Neville Chamberlain, Keith Feiling, *The Life of Neville Chamberlain* (London: Macmillan, 1946) is standard. Feiling includes several important excerpts from Chamberlain's diary and personal correspondence. Iain Macleod, *Neville Chamberlain* (London: Frederick Muller, 1961), and William R. Rock, *Neville Chamberlain* (New York: Twayne, 1969), add little that is new. Simon's memoirs, *Retrospect: The Memoirs of the Rt. Hon. Viscount Simon* (London: Hutchinson, 1958), are not at all useful, and a scholarly study of his important role in the 1930's has yet to be written. Viscount Templewood (Sir Samuel Hoare), *Nine Troubled Years* (London: Collins, 1954), is essential reading for anyone dealing with the question of appeasement. Hoare's own views were firmer than one might gather from a perusal of his memoirs.

The memoirs and biographies of the less prominent members of the Chamberlain Cabinet contain some points of interest. The Earl of Swinton, *Sixty Years of Power* (London: Hutchinson, 1966), provides sketches of Chamberlain and Eden. Swinton was Secretary of State for Air until May 1938. Marquess of Zetland, *"Essayez"* (London: John Murray, 1956), makes some references to the East Asian situation in 1937. R. F. V. Heuston, *Lives of the Lord Chancellors, 1885-1940* (London: Oxford University Press, 1964), includes a few extracts from Sir Thomas Inskip's papers. Debates within the government over rearmament can be followed in R. J. Minney, *The Private Papers of Hore-Belisha* (London: Collins, 1960). Hore-Belisha was the War Minister from 1937 to 1940. Alfred Duff Cooper, *Old Men Forget* (London: Rupert Hart-Davis, 1953), discusses the disputes between the Admiralty and the Treasury over spending on the Royal Navy.

Keith Middlemas and John Barnes, *Baldwin: A Biography* (London: Weidenfeld and Nicolson, 1969), pay much attention to the beginning of Britain's rearmament effort in the 1933-34 period, but their view of Baldwin's role is open to question. The failure to rearm more quickly is bemoaned in Lord Chatfield, *It Might Happen Again* (London: William Heinemann, 1947). Chatfield was the key figure on the Chiefs of Staff subcommittee until 1939, when he became the Minister for the Coordination of Defence. Also of interest are Col. Roderick Macleod and Denis Kelly, eds., *The Ironside Diaries 1937-1940* (London: Constable, 1962); and Lord Ismay, *Memoirs* (London: Heinemann, 1960). For glimpses into the minds of some "appeasers," see Thomas Jones, *A Diary with Letters, 1931-1950* (London: Oxford University Press, 1954); John Evelyn Wrench, *Geoffrey Dawson and Our Times* (London: Hutchinson, 1955); and J. R. M. Butler, *Lord Lothian* (London: Macmillan, 1960). Both Dawson, who was editor of *The Times,* and

Lothian favored a conciliatory line toward Germany but pressed for a firm stand against Japan. Jones was on close terms with many leading politicians, and he provides a good picture of their views. Critiques of Britain's German policy can be found in Winston S. Churchill, *The Gathering Storm* (Boston: Houghton Mifflin, 1948); Leopold S. Amery, *My Political Life*, vol. 3: *The Unforgiving Years, 1929-1940* (London: Hutchinson, 1955); and Hugh Dalton, *The Fateful Years: Memoirs, 1931-1945* (London: Frederick Muller, 1957). None of these three works says much about East Asia.

There are some diaries, memoirs, and biographies of Foreign Office officials in the 1930's. By far the most useful is David Dilks, ed., *The Diaries of Sir Alexander Cadogan, 1938-1945* (London: Cassell, 1971). Lord Vansittart, *The Mist Procession* (London: Hutchinson, 1958), is difficult to read and covers only the period before 1937, but is nonetheless important. Ian Colvin, *Vansittart in Office* (London: Gollancz, 1965) promises more than it accomplishes. Lord Strang, *Home and Abroad* (London: Andre Deutsch, 1956), contains some perceptive general remarks about the limits on British diplomacy in the 1930's. Also to be noted are Lord Butler, *The Art of the Possible: The Memoirs of Lord Butler* (London: Hamish Hamilton, 1971); and Lord Gladwyn, *The Memoirs of Lord Gladwyn* (London: Weidenfeld and Nicolson, 1972). Of the works by ambassadors, the most revealing is Sir Nevile Henderson, *Failure of a Mission: Berlin 1937-1939* (London: Hodder and Stoughton, 1940). Ivone Kirkpatrick, *The Inner Circle* (London: Macmillan, 1959), is an uninformative account by a diplomat who served under Henderson at the embassy in Berlin.

Of the memoirs that discuss in detail the East Asian situation, the most important is Robert L. Craigie, *Behind the Japanese Mask* (London: Hutchinson, 1946). The picture Craigie gives of his own views is not entirely in accord with the one that emerges from the unpublished Foreign Office records, but, even so, the book contains some significant information. Sir Hughe Knatchbull-Hugessen has also written memoirs: *Diplomat in Peace and War* (London: John Murray, 1949). Sir Hughe's rather peculiar reconstruction of the Sian Incident reflects his difficulty in distinguishing reality from illusion in East Asian politics. F. S. G. Piggott, *Broken Thread: An Autobiography* (Aldershot: Gale & Polden, 1950), has some points of interest. Piggott, who was the British military attaché in Tokyo, sympathized with Japan's point of view regarding the Sino-Japanese conflict. Sir Frederick Leith-Ross discusses his mission to China in his book *Money Talks: Fifty Years of International Finance* (London: Hutchinson, 1968). The observations of the British minister to Thailand are recorded in Josiah Crosby, *Siam: The Cross-*

roads (London: Hollis and Carter, 1945). For the views of three other officials concerned with East Asian problems, see Sir Eric Teichman, *Affairs of China: A Survey of Recent History and Present Circumstances in the Republic of China* (London: Methuen, 1938); Simon Harcourt-Smith, *Japanese Frenzy* (London: Hamish Hamilton, 1942); and Sir Victor Wellesley, *Diplomacy in Fetters* (London: Hutchinson, 1944).

The memoirs, biographies, and papers of American officials contain valuable information about Washington's response to the Sino-Japanese War and also throw light on Anglo-American relations. For this study I used the collected papers of Norman Davis (Library of Congress), Joseph Grew (Houghton Library, Harvard University), Cordell Hull (Library of Congress), Nelson Johnson (Library of Congress), William Leahy (Library of Congress), Jay Pierrepont Moffat (Houghton Library, Harvard University), Henry Stimson (Sterling Memorial Library, Yale University), and Harry Yarnell (Library of Congress). The most helpful collections were those of Davis, Grew, and Moffat.

Sections of the Grew Papers are included in two books by Joseph C. Grew: *Ten Years in Japan* (New York: Simon and Schuster, 1944), and *Turbulent Era: A Diplomatic Record of Forty Years, 1904-1945*, ed., Walter Johnson, 2 vols. (Boston: Houghton Mifflin, 1952). Grew's evaluation of Japanese foreign policy is admirably assessed by Waldo Heinrichs, Jr., *American Ambassador: Joseph C. Grew and the Development of the United States Diplomatic Tradition* (Boston: Little, Brown, 1966). Excerpts from the Moffat Papers can be found in Jay Pierrepont Moffat, *The Moffat Papers: Selections from the Diplomatic Journals of Jay Pierrepont Moffat*, ed., Nancy H. Hooker (Cambridge, Mass.: Harvard University Press, 1956). No satisfactory biography of Davis has been written, but many scholars have analyzed Stimson's career. In particular, see Elting E. Morison, *Turmoil and Tradition: A Study of the Life and Times of Henry L. Stimson* (Boston: Houghton Mifflin, 1960), which is favorable to Stimson; and Armin Rappaport, *Henry L. Stimson and Japan, 1931-33* (Chicago: University of Chicago Press, 1963), which is critical of his diplomacy. Stimson's controversial account of the Anglo-American misunderstandings during the Manchurian crisis is presented in his book *The Far Eastern Crisis* (New York: Harper, 1936). Also to be noted is Henry L. Stimson and McGeorge Bundy, *On Active Service in Peace and War* (New York: Harper, 1948). A biography of Nelson Johnson, the American ambassador to China during the 1937-39 period, has been written by Russell D. Buhite, *Nelson T. Johnson and American Policy Toward China, 1925-1941* (East Lansing: Michigan State University Press, 1968). On Cordell

Hull, see *The Memoirs of Cordell Hull,* 2 vols. (New York: Macmillan, 1948); and Julius M. Pratt, *Cordell Hull, 1933-1944* (New York: Cooper Square, 1964).

Hull's views on foreign policy were often challenged by the Secretary of the Treasury, Henry Morgenthau, who is the subject of a biography by John M. Blum. Blum's first two volumes, *From the Morgenthau Diaries: Years of Crisis, 1928-1938* (Boston: Houghton Mifflin, 1959) and *From the Morgenthau Diaries: Years of Urgency, 1938-1941* (Boston: Houghton Mifflin, 1965), are especially important, though his analysis is uncritical of Morgenthau's simplistic judgments about the crisis in East Asia. Other useful memoirs and biographies are Harold L. Ickes, *The Secret Diary of Harold L. Ickes,* vol. 2: *The Inside Struggle, 1936-1939* (New York: Simon and Schuster, 1954); Sumner Welles, *Seven Decisions That Shaped History* (New York: Harper, 1950); and Sumner Welles, *The Time for Decision* (New York: Harper, 1944).

Memoirs and biographies in English that deal specifically with the policies of powers other than America and Britain are rare. There are no adequate studies of Chiang Kai-shek in the 1930's. Earl A. Selle, *Donald of China* (Sydney: Invincible Press, 1948), is a journalistic sketch of an Australian who advised Chiang. C. L. Chennault, *Way of a Fighter,* ed., Robert Hotz (New York: Putnam, 1949), contains information about Nanking's reaction to the events of July 1937. Hallett Abend, who was a *New York Times* reporter, presents some observations on Chinese politics in his book *My Life in China, 1926-1941* (New York: Harcourt, Brace, 1943). On the Japanese side, there are four rather mediocre memoirs in English: Shigemitsu Mamoru, *Japan and Her Destiny: My Struggle for Peace,* ed., F. S. G. Piggott, tr., O. White (New York: E. P. Dutton, 1958); Togo Shigenori, *The Cause of Japan,* ed. and tr., Togo Fumihiko and B. B. Blakeney (New York: Simon and Schuster, 1956); Toshikazu Kase, *Journey to the Missouri,* ed., D. N. Rowe (New Haven, Conn.: Yale University Press, 1950); and Yoshida Shigeru, *The Yoshida Memoirs: The Story of Japan in Crisis,* tr., Kenichi Yoshida (Boston: Houghton Mifflin, 1962). For a short account of an abortive attempt to negotiate an end to the Sino-Japanese conflict during Ugaki's tenure as Foreign Minister, see Ugaki Kazushige, "Sino-Japanese Peace Talks, June-September, 1938," tr., E. H. M. Colegrave, *St. Antony's Papers, No. 2: Far Eastern Affairs, No. 1,* ed., G. F. Hudson (London: Oxford University Press, 1957), pp. 94-104. Also to be noted is Hugh Byas, *Government by Assassination* (New York: Knopf, 1942). Byas was a correspondent in Tokyo for both *The Times* of London and the *New York Times.*

Germany's East Asian policy is treated sketchily in Herbert von Dirksen, *Moscow, Tokyo, London* (London: Hutchinson, 1951), and Ernst von Weizsäcker, *Memoirs of Ernst von Weizsäcker* (London: Gollancz, 1951). There are some interesting remarks on Italy's relations with Japan in two collections of Count G. Ciano's writings: *Ciano's Diplomatic Papers*, ed., Malcolm Muggeridge, tr., Stuart Hood (London: Odhams, 1948), and *Ciano's Diary, 1937-1938*, tr., Andreas Mayor (London: Methuen, 1952). For commentaries on both Dirksen and Ciano, see Gordon A. Craig and Felix Gilbert, eds., *The Diplomats 1919-1939* (Princeton, N.J.: Princeton University Press, 1953).

E. SECONDARY WORKS AND ARTICLES

Britain's reaction to the crisis that developed in East Asia after July 1937 needs to be placed in proper perspective. There are some surveys that are helpful in this respect. G. F. Hudson, *The Far East in World Politics* (London: Oxford University Press, 1937), is still of use. John T. Pratt, *War and Politics in China* (London: Jonathan Cape, 1943), is an interesting though contentious overview of Britain's China policy. Anglo-Japanese relations are ably sketched by Ian H. Nish, "Japan's Relations with Britain," *Conference on Japanese Foreign Policy: The Agenda for Research*, vol. 3, mimeographed (Buck Hill Falls, Pa.: East Asian Institute, Columbia University, 1963). Another useful survey is Evan Luard, *Britain and China* (Baltimore: Johns Hopkins University Press, 1962), which should be read in conjunction with Saul Rose, *Britain and Southeast Asia* (Baltimore: Johns Hopkins University Press, 1962). For a social history of British nationals in China, see George Woodcock, *The British in the Far East* (New York: Atheneum, 1970), which is aimed at general readers.

Works that focus on a shorter period of time are more numerous. Of the studies that deal with the era before the Washington Conference, four are especially important: William L. Langer, *The Diplomacy of Imperialism, 1890-1902*, 2d ed. (New York: Knopf, 1951); L. K. Young, *British Policy in China, 1895-1902* (London: Oxford University Press, 1970); Ian H. Nish, *The Anglo-Japanese Alliance: The Diplomacy of Two Island Empires, 1894-1907* (London: Athlone, 1966); and Ian H. Nish, *Alliance in Decline: A Study in Anglo-Japanese Relations, 1908-23* (London: Athlone, 1972). Also of interest are Peter Lowe, *Great Britain and Japan, 1911-1915: A Study of British Far Eastern Policy* (London: Macmillan, 1969); Robert Joseph Gowen, "Great Britain and the Twenty-One Demands of 1915: Cooperation Versus Effacement," *The Journal of Modern History*, 43.1 (Mar. 1971): 76-106; V. H. Rothwell, "The British Government and Japanese Military Assistance, 1914-

18," *History*, 56.186 (Feb. 1971): 35-45; and Ian H. Nish, "Britain and the Ending of the Anglo-Japanese Alliance," *Bulletin of the Japan Society of London*, 53 (Oct. 1967): 2-5.

An important and lucid work on British policy in the interwar years is William Roger Louis, *British Strategy in the Far East, 1919-1939* (London: Oxford University Press, 1971). Louis emphasizes the economic and racial causes of friction in East Asia. His treatment of the 1919-35 period is more substantial than his coverage of developments after 1935. For an argument that the Anglo-Japanese alliance should not have been abrogated, see Malcolm D. Kennedy, *The Estrangement of Great Britain and Japan, 1917-35* (Manchester, Eng.: Manchester University Press, 1969). Kennedy was once a British army officer in Japan and later did research for the Foreign Office. Britain's lack of power in East Asia after World War I is noted by A. P. Thornton, *The Imperial Idea and Its Enemies: A Study in British Power* (London: Macmillan, 1963). On the problems of the 1920's, two monographs deserve close attention: Stephen Roskill, *Naval Policy Between the Wars*, vol. 1: *The Period of Anglo-American Antagonism, 1919-1929* (London: Collins, 1968); and Akira Iriye, *After Imperialism: The Search for a New Order in the Far East, 1921-1931* (Cambridge, Mass.: Harvard University Press, 1965). Chapter 9 of David Carlton, *MacDonald Versus Henderson: The Foreign Policy of the Second Labour Government* (London: Macmillan, 1970), deals with the Sino-British negotiations of 1929-31 over the unequal treaties. Reginald Bassett, *Democracy and Foreign Policy: A Case History, the Sino-Japanese Dispute, 1931-1933* (London: Longmans, 1952), traces the evolution of British opinion during the Manchurian crisis. This work will no doubt be superseded by Christopher Thorne's book *The Limits of Foreign Policy: The West, the League and the Far Eastern Crisis of 1931-1933*, which was scheduled to be published by Hamish Hamilton in late 1972, about the time my own book was going to press. For some of his preliminary findings, see his articles "The Shanghai Crisis of 1932: The Basis of British Policy," *The American Historical Review*, 75.6 (Oct. 1970): 1616-39; "The Quest for Arms Embargoes: Failure in 1933," *Journal of Contemporary History*, 5.4 (Oct. 1970): 129-49; and "Viscount Cecil, the Government, and the Far Eastern Crisis of 1931," *Historical Journal*, 14.4 (Dec. 1971): 805-26. Also of interest is Robert A. Hecht, "Great Britain and the Stimson Note of January 7, 1932," *Pacific Historical Review*, 38.2 (May 1969): 177-91. Gerald E. Wheeler, "Isolated Japan: Anglo-American Diplomatic Cooperation, 1927-1936," *Pacific Historical Review*, 30 (1961): 163-78, stresses instances of Anglo-American collaboration but overlooks important disagreements between Washington and London.

D. C. Watt, *Personalities and Policies: Studies in the Formulation of British Foreign Policy in the Twentieth Century* (London: Longmans, 1965), includes an analysis of the Cabinet debate in 1934 over the desirability of a rapprochement with Tokyo.

The only recent book on Britain's reaction to the crisis in East Asia after July 1937 is Nicholas Clifford, *Retreat from China: British Policy in the Far East, 1937-1941* (Seattle: University of Washington Press, 1967). This work is both perceptive and gracefully written, but it suffers from a serious handicap: Clifford did not have access to the unpublished British records and hence had to make heavy use of American documents. This limitation led him to stress Anglo-American relations at the expense of such crucial issues as the British evaluations of Japan and China and the interaction between Britain's East Asian and European problems. Clifford has written two articles as well: "Britain, America and the Far East, 1937-1940: A Failure in Cooperation," *Journal of British Studies*, 3 (1963): 137-54, which summarizes the main themes of his book; and "Sir Frederick Maze and the Chinese Maritime Customs, 1937-1941," *Journal of Modern History*, 37 (1965): 18-34. Also noteworthy is Lawrence Pratt, "The Anglo-American Naval Conversations on the Far East of January 1938," *International Affairs*, 47.4 (Oct. 1971): 745-63, an insightful article based on the British archives.

Three analyses of Britain's response to the Sino-Japanese conflict were published in the early 1940's: Irving S. Friedman, *British Relations with China, 1931-1939* (New York: International Secretariat, Institute of Pacific Relations, 1940); G. E. Hubbard, *British Far Eastern Policy* (New York: International Secretariat, Institute of Pacific Relations, 1943); and Chin-lin Hsia, *British Far Eastern Policy, 1937-1940* (Chungking: China Information Publishing Co., 1940). Of these three books, only Friedman's volume merits any attention from historians. Summaries of events in East Asia can be found in the *Survey of International Affairs*, and some useful documents are collected in *Documents on International Affairs*. Both series were sponsored by the Royal Institute of International Affairs (Chatham House).

Perhaps the three most popular contemporary accounts touching on the Sino-Japanese conflict and Britain's role in East Asia were Norman Angell, *The Defence of the Empire* (New York: Appleton, 1937); Freda Utley, *Japan's Feet of Clay* (London: Faber and Faber, 1936); and Freda Utley, *Japan's Gamble in China* (London: Secker and Warburg, 1938). Both writers called for a hard-line British policy against Japan. Also of interest are several articles by contemporary observers: R. T. Barrett, "British Responsibilities in South China," *Asiatic Review*, 24 (1938):

147-56; O. M. Green, "Great Britain's Chance in the Far East," *Empire Review and Magazine*, 65 (1937): 12-18, and "An Anglo-Japanese Entente?" *ibid.*, pp. 365-69; Malcolm D. Kennedy, "The Future of Anglo-Japanese Relations," *Asiatic Review*, 35 (1939): 777-85; John T. Pratt, "America, Britain and China," *Contemporary Review*, 158 (1940): 47-55; and H. G. W. Woodhead, "Sino-Japanese Hostilities: A Frank British Opinion," *Contemporary Japan*, 6 (1937): 411-18. For a scholarly analysis of opinion in Britain, see Tai Erh-ching, "British Opinion of the Sino-Japanese War, 1937-1941," unpublished Ph.D. dissertation, 1952, London University.

As many observers in the late 1930's pointed out, Japanese expansion posed a serious threat to Britain's economic interests in China and to the security of the British Empire. The best estimate of the magnitude of Britain's economic interests is probably to be found in E. M. Gull, *British Economic Interests in the Far East* (New York: International Secretariat, Institute of Pacific Relations, 1943). Also helpful is C. F. Remer, *Foreign Investments in China* (New York: Macmillan, 1933). The damage done to these interests by Japan's advance is discussed in detail in F. C. Jones's valuable work *Shanghai and Tientsin, with Special Reference to Foreign Interests* (London: Oxford University Press, 1940). Two other studies are useful: Robert W. Barnett, *Economic Shanghai: Hostage to Politics, 1937-1941* (New York: International Secretariat, Institute of Pacific Relations, 1941); and A. G. Donnithorne, *Economic Developments Since 1937 in Eastern and Southeastern Asia and Their Effects on the United Kingdom* (Lucknow, India: Eleventh Conference, Institute of Pacific Relations, 1950). Some of the strategic and military dimensions of the East Asian crisis are explored in Arima Seiho, "The Anglo-American Naval Program," *Contemporary Japan*, 7 (1938): 58-67; and Hector C. Bywater, "Britain on the Seas," *Foreign Affairs*, 16 (1938): 210-21. Britain's strategy in the Far East before December 1941 is criticized in Russell Grenfell, *Main Fleet to Singapore* (London: Faber and Faber, 1951); and S. Woodburn Kirby, *Singapore: The Chain of Disaster* (London: Cassell, 1971). The shaping of British defense policy is examined in F. A. Johnson, *Defence by Committee: The British Committee of Imperial Defence, 1880-1959* (London: Oxford University Press, 1960).

Very few historians have tried to discuss the relationship between Britain's policy in Europe and her reaction to the East Asian crisis. W. N. Medlicott pays some attention to this question in two works: *Contemporary England, 1914-1964* (London: Longmans, 1967), and *British Foreign Policy Since Versailles, 1919-1963*, rev. ed. (London: Methuen, 1968). So does F. S. Northedge in *The Troubled Giant:*

Britain Among the Great Powers, 1916-1939 (London: Bell, 1966). For some astute observations on this problem by a contemporary observer, see E. H. Carr, *Britain: A Study of Foreign Policy from the Versailles Treaty to the Outbreak of War* (London: Longmans, 1939), and his Cust Foundation Lecture, *Great Britain as a Mediterranean Power* (Nottingham: University College, 1937).

A. J. P. Taylor, *The Origins of the Second World War*, 2d ed. (Greenwich, Conn.: Fawcett, 1961), contains some perceptive remarks about Britain's troubles in East Asia but is more important for its provocative reassessment of the road to war in Europe. Incisive criticism of Taylor's thesis can be found in E. M. Robertson, ed., *The Origins of the Second World War* (London: Macmillan, 1971), and in chapter 15 of F. H. Hinsley, *Power and the Pursuit of Peace* (Cambridge, Eng.: Cambridge University Press, 1967).

A number of monographs focus on the problem of British appeasement; only the most recent will be cited here. Martin Gilbert, *The Roots of Appeasement* (London: Weidenfeld and Nicolson, 1966), traces the origins and evolution of an appeasement policy, and Margaret George, *The Warped Vision: British Foreign Policy, 1933-1939* (Pittsburgh: University of Pittsburgh Press, 1965), probes the Conservatives' outlook on foreign affairs. Both Ian Colvin, *The Chamberlain Cabinet* (London: Gollancz, 1971), and Roger Parkinson, *Peace for Our Time: Munich to Dunkirk—The Inside Story* (London: Rupert Hart-Davis, 1971), are based on unpublished British records, but neither is particularly penetrating. A. L. Rowse, *Appeasement: A Study in Political Decline, 1933-1939* (New York: Norton, 1961), stresses the anti-communism of the Conservative leaders, whereas Donald N. Lammers, *Explaining Munich: The Search for Motive in British Policy* (Stanford, Calif.: Hoover Institution, 1966), criticizes historians who argue that appeasement was a product of the Conservatives' antipathy to the Soviet Union. In his article "Fascism, Communism, and the Foreign Office, 1937-39," *Journal of Contemporary History*, 6.3 (1971): 66-86, Lammers seeks to demonstrate that the British Foreign Office took an "unideological approach" to international politics. Martin Gilbert and Richard Gott, *The Appeasers* (Boston: Houghton Mifflin, 1963), have chapters on economic and colonial appeasement, but the rest of their study is rather unenlightening, as is William R. Rock, *Appeasement on Trial: British Foreign Policy and Its Critics, 1938-1939* (Hamden, Conn.: Archon, 1966). Christopher Thorne, *The Approach of War, 1938-1939* (London: Macmillan, 1967), is a competent synthesis. An admirable summary of the controversy among historians over appeasement and the origins of war in Europe is offered in D. C. Watt, "Appeasement:

The Rise of a Revisionist School?" *Political Quarterly*, 36 (1965): 191-213. For three recent "revisionist" studies, see Keith Robbins, *Munich 1938* (London: Cassell, 1968); Neville Thompson, *The Anti-Appeasers: Conservative Opposition to Appeasement in the 1930's* (London: Oxford University Press, 1971); and W. N. Medlicott, *Britain and Germany: The Search for Agreement, 1930-1937* (London: Athlone, 1969). Medlicott's stimulating essay, which examines the Foreign Office's views on the German problem, should be contrasted with, for example, John Connell (pseud. for John Henry Robertson), *The "Office": A Study of British Foreign Policy and Its Makers, 1919-1951* (London: Allan Wingate, 1958). Several interesting studies appeared while my book was in press: Corelli Barnett, *The Collapse of British Power* (London: Methuen, 1972); Michael Howard, *The Continental Commitment* (London: Temple Smith, 1972); Keith Middlemas, *Diplomacy of Illusion: The British Government and Germany, 1937-39* (London: Weidenfeld and Nicolson, 1972); F. Coghlan, "Armaments, Economic Policy and Appeasement: Background to British Foreign Policy, 1931-7," *History*, 57.190 (June 1972): 205-16; and Robert Skidelsky, "Going to War with Germany: Between Revisionism and Orthodoxy," *Encounter*, 39.1 (July 1972): 56-65.

No bibliography that touches on the 1919-39 period would be complete without taking note of two brilliant works: A. J. P. Taylor, *English History, 1914-1945* (London: Oxford University Press, 1965), and E. H. Carr, *The Twenty Years' Crisis, 1919-1939: An Introduction to the Study of International Relations*, reprint (New York: Harper and Row, 1964). Taylor's book has in many respects superseded Charles L. Mowat's masterly *Britain Between the Wars, 1918-1940* (Chicago: University of Chicago Press, 1955) as the most important account of the interwar era in Britain. Carr's study has been called (by Taylor) "a brilliant argument in favour of appeasement."

The history of America's relations with Japan and China has received far more scholarly attention than Britain's involvement in East Asian affairs. The standard introduction to the evolution of American policy is A. Whitney Griswold, *The Far Eastern Policy of the United States* (New York: Harcourt, Brace, 1943), though it should be noted that many of Griswold's interpretations have been revised by recent scholarship. Three very interesting books that deal with American attitudes and assumptions are Akira Iriye, *Across the Pacific: An Inner History of American-East Asian Relations* (New York: Harcourt, Brace, 1967); William L. Neumann, *America Encounters Japan: From Perry to MacArthur* (Baltimore: Johns Hopkins University Press, 1963); and Warren I. Cohen, *America's Response to China: An Interpretative His-*

tory of Sino-American Relations (New York: Wiley, 1971). For a careful study of "isolationism," see Manfred Jonas, *Isolationism in America, 1935-1941* (Ithaca, N.Y.: Cornell University Press, 1966). George Kennan emphasizes American "moralism" and "legalism" in his extended essay *American Diplomacy, 1900-1950* (Chicago: University of Chicago Press, 1951). Economic and ideological factors are stressed in three analyses of America's policy: William A. Williams, *The Tragedy of American Diplomacy*, rev. ed. (New York: Dell, 1962); Lloyd C. Gardner, *Economic Aspects of New Deal Diplomacy* (Madison: University of Wisconsin Press, 1964); and Robert F. Smith, "American Foreign Relations, 1920-1942," in Barton J. Bernstein, ed., *Towards a New Past: Dissenting Essays in American History* (New York: Random House, 1967), pp. 232-62. John W. Masland, "Commercial Influences Upon American Far Eastern Policy, 1937-1941," *Pacific Historical Review*, 11 (Sept. 1942): 281-99, argues that economic considerations did not greatly influence American policy before the Second World War.

On the 1920's, Dorothy Borg, *American Policy and the Chinese Revolution, 1925-1928* (New York: Macmillan, 1947) is a helpful point of departure. Her book *The United States and the Far Eastern Crisis of 1933-1938* (Cambridge, Mass.: Harvard University Press, 1964) is an exhaustive treatment of the Roosevelt administration's East Asian policy in the mid-1930's. For Dr. Borg's persuasive interpretation of Roosevelt's "Quarantine" Speech, see her article "Notes on Roosevelt's 'Quarantine' Speech," *Political Science Quarterly*, 72 (Sept. 1957): 405-33. A different point of view can be found in three articles by John McV. Haight, Jr.: "France and the Aftermath of Roosevelt's 'Quarantine' Speech," *World Politics*, 14 (Jan. 1962): 283-306; "Roosevelt and the Aftermath of the Quarantine Speech," *The Review of Politics*, 24.2 (Apr. 1962): 233-59; and "Franklin D. Roosevelt and a Naval Quarantine of Japan," *Pacific Historical Review*, 40.2 (May 1971): 203-26. Also of interest are Travis Beal Jacobs, "Roosevelt's 'Quarantine Speech,'" *The Historian*, 24.4 (Aug. 1962): 483-502; and William E. Leuchtenburg, "Franklin D. Roosevelt, 'Quarantine' Address, 1937," in Daniel J. Boorstin, ed., *An American Primer* (Chicago: University of Chicago Press, 1966). The Panay Incident and its aftermath are examined in Manny T. Koginos, *The Panay Incident: Prelude to War* (Lafayette, Ind.: Purdue University Studies, 1967); and Thaddeus V. Tuleja, *Statesmen and Admirals: Quest for a Far Eastern Naval Policy* (New York: Norton, 1963). For an account by a participant in the incident, see Masatake Okumiya, "How the Panay Was Sunk," *United States Naval Institute Proceedings*, 79 (June 1953): 587-96. Arnold A. Offner, *American Appeasement: United States Foreign Policy and Ger-*

many, 1933-1938 (Cambridge, Mass.: Harvard University Press, 1969), is very good on Anglo-American relations in the 1930's. See also Francis L. Loewenheim, "An Illusion That Shaped History: New Light on the History and Historiography of American Peace Efforts Before Munich," in D. R. Beaver, ed., *Some Pathways in Twentieth-Century History: Essays in Honor of Reginald Charles McGrane* (Detroit: Wayne State University Press, 1969).

Of the many works that deal specifically with the part played by the United States in the origins of the Pacific war, the following deserve special attention: William L. Langer and S. Everett Gleason, *The Challenge to Isolation* (New York: Harper, 1952), and *The Undeclared War* (New York: Harper, 1953); Herbert Feis, *The Road to Pearl Harbor: The Coming of the War Between the United States and Japan* (Princeton, N.J.: Princeton University Press, 1950); and Paul W. Schroeder, *The Axis Alliance and Japanese-American Relations* (Ithaca, N.Y.: Cornell University Press, 1958). Langer and Gleason generally defend American policy, as does Feis, whereas Schroeder is rather critical of the Roosevelt administration.

A good introduction to Japanese foreign policy from the mid-nineteenth century to the Second World War is Chitoshi Yanaga's survey *Japan Since Perry* (New York: McGraw, 1949). Various perspectives on Japanese imperialism are presented in Grant K. Goodman, comp., *Imperial Japan and Asia: A Reassessment* (New York: East Asian Institute, Columbia University, 1967). For Japan's policy at the time of the Washington Conference, see Sadao Asada, "Japan's 'Special Interests' and the Washington Conference, 1921-1922," *American Historical Review*, 67 (Oct. 1961): 62-70; and Ian H. Nish, "Japan and the Ending of the Anglo-Japanese Alliance," in K. Bourne and D. C. Watt, eds., *Studies in International History* (London: Longmans, 1967), pp. 369-84. Akira Iriye, *After Imperialism* (cited above), traces Japanese diplomacy from 1921 to 1931, and Sadako N. Ogata, *Defiance in Manchuria: The Making of Japanese Foreign Policy, 1931-1932* (Berkeley: University of California Press, 1964) analyzes the Manchurian crisis in detail.

Japan's "road to Pearl Harbor" has been the subject of a lively debate among historians. The conventional interpretation, which focuses on "conspiracies" perpetrated by certain Japanese militarists, can be found in Yale C. Maxon, *Control of Japanese Foreign Policy* (Berkeley: University of California Press, 1957); and Richard Storry, *The Double Patriots* (Boston: Houghton Mifflin, 1957). See also Storry, "Konoye Fumimaro, the Last of the Fujiwara," in G. F. Hudson, ed., *St. Antony's Papers, No. 7: Far Eastern Affairs, No. 2* (London: Oxford University Press, 1960), pp. 9-33; and Masao Maruyama, *Thought and*

Behavior in Modern Japanese Politics, ed., Ivan Morris (London: Oxford University Press, 1963), which probes *inter alia* the Japanese military mind.

The orthodox view has been undermined by James B. Crowley in his important study *Japan's Quest for Autonomy: National Security and Foreign Policy, 1930-1938* (Princeton, N.J.: Princeton University Press, 1966), which stresses that on the whole political leaders in Tokyo, not the field armies or junior officers, played the central role in the making of Japanese foreign policy. A convincing reappraisal of the outbreak of the Sino-Japanese war is offered in his article "A Reconsideration of the Marco Polo Bridge Incident," *Journal of Asian Studies*, 22.3 (May 1963): 277-91. Two other interesting essays by Crowley are "Japanese Military Foreign Policy, 1868-1941: An Explorative Analysis of the Influence of the Military on Japanese Foreign Policy," *Conference on Japanese Foreign Policy: The Agenda for Research*, vol. 2, mimeographed (Buck Hill Falls, Pa.: East Asian Institute, Columbia University, 1963); and "A New Deal for Japan and Asia: One Road to Pearl Harbor," in James B. Crowley, ed., *Modern East Asia: Essays in Interpretation* (New York: Harcourt, Brace, 1970).

A recent view of Japan's China policy after July 1937 can be found in John H. Boyle, "Japan's Puppet Regimes in China, 1937-1940," Ph.D. dissertation, 1968, Stanford University; and in his *China and Japan at War, 1937-1945: The Politics of Collaboration* (Stanford, Calif.: Stanford University Press, 1972), a heavily revised version of his dissertation, which was published while my book was in press. Two articles by Akira Iriye are very important for evaluating Japanese policy in the 1937-41 period: "Japanese Imperialism and Aggression: Reconsiderations, II," *Journal of Asian Studies*, 23.1 (Nov. 1963): 103-13; and "Japan's Foreign Policies Between World Wars—Sources and Interpretations," *Journal of Asian Studies*, 26.4 (Aug. 1967): 677-82. Also useful are F. C. Jones, *Japan's New Order in East Asia: Its Rise and Fall, 1937-45* (London, Oxford University Press, 1954); David J. Lu, *From the Marco Polo Bridge to Pearl Harbor: Japan's Entry into World War II* (Washington, D.C.: Public Affairs Press, 1961); and Robert J. S. Butow, *Tojo and the Coming of the War* (Princeton, N.J.: Princeton University Press, 1961).

Japan's military problems and successes in China after 1937 are traced in Alvin D. Coox, *Year of the Tiger* (Philadelphia: Orient/West, 1964); and in his article "Effects of Attrition on National War Effort: The Japanese Army Experience in China, 1937-1938," *Military Affairs*, 32.2 (Oct. 1968): 57-62. Coox collaborated with Saburo Hayashi in writing *Kōgun: The Japanese Army in the Pacific War* (Quantico, Va.:

Marine Corps Association, 1959). Assessments of the origins and outcome of the Soviet-Japanese border conflicts during 1938 and 1939 are
provided by Coox, "High Command and Field Army: The Kwantung
Army and the Nomonhan Incident, 1939," *Military Affairs*, 33.2 (Oct.
1969): 302-11; Katsu H. Young, "The Nomonhan Incident: Imperial
Japan and the Soviet Union," *Monumenta Nipponica*, 22 (1967): 82-
101; and Martin Blumenson, "The Soviet Power Play at Changkufeng,"
World Politics, 12.2 (Jan. 1960): 249-63. On Japan's claim to be an
anti-communist bulwark in East Asia, see Shibata Yuji, "Britain's
Choice: Japan or Red China," *Contemporary Japan*, 6 (1937): 454-63.

   Chinese foreign policy since the 1890's is surveyed by Werner Levi,
Modern China's Foreign Policy (Minneapolis: University of Minnesota
Press, 1953). Also to be noted are O. Edmund Clubb, *Twentieth Century China* (New York: Columbia University Press, 1964); and Wesley
R. Fishel, *The End of Extraterritoriality in China* (Berkeley: University
of California Press, 1952). There is no adequate English-language study
dealing specifically with China's foreign policy during the 1931-37 period, but a considerable body of work has been done on the Sino-
Japanese War. Chalmers A. Johnson, *Peasant Nationalism and Communist Power: The Emergence of Revolutionary China, 1937-1945*
(Stanford, Calif.: Stanford University Press, 1962), explores the impact
of the war on the Chinese peasantry. Though Donald Gillin and Mark
Selden have challenged Johnson's "peasant nationalism" thesis, his
book is still the leading analysis of the conflict between Japan and
China. Five other works need to be mentioned: F. F. Liu, *A Military
History of Modern China, 1924-1949* (Princeton, N.J.: Princeton Uni-
versity Press, 1956); T. H. White and A. Jacoby, *Thunder Out of China*
(New York: William Sloane Associates, 1946); T. A. Bisson, *Japan in
China* (New York: Macmillan, 1938); John Goette, *Japan Fights for
Asia* (New York: Harcourt, Brace, 1943); and George E. Taylor, *The
Struggle for North China* (New York: International Secretariat, Insti-
tute of Pacific Relations, 1940). Kimitada Miwa's article on the origins
of the Sino-Japanese War, "The Chinese Communists' Role in the
Spread of the Marco Polo Bridge Incident into a Full-Scale War,"
Monumenta Nipponica, 18 (1963): 313-28, is contentious and poorly
documented. His article "The Wang Ching-wei Regime and Japanese
Efforts to Terminate the China Conflict," in Joseph Roggendorf, ed.,
Studies in Japanese Culture (Tokyo: Sophia University Press, 1963), is
more helpful. On Wang Ching-wei, see also Gerald E. Bunker, *The
Peace Conspiracy: Wang Ching-wei and the China War, 1937-1941*
(Cambridge, Mass.: Harvard University Press, 1972); Howard L. Boor-

man, "Wang Ching-wei: China's Romantic Radical," *Political Science Quarterly*, 79 (Dec. 1964): 504-25; and John H. Boyle, "The Road to Sino-Japanese Collaboration: The Background to the Defection of Wang Ching-wei," *Monumenta Nipponica*, 25 (1970): 267-301.

The best points of departure for a study of Chinese politics in the 1930's are Lyman P. Van Slyke, *Enemies and Friends: The United Front in Chinese Communist History* (Stanford, Calif.: Stanford University Press, 1967); Mary C. Wright, "From Revolution to Restoration: The Transformation of Kuomintang Ideology," *The Far Eastern Quarterly*, 14.4 (Aug. 1955): 515-32; and Lucien Bianco, *Origins of the Chinese Revolution, 1915-1949*, tr. Muriel Bell (Stanford, Calif.: Stanford University Press, 1971). Parts of James C. Thomson, *While China Faced West* (Cambridge, Mass.: Harvard University Press, 1969), and Y. C. Wang, *Chinese Intellectuals and the West, 1872-1949* (Chapel Hill: University of North Carolina Press, 1966), are also useful.

Of the numerous studies on China's economy in the 1930's, the most helpful are Douglas S. Paauw, "The Kuomintang and Economic Stagnation, 1928-1937," *Journal of Asian Studies*, 16.2 (Feb. 1957): 213-20; John K. Chang, "Industrial Development of Mainland China, 1912-1947," *Journal of Economic History*, 27 (Mar. 1967): 56-81; Arthur N. Young, *China's Nation-Building Effort, 1927-1937: The Financial and Economic Record* (Stanford, Calif.: Hoover Institution, 1971); T. C. Liu and K. C. Yeh, *The Economy of the Chinese Mainland: National Income and Economic Development, 1933-1959* (Princeton, N.J.: Princeton University Press, 1965); and Albert Feuerwerker, *The Chinese Economy, 1912-1949* (Ann Arbor: University of Michigan, Center for Chinese Studies, 1968). See also a review article by Ramon Myers, "Studies in Modern Chinese Economic History," *Journal of Asian Studies*, 29.4 (Aug. 1970): 897-905; and the rather one-sided essays in Paul K. T. Sih, ed., *The Strenuous Decade: China's Nation-Building Efforts, 1927-1937* (New York: St. John's University Press, 1970). On the economic interaction between China and the West, see G. C. Allen and Audrey G. Donnithorne, *Western Enterprise in Far Eastern Economic Development* (New York: Macmillan, 1954); G. E. Hubbard, *Eastern Industrialization and Its Effect on the West*, 2d ed. (London: Oxford University Press, 1938); and Chi-ming Hou, *Foreign Investments in China, 1840-1937* (Cambridge, Mass.: Harvard University Press, 1965). Arthur N. Young, *China's Wartime Finance and Inflation, 1937-1945* (Cambridge, Mass.: Harvard University Press, 1965), analyzes China's economic difficulties after July 1937. Young, who was a financial adviser to the Chinese government, discusses the assistance given to Chiang Kai-shek by the West in *China and the Helping Hand* (Cambridge, Mass.: Harvard University Press, 1963).

E. M. Robertson, *Hitler's Pre-War Policy and Military Plans 1933-1939* (London: Longmans, 1963), is an excellent introduction to Germany's foreign policy in the 1930's. A number of monographs deal specifically with German policy in East Asia: Kurt Bloch, *German Interests and Policies in the Far East* (New York: International Secretariat, Institute of Pacific Relations, 1939); Frank W. Iklé, *German-Japanese Relations, 1936-1940* (New York: Bookman Associates, 1956); Johanna Meskill, *Hitler and Japan: The Hollow Alliance* (New York: Atherton, 1966); Ernst L. Presseisen, *Germany and Japan: A Study in Totalitarian Diplomacy, 1933-1941* (The Hague: Martinus Nijhoff, 1958); and Theo Sommer, *Deutschland und Japan zwischen den Mächten 1935-1940* (Tübingen: J. C. B. Mohr, 1962). See also James T. C. Liu, "German Mediation in the Sino-Japanese War, 1937-1938," *Far Eastern Quarterly*, 8.2 (Feb. 1949): 157-71. Mario Toscano, *The Origins of the Pact of Steel* (Baltimore: Johns Hopkins University Press, 1967), throws light on Italy's relations with Japan. French policy in East Asia is surveyed in Roger Levy, Guy Lacam, and Andrew Roth, *French Interests and Policies in the Far East* (New York: International Secretariat, Institute of Pacific Relations, 1941).

John Erickson, *The Soviet High Command: A Military-Political History, 1918-1941* (London: Macmillan, 1962); and Charles B. McLane, *Soviet Policy and the Chinese Communists, 1931-1946* (New York: Columbia University Press, 1958) are helpful on the Soviet Union's involvement in East Asian politics in the 1930's. Aitchen K. Wu, *China and the Soviet Union* (London: Methuen, 1950); Max Beloff, *The Foreign Policy of Soviet Russia, 1929-1941*, 2 vols. (London: Oxford University Press, 1947-1949); and Henry Wei, *China and Soviet Russia* (Princeton, N.J.: Van Nostrand, 1956), are also adequate; David J. Dallin, *Soviet Russia and the Far East* (New Haven, Conn.: Yale University Press, 1948), is not.

Finally, the attitudes of the Dominions toward events in East Asia are touched on in Gwendolen Carter, *The British Commonwealth and International Security: The Role of the Dominions, 1919-1939* (Toronto: Ryerson, 1947); and Nicholas Mansergh, *Survey of British Commonwealth Affairs: Problems of External Policy, 1931-1939* (London: Oxford University Press, 1952). Also to be noted is Maurice Ollivier, ed., *The Colonial and Imperial Conferences from 1887 to 1937*, vol. 3: *Imperial Conferences*, part 2 (Ottawa: Edmond Cloutier, 1954). Raymond A. Esthus, *From Enmity to Alliance: United States–Australian*

Relations, 1931-1941 (Seattle: University of Washington Press, 1964); and Jack Shepherd, *Australia's Interests and Policies in the Far East* (New York: International Secretariat, Institute of Pacific Relations, 1940), throw light on Australian policy. Ian M. Drummond, *British Economic Policy and the Empire, 1919-1939* (London: Allen and Unwin, 1972) appeared while my book was in press.

Index

Index